THE WHISTLER
STEPPING INTO THE SHADOWS

A COLUMBIA FILM SERIES

by **DAN VAN NESTE**
Foreword by **ROBERT DIX**

THE WHISTLER: STEPPING INTO THE SHADOWS
THE COLUMBIA FILM SERIES
©2011 DAN VAN NESTE

ALL RIGHTS RESERVED.

All rights reserved. No part of this book may be reproduced or distributed, in print, recorded, live or digital form, without express written permission of the copyright holder. However, excerpts of up to 500 words may be reproduced online if they include the following information, "This is an excerpt from *The Whistler: Stepping into the Shadows* by Dan Van Neste."

Published in the USA by:

BEARMANOR MEDIA
P.O. BOX 71426
ALBANY, GEORGIA 31708
www.BearManorMedia.com

ISBN-10: 1-59393-402-5 (alk. paper)

ISBN-13: 978-1-59393-402-6 (alk. paper)

DESIGN AND LAYOUT: VALERIE THOMPSON

TABLE OF CONTENTS

FOREWORD BY ROBERT DIX . . . **1**

INTRODUCTION & ACKNOWLEDGEMENTS . . . **3**

CHAPTER ONE . . . **10**
BEGETTING A WHISTLER — ORIGINS, FAMILY TREES, INFLUENCES, INSPIRATIONS

CHAPTER TWO . . . **20**
HOME OF THE WHISTLER — COHN, COLUMBIA, AND CORN BEEF AND CABBAGE

CHAPTER THREE . . . **34**
MR. WHISTLER TAKES TO THE AIR

CHAPTER FOUR . . . **41**
UNDER THE TRENCH COAT — ANATOMY OF THE WHISTLER ON FILM
THE WHISTLER (1944) . . . **48**
THE MARK OF THE WHISTLER (1944) . . . **60**
THE POWER OF THE WHISTLER (1945) . . . **71**
VOICE OF THE WHISTLER (1945) . . . **82**
MYSTERIOUS INTRUDER (1946) . . . **93**
THE SECRET OF THE WHISTLER (1946) . . . **110**
THE THIRTEENTH HOUR (1947) . . . **121**
THE RETURN OF THE WHISTLER (1948) . . . **131**

CHAPTER FIVE . . . 141
IN THE SHADOW OF THE WHISTLER—
THE END OF THE SERIES AND BEYOND
(INCLUDING ANALYSIS OF THE WHISTLERS AS NOIR BY
FILM HISTORIAN KAREN BURROUGHS HANNSBERRY)

CHAPTER SIX . . . 153
THE WHISTLER FAMILY ALBUM—
50 PROFILES OF WHISTLER FILMMAKERS:
THE LEADS, LEADING LADIES, CHARACTER PLAYERS,
BEHIND THE SCENES

BIBLIOGRAPHY . . . 378

INDEX . . . 386

FOREWORD
BY ROBERT DIX

I was eight years old when my dad, Richard Dix, starred in the first Whistler movie, quite naturally entitled *The Whistler*. I remember it well. When he was in the library of our home with the door closed, he was not to be disturbed. It was a standing house-rule we all obeyed.

Being the son of a movie star did not seem unusual to me. As a kid, I didn't know the difference between me and the other kids in my grammar school, many of them also the sons and daughters of famous movie people. As the years went by, I learned the difference. My dad was loved and respected around the world as an American actor. During the "Whistler Years," he brought his talent to the silver screen for Columbia Pictures in a classic series of movies which became a special part of Hollywood history. My friend, author of *Stepping Into the Shadows*, Dan Van Neste has revealed the history of the *Whistler* films and the years that my dad and a wonderfully creative team of directors, supporting actors and motion picture crews made the series. They painted with light and wove spine-tingling mystery and often blood-curdling stories of human tragedy and loss, winning and losing, living and dying.

Dan is gifted as a writer and a historian. He brings his ability to tell the background of each of the eight *Whistler* movies to the forefront, one at a time, and in the sequence as they were produced. He goes back in time to give us the birth of *The Whistler* radio shows and their success through the 1940s and 1950s. Harry Cohn at Columbia Pictures decided to make the stories into what became the series of eight movies. No head of production or studio head ever starts out to make a series of movies. If the motion picture is well received, is liked by audiences and, most important, does well at the box office, then the second movie is scheduled for production, not before. They do not sit down and say, "Okay, guys, we're going to make eight movies." They start with the first one. When Mr. Cohn signed Richard Dix to play the lead in the first *Whistler* movie he was insuring his bet that with a decent screenplay the movie would be successful. And he was right.

An important point about Richard Dix's career as an actor is underscored by Dan: It is his versatility. Many of his fans still do not know the breadth of his work from stage, silent movies and the years of making "talkies." When sound came into the motion picture business, it was as dramatic a change as TV was to the motion picture industry. Dad's stage experience in New York and Los Angeles and his ability to "speak to the last row" helped him to easily make the transition. In the process and with the Oscar nomination for Best Actor in 1931 for *Cimarron* (the movie won Best Picture) it followed that Richard Dix was thought of as a western star. He went on to make seventeen westerns, many of them Zane Grey stories, but out of over 100 movies, there were comedies and action/adventure movies and many about love and relationships.

To clarify for any and all, simply look at any of the characters Dad played in the seven *Whistler* movies he starred in. The answer is that he was one of the most diversified American actors ever to grace the silver screens of the world. I thank Dan for being one of the few Hollywood historians to point out this commonly unknown fact.

And it is not just my beating Dad's drum. The many actors and crew members I have worked with in Hollywood in both motion pictures and television attest to Dad being an accomplished actor and a fine human being. Without exception, people have come up to me at Paramount, MGM, Universal, Columbia, 20th Century-Fox, Warner Brothers and locations around the world and spoken about what a wonderful time they had with my dad, as a man. He was loved and respected by both men and women, which is rare. Usually it is one or the other.

You are now going to read Dan's book but you should also see one or two (if not all) of the *Whistler* movies now available on DVD as well. You are guaranteed a scary, emotional and lasting trip down one of the rare memory lanes of Hollywood. Be scared and enjoy!

Introduction & Acknowledgments

Preface:
The setting is a dark, menacing big city street. A dim street lamp is the only light, the only thing between us and the all-enveloping blackness. There is a quiet sense of foreboding in this lonely, dangerous place. Out of the damp darkness a silhouette is seen clothed in a trench coat and slouched fedora. As it approaches an eerie, otherworldly whistle is heard from the mysterious, amorphous being. Its song is strange, unmelodic, unlike any heard before or since. As the disembodied stranger crosses our path we hear his unearthly soliloquy delivered in a silky, terrifying sneer.

"I am the Whistler and I know many things for I walk by night. I know many strange tales, many secrets hidden in the hearts of men and women who have stepped into the shadows. Yes, I know the nameless terrors of which they dare not speak!"

Strange tales, hidden secrets, nameless terrors? Who is this being who walks by night? What is his purpose? Is he the voice of fate, an angel of mercy, or a messenger from hell?

Hypnotized by this fearsome nocturnal entity we fix our attention on his chosen tales each introduced briefly, cryptically. There are eight in all. Frightening, spine-tingling stories of crime victims, thieves, paranoiacs, psychotics, cold-blooded murderers, all of whom share one thing in common. Each made a fateful decision or committed a life-altering act for which they must atone. Will they escape the clutches of the grim reaper or become the bloody victims of his deadly scythe? Soon we will know what fate awaits those who have stepped into the shadows.

At first glance *The Whistler* series, eight low-budget feature films produced by Columbia Pictures during a four-year period in the mid- to later 1940s, may seem a rather odd, trivial subject to be memorialized in book form. After all they *were* merely B crime thrillers made quickly and cheaply by a studio who produced them solely for the purpose of filling the bottom half of a mandatory double bill. If what records we have are to be believed there was little planning given to their production, and precious little effort made to showcase or promote them. In comparison to many contemporary film series like MGM's *Thin Mans* and Fox's *Charlie Chans*, the *Whistler* pictures were in many respects inferior. Save their star, former silent heartthrob Richard Dix, there were no big-name actors or directors associated with them, no fancy costumes, expensive sets, and location shots. Unlike almost all competing series, the films featured no continuing characters with which audiences could attach to or identity with. So why the book? Why should we care? Let me tell you.

The first reason is simple. Despite the handicaps all eight are good movies; innovative productions with intriguing characters, haunting themes, and excellent performances which appeal to a broad cross section of movie fans. After 60+ years all remain highly watchable, entertaining, sometimes compelling films which utilize an economy of activity and dialogueue to maximum effect.

To all who enjoy the crime, mystery, horror, suspense genre the *Whistler* films have much to offer. All eight have a stylish, tense, atmospheric quality. While the dingy settings, dark shadowy lighting may not always have been the result of the brilliant machinations of filmmakers, but a necessary contrivance reflecting Columbia's budgetary restrictions, somehow it all worked. Producer Larry Darmour's pedestrian interior sets may not have been anything to write home about, but in these pictures they were appropriate backdrops for the fated tales of terror and doom depicted. And of course to all who enjoy suspense and the supernatural there is the title character. His eerie whistle, his shadowy, otherworldly appearance, and cynical, whining voice are exceedingly provocative. Does he represent fate or judgment? Is he a savior attempting to rescue the morally conflicted characters depicted in his tales, or a terrifying fiend who takes pleasure in their pain? The answer is not entirely clear.

The burgeoning fascination with *film noir* also makes these films of interest. Although not traditionally listed in major reference books on the subject, in recent years the *Whistler* movies have been singled out as early, innovative examples of the genre by an increasing number of *noir* experts and film historians, one of whom will share her impressions in this volume.

To those (like me) who are interested in the history of B movies and B film series, the *Whistlers* are among the best examples of low-budget product being churned out by the studios during and after World War II, more specifically by Columbia's B assembly line which had a legendary reputation as one of the foremost producers of quality low-budget features.

In addition to the all the above, still another major reason to care about the series is it featured the artistry of superb actors, directors, and technicians. Of special note is the work of legendary star Richard Dix whose maturity as an actor reached full fruition in the *Whistler* films, the last of roughly 100 motion pictures he made during his career. Also of interest are performances by several unsung leading ladies such as Gloria Stuart, Karen Morley, Leslie Brooks, and some of the best character actors of all time; among them J. Carrol Naish, Richard Lane, and Kathleen Howard. Last, but by no means least, the *Whistlers* showcased the work of many gifted, behind-the-scenes craftsman, B directors like William Castle, Lew Landers, George Sherman; writers such as Eric Taylor, Raymond Shrock; cinematographers Philip Tannura, L.W. McConnell, and many others.

Having explained the "whys" of the volume let me say a few words about the "hows." *Stepping Into the Shadows* has been structured in such a way as to share all available information regarding the series as well as address certain key unknowns. Tragically, unlike the majority of major studios, there exists no formal Columbia archive. Vital records and correspondence detailing the making of the *Whistlers* are missing or incomplete. According to informed sources the majority of Columbia's production records and office files were discarded when the studio moved from Gower Street to Burbank to join Warners in 1972. There is a smattering of information scattered about in various personal collections and 36 boxes of Columbia memorabilia preserved at the American Heritage Center at the University of Wyoming at Laramie (primarily consisting of transcribed teletypes of communications between Columbia's East and West Coast offices), but most of these materials deal with Columbia's high-end productions, not its Bs. The point is we do not know key background information regarding the decision to make the first *Whistler* film and the backstories of each of the eight *Whistlers*.

The problem is exacerbated by the absence of interviews, records, and papers from *Whistler* creator J. Donald Wilson which would undoubtedly shed light on how the Whistler character was conceived, and how it found its way on the airwaves and later to the silver screen. No one seems to remember much about this talented, enigmatic man. A couple of notes from his wife at the time of his death from a heart attack in 1984 shed some light on his multi-faceted career, but say nothing about his greatest creation, the Whistler.

With these impediments in mind it is no wonder few books have been written on Columbia Pictures and fewer still on their low-budget films. Writing this volume was something akin to working a 10,000-piece jigsaw puzzle with no picture on the box. The overall organization of the book reflects the lack of key information as well as my passion (developed over decades of writing film-related articles) for providing context. To me contextual information is an essential prerequisite to a thorough understanding of a particular subject, and doubly so when other critical data is missing. Chapters One and Two are attempts to address the aforementioned deficiencies.

Chapter One provides a brief history of the mystery suspense genre in books, radio, and motion pictures to help readers understand what may have influenced and impacted Wilson's creation of the Whistler, and inspired those who brought the character to radio and to the silver screen.

Chapter Two provides a concise history of Columbia Pictures from its founding to the production of the *The Whistler* in 1944, particularly its legendary B unit. An emphasis has been placed on how B films like the *Whistlers* were made and how the series fits into the broad scheme of things at Columbia. Included in the latter discussion is a brief description of the various types of B films being manufactured by the studio at the time the *Whistler* series was born. Eyewitness accounts by former Columbia employees are provided whenever possible to add depth and meaning.

Chapter Three covers the production of *The Whistler* radio series, which commenced in 1942 and ran 13 years until 1955. A short overview of the series is offered along with particulars regarding the writers, casts, and overall subject matter. A sample episode is discussed to give readers an overall sense of the series.

The heart of the book is found in Chapter Four which begins with information on events leading up to the production of the first *Whistler* film, and an analysis of the eight *Whistler* motion pictures as a group; stressing common themes and characteristics. Eight separate sections follow corresponding to the eight *Whistler* films. Under each title are several subsections which include relevant production and credit information, plot synopsis (including the beginning and concluding statements of the Whistler character), reviews, expert opinions, interesting facts/trivia, and "my take." The expert opinion section is comprised of more recent reviews of the *Whistlers* by prominent contemporary movie scholars. The interesting facts and trivia section houses all the extent background information on the making of the *Whistlers* as well as some intriguing facts about the films and their makers. "My take" is simply my own analysis of each film in which I endeavored to present both its strengths and weaknesses. For comparative purposes, and as a fun way of provoking debate and discussion, I concluded each review with a rating. A number 1 rating is the best of the series; and number 8 the weakest. I based the rating on the following criteria: script, direction, acting, technical expertise, and entertainment value.

Chapter Five: "In the Shadow of the Whistler" chronicles events immediately following the demise of the film series, and briefly discusses the impact and influence of the Whistler on motion pictures, radio, and television. Among the topics is *The Whistler* television series, a well-done 30-minute syndicated anthology which fizzled after only a few months on the air. The chapter concludes with a discussion of *film noir*. An approximate definition of the term is followed by opinions and analysis from renown film historian, *noir* expert Karen Burroughs Hannsberry the author of *Femme Noir* (1998), *The Bad Boys of Film Noir* (2003), and the monthly *noir* newsletter, *The Dark Pages*.

One of my favorite parts of the book is Chapter Six: "The Whistler Family Album," a fond, respectful look back at the lives and careers of the filmmakers who made this B movie series one to remember. Profiles are offered on 50 talented individuals, including an expansive bio tribute to one of filmdom's most underrated actors, Richard Dix. Although important details of each individual's personal life are covered, a special emphasis has been placed on their careers, their screen personas, and significant credits in order to help readers assess the filmmaker's overall legacy. As you will see the length of the character player profiles varies considerably, roughly corresponding to the importance of the person's work in the series, and the availability of information. In addition, I have purposely created lengthier bios on certain individuals whose long and distinguished careers have long been undervalued. At the end of the Chapter Six vital stats are provided on other contributors not covered previously. I sincerely regret I was unable to determine the whereabouts/and or fate of two important *Whistler* players: Nina Vale and Helen Mowery.

Let me conclude by acknowledging the efforts of many kind people who helped me with this project. Without their contributions the book would not be possible. I want to sincerely thank Janet Lorenz and librarians at the Academy of Motion Picture Arts and Sciences (Margaret Herrick Library), Shannon Bowen of the University of Wyoming's American Heritage Center, Dorinda Hartman, Assistant Archivist at the Wisconsin Center for Film and Theater Research, the staff of the Library of the Performing Arts in New York, Gary Haman, Tony Greco, David Siegel, Frank Reichter, Martin Halperin of the Pacific Pioneer Broadcasters, Ben Ohmart, Sandy Grabman, Martin Grams Jr., Jim Cox, Bill Cappello, Marvin Paige, Laura Wagner, Claire Brandt of Eddie Brandt's Saturday Matinee, Blackie Seymour and his Pentagram Library, Hal Snelling, Daniel Bubbeo, John Gettman, Betty Heater, David Smith, Caroline Marsh, Oscar Van Neste, and Cherie Van Neste. I must also thank *Classic Images/Films of the Golden Age* editor Bob King, a great guy and genuine classic film devotee for his support of my writings low these many years.

Special thanks to several very fine actors, filmmakers, and family members whose motion picture memories (shared with me for this project and others in the past) I have used in this volume. They include: Ann Rutherford, Ted Donaldson, Will Hutchins, the late

Edward Norris, the late Adele Jergens, the late Jeanne Bates, the late Gloria Stuart, and the late Karen Morley. Very special thank yous are also in order to three friends: actor, producer, author, and all-around good guy Robert Dix, (son of Richard) who generously shared some of his unique memories of his father for this book, the gracious Nicholas McKinney, son of Michael Duane for providing vital facts and remembrances of his father, and my longtime pal, author/*film noir* expert, Karen Burroughs Hannsberry for her encouragement, and for all the valuable time she took offering her articulate and perceptive commentary. This book is dedicated to the memory of my wonderful mother, Bessie Glossop (1921–2008) who passed away a month after I signed the contract to write it. A talented singer and musician, she was an inspiration to all those who knew her—most especially her youngest son. She spent a lifetime lighting my way and keeping the light shining. Whatever I've achieved in life I owe to her love and sacrifice. I love you, Mom.

Guess that's about it for now. So settle back and enjoy this trip back in time to the 1940s when a mysterious shadowy entity entered American's living rooms, and later its theaters with the unforgettably ominous refrain, "I am the Whistler and I know many things . . ."

CHAPTER ONE
BEGGETING A WHISTLER
ORIGINS, FAMILY TREES, INFLUENCES, INSPIRATIONS

Before delving into known details of the radio and film Whistler it is important to have some understanding of his origins. Several key questions immediately come to mind. For starters how was the Whistler character conceived, and how and why was it brought to radio? What influenced Columbia to produce the *Whistler* film series; and how was each *Whistler* film made? Under ordinary circumstances these questions might be answered by perusing the personal papers and/or memoirs of *Whistler* creator J. Donald Wilson and visits to the archives of Columbia Pictures who produced all eight features. Unfortunately, neither is available so we are compelled to search for answers elsewhere. One of the best ways is through history and context; more specifically a brief review of the history of suspense and crime in books, radio, and film, *and* a look back at the low-budget filmmaking process and product of Columbia. If we cannot know with certainty the true origins of Wilson's radio and film *Whistler* and the particulars of how each *Whistler* motion picture was made from those involved, we can certainly arrive at some highly educated guesses based on an examination of the environment in which the Whistler was born.

There is little doubt as long as humans have inhabited the earth they have been fascinated and entertained by mystery and suspense tales. Certainly, the Greeks and Romans loved a good blood-and-guts story. The invention of the printing press and the mass production of books helped feed the public's hunger for murder and crime tales. By the 19th century inventive authors like Poe, Hawthorne, Dickens, Shelley, to name a few, were busy making a name for themselves as crime/mystery/horror writers. Poe, in particular, can be seen as one of the "great-granddaddies" of the *Whistler* stories and all the suspense and detective fiction which would follow. His 1841 story, *Murders in the Rue Morgue*, with its brilliant crime-solving protagonist, Auguste C. Dupin, is widely acknowledged as the first modern mystery novel. The published works of Victorian English authors Wilkie Collins: *The Woman in White* (1860), *The Moonstone* (1868); Anna Katherine Green: *The Leavenworth Case* (1878); Sir Arthur Conan Doyle: *A Study in Scarlet* (1887), *Adventures of Sherlock Holmes* (1892), *The Hound of the Baskervilles* (1902), and others were also important influences on the stories and characters of crime/suspense radio and motion pictures.

The 20th century ushered in the "golden age" of the mystery and crime novel in Europe and America. Of particular note were the stories of English mystery icon Agatha Christie and Americans Manfred Lee and Fredric Dannay. The popular Miss Christie's name has become synonymous with the mystery/suspense genre thanks to a multitude of bestselling novels like *The Mysterious Affair at Styles* (1920) and *The Murder of Roger Ackroyd* (1926). On the other side of the Atlantic, Lee and Dannay's *The Roman Hat Mystery* (1929), chronicling the exploits of amateur detective Ellery Queen, helped initiate America's "golden age." The works of novelist and playwright Earl Derr Biggers: *House Without a Key* (1925), *The Black Camel* (1929); and Earle Stanley Gardner: *The Case of the Sulky Girl* (1933), *The Case of the Curious Bride* (1935) was also significant. Biggers' Asian sleuth Charlie Chan and Gardner's crime-solving attorney Perry Mason enjoyed enormous success with readers, eventually inspiring popular radio and television series.

The 1920s saw the rise of pulp-fiction magazines like *Black Mask, Dime Detective,* and *Thrilling Detective* showcasing hard-boiled, reality-based crime stories with tough-edged protagonists like Dashiell Hammett's Sam Spade and Raymond Chandler's Philip Marlowe, both of whom found their way to the silver screen. Hammett, Chandler and other pulp-fiction writers were "granddaddies" of the *Whistler* radio programs and the enormously popular *noir* motion pictures which flooded theaters following the end of World War II. In fact, some of the *Whistler* radio and movie scripts (including those written by Cornell Woolrich) were originally penned for *Black Mask* and other publications. It is also important to note that some of Columbia's scenarists, including Eric Taylor, did pulp-fiction work. The point is that Wilson and others involved in the creation and production of the radio and film *Whistler* were undoubtedly influenced directly or indirectly by many of the above literary works.

The invention of radio and the motion picture camera in the late 19th century precipitated revolutionary changes in all aspects of the entertainment industry on both the North American and European continents. Soon high growth industries developed and thrived around the production and distribution of radio and motion pictures. By the 1930s people could indulge their passion for mayhem not only by reading books, but by listening to their favorite suspense novels and detective stories in the comfort of their living rooms via radio, or see them literally spring to life on a theater screen. Suddenly, crime and murder had a face and a voice.

The late 19th century wireless communication inventions of Popov, Fessenden, and Marconi, etc., set in motion the radio revolution which culminated in America's "golden age of radio" roughly spanning 30 years from the mid-1920s through the mid-1950s. Before 1925 radio was considered only as a one-way wireless telephone offering news, information, and live music; but by the latter 1920s independent stations developed producing programs built around specific ideas and utilizing announcers. Soon stations had their own stars and were broadcasting original stories or dramatized versions of popular novels. Because these stations could not always be heard in all parts of the U.S., networks (made up of collections of stations) were formed which improved the quality and variety of programming. The 1930s saw the production of an amazing array of radio programs funded by national advertisers whose names became associated with them.

By the time J. Donald Wilson's *The Whistler* came along in the 1940s the mystery/crime/suspense radio program had already carved a unique niche. Fictional detectives were a special favorite. By 1942 (the year radio's *The Whistler* debuted) several of suspense literature's most popular crime-solvers had found their way to the airwaves, notably Doyle's Sherlock Holmes, Bigger's Charlie Chan, Lee and Dannay's Ellery Queen, as well as ace criminologists Bulldog Drummond and The Thin Man. Other significant 1930s crime/suspense/horror programming included *Shadow of Fu Manchu* (1932–39), *Lights Out!* (1934–47), *Hermit's Cave* (1935–44), and *I Love a Mystery* (1939–52).

Two particular programs which preceded radio's *The Whistler* likely influenced Wilson's conception of the character and/or the decision to broadcast the radio show. Produced in New York, *Inner Sanctum Mysteries* was first broadcast by the NBC network on January 7, 1941. Created by Himan Brown, the supernatural anthology series lasted 11 years and 526 episodes. Each program began with the opening of a creaking door accompanied by a spooky, melodramatic organ score. A creepily sardonic host, known as "Raymond," introduced each tale and provided concluding comments utilizing ghoulish puns. His chilling sign-off, "Pleasant dreeeeeeams!!" became legendary, as did the program's casts which included the likes of Boris Karloff, Orson Welles, and Frank Sinatra.

Although technically a mystery/horror series with supernatural themes in contrast to *The Whistler* which emphasized crime over horror, the *Inner Sanctum* programs shared many common elements with Wilson's creation. Both effectively weaved tales of terror and paranoia aided by proficient writing, excellent direction, and good acting. Both were so successful they were spun-off into motion pictures and later television series. The atmospheric quality of each was also comparable. Like *The Whistler* (which featured the sound of footsteps accompanied by spooky whistling) the creaking door and organ music of *Inner Sanctum Mysteries* had Mr. and Mrs. John Q. Public on the edge of their seats. The most striking similarity, however, was the narration. The mass popularity of the spine-tingling Raymond inevitably influenced many subsequent radio and film characters. It certainly would not be a stretch of the imagination to believe Raymond and his *Inner Sanctum Mysteries* might well have inspired Wilson to create the Whistler, and may also have been a factor motivating CBS's decision to give Wilson's program a shot in 1942.

Classic radio's *The Shadow* (1930–54) appears to have had an even greater impact on the development and creation of the Whistler and a whole host of literary, radio, and filmic characters and productions from the 1930s to the present day. Of all Wilson's influences (literary, radio, and cinematic) none may be as important. First heard in 1929 and 1930 as the sinister host of pulp-fiction publisher Street and Smith's radio dramatizations of their magazine stories, by the mid-1930s *The Shadow* had become a pulp-fiction icon thanks to legendary writer Walter Gibson's colorful, ghost-written stories which transformed the character into an anti-heroic, black-cloaked, crime-fighting avenger armed with two .45 pistols, and assisted by a network of agents. The mass popularity of Gibson's tales published in *Shadow* magazine made it almost inevitable the character would become a radio star.

Premiering on the Mutual Broadcasting System in 1937 *The Shadow* radio series, starring young Orson Welles and Agnes Moorehead, further developed Gibson's character to suit the needs and demands of the medium. Instead of pistols and a network of agents, radio's less sinister Shadow developed the art of invisibility and the knack of "clouding men's minds." He took over the mind and body of wealthy bon vivant Lamont Cranston (played by Welles, later Bill Johnstone, etc.), who did his crime battling capably assisted by girl Friday Margo Lane (Moorehead, later many others)— the only person to know his true identity. Their adventures combined crime, suspense, and supernatural themes to great effect, making *The Shadow* one of the most enduring and successful programs in radio history. The classic introduction, "Who knows what evil lurks in the hearts of men . . . The Shadow knows!" accompanied by Frank Readick's otherworldly laugh, and the haunting theme song, "Le Rouet d'Omphale" composed by Camille Saint Saens, still resonates.

If not a direct descendent of the "black-cloaked one," certainly Wilson's radio Whistler was a first cousin; strikingly analogous in several important ways. Firstly, both series had criminal themes which on occasion veered off into the supernatural. Both characters possessed otherworldly powers which were used to obliterate crime for the betterment of society. The theme song of *The Shadow* and his memorable recitations were distinctly akin to the whistling refrain and opening "monologue" of *The Whistler* both in mood and substance. On a strictly superficial note, both Gibson's magazine Shadow (on which the radio character was based) and the Whistler wore similar attire, and both spent their time in the shadows.

There were differences. Clearly, the Whistler was more a "hands off" character rarely involving himself in his tales. Although he does speak to his protagonists and occasionally intervenes, his primary function appears to be as a spooky, rather sadistic voice of destiny, providing opening and closing commentary, and occasionally telling the viewer via voiceover what a person is thinking and feeling at critical moments. His kin the Shadow was very different in both radio and film. An active participant in his adventures, he not only commented on the fate of others but intervened (through Cranston) to make their fate a reality. Despite the differences it is virtually impossible to envision a Whistler radio and film series without the existence and success of its iconic predecessor.

As radio enjoyed the enthusiastic embrace of an entertainment hungry American public, the motion picture industry was on a parallel track to an even greater, more sustained success. By the 1920s the infant film industry was rapidly maturing in size and scope. The demise of the nickelodeons had paved the way for the erection of elaborate movie palaces. The patent war, which had sidetracked movie entrepreneurs for years, was largely over, unleashing inventive independent movie producers who offered more sophisticated motion pictures. New important companies sprang up which moved the creative center of the industry from the east (New York and Chicago) to west coast (Hollywood), attracting and employing an incredible variety of young, imaginative artists and technicians.

These geniuses helped their ruthless, risk-taking bosses, a.k.a. the moguls, to consolidate the industry and perfect their product, setting in motion revolutionary alterations in the creative process of making movies, the totality of which came to be known as the "studio system": a complex network of motion picture production, distribution, and exhibition. The 1930s saw the vast majority of the movie business concentrated in the hands of the big five studios: Warner Brothers, MGM, Twentieth Century-Fox, Paramount, and RKO, and the little three: Columbia, United Artists, and Universal, who not only controlled content but every aspect of filmmaking.

The secret of the moguls' amazing success had much to do with savvy business acumen and efficiency. The big five purchased the theaters where eager film connoisseurs flocked to see their product. They invented an assembly line organization of their staffs which decentralized the filmmaking process among many creative artists, and created a "star system" by nurturing and exploiting talented actors from the theater, radio, and the concert stage whose names became associated with their studios. To meet the demands of an increasingly sophisticated and diverse audience, the studios scoured the literary and radio worlds for material. The evolution of distinct film genres, which began a decade earlier, intensified.

The advent of sound motion pictures in the late 1920s coincided with America's "Great Depression." At first the financial and societal calamity worked to the benefit of the moviemakers who temporarily prospered by providing a desperate, downtrodden nation a temporary escape from their troubles; but by the early 1930s the Depression began taking a toll. Between 1931 and 1934, movie attendance plummeted and many theaters went dark. The tough, resilient moguls knew they had to take decisive action to save their businesses.

One of their innovative responses to the calamity was the B movie, a.k.a. the second feature, a.k.a. the programmer. When roster and salary trimming proved insufficient, the studios lowered ticket prices, promoted giveaways, and began offering two-for-one specials, a.k.a. the double bill. For the price of admission filmgoers would not only have the pleasure of viewing big-budget favorites, but also a secondary picture starring less familiar actors and actresses. There had always been low-budget pictures, but during the early 1930s their numbers and significance grew immeasurably.

Coinciding with the rise to prominence of the B movie was the resurgence of the mystery/crime thriller. Although moviemakers presented many exceptional suspense features during the silent period, it wasn't until the Depression era that the genre appeared to come of age. Why? There were many reasons. Certainly, crime thrillers provided great escapist fare for weary audiences; but even more importantly, the advent of talking pictures provided the perfect venue to present the genre. In his excellent book *Suspense in the Cinema*, author Gordon Gow offers a succinct explanation for the success of suspense movies: "The cinema is a medium that can induce suspense more readily than any other. It might be argued that many films have derived their plots and ideas from novels. But the images and sounds of the cinema are another language. A transformation is wrought; the ideas impinge in a different manner, and more strongly . . ."

Gow goes on to explain that no matter how powerful a spell is cast by radio and the written word, daily distractions intervene to interrupt the experience. He posits films have a way of manipulating and focusing attention like no other medium because filmgoers are physically removed from distractions; and because the sound motion picture lends itself to the manipulation of both audio and visual aspects as a way of concentrating our attention and "power of reasoning."

All major and minor studios contributed notable mystery, crime, and suspense motion pictures of both A and B varieties throughout the 1930s and 1940s. Although the German Expressionist movement of the 1920s and the early British films of Alfred Hitchcock can rightly be seen as influencing all the suspense and crime films which followed, for the purposes of our examination of how and why the *Whistler* movies were made, we will confine our discussion to the productions of Hollywood studios. Three in particular: Warner Brothers, Universal, and Columbia influenced the eight *Whistler* films in three very different ways.

It's hard to imagine a *Whistler* film series would have been made were it not for the success of Warner Brothers' gritty, groundbreaking melodramas of the 1930s and early 1940s. Beginning with Bryan Foy's *Lights of New York* (1928), WB made an unparalleled string of significant crime and gangster thrillers depicting the rise and fall of charismatic, largely one-dimensional hoodlums who turned to a life of crime to survive in Depression-era America. Set on the ominous, shadowy big city streets, these criminals fought for power and dominance armed with an amoral ingenuity, and an arsenal of guns. Mervyn LeRoy's *Little Caesar* (1931), William Wellman's *The Public Enemy* (1931), Michael Curtiz's *Angels With Dirty Faces* (1938), and Raoul Walsh's *The Roaring Twenties* (1939) were the most notable of many examples.

The emergence of more complex multi-dimensional antiheroes in the 1940s was WB's response to the demands of an increasingly discriminating film-going public. John Huston's *The Maltese Falcon* (1941) and Walsh's *High Sierra* (1941) carried on the WB criminal tradition, but with a twist. Both featured conflicted criminal protagonists whose good and evil aspects appeared to be at war.

All crime and *noir* films which followed owe much to WB's legacy. The eight *Whistler* pictures are no exception; exhibiting many similarities. Like Warners' crime thrillers they were produced frugally and featured criminal themes. All were morality tales; the ultimate lesson being a life of crime has dire, often fatal, consequences. Those who choose to harm others and/or society can expect to pay a heavy price not only in physical but psychological terms. Most of the *Whistlers* were set on the dark, seedy streets of the big city and featured protagonists who ranged from deeply flawed to remorseless monsters. Like their WB counterparts many of the *Whistler* main characters were at war with themselves, battling demons which sometimes engulfed them.

Speaking of monsters, Carl Laemmle's Universal Studios left its own mark on the *Whistler* pictures through its string of hit supernatural thrillers during the 1930s, many adapted from classic suspense literature. Tod Browning's *Dracula* (1931), James Whale's *Frankenstein* (1931), *The Invisible Man* (1932), and *Bride of Frankenstein* (1935), etc., established the studio as the prime purveyor of the horror fantasy, a popular genre which endured. Universal influenced the creation and production of the *Whistler* series in many ways. Like the titled monsters Wilson's Whistler was basically a supernatural being who appeared to exhibit both good and evil. Although he oversaw justice, he often acted in a sinister manner, laughing and taking fiendish pleasure in the pain inflicted on the characters in his tales. The studio's impact was also felt through Harry Cohn. Harry's experiences as an executive secretary to Laemmle at the outset of his movie career left a lasting impact on him. Harry not only patterned his private life after his old boss, among others, but adopted and perfected Universal's business model emphasizing economy and ingenuity in motion picture production.

For obvious and not-so-obvious reasons the *Whistler's* home studio had the most profound impact on the pictures bearing his name. Any attempt to explore the hows and whys of the filmic *Whistler*, via history and context, inevitably ends inside the formidable double doors of Harry Cohn's Columbia Pictures Corporation which produced all eight entries. Although little detail (i.e. productions notes, etc.) exists on any particular Columbia feature (especially its Bs), a good deal of valuable information is known about the studio, its founder, its product, and the filmmaking process of its famed B unit which will help us understand how and why films like the *Whistlers* were made.

CHAPTER TWO
HOME OF THE WHISTLER
COHN, COLUMBIA, AND CORN BEEF AND CABBAGE

No examination of the inner workings of Columbia could possibly commence without briefly discussing the life and times of the controversial man who co-founded the company and became its face. Also known as "White Fang" and "His Crudeness," Harry Cohn possessed qualities resembling J. P. Morgan, Arthur Godfrey, and Sadaam Hussein all wrapped up in one boorish package. A profane, ruthless, skinflintty, egocentric s.o.b., Harry was also a brilliant businessman who built his empire through audacious ingenuity, determination, shrewdness, and an eye for talent, ultimately leaving behind an indelible, highly meritorious imprint on an industry which both loved and reviled him.

Harry Cohn was born to be a Hollywood mogul. A former pool hustler, trolley car operator, and song plugger, at age 27 he entered the film business in the employ of Universal studio head Carl Laemmle, thanks to an intervention from older brother (and frequent rival) Jack who worked for Universal as an editor and producer of film shorts. In 1919 Harry, Jack, and mutual friend Joe Brandt struck out on their own, establishing C.B.C. Productions. Leasing space near the corner of Sunset Boulevard and Gower Streets on Hollywood's Poverty Row (a collection of small independent and fly-by night firms attempting to compete with the big guns), the new company flourished by producing entertaining two-reel shorts on barebones budgets. So "economical" was their technique the big studios snidely referred to C.B.C as "Corn Beef and Cabbage Productions"; but the Cohns persevered and their company prospered. In 1924 the trio purchased a tiny Gower Street studio, renamed their company Columbia Pictures Corporation, came up with a new logo (which eventually morphed into Columbia's famous "proud lady"—a torch-bearing woman draped in a flag standing on a pedestal), and began producing full-length feature films. An amiable agreement was eventually forged between the three partners which ceded the studio's West Coast operation to Harry while the elder Cohn and Brandt remained in New York handling the financial and distribution end. Both Jack and Joe would soon regret the decision to give Harry so much authority, but by then it was too late.

An authoritarian who ruled his mini-fiefdom with iron-handed intimidation, by the early 1930s Harry Cohn was on the fast track to becoming known as the meanest man in Hollywood, *and* one of the most successful. After winning a power struggle with brother Jack (whose influence was permanently diminished) and Brandt (who exited the company in 1932), Harry literally became the symbol of Columbia Pictures as company president and head of production, the only mogul to hold both positions. Free of East Coast interference, Cohn set out on a single-minded quest to make his company a major player. One of his shrewdest moves was to assemble a top-drawer staff: smart, savvy executives, assistants, and craftsman who understood both the business and the artistic ends of making movies; and who shared his work ethic. For all his faults, throughout his tenure at Columbia, Harry displayed an uncanny ability to spot and promote gifted young moviemakers. "I kiss the feet of talent!" and "If you've got talent I'll kiss your ass, if you haven't I'll kick it!" were two memorable quotations attributed to Harry C. by author Bob Thomas in his unforgettable biography, *King Cohn*.

Gradually lessening, but never obliterating, his company's corn beef and cabbage image, during the early 1930s Harry and company began making two or three "prestige" pictures per year as he churned out scores of lesser entries (both one- and two-reelers). High-end pictures were subdivided into two categories according to the approximate cost of each. Harry's "As" were films budgeted between $500,000-$750,000, and his "AAs" were those exceeding $750,000. Most of Columbia's initial "prestige" productions were helmed by Cohn's most illustrious employee, director Frank Capra. Aided by literate scripts from Robert Riskin, and top-flight acting supplied by first-tier movie stars, mostly on loan from other studios, Capra

Frank Capra's scintillating comedy *It Happened One Night* (1934) starring Clark Gable and Claudette Colbert was a milestone for Columbia, netting multiple Oscars and the grudging respect of the movie industry.

made such acclaimed features as *Ladies of Leisure* (1930), *The Last Parade* (1931), *American Madness* (1932), *The Bitter Tea of General Yen* (1933), and *Lady for a Day* (1933). In 1934 his classic romantic comedy *It Happened One Night* won raves, netting Columbia Academy Awards for best picture and director. Capra's genius for story telling and depicting basic American decency continued to bring prestige and multiple honors to Cohn and company throughout the 1930s, until his departure in 1939. By then such Capra classics as *Mr. Deeds Goes to Town* (1936), *You Can't Take It With You* (1938), and *Mr. Smith Goes to Washington* (1939); George Cukor's *Holiday* (1938), Leo McCarey's *The Awful Truth* (1937), and Howard Hawks' impressive threesome *Twentieth Century* (1934), *Only Angels Have Wings* (1939), and *His Girl Friday* (1940) had established Columbia as a studio to be reckoned with, one which could compete at all levels.

While Harry was justifiably proud of his acclaimed filet mignon features, he was wise enough to realize the awards and recognition would never have been possible were it not for the substantial profits he netted from "corn beef and cabbage," a.k.a. "those lousy little B pictures" produced in mass and sold as part of a block (the total output at a given time). Unlike his competitors Cohn never operated his studio in the red even in the darkest days of the Great Depression, or when his Grade A productions like 1937's *Lost Horizon* were monetary failures; and he knew why. Throughout Hollywood's "golden age" (from the mid-1930s to the early 1950s) Cohn led the way in the production of low-budget feature films of all shapes and sizes. All other studios produced Bs, but no one did it more efficiently, economically, and enthusiastically than Columbia. In retrospect it appears as if the studio perfected the low-budget program picture into something akin to an art form, grinding out scores of entertaining second features via an assembly line method which employed the studio's hardworking B unit staff made up of artists and technicians who specialized in making low-budgeters.

Acquiring adjacent poverty row properties, which eventually constituted a square lot (114 ft. on Gower Street; 114 ft. on Beachwood, with a 270 ft. depth), and a 35-acre ranch near Burbank (where most of his low-budget westerns were produced), by the mid-1930s the studio was cranking out 40–50 programmers per year excluding short subjects. Most were fast-paced and action-packed. What they lacked in size and scope they made up in profitability, craftsmanship, and in sheer entertainment value. While most had major flaws and were not great art, they filled the bottom half of the mandatory double bill and provided escapist fare to a weary American public who had endured a depression. As author/B movie historian Don Miller said so succinctly in his quintessential volume *B Movies*, "The whole studio [Columbia] may have been run on a shoestring, but Harry Cohn knew what he was doing."

Indeed, Harry *did* know what he was doing; and he did it on the cheap. The well-worn motto "making the most with the least" applied to all Cohn's productions, particularly his lesser entries which he entrusted to second-in-command Irving Briskin. It was Briskin's job to keep churning out B product while keeping a tight budgetary lid on the process, especially pictures farmed out to independent producers like Sam Katzman and Larry Darmour. All Columbia Bs were budgeted under $250,000, with most being made for $150,000 or less. Many, including all the *Whistlers*, came in well under $100,000—roughly comparable to what Twentieth Century-Fox spent on sets!

The vast majority of Columbia's second features were between 60–70 minutes in length. All were shot on tight schedules (usually 10 to 21 days). Directors limited the number of takes and did not tolerate production delays. Virtually all B footage was filmed on studio soundstages, the Columbia ranch, and/or studios rented from independent producers. Stock footage was substituted for exotic locales, and liberally inserted into programmers to maximize the effect of a particular scene. Some of the stock footage was used so frequently it became as familiar to the discerning fan as the pictures' stars.

Harry Cohn's rough-hewn genius as a talent scout and promoter was reflected in his B unit. Most of Columbia's low-budget product was helmed by gifted contract directors; old hands like Lew Landers, D. Ross Lederman, Charles Barton, Arthur Dreifuss, George Sherman, Lambert Hillyer, and young talents like Edward Dmytryk, Michael Gordon, and William Castle. Overworked, underpaid, and under the gun they had the unenviable task of making respectable pictures within the budgetary structure and time constraints imposed from on high. This became particularly challenging when they received undernourished scripts from company writers who were afforded little time to write literate, well-constructed screenplays. This is by no means a harsh critique of Columbia's crack team of scenarists. Quite the contrary. Such gifted pros as Eric Taylor, Aubrey Wisberg, and Ray Schrock often worked miracles under trying circumstances. Those "circumstances" were outlined by film historian/critic Leonard Maltin in his informative foreword to Miller's *B Movies*. In it he recalled hearing about the scriptwriting process at Columbia's B division from various Hollywood veterans. "Supervisor Irving Briskin would take prospective writers to an outer office where there was a list of titles on a blackboard—*Two Senoritas from Chicago, Boston Blackie Meets a Lady*, etc. Briskin would ask the writer to pick a title that sounded interesting and do sample pages. On that basis, a screenplay would be assigned but the title came first."

All too frequently problems arose requiring rewrites by authors and/or directors. "Sometimes they literally made up the story as we were shooting," says actress Ann Rutherford, a veteran of innumerable Bs from various studios including Columbia.

When the direction and writing were uninspired, many a Columbia B was rescued by the competence and professionalism demonstrated by able, inventive technicians like cinematographers Benjamin Kline, Henry Freulich, Philip Tannura, George Meehan, Lucien Ballard; editors Reginald "Reg" Browne, and Dwight Caldwell; art directors Hans Radon and Lionel Banks, all of whom developed new approaches to filmmaking to satisfy their tightfisted bosses. Set designers and art directors made do with smaller soundstages and sets, even painting both sides of the scenery. Costume design was extremely limited or non-existent. Veteran character actor Edward Norris, who made several films for Columbia, recalled often wearing his own apparel in B films, and said he won many a B role because "I owned the right clothes and wore them to work!" When Harry was forced by necessity to construct costly sets, props, and purchase expensive costumes for his high-bracket pictures, he did what any respectable penny-pinching financial genius would do: he recycled them again and again in low-budgeters, giving many of his Bs an added aura of respectability and class.

There was no area where Cohn's thrift and legendary eye for talent were more apparent than in his contract actors. At Columbia Pictures Corporation there were no overpaid, pampered superstars. The studio limited its roster to "affordable talent," which roughly fell into two categories: upwardly mobile young players looking for their first major break in films, like Evelyn Keyes, Nina Foch, Adele Jergens, Jeanne Bates, Larry Parks, Lloyd Bridges; and aging veteran grade A stars such as Warner Baxter, Chester Morris, and Richard Dix who swallowed their pride and accepted employment in Bs out a desire to continue working and/or financial need. Cohn did employ a tiny group of A-level actors like Jean Arthur and later Rita Hayworth but they received considerably less money than comparable talent at other studios.

Actors employed by Cohn's B unit often worked in multiple films concurrently. It was not unusual for them to put in 12 to 18-hour days. There were few if any rehearsals. Actors were expected to report for work prepared to make the first take a good one. It is not an exaggeration to liken Columbia B movie sets to pressure cookers!

In a 2008 interview published in the *Los Angeles Times*, Columbia contractee Nina Foch recalled her apprenticeship in Harry Cohn's B unit. "It's extraordinary how fast we made them [the Bs]. You'd shoot an entire picture in 10 or 12 days. We worked six days a week. There was no turn-around time back then, so you'd work into the evening, go home for six hours and then come back to work again. The movies were called noir because no one had the time to light anything."

Despite the hard work and Cohn's reputation as a tough taskmaster, most of his employees were surprisingly loyal and appreciative. One such player was actress Adele Jergens, who shed a favorable light on the studio in an interview with the author first published in *Films of the Golden Age* magazine in 2002. "I was under contract to Columbia for about five years. I liked working there very much. It was my home studio and I knew everyone and they knew me. Everybody was very nice, but they worked us hard. I only recall one film in which we were able to rehearse. They would put me in three pictures at one time, but I didn't mind [*laughter*]. I enjoyed it; and besides it was a steady income. Columbia was really a learning experience for me. I had been on the stage but never acted in films before. I was learning with each movie I made even though many were B pictures."

Another 1940s Columbia contract player, Jeanne Bates, also expressed gratitude to Cohn and company for the opportunity to appear in motion pictures in a 1994 interview with author/interviewer Tom Weaver published in his book *They Fought in the Creature Features*. "I was just one more Columbia starlet. Max Arnow was the head casting man and it was he who took me in to meet Mr. Cohn, the head of Columbia. Mr. Cohn looked up at me for a couple seconds, and then went right back to what he was doing [*laughs*]. But even though I knew they had no 'big plans' for me, I did do about twenty-two films in the short time I was there. There was a nice man in charge of Columbia's B unit [Briskin] and he liked me a lot, and he put me into some films."

Although never formally under contract to Cohn, actor Edward Norris said in separate interviews (conducted by the author in 2000 and 2001) that he also enjoyed working at Columbia in such films as *Scandal Sheet* (1940), *Sabotage Squad* (1942), *Trapped By Boston*

Edward Norris (left) and Sidney Blackmer in the Columbia action adventure *Sabotage Squad* (1942).

Blackie (1948), *Shadows In the Night* (1944), and *Close Call For Ellery Queen* (1942). "I worked for many B movie studios at that time. Although there were severe time constraints involved in all minor productions, in general Columbia scripts were of a higher quality and their directors took greater pains to make good films. I appreciated that and always looked forward to making pictures there."

Of course, not all the studio's players were content. Nina Foch put it bluntly, "I wasn't very happy at Columbia. I didn't like Harry Cohn and his ilk. They wished I was prettier, had luscious lips and big tits, but I didn't. But when you were under contract to a studio, you were stuck."

All film genres (both shorts and feature length) were represented by Columbia low-budget productions. Similar to his prestige pictures, Cohn developed a rough hierarchy for his Bs which corresponded to their budgets. At the top of the heap was the western followed by serials, short subjects, series films, and other studio productions which included adventures, crime dramas, and musicals. Unlike most studios Columbia distinguished itself in all categories. The following is a brief description of Columbia's eclectic mix of pre-*Whistler* B product in the order of their importance to "King" Cohn.

Given its reputation for producing memorable film short subjects and series, many find it surprising that westerns topped Cohn's B unit priority list. In his volume *The Merchant Prince of Poverty Row, Harry Cohn of Columbia Pictures*, Bernard Dick provided an explanation. "Although it may seem odd that Harry ranked the western second to the high bracket pictures, westerns played such an important role in Columbia history that its first Technicolor film was a western, *The Desperadoes* . . ." At one time or another Columbia employed many of the movieland's most successful cowboy actors, including Charles Starrett, Buck Jones, Ken Maynard, Gene Autry, and Tim McCoy. Because of the presence of recurring characters such as Starrett's "Durango Kid," some Columbia westerns technically qualify as series films.

Although they never achieved the renown of rivals Universal and Republic in the production of motion picture serials, the sheer magnitude of Columbia's serial output (192 titles) was impressive. Deemphasizing strong scripts, acting, and directing in favor of "thrilling action" and ingenious escapes, during the 1940s the studio mesmerized young movie patrons with the exciting adventures of comic book heroes like *Batman* (1943), *Superman* (1948), and *The Shadow* (1940), as well as the exploits of *Captain Midnight* (1942). Western shoot-'em-ups and jungle adventures were also popular fodder for Columbia cliffhangers, featuring such noted serial actors as Buster Crabbe, Kane Richmond, Robert Lowery, Kirk Alyn, and cowboys Clayton Moore and Jock Mahoney.

Following a tradition established during the silent era when it released its famed Hall Room Boy photoplays, Cohn and company produced a stunning variety of one- and two-reelers throughout the 1930s and 1940s (529 in all). Although there were documentaries, travelogues, musicals, newsreels, sports reels, and cartoons, the studio's most memorable short subjects were comedies, notably those starring Larry Fine and the Howard Brothers, (Moe, Curly, later Shemp) better known as the Three Stooges. With a major assist from producer Jules White and his ace technical team, the iconic trio made 190 short comedies (1934–57) for Columbia, tackling subjects ranging from the exceedingly silly to Nazism and anti-Semitism. Under White's guidance such comedy talents as Leon Errol, Vera Vague, Andy Clyde, Charlie Chase, and even Buster Keaton also contributed comic short subjects for Harry Cohn. In the cartoon category Columbia distinguished itself as the home of the Oscar-winning Mr. Magoo, and for the early work of the legendary Walt Disney.

The bottom rung on Harry's ladder was occupied by a disparate group of second features, many of which are fondly remembered for their innovation, pace, and utilization of unheralded talent. Besides series pictures there were musicals, comedies, mysteries, adventures, melodramas, dramas, and horrors. Notable pre-*Whistler* examples included thrillers *The Man They Could Not Hang* (1939), *The Devil Commands* (1941), and *The Face Behind the Mask* (1941); the crime comedy *There's Always a Woman* (1938), musical comedies *Sweetheart of the Fleet* (1942), and *Reveille With Beverly* (1943); the macabre melodrama *The Black Room* (1935); the aerial meller *Devil's Squadron* (1936); and the dramatic *Adventures of Martin Eden* (1942).

Among the lowest of Cohn's low-budgeters was the series film. It is more than ironic given the fame and popularity of Columbia's series then and now. Based on various sources we know the visionary Harry was uncharacteristically late to realize the full potential of the non-western film series. He'd dabbled in detective series pictures for years; producing a few silents and early talkies featuring author Louis Joseph Vance's reformed jewel thief, the Lone Wolf, and Rex Stout's orchid-growing criminologist, Nero Wolfe; but it wasn't until 1938 he made a decisive move to enter the movie series competition. By then many rivals had beaten him to the punch; winning plaudits and striking box-office gold producing groups of feature-length motion pictures with characters adapted from popular mystery/suspense literature and radio like Charlie Chan and Mr. Moto (Fox), Perry Mason and Philo Vance (WB), The Thin Man (MGM), Tarzan (MGM, RKO), and Bulldog Drummond (Paramount). Undoubtedly, the success of the Chan and Tarzan films were influential in Cohn and company's decision to enter the fray.

While Harry may have been a late convert to the film series, by the 1940s he was churning them out with a vengeance. Excluding

One of Columbia's most popular and enduring series was devoted to the adventures of comic book heroine Blondie and her husband Dagwood (Penny Singleton and Arthur Lake). A scene from *Blondie Goes to College* (1942).

B westerns, Columbia made 11 motion picture series in the period (1938–55). Similar to its other B movie product, the studio did not specialize in a particular type. There were comedies (Blondie, Gasoline Alley), warm family dramas (Five Little Peppers, Rusty), adventures (Jungle Jim), detective whodunits (Ellery Queen, Lone Wolf, Boston Blackie, Crime Doctor) and crime thrillers (Whistler, I Love a Mystery). Some were hits, some were misses, but all had redeeming qualities.

Three of the most popular Columbia series produced in the period just prior to the *Whistler*, Lone Wolf (1926–49), Boston Blackie (1941–49), and Crime Doctor (1943–49), were of the crime mystery genre. Their success undoubtedly influenced Columbia's decision to produce a similar series. The Crime Doctor pictures, in particular, appear to have paved the way for the *Whistler* films by engendering great fan support and even an occasional "tip of the hat" from critics.

Debonair Warren William (second from left) impersonated fictional sleuth Michael Lanyard, known as the Lone Wolf in a long-running Columbia series. A scene from the *Passport to Suez* (1943), costarring Lloyd Bridges (center right) and series regular Eric Blore (far right).

The adventures of a reformed jewel thief named Boston Blackie (played by charismatic Chester Morris) was the focus of another popular Columbia mystery detective series. From left to right: Adele Mara, Morris, and series regulars George E. Stone and Richard Lane in a publicity shot for *Alias Boston Blackie* (1942).

The daring exploits of gangster-turned-psychiatrist/sleuth Robert Ordway, known as the Crime Doctor (Warner Baxter), became the sixth major Columbia series in 1943. From left to right: Baxter, Gloria Dickson, Sam Flint, Rose Hobart, Virginia Brissac, Reginald Denny in *The Crime Doctor's Strangest Case* (1943).

CHAPTER THREE
MR. WHISTLER TAKES TO THE AIR

The date is May 16, 1942. It's early evening on the U.S. West Coast and a war weary Mr. and Mrs. America and their children are huddled around their radios hoping for a respite from their worries if only for a few moments. An announcer interrupts the silence. "Wait a minute, have you heard the Whistler?" They don't know it yet but these lucky listeners are about to become transfixed on terror; about to witness the debut broadcast of one of the most successful programs in all radio history, one which would not only tingle their spines but challenge their brains.

Suddenly, a hauntingly, discordant 13-note whistle is heard which becomes progressively louder as a suspenseful music score is played. Out of the blue a sinister voice proclaims, "I am the Whistler" followed by a brief, terrifying preview of the program, and a formal announcement, "Tonight, CBS presents a new mystery series, The Whistler." Then the macabre voice takes the microphone again to identify himself and state his mission: "I am the Whistler and I know many things for I walk by night. I know many strange tales, many secrets hidden in the hearts of men and women who have stepped into the shadows. Yes, I know the nameless terrors of which they dare not speak! And so I tell you tonight the strange mystery of 'Retribution' . . ."

The story involved convicted killer John Hendricks, sentenced to life for hacking up his wife and stepson in order to lay claim to her money. After 10 years of incarceration he escapes from prison and returns home on a stormy, windswept night to retrieve a large sum hidden in the fireplace. All does not go as planned. As he attempts to leave the old abandoned house with the cash, he is confronted and killed by what he believes to be the spirits of his wife and stepson returned from their graves to avenge their gruesome deaths. In reality, the vengeful spirits are merely murderous mortals hired by John's greedy cellmate who intends to claim the money for himself.

Although it's impossible to say just how many shudders cascaded down the backs of the radio audience that night as they listened to the horrific tale of ax murders and vengeance, we do know the unique 30-minute program created quite a stir, guaranteeing there would be many more to follow. In fact, "Retribution" would be the first of 692 West Coast *Whistler* episodes in a series which would be heard each week for the next 13 years, until September 22, 1955.

Broadcast on CBS, sponsored until 1955 by the Signal Oil Company (later by Lever Brothers), the program was the brainchild of writer, actor, producer, pioneer broadcast executive J. (John) Donald Wilson, who penned the initial episodes, and produced and directed the series for two years. In 1944, he turned over the directorial and production duties to George W. Allen so he could oversee Columbia's *Whistler* films and other projects.

The amazing success of the *Whistler* on radio is often attributed to a combination of traditional and non-traditional elements. An anthology series with different characters and storylines each week, *Whistler* episodes nonetheless followed a familiar formula. Like "Retribution," each program began with the spooky 13-note theme, the Whistler's trademark recitation, immediately followed by a brief introduction. Throughout each half-hour episode, the Whistler character often interrupted proceedings to make comments or voice the thoughts of characters. He concluded each broadcast with an explanation of events which were ordinarily not as they seemed.

The Whistler radio programs frequently contained supernatural elements, but the tales spun by the omniscient Whistler were primarily crime stories chronicling the experiences of ordinary individuals who wander outside the boundaries of law, propriety, and morality to achieve an unsavory objective. The program's tragic protagonists were oft-times driven to their crimes by a confluence of unfortunate circumstances and by the corruption of others, but theirs is a conscious decision to violate, one for which they must a pay a price. Greed, selfishness, desperation, and madness were often motivating factors. Most perpetrators make a valiant attempt to avoid detection and punishment. Many seem to have succeeded when fate inevitably intervenes. In the end most are undone by their own avarice, carelessness, stupidity, and the hand of destiny guided by the all-knowing Whistler.

Narrated in the highly distinctive second person, present tense (from the perpetrator's viewpoint), the liberal use of irony and innumerable plot twists and turns lent the "crime does not pay" morality tales a unique aura of disquietude which kept listeners interested and entertained. Unlike traditional whodunits, and most suspense programs, the criminal's and/or killer's identity was known at the outset. Mystery and suspense was derived from how they would be caught. The series' surprise endings (a la O. Henry) were also a major source of popular appeal and a challenge to its creators. Trying to guess the outcome of each thriller became a favorite pastime, one which kept dedicated fans glued to their radios and series' writers and directors on their toes. In a 1948 *Radio World* interview, director George Allen discussed this professional challenge. "We know that many of the listeners play the game along with us and we love to have them do it . . . We don't pull our twists out of left field. We try to make them surprising but logical. Two thirds of the scripts submitted don't have a Whistler ending. We have to dream those up ourselves."

Of *The Whistler's* many distinct elements none was more important to its phenomenal success than its secret weapon: its sinister, silk-voiced star/host, exceptionally portrayed by Bill Forman. Similar to his soul brother, *Inner Sanctum's* fiendish Raymond, the character was literally the glue which held the productions together. Like a Greek chorus he introduced the tale, interacted with his characters, commented on their activities, and wrapped up the story with a chillingly cryptic summation. Resembling the Shadow, Wilson's Whistler was a supernatural being with exceptional powers to read minds and see the future, entering and exiting situations without being seen. Also like the original Walter Gibson Shadow, the Whistler had a mean, vengeful streak. He delighted in the misery of his protagonists, laughed at their predicaments, and expressed a snide satisfaction in their punishment and/or deaths. Most believe the Whistler represented destiny, judgment. There is ample evidence to support this thesis; but it is a fate tinged with cruelty, a judgment untempered by mercy, meted out in a retaliatory manner befitting a lynch mob not the steady, even-handed restraint we have come to associate with jurisprudence.

In an effort to heighten the suspense and improve the broadcasts, the innovative Mr. Allen, who helmed the radio series for 11 years, continually altered the program to keep it fresh. He eventually discontinued the Whistler's dialogue with characters, and began relying on his cast to deliver each story's denouement instead of a Whistler epilogue. In a *Radio Life* magazine interview Allen described the uniqueness of his program, and paid tribute to his writers and actors. "Listeners are always commenting on the fact that there is no real horror portrayed on the show—killings, screams, and attendant horrific elements are never played on mike. It is the actors themselves who deliver the impact of these dramatic elements through their own convincing interpretations."

For those unfamiliar with the on-air *Whistler*, the following is a sample of the program's opening and ending narration from an early, George W. Allen-directed episode entitled, "The Last of the Devereaux," a tale of murder and revenge in the American South. Broadcast on July 23, 1944 (before Allen discontinued the Whistler's epilogue), it chronicled the evil machinations of a nouveau riche man who achieved his most cherished wish by ruthlessly obtaining a plantation from an aristocratic family, only to be undone by an unlikely foe who is as cunning as he. It is included here to give readers a rough sense of the mood and atmospherics of each *Whistler* story.

The program begins with the standard whistle, "I am the Whistler" recitation, then an introduction to the story.

"THE LAST OF THE DEVEREAUX" INTRODUCTION:

THE WHISTLER: "In the bayou country of the deep South, a land inhabited by the descendents of early French settlers stands an ancient mansion called the Cypresses. Owned for generations by the aristocratic Devereaux family, the plantation boasts acre upon acre of sugar cane bending to the warm river breezes. Life goes on much as it has in the past. Beauty is everywhere, but danger, too; like the treacherous morasses which lie beneath innocent flowers. Paul Viertel, who is definitely not aristocratic, has long wanted the Cypresses for his own; hopelessly it seems. Ah, but times have changed. Paul is now rich and today as the heavy door of the Devereaux mansion opens he believes his ambitions are about to be realized."

A short scene follows in which Viertel hastens the death of aged, sickly Mr. Devereaux, who places a curse on him. The Whistler returns to the microphone.

THE WHISTLER: "Poor old Mr. Devereaux; but how very fortunate for Paul Viertel, now the master of the Cypresses. Paul is quite pleased with the way things are going. By nightfall Doctor Carson has already signed a death certificate. An inquest would have been such an annoyance! Then, too, there is this Miss Anne, young fascinating Miss Anne, who at the dinner table identifies herself as Anne Martin, the Devereaux's housekeeper with a strong love for the Cypresses, its gloomy old house, and its swamps."

As it turns out the lovely, innocent appearing Anne is really Devereaux's daughter out to avenge her father's death and keep the estate in the Devereaux family. She succeeds but her victory is pyrrhic.

"THE LAST OF THE DEVEREAUX" EPILOGUE:

THE WHISTLER: "And so Anne Devereaux got the Cypresses back in the family. [*snide laughter*] Yesss, she tricked Paul Viertel using every means at her command to break him in body and mind. She had an ally in the malaria, of course, but Anne helped that along by giving Paul capsules of plain flour instead of quinine. Unfortunately for her, people cannot store up as much hatred as Anne without hurting themselves. And that's why when they found her after the storm she was still laughing, quite insane."

STANDARD CLOSING: Concluding whistle.

The following is a partial list of cast and credits for radio's *The Whistler*.

CAST: For the greater portion of its 13-year run (1942–55), the Whistler was brilliantly portrayed by Bill Forman, whose name was not revealed until 1951. Dripping with macabre irony, Forman's spooky, expressive tenor voice added an amazing air of suspense to the productions. When Forman served in the armed forces during the war years, the character was played at various times by Gale Gordon, Joseph Kearns, Marvin Miller, Bill Johnstone, and Everett Clarke. Supporting casts included many regulars who made so many appearances on the program they became known as "Whistler's children." Rotating assignments, according to the needs of the script, were Bill & Cathy Elliott, Betty Lou Gerson, Wally Maher, Joseph Kearns, Joan Banks, John Brown, Hans Conried, Gerald Mohr, Lurene Tuttle, Gloria Blondell, John McIntire, and Jeanette Nolan, among others. During its many years on the air *The Whistler* series also featured appearances by several actors who would enjoy notable film careers. Among them were Jeff Chandler, Frank Lovejoy, Howard Duff, Donald Woods, and Mercedes McCambridge.

MUSIC: The Wilbur Hatch orchestra. Hatch not only composed the music but also wrote the haunting *Whistler* theme: an unusual two-octave whistle impeccably delivered each week for 13 long years by Dorothy Roberts.

PRODUCER-DIRECTOR: J. Donald Wilson (1942–44), George W. Allen (1944–55). Other directors included Sterling Tracy, and Sherman Marks.

WRITERS: J. Donald Wilson created the Whistler character and wrote many of the initial stories. Countless other writers contributed through the years. Final scripts were furnished by Harold Swanton and Joel Malone.

ENGINEER: Robert Anderson.

SOUND EFFECTS: Berne Surrey, Gene Twombly, and Ross Murray.

The popularity of *The Whistler* eventually spread beyond the West Coast. On August 21, 1946, an East Coast broadcast commenced on the CBS network, sponsored by the Household Finance Corporation, with Everett Clarke as the Whistler. It lasted two years and 77 episodes until September 1948 when it was discontinued. In 1946, at the height of its popularity, a local Chicago version of *The Whistler* was also produced on WBBM featuring local actors, sponsored by Meister Brau beer.

There are several websites which contain information and semi-complete logs of all known West and East Coast episodes of radio's *The Whistler* and broadcast dates. Two of the best are Jerry Haendiges Vintage Radio Logs and Radio Goldindex by J. David Goldin.

CHAPTER FOUR
UNDER THE TRENCH COAT
ANATOMY OF THE WHISTLER ON FILM

In the summer of 1943, the stars appeared perfectly aligned for the birth of *The Whistler* on film. On the heels of Columbia's successful adaptation of radio's *Crime Doctor* studio execs were contemplating another series and the airwaves appeared the perfect place to find one. From the beginning, radio's *Whistler* seemed destined to find its way to the silver screen. Since its 1942 debut the program had become a fixture with listeners and was on a fast track to becoming the most popular on the West Coast. While the destruction of Columbia's production and office records in 1972 prevents us from learning all the background details of how the series came to be, the popularity of the radio program was surely the number one motivator which led producer Rudolf Flothow to propose an initial *Whistler* picture to Irving Briskin who brokered it to Harry Cohn.

By July 1943 a preliminary agreement had been reached to purchase the screen rights from Wilson, who agreed to furnish the initial story and oversee the first film. One month later Columbia contract scenarist Eric Taylor received the assignment to write the screenplay based on Wilson's story; and veteran actor Richard Dix was signed to star.

Production began on January 21, 1944. Directed with panache by young, exuberant William Castle, *The Whistler* was released five weeks later to virtually unanimous popular and critical approval. By July 1944, Columbia's commitment to a *Whistler* series became official when a delighted Cohn acquired the screen rights to famed pulp-fiction writer Cornell Woolrich's unusual story "Dormant Account" and began filming series entry # 2, *The Mark of the*

Whistler, which reteamed Castle with newly-signed Columbia contractee Dix. Released in November 1944, *Mark* also engendered positive notices. Some influential critics and columnists compared it favorably to its predecessor; even declaring it one of the best low-budgeters ever made.

During the next three years, the studio would make six more *Whistler* features (roughly two per year), shot in the period between December 1944 and October 1947. None were artistic masterpieces, but many historians often cite them as examples of how good low-budget films could be given the right mix of craftsmanship and commitment. One of the series' most ardent admirers was Oscar-winning director Robert Wise, who expressed his fondness for the *Whistlers* in a book about his mentor, Val Lewton, *Fearing the Dark: The Val Lewton Career* (authored by Edmund G. Bansak and published in 1995). In a two-page salute, Wise spoke for many experts and industry professionals when he described the eight *Whistler* features as "examples of budget filmmaking at its very best . . . though they were designed as second bill fodder, they were at times preferable to the feature films with which they played."

Before evaluating the *Whistler* pictures on an individual basis, it is important to take stock of the series as a whole; emphasizing common elements which bound all the entries into a semi-cohesive unit, including details and characteristics relating to their production (i.e. budgets, shooting schedules, etc.), themes, atmospherics, characters, storylines, casts, and various personnel.

Despite the acclaim and the box-office appeal generated by the *Whistler* films, there is absolutely no evidence any of them were considered special by Columbia. In fact, the opposite is true. Designed solely for the purpose of filling the bottom half of a double bill, all were produced (in the fashion described in Chapter 2) by Darmour Inc. This company was founded by low-budget indie producer Lawrence J. "Larry" Darmour, who ran poverty row's Majestic Pictures and made programmers for Republic before subcontracting with Columbia in the latter 1930s. When Darmour died prematurely in 1942, he was succeeded by his assistant, German-born Rudolph Flothow, who supervised the *Whistler* films. All were shot on the Darmour Lot located at 5821 Santa Monica Boulevard (the corner of Santa Monica Blvd. and Gower across from the Hollywood Cemetery) utilizing Columbia personnel.

Thanks to the time-tested talents of Columbia's well-oiled B machine, all eight *Whistler* features were manufactured quickly (10–19 days) and cheaply (budgets ranged from $65,000 to $75,000) utilizing Darmour's cityscapes and pedestrian interior sets. To save precious pennies stock footage was substituted for location shots; and art directors and set designers used scenery and sets constructed for other motion pictures. *Whistler* scripts were produced by company scenarists in days rather than weeks and often "evolved" as filming progressed. Since most of the screenplays involved bleak, big city settings and working-class characters they could be darkly lit and inexpensively costumed. Wilbur Hatch's memorable Whistler theme was retained, and Dorothy Roberts was brought in to record her famous 13-note whistle, but most of the series' music was unoriginal; composed previously for other productions. Substantial savings was also netted on creative personnel. With the exception of Dix, no special contracts were proffered to big-named actors and technicians. Writers, directors, cinematographers, supporting casts, etc., came primarily from the studio stable at Columbia's cut-rate salaries.

If the *Whistler* pictures reflected the economical efficiency of the typical Columbia cluster production, they were exceptional in many important respects as well. Unlike other movie series the *Whistlers* was an anthology with distinct characters and stories. Given the desire of filmgoers to attach themselves to familiar characters this might have become a disadvantage were it not for the series' other distinguished elements. Among them were an intriguing premise, a mysterious host/narrator, and atmospheric screenplays featuring provocative protagonists and ironic climaxes, and the superb craftsmanship of accomplished filmmakers.

Although the *Whistler* film series was not an exact replica of its radio predecessor, the hit program's most compelling elements were retained by Cohn, Flothow, and company, who wisely recognized it would be foolhardy to tamper with its successful formula. Parroting the radio program, each 60 to 70-minute film established an air of unpredictability and foreboding early on. Each commenced with familiar footsteps, the appearance of a shadowy figure who whistled his mournful 13 notes, then recited his trademark speech, ("I am the Whistler and I know many things . . .") followed by a brief introduction to the main character and story. In the tradition of his radio blood brother, the cinematic Whistler, portrayed by silk-tongued, uncredited Otto Forrest, served multiple functions. As host and framing device he introduced the protagonists and concluded each feature by tying up all the stories' loose ends. As a superhuman voice of conscience and fate he provided advice to his main characters, commented on their activities, and on rare occasions, interceded on their behalf. And lastly, as an avenging angel he meted out severe, often deadly punishment with a vindictive delight reminiscent of both the radio Whistler and his contemporary, the Shadow.

As on radio filmgoers knew at the outset who the culprit was. The element of mystery was derived from how he would be apprehended and punished. The eight protagonists featured in the *Whistler* films were also similar to their radio counterparts. An eclectic mix of "ordinary" and "extraordinary" individuals each tested the fates by making life-altering decisions or committing immoral and/or unlawful acts. More akin to the antiheroes of late 1940s *film noir* than the paragons of virtue traditionally featured in traditional series cinema, those who "stepped into the shadows" of the filmland's Whistler were conflicted, desperate people, some victims of circumstances others hostages to greed, and unhealthy desires. The pitched battle between their good and evil sides was a fundamental key to their personalities and their stories. Seven of the eight suffer severe physical and psychological ailments which complicate their lives and often motivate them to make bad decisions. Most end up as physical and psychological fugitives who seek relief and refuge wherever they can find it. Some end up on the dark, dangerous streets of the big city where they fight for their sanity and survival in a nightmarish scenario of felons, crazies and murderers. Four of them narrowly escape with their lives in thrilling, often ironic climaxes, but none avoids their fate as predetermined by the ominous Whistler.

Not all the exceptional qualities found in the film series came from radio. Some fascinating aspects (both thematic and atmospheric) were unique to the visual medium of the cinema. For instance, many of the ironic, suspenseful stories featured in the *Whistler* films were enhanced by a *noir*-like mood of disillusionment and pessimism created by skilled directors and cameramen. Tension was heightened through the utilization of unusual camera angles and manipulation of lighting. The use of chiaroscuro (shadows and dark light) was particularly effective in depicting the bleakness of scenes which often took place in sinister locations like dimly-lit hotel rooms, flop houses, waterfront dives, and old storerooms. These visual settings not only enhanced the suspenseful atmosphere, and functioned as embodiments of the thematic despair depicted in the stories, but often appeared to be characters in their own right. Symbolizing urban poverty, decay, and violence, they provide (no doubt unintentionally) a rich subtext of social commentary to the features. Still another important difference between the filmic and radio series was obvious. Thanks to the visual medium of film, audiences had a chance to see the mysterious entity known as the Whistler (in shadow attired in a trench coat and fedora).

The uniqueness of the film series was also apparent in the personnel department. In order to give it necessary continuity, Columbia hired a single actor to star in all the *Whistler* films in contrast to the radio program which featured different leads each week. That honor went to former silent heartthrob Richard Dix, an Academy Award-nominated star who'd gained lasting fame playing staid, square-jawed heroes. A gifted actor whose age and unhealthy habits had begun to catch up with him, Dix had been working in Bs for several years when he opted to cast off the shackles of his status as a movie hero and accept lead roles in the *Whistler* series in 1944. Alternating between anti-heroes and outright villains, he contributed superb performances in seven of the eight entries. His characterizations contain an edgy, unsettling quality perfectly in keeping with the films' moods and dark themes. With a face etched in sadness and melancholy, he was particularly effective in portraying the duality of the *Whistler* protagonists who appear refined and outwardly passive, but who harbor dark secrets which often manifest themselves in desperate acts. When deteriorating health forced him to retire in 1947, he was replaced (for only one film) by Columbia contractee Michael Duane.

In all eight films Dix and Duane were ably supported by a group of seasoned veteran actors and talented newcomers like J. Carrol

Naish, Gloria Stuart, Karen Morley, Lynn Merrick, Porter Hall, John Calvert, Janis Carter, Leslie Brooks, Barton MacLane, and Kathleen Howard. These experienced thespians and many others contributed essential performances to the series; adding meat to the skinny screenplays by breathing life into a incredible variety of characters, from sympathetic heroes and pitiable victims to a veritable rogue's gallery of crooks, con artists, *femme fatales*, and remorseless killers. Because there was so little time in each 60 to 65-minute picture for character development, it is a testament to their abilities that so many striking supporting performances surfaced. The superb craftsmanship of Columbia cinematographers like Philip Tannura, George Meehan, and L.W. O'Connell, and art directors such as John Datu, and Hans Radon, etc., added further depth and dimension to the productions.

The contributions of expert directors also distinguished the series. Half the *Whistler* films were helmed by William Castle, a talented young up-and-comer who had only one film to his credit prior to directing the series' first entry. Combining an action-packed style, innovative use of lighting, unusual camera angles, and a cornucopia of gimmicks and contrivances (that would later become his trademark); Castle pushed every possible button in order to enhance the tension and entertain his audiences. Seasoned veteran directors Lew Landers, William Clemens, and George Sherman also contributed respectable films in the series. Landers' *The Power of the Whistler* was a particularly strong entry which demonstrated the veteran director's consummate skill and professionalism.

The following consists of eight separate sections corresponding to the each *Whistler* film arranged in the order of release. Under each title heading are several subsections listing all pertinent information regarding the production. As part of the plot summary the entirety of each Whistler introduction and epilogue is included. The "expert opinions" section consists of critical assessments taken from several authoritative sources, including Don Miller's *B Movies*, Jon Tuska's *The Detective in Hollywood*, Arthur Lyon's *Death on the Cheap*, John Cocchi's, *Second Features*, Leonard Maltin's *Movie Video Guide*, Michael Pitts' *Famous Movie Detectives II*, and Edmund Bansak's *Fearing the Dark: The Val Lewton Career*. "My take" is a short summation of the author's overall opinion followed by an

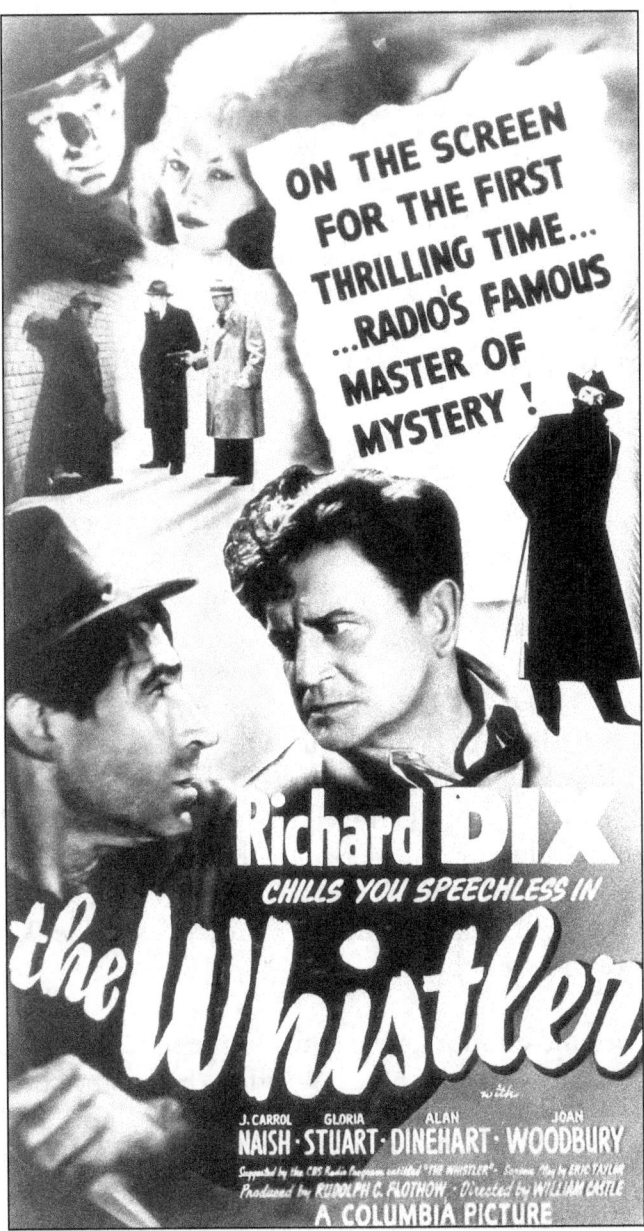

Poster for *The Whistler*.

in-depth analysis of each film. The numerical ratings at the end of each subsection are provided as a means of comparing the films and provoking debate. Number one is my choice as the best of the series, number eight the weakest.

THE WHISTLER (COLUMBIA – 1944)

PRODUCTION: January 21, 1944 – February 7, 1944
RELEASE: March 30, 1944.
RUNNING TIME: 59 minutes.
TAGLINES: "Men shudder at the mere sound of him! Women scream at the mere thought of him!"

"WHEN HE WHISTLES, SOMEONE DIES!"

CREDITS: Rudolph C. Flothow (Producer), William Castle (Director), Eric Taylor (screenplay) based on a story by J. Donald Wilson, suggested by the radio program, "The Whistler" created by J. Donald Wilson, James S. Brown (photography), Wilbur Hatch (Music), Jerome Thoms (editing), George Van Marter (art direction), Sidney Clifford (set decoration).

CAST: Richard Dix (Earl Conrad), J. Carroll Naish (The Killer), Gloria Stuart (Alice Walker), Alan Dinehart (Gorman), Joan Woodbury (Toni Vigran), Cy Kendall (Bartender), Trevor Bardette (The Thief), Don Costello (Lefty Vigran), Clancy Cooper (Briggs), Byron Foulger (Flophouse Clerk), Robert E. Keane (Charles McNear), George Lloyd (Bill Tomley), Charles Coleman (Jennings), Robert E. Homans (Dock Watchman), Otto Forrest (The Whistler), Billy Benedict (Delivery boy).

The Whistler and all subsequent films in the series begin with the sound of footsteps, the 13-note Whistler theme (performed by Dorothy Roberts), and the standard recitation: "I am the Whistler and I know many things for I walk by night. I know many strange tales, many secrets hidden in the hearts of men and women who have stepped into the shadows. Yes, I know the nameless terrors of which they dare not speak." This is followed by an introduction to each story.

The Whistler Introduction:

The Whistler: "The man sitting alone is a stranger here. He has means and a responsible position in society. He's a man who's more at home in a fashionable club than a waterfront bar. But tonight he has turned from the comfort and security of his own world to meet a man whose business is death!"

Plot Summary: Despondent and guilt ridden over his wife's apparent drowning death, while on a cruise attempting to salvage a crumbling marriage, wealthy merchant Earl Conrad (Richard Dix) decides to commit suicide. Fearful of doing the job himself, for $10,000 he hires local thug Lefty Vigran (Don Costello), whom he meets at the waterfront dive "The Crows Nest." Vigran pockets half the cash and sends the remainder along with Conrad's address via deaf mute currier (Billy Benedict) to professional assassin (J. Carrol Naish), a cold-blooded killer obsessed with the idea of murdering a person by scaring them to death. When Conrad learns from his devoted secretary, Alice (Gloria Stuart), that his wife is alive in a Japanese prison camp, he regrets his deadly decision and sets out on a quest to prevent his own murder. The problem is Vigran is now deceased (killed in a shoot-out with police) and Conrad never learned the identity of his would-be killer.

A match of wits ensues between the intelligent, resourceful Conrad and his determined and demented assassin. As the hours and days pass a psychologically distressed Earl confronts a bewildering array of coincidences, imagined and real foes, including the killer disguised as a slick insurance salesman, Vigran's vengeful widow (Joan Woodbury), and a dangerous, desperate vagrant (Trevor Bardette) who attempts to murder him in order to steal his wallet. Meanwhile, the maniacal killer continues to shadow his intended victim, gradually showing his face, waiting for a panicked Conrad to die of fright.

The final sequences find the exhausted Conrad preparing to escape his assailant by stowing away on a Red Cross mercy ship. When he collapses of exhaustion at the harbor, he is rescued by a dock watchman who summons Alice, calls the police, then takes the sick man to the harbor master's office. As Alice is preparing to take her boss home, the killer, lurking outside, aims and fires at Conrad from the window. He misses his mark and is killed by police. In the end good fortune smiles on Conrad. Not only has he escaped death, but Alice informs him his wife died in a Japanese internment camp, which leaves the unhappy man free to start a new life with Alice.

THE WHISTLER EPILOGUE:

THE WHISTLER: "It was this man's destiny to die tonight. Earl Conrad lives because man cannot change his destiny. After this dark night he will recover from his mental illness and there will come a new chapter in his life which will bring happiness to him. I know because I am the Whistler."

The film concludes with the 13-note Whistler theme. All seven subsequent films would end similarly.

REVIEWS FOR THE WHISTLER:

Variety: "A new type of gangster-killer melodrama . . . an exciting bout of wits to see whether Dix will crack under the strain of being shadowed by a pro-killer or be able to bring the man to terms."

Film Daily: "Ace melodrama, developed with great tautness and suspense, is a model of simplicity . . . The straightforward direction of William Castle is praiseworthy indeed . . . Dix and Naish are outstanding in top roles."

New York World Telegram: "This is one of the year's most compact and movingly narrated manhunts . . . William Castle, a new name among directors, has assembled a good cast and drawn the most from them in a picture full of his dexterous skill."

Brownsville Herald: "*The Whistler* lives up to its air reputation. It clicks in every department which fans demand of their mysteries. It has suspense, twists and turns of plot, and an original, thought provoking idea on which its action is based…Richard Dix gives a convincing portrayal of a man whose nerve is broken by constant fear of death. Gloria Stuart as his secretary is a lovely contrast to the grimness of the Dix characterization . . . J. Carrol Naish is an acting standout in the role of the warp minded killer . . ."

Expert Opinions:

Don Miller: "Taylor's script was suspenseful and without waste motion. Castle heightened the tenseness with excellent economy of means while eliciting exemplary performances from Dix and J. Carrol Naish as the killer."

Leonard Maltin: "Tense, moody tale of fate sets the ironic tone for the rest. Naish shines as the principle hit man."

Movie Morlocks.com: "Structurally, it's typical B-unit stuff, running under an hour and confined for the most part to the back lot. But those generic, nameless city streets and storefronts actually add to the atmosphere of mental degeneration, reminding me of the sad paintings of Edward Hopper and the bleak cityscapes of the nascent *film noir* movement . . ."

Michael Pitts: "The film was well written, and William Castle's direction was tight and supplied the film with an aura of suspense and horror."

Motion Picture Guide: "Director Castle made his first big impression with this tense little B programmer . . . A perfect example of the art that could be created within the strictures of studio B-unit production.

Interesting Facts/Trivia — The Whistler

1. According to William Castle's autobiography, *Step Right Up, I'm Gonna Scare the Pants Off America* (Putnam, 1976), he was first handed the script of *The Whistler* directly from Harry Cohn immediately after receiving scathing reviews for his first Columbia feature, *Chance of a Lifetime*. After a tongue lashing Cohn rewarded his frightened young director with what Castle described as, "one of the most terrifying screenplays I'd ever read." When he telephoned Cohn later that day, Castle made the mogul a promise. "I'll scare the shit out of audiences."

2. Later in his autobiography, Castle discussed various aspects of filming *The Whistler*.
"I tried every effect I could dream up to create a mood of terror: low key lighting, wide-angle lenses to give an eerie feeling, and a hand-held camera in many of the important scenes to give a sense of reality to the horror. To achieve a mood of desperation I insisted that Dix give up smoking and go on a diet. This made him nervous and irritable, particularly when I gave him early-morning calls and kept him waiting on the set, sometimes for an entire day before using him in a scene. He was constantly off-center, restless, fidgety, and nervous as a cat. When I finally used him in a scene, I'd make him do it over and over until he was ready to explode. It achieved the desired effect, that of a man haunted by fear and trying to keep from being murdered."

3. According to Castle's autobiography, as a means of promoting *The Whistler*, he suggested Cohn hire an actor to dress up like the Dix character and run up and down theater aisles screaming while several paid audience plants fainted. Cohn flatly refused.

4. Harry Cohn rewarded Castle for his work on the acclaimed movie by loaning him to the King Brothers at Monogram at a profit of $400 a week. Castle would have the last laugh, however. The film, made in seven days at a total cost of $50,000, was the B-movie classic *When Strangers Marry* starring young Robert Mitchum.

5. In an interview with author Tom Weaver in his book *It Came from Weaver Five* (McFarland, 1996), leading lady Gloria Stuart recalled filming *The Whistler*. "That was purely freelance. I did *The Whistler* because Bill Castle asked me to do it, and I thought maybe I might want to go back to film acting. (I decided I didn't.) Bill was very young and very gung-ho, and very talented, I thought. It was a very pleasant engagement."

6. *The Whistler* (1944) contains two separate interventions by the mysterious titled character to save the life of the unfortunate Dix. This is significant because apparently the contrivance concocted by scenarist Eric Taylor was considered ill-advised or unnecessary and was discontinued. The Whistler whistled, provided narration and commentary in succeeding entries, but he never intervened to help the protagonist again.

7. For the first and last time during the series filmgoers saw the back of the Whistler's head. From here on out, in order to make him more sinister and otherworldly, Columbia decided to show him only as a shadowy silhouette.

8. The film contains the two best lines of dialogueue in all eight pictures. The most famous is homeless psychotic's (Trevor Bardette) famous admonition to Dix as he leads the exhausted man to an abandoned storefront where he hopes to murder him for his billfold.

THE THIEF: "There's rats in here as big as beavers. They won't hurt you, but you're liable to trip over them in the dark."

The other memorable line is delivered by Dix's would-be assassin (J. Carrol Naish), who expresses an obsession with the idea of scaring someone to death.

THE KILLER: "Maybe I'm on to something in the art of murder, 'No fuss, no muss.'"

9. In *The Whistler* the psychotic killers' macabre preoccupation with death is reinforced by his favorite book, *Studies in Necrophobia, An Exaggerated Fear of Death*. Interestingly, the same book turns up in the hands of a heroic young boy in the sixth series entry, *The Thirteenth Hour*.

10. Sadly and ironically, actor Don Costello, who played Lefty Vigran the criminal middle man who is killed in a shoot-out in *The Whistler*, died suddenly just one year and nine months after filming it (October 1945).

My Take:

The Whistler is a creepy, unnerving rollercoaster ride of a film chock full of chills, thrills, and hairpin turns with enough kooky characters to keep a dozen funhouses in business. If you're a fan of the Bs it is a must-see.

A praiseworthy script, some excellent photography, first-rate acting, and superb direction helped give *The Whistler* series a great sendoff. There is much to like in this film, beginning with its screenplay. Although scenarist Eric Taylor had little time to write a well-developed script based on Wilson's story, he did manage to create a compelling sketch from which Castle and his actors could paint a detailed picture. His creative use of character and setting was particularly effective in energizing and refreshing an old chestnut of a plot. Utilizing big city streets as a backdrop, the former *Black Mask* writer built chills and tension by sending his wealthy protagonist, Conrad, on a *noirish* journey into an urban netherworld of sleazy flophouses, dingy hotel rooms, abandoned warehouses; an environment populated by dangerous, often hostile eccentrics. Forced to confront the nightmarish realities of society's "underbelly" while in flight from a determined assassin, the increasingly paranoid, exhausted protagonist comes to a realization of the profundity and folly of his decision to commit suicide as he fights for survival.

Taylor weaved his frightening tale by inventing a dizzying array of minor characters who added texture to the story and moved the plot along. Although there were too many for a 60-minute feature, they were a decidedly interesting, evocative mixture of individuals, including a cop-killing mobster, a vengeance-seeking widow, a comic book-reading deaf mute, a psychopathic vagrant, a devoted manservant, a loving secretary, and a kindly night watchman. Particularly memorable was Taylor's villain. Referred to only as "the killer," the unnamed assassin was a subhuman, incendiary character who spent his free time collecting rats and reading about new, creative ways of committing murders.

Effective performances fill in some of the gaps left in Taylor's story/sketch. Dix is first rate as Conrad. With simplicity of style and manner he created a full-bodied characterization; one which required him to make a 180-degree change in attitude, from a man willing to give up on life, to one who fights a tenacious battle to stay alive. Discarding the tough guy veneer of his previous heroic impersonations, Dix brought a combination of vulnerability, reserve, and determination to his performance which made it both appealing and real. He was especially effective toward the end of the picture when fear and paranoia overcame Conrad's mask of respectability and reserve leaving him exposed and defenseless. Matching his excellence was J. Carrol Naish. One of the cinema's finest character players, his portrayal of the deranged miscreant was mesmerizing. Although his character is hardly someone to identify with, Naish made him so fascinating we find ourselves wanting to know more. What was his background? How did he turn out this way? Was he the personification of an urban nightmare, or its demented victim? Other standout supporting performances were contributed by lovely Gloria Stuart, tender and believable as Dix's devoted secretary; Robert Homans, sincere as a kindly dock watchman; Don Costello, menacing as a cop-killing mobster, and underrated Joan Woodbury, calculatingly crazy as the mobster's grieving widow.

As distinguished as these contributions were it is director Castle who deserves the lion's share of credit for making *The Whistler* a success. A true showman possessed of an imaginative mind, a thorough knowledge of his audience, and a commitment to do good work, he transformed Taylor's script into a taut, suspenseful, and coherent film. His action-packed style and technical expertise lifted this entry and three others in the series. In *The Whistler* Castle missed no opportunity to create a tense, apprehensive mood. Like a hungry python, he literally squeezed every possible smidgeon of pathos and terror from the story; utilizing each scene and bit of dialogueue to maximize its impact. No easy fete when one considers the oppressive money and time structure under which he operated.

Castle's unique style and commitment were most evident in his use of imagery and attention to detail. Not satisfied with telling the story in a strictly conventional manner, he and ace cinematographer James S. Brown, armed with a hand-held camera, enhanced the dark mood of unpredictability and angst found in Taylor's script by utilizing dim light, unusual camera angles, a plethora of contrivances (such as a cat kicking over a trash can, Naish showing himself to Dix in a mirror, etc.), and eliciting believable performances from a large cast. It is a tribute to Castle's ability so many of the minor characters who constantly wander in and out of the movie seem to make sense, and leave lasting impressions. A case in point is the two-minute bit contributed by veteran actor Trevor Bardette, who portrayed a murderous hobo who meets Conrad at a 25-cent-per-night flophouse. After unsuccessfully attempting to lift his wallet, Bardette's character lures the exhausted man (who is looking for a place to rest and hide from police) to an abandoned warehouse. In one of the film's most chilling scenes he lights a candle, warns Conrad of, "rats as big as beavers," and shows him a bed of shredded newspapers. In a soft soothing voice he offers the vulnerable man comfort and solace. "There you are, Mister, between those cases, that's my bedroom. Hop right down on 'em. Nothing like newspapers to keep you warm. You look verrrry tired. Yessssss, you look verrrrrrry tired." As Conrad prepares to lie down, the hobo picks up a large stick to club him to death. Luckily for Conrad (at least for now), the killer is lurking outside. Determined to be the one responsible for Conrad's death, he shoots the hobo from a broken window. As Bardette's character falls dead on the floor, his body extinguishes the candle and the scene goes completely dark.

With all its positive qualities *The Whistler* could have been better. Ironically, some of its strengths are also its weaknesses. Although they *do* keep the action moving and the pot stirred, *and* most are surprisingly memorable, there are too many characters. It would have been better if some had been eliminated and extra time spent developing others. One of my candidates for elimination would have been Alan Dinehart's character, Gorman. The one-note, nonsensical role of Naish's unscrupulous friend not only wasted valuable screen time but squandered the talents of one of B movies' best screen villains: the capable Mr. Dinehart. While watching *The Whistler* one wonders if Dinehart's 4th-billed role was cut substantially prior to release.

The film's length was also limiting. In the hands of the innovative Mr. Castle an extra 10-15 minutes of footage would have done wonders in the area of plot and character development; helping us understand the motivations and decisions of some of the characters. *The Whistler's* abrupt ending was also a weakness. Castle's suspenseful buildup seems to presage a more creative, exciting conclusion than the one offered. Although the assassin's attempt to shoot Conrad through the harbor master's window did make sense, and was in keeping with the ironic denouements which were the hallmark of the *Whistler* radio series, somehow it lacked the wallop the audience anticipates.

RATING: 2

THE WHISTLER PHOTO GALLERY

The psychotic killer (J. Carrol Naish) impersonates a life insurance salesman to scare his victim in *The Whistler*. Here with Gloria Stuart.

A violent hobo (Trevor Bardette) waits for the right moment to relieve the exhausted Conrad (Richard Dix) of his wallet as he rests in a 25-cent-per-night flophouse.

The killer (Naish, left) temporarily loses his cool while dining with his friend Gorman (Alan Dinehart).

Richard Dix in *The Whistler*.

THE MARK OF THE WHISTLER (Columbia–1944)

Production: July 31, 1944 – August 14, 1944
Release: November 2, 1944.
Running Time: 60 minutes.
Taglines: "He lived another man's life! He stole another man's money. He loved another man's woman!" "$30,000 and

AN ALIAS WILL BE THIS MAN'S PASSPORT TO DEATH!"

Credits: Rudolph C. Flothow (Producer), William Castle (Director), Harold Godsoel (Assistant Director), George Bricker (screenplay) based on story "Dormant Account" by Cornell Woolrich suggested by the radio series, "The Whistler" created by J. Donald Wilson, George Meehan (photography), Frank Titus (second camera operator), Wilbur Hatch (music), Reginald Browne (film editing), John Datu (art direction), Sidney Clifford (set decoration), Hugh McDowell Jr. (sound).

Cast: Richard Dix (Lee Selfredge Nugent), Janis Carter (Patricia Henley), Porter Hall (Joe Sorsby), Paul Guilfoyle (Limpy Smith a.k.a. Lee Nugent), John Calvert (Eddie Donnelly), Matt Willis (Perry Donnelly), Walter Baldwin (Fireman), Willie Best (Men's room attendant), Edgar Dearing (Bank Guard), Otto Forrest (The Whistler), Howard Freeman (M.K. Simmons), Edna Holland (Children's Aid Society Administrator), Eddie Kane (Haberdasher), Donald Kerr (Newspaper Photographer), Matt McHugh (Tom, reporter), Bill Raisch (Truck Driver), Jack Rice (Mailman), Arthur Space (Sellers, Bell Captain), Minerva Urecal (Woman Sweeping Front Stair).

THE MARK OF THE WHISTLER INTRODUCTION:

THE WHISTLER: Standard Recitation. "Tonight I'm keeping a strange rendezvous. This man is a human derelict, broke, discouraged, unable to hold a job because of ill health. His name is Lee Selfredge Nugent. I knew him in better days when he possessed money, power, influence, but fate decreed that those material things should slip away and I, the Whistler, should find him alone tonight in a strange city on this park bench. What can the future hold for a man like this?"

A brief scene follows in which Nugent reads a newspaper article about unclaimed bank accounts and comes upon one reserved for "Lee Nugent."

THE WHISTLER: "Ironic, isn't it? These people all have money in the bank waiting for them and for some reason they do not come to claim it. Coincidence, that's all it is. You're not the Lee Nugent they are looking for. You are Lee Selfredge Nugent. Your mother's name was Mary, not Stella. Forget about it. Desperation prompts this man to think that he can compromise with his conscience. We shall see how he fares."

PLOT SUMMARY: Formally a man of means and influence, now a penniless and desperate drifter, Lee Selfredge Nugent (Richard Dix) hatches a scheme to lay false claim to a dormant bank account listed under the name Lee Nugent. With the help of some careful research and a new suit of clothes supplied by miserly storekeeper Joe Sorsby (Porter Hall), who extracts a promise of a 100% return on his investment, the fake Nugent manages to convince the bank he is the man they are looking for, and claim the princely sum of $29,000. Unfortunately for him, in doing so he attracts the attention of a local newspaper reporter, Patricia Henley (Janis Carter), who takes his picture and accompanies it with a story.

While attempting to avoid the press, Nugent accidentally runs into a crippled peddler, Limpy Smith (Paul Guilfoyle), who befriends the imposter and alerts him to the suspicious intentions of the

Donnelly brothers, Eddie and Perry (John Calvert, Matt Willis), who read the newspaper story and vow to kill the man who claimed the account to avenge wrongs done to their father years before. The dogged Eddie Donnelly eventually captures the imposter at the bus station and takes him to the brothers' apartment.

In spite of the fake Lee's protestations he is not the man they are searching for, Eddie and Perry introduce him to their mentally and physically incapacitated father, then force the imposter into a car to transport him to an undisclosed location where they intend to torture him to death. Involved in an auto accident on route (near Limpy's apartment), Nugent escapes. Although wounded by Eddie, Nugent manages to reach Limpy's abode with the Donnelly brothers in hot pursuit, followed by the police who were alerted by gunfire. After Limpy informs his pal he is Lee Nugent, the rightful owner of the account, police shoot Eddie and arrest Perry as they attempt forcible entry. Hospitalized but grateful to be alive, Lee Selfredge Nugent is informed by Limpy and Pat he will be prosecuted by the bank. There is a silver lining, however. The generous Limpy vows to use his inheritance to start a business and make his friend a partner after he completes his prison term.

THE MARK OF THE WHISTLER EPILOGUE:

THE WHISTLER: "I am the Whistler and I know many things. I know many strange tales. Yes, the amazing story of how fate dealt with Lee Selfredge Nugent who learned the hard way that there is no compromise with conscience. Now he will pay his debt to society, and after he has paid that debt fate will be kinder to him. I know because I am the Whistler."

REVIEWS FOR THE MARK OF THE WHISTLER:

Film Daily: "A gripping, engrossing thriller that holds interest to the end. It has been given splendid direction by William Castle . . . The acting is top notch."

New York Herald Tribune: "For the second time the directorial hand of William Castle has brought a Columbia mystery drama out of the usual slough of whodunits...The script doesn't quite match up to the first one in the matter of suspense and terror, nevertheless, this latest corpse festival proves again that capable actors and a smart director can work wonders with run-of-the-mill material."

The Hollywood Reporter: "A slick job of picture making on all counts . . . The picture is exciting and excellently done, with director Castle impressing again with the importance he makes every character mean to his drama . . . Richard Dix is, again, topflight . . ."

Zanesville Sunday Times: "An exciting, and entertaining hour of screen fare . . . To those who saw the first film in Columbia Pictures' series of thrillers taken from the radio program, the second, '*The Mark of the Whistler*' should prove a must see . . ."

EXPERT OPINIONS:

DON MILLER: "Cornell Woolrich's original story was expertly adapted by George Bricker and director Castle guided the suspense-filled plot over a brief sixty minutes. In many ways *The Mark of the Whistler* is superior to the first one. The plot is neater, less familiar, and contains unexpected turns. Production values, rather noticeably skimpy in the opener, were more in keeping, and the performances matched those in the first one with Janis Carter, Porter Hall, Paul Guilfoyle, John Calvert, and Matt Willis all fine in their roles as was Dix."

JON TUSKA: "If anything, it was even better than the first picture. The original story was by Cornell Woolrich, whose tales of suspense were having, and would continue to have, a tremendous effect on *film noir* of the Forties."

Interesting Facts/Trivia — The Mark of the Whistler

1. Both producer Rudolph Flothow and star Richard Dix requested William Castle to direct *The Mark of the Whistler*. For his work on the picture, Castle was paid $100 a week.

2. "Dormant Account," the story on which *The Mark of the Whistler* was based, was written by noted pulp-fiction writer Cornell Woolrich (1903–68) and first published in *Black Mask* in May 1942.

3. Perhaps to better suit the sympathetic, low-key screen image of star Richard Dix, Columbia scriptwriter George Bricker chose to soften Woolrich's protagonist. In the original story, George Palmer (Nugent) was totally reckless and remorseless, and the journalist was a man. Bricker apparently substituted the character of Patricia Henley (Janis Carter) to inject an element of romance into the grim proceedings.

4. Another departure from the Woolrich short story was the film's conclusion. In "Dormant Account" Palmer escapes punishment and reunites with Limpy, who shares his money with his friend. Of course, that could not happen in a 1940s motion picture. According to the Production Code crime could never be left unpunished.

5. On three separate occasions during the 60-minute film the Whistler character whistles his mournful 13-note tune, and then inserts himself in the story by speaking to Nugent as his conscience. On all three occasions Lee S. Nugent appears to hear the whistle. This would not happen again.

6. In his first substantive film role, as the vengeful kidnapper Eddie Donnelly, magician John Calvert won raves and had the film's best lines, delivered to his unfortunate captive.

EDDIE: "I suppose you're wondering how you're going to die. Maybe you think I'm going

	to shoot you and it will be all over all of a sudden. But it's not gonna be like that, Nugent . . ."
EDDIE:	"Oh, you'll die all right, but your mind will go first."

My Take:

This is a suspenseful, technically proficient B film, based on an unusual story. Another notch in the belt of director William Castle, who is aided by fine technical support and an expert cast.

Crime's unintended consequences were the theme of the second series entry, *The Mark of the Whistler*. While not quite as good as the first, it has much to recommend it, including a first-rate script/sketch, standout performances, superb editing, and adroit direction. Based on Woolrich's unusual story of ill-gotten gains, scenarist George Bricker skillfully crafted a tension-filled scenario with interesting characters, several twists and turns, and an ironic denouement. To accomplish this, he changed and in some ways improved on the original Woolrich tale by creating a multidimensional, more sympathetic lead character, and by giving him a romantic interest.

Richard Dix is a revelation as Lee Selfredge Nugent, the down-on-his-luck rambler who turns to a life of crime. His performance strikes the right balance at all times; insinuating the alternating sadness, greediness, paranoia, and fear of a desperate man who trades honor for money and almost loses his life as a result. He is extremely effective early on in the film when he researches the identity of the real Lee Nugent, then deceives bank manager L.W. Simmons (Howard Freeman). In these scenes we witness both the good and evil sides of this deeply flawed individual who, on one hand, seems genuinely touched by the plight of a wheelchair-bound boy; while on the other, appears to have no qualms about ruthlessly pursuing a bogus claim on another's rightful inheritance (ironically a handi-capped person's). With an economy of dialogue Dix conveys the complexity of his character through expressions, posture, and body language.

Acting honors are shared by an extraordinary supporting cast headed by lovely Janis Carter who is effective as the nosy reporter, Howard Freeman properly suspicious as the bank official, and Paul Guilfoyle convincingly sympathetic as the peddler. Special kudos go to veteran actor Porter Hall and newcomer John Calvert for their finely etched villainous turns. With only a few minutes of screen time both created indelible impressions. Hall almost runs away with the film as the delightfully nasty skinflint, Joe Sorsby, a clothier who supplied the fake Lee Nugent with a suit of clothes then accompanied him on his unethical mission to collect his reward. Magician Calvert also scores. As a loving son driven to madness and sadism by dirty deeds perpetrated on his beloved father, Calvert skillfully projected insanity and evil. Like its predecessor, *Mark* also showcased several talented character actors in memorable cameos. Among them were some of B movies' best loved "types," including Edgar Dearing as a bank guard, Minerva Urecal as a cantankerous landlady, and Willie Best as a resourceful men's room attendant.

Even with a good script and performances, *The Mark of the Whistler* would have been little more than a reasonably entertaining series entry were it not for the talent of Bill Castle. With an uncommon abundance of style, humor, and impressive attention to detail, Castle took an unconventional story, which featured several unsympathetic roles, and made it into a compact, intensely interesting, action-oriented motion picture with characters we care about. Once again he utilized unusual camera angles and low-key lighting to enhance a mood of apprehension, while placing special emphasis on several minor characterizations which add interest and advance the plot. In these endeavors he was aided by assistant director Harold Godsoel and three talented Columbia technicians: cinematographer George Meehan, art director John Datu, and editor Reginald Browne. Mr. Brown, in particular, deserves a great deal of credit for organizing the disparate elements of the movie (including stock footage) into a tight, well-structured motion picture.

As good as it is *Mark* does have significant flaws associated with its low-budget production values, and the incredibility of certain plot elements, what one critic referred to as the "beatitudes" of the Bs. An example of the latter is a multitude of coincidences which permeate the film and destroy some of its realism. For instance, it *is* beyond belief that the imposter, Lee Selfredge Nugent, ran into the real Lee Nugent (Limpy) as he left the bank after claiming the latter's money. And, even if one accepts the event as a Whistler intervention, it is even more incredible the Donnelly brothers accompanied by their captive just happen to be involved in an auto accident on the very street on which Limpy resides.

RATING: 4

THE MARK OF THE WHISTLER PHOTO GALLERY:

While attempting to avoid a nosy reporter Lee Selfredge Nugent (Dix) accidentally knocks a crippled peddler to the pavement in *The Mark of the Whistler*. Left to right: Paul Guilfoyle, Richard Dix, and Janis Carter.

Guilfoyle and Dix.

After impersonating another and stealing his inheritance, Nugent (Dix) decides to celebrate with a night on the town. At a fancy restaurant he runs into reporter Pat Henley (Janis Carter) and a lot of trouble.

John Calvert (left) and Matt Willis play brothers bent on revenge in *The Mark of the Whistler*.

Willis, Calvert, and Dix.

THE POWER OF THE WHISTLER (COLUMBIA – 1945)

PRODUCTION: December 6, 1944 – December 20, 1944
RELEASE: April 19, 1945.
RUNNING TIME: 66 minutes.
TAGLINES: "MURDER BY A MADMAN WHO LOVED . . . TO KILL!"

CREDITS: Leonard S. Picker (Producer), Lew Landers (Director), Leonard J. Shapiro (Assistant Director), Irvin Berwick (Dialogueue Director), Aubrey Wisberg (screenplay) suggested by the radio series, "The Whistler" created by J. Donald Wilson, L.W. O'Connell (photography), Wilbur Hatch (theme music), Paul Sawtell (original music), Reginald Browne (film editing), John Datu (art direction), Sidney Clifford (set decoration), Hugh McDowell Jr. (sound).

CAST: Richard Dix (William Everest), Janis Carter (Jean Lang), Jeff Donnell (Frances "Francie" Lang), Loren Tindall (Charlie Kent), Tala Birell (Constantina Ivaneska), John Abbott (Kaspar Andropolous), Murray Alper (Joe Blainey), Walter Baldwin (Western Union agent), Margia Dean (bit role), Otto Forrest (The Whistler), Jack George (Locksmith), Frank Haney (Cake Delivery), I. Stafford Jolley (Motorist), Cy Kendall (Druggist), Kenneth MacDonald (Dr. John Crawford, Mental Hospital), Nina Mae McKinney (Flotilda, Constantina's maid), Eddie Parker (Motorcycle Patrolman), Stanley Price (Richards, the printer), Frank J. Scannell (Highway Patrolman), John Tyrell (Clerk), Crane Whitley (Police Captain).

THE POWER OF THE WHISTLER INTRODUCTION:

THE WHISTLER: Standard Recitation. "Tonight I'm keeping a strange rendezvous. Here is a strange man formed in God's image according to the Bible but how far is image from mirage. The two words sound alike. This man looks like all others but what separates him from his fellows? It cannot be seen by the naked eye. His name is William Everest and he is a man with a ghastly mission which will not let him rest until it is successfully accomplished. But the best laid plans which men sometimes make have a habit of going astray. Whether in this case for good or evil only the events of the night can foretell." A brief scene follows in which William Everest is struck by a car when he attempts to cross the street. Stunned, he stumbles into a café.

THE WHISTLER: "He hesitated, a thought must have run through his mind. It took no longer than a second or two, yet whose destiny may have been changed by this sudden impulse which took William Everest through the door of this little café down here in Greenwich Village; and how will the fate of William Everest be affected?"

PLOT SUMMARY: While attempting to cross the street, escaped mental patient William Everest (Richard Dix) is struck by a car. Dazed and confused, he wanders into a café where his presence is noted by three people: Jean Lang, her sister Francie, and Francie's fiancé Charlie (Janis Carter, Jeff Donnell, Loren Tindall) sitting at a table playing cards. Attracted to Everest, Jean decides to use the deck to tell his fortune. When she turns up the death card twice, she follows Everest out of the café to warn him. Intrigued by his refined manner, the kindly Jean agrees to help the confused man (who does not remember who he is) learn his identity. There are several clues in his pockets: a license plate number, a railroad schedule, a prescription, a skeleton key, and orders for a birthday cake, and a dozen roses to be sent to a renowned dancer.

Their search begins with a visit to dancer Constantina Ivaneska (Tala Birell), who denies knowing Everest. The couple then proceeds to the doctor's address printed on the prescription, which turns out to be a bookstore. The bookstore owner (John Abbott) recognizes Everest, and says he came in looking for books on poisons.

When no breakthrough is made after a few hours, generous Jean offers to let the accident victim sleep on her couch in the apartment she shares with her sister Francie. There both sisters vow to help the unfortunate man discover who he is. As he lies on the makeshift bed in Jean's apartment, Everest gradually begins to regain his memory; and the kindly, dazed look on his face turns into the terrifying gaze of a determined killer.

The next morning the sisters awaken to find their breakfast prepared by Everest. Their pleasure turns to horror when Francie finds her pet bird dead in its cage. Despite the trauma, she, her sister, and Everest divvy up the remaining clues and set out on a quest to learn the amnesiac's identity. Francie discovers the prescription is for poison, and the bakery order is to be delivered to John Crawford (Kenneth MacDonald), warden of the Hudson Mental Institution. Alarmed, she contacts a startled Charlie, who summons all involved parties to police headquarters to convince authorities Everest should be arrested. Eventually, the police are persuaded to take action, and put out an all points bulletin. Meanwhile, Everest has not only learned his true identity (after checking out the license plate number at the Department of Motor Vehicles), but has resumed his quest to murder those who had a part in his institutionalization, including Warden Crawford and Judge Nesbitt.

Everest does not inform Jean he has regained his memory when they meet in a park later in the day to compare notes. Instead, he professes love for her, and persuades her to accompany him on a trip to the country to visit Nesbitt who he claims is the only person he remembers from his past. Innocently, she agrees. From the train station they borrow a car to drive to the judge's home in a remote area. On the way they are stopped by the police. When Everest identifies himself as Warden John Crawford, they believe him and proceed on their way. Jean becomes alarmed, however, and confronts Everest. Increasingly agitated, the psychotic Everest grabs Jean intending to stab her, but she escapes his grasp and flees into the woods with the maniacal Everest and the newly summoned police in pursuit. Jean eventually comes upon a barn where she hopes to find a hiding place. Everest finds her there, and prepares to murder her when she grabs a pitchfork and stabs him to death.

Poster for *The Power of the Whistler*.

THE POWER OF THE WHISTLER EPILOGUE:

THE WHISTLER: "In a city full of strange adventures, this, what happened to Jean Lang, has been one of the most amazing. Protected by the resilience of youth, Jean Lang will carry no scars on her soul from her encounter with William Everest. And as time passes even the nightmare memory will not disturb her innocent sleep. She will marry in time a man destined for her and live long and happy in the fullness of her years. I know because I am the Whistler."

Reviews for The Power of the Whistler:

Motion Picture Herald: "The latest offering in the Whistler series is a chilling, hair-raising melodrama. Richard Dix plays the part of the madman to the hilt. Dix's facial expressions and the manner in which he speaks his lines give an eerie effect to the film. This picture is the type that is intended to send chills up and down ones' spine and it does it very well . . ."

The Independent: "This newest in the 'Whistler' series is a better than average psychological thriller in the program class . . . Richard Dix does a superb job of the maniac and Janis Carter is equally outstanding as the gal. Lew Landers' direction is pointed and deliberate, and accomplishes believability by cutting corners for speedier bits of suspense."

Variety: "*The Power of the Whistler* shapes up as an okay entry for supporting positions. There are plenty of thrills and suspense crowded into its short footage by Lew Landers' direction, which treats the melodramatic factors seriously for the best results, and the cast goes about its assignments for the satisfaction of thriller fans . . . Richard Dix does a thoroughly satisfactory job of the maniac, a man with several personalities, some of them kind . . ."

Expert Opinions:

John Cocchi: "The third entry, and best of the group . . . A well-developed plot moves things along to a smash climax. One of Dix's most impressive portrayals."

Don Miller: "Aside from an excellent bit of photography by L. W. O'Connell introducing the Dix character in full close-up, *The Power of the Whistler* failed to approach the story and entertainment values set by the first two. Significantly or not Castle did not direct, but the task was taken on by a familiar name, Lew Landers."

Interesting Facts/ Trivia — The Power of the Whistler

1. While making *The Power of the Whistler*, filming was halted briefly for an impromptu party commemorating the 22nd anniversary of star Richard Dix's entry into films.

2. In the tradition of the first *Whistler* series entry, which commenced in a dingy San Francisco bar named The Crow's Nest, *Power* begins in a crowded Greenwich Village café called The Salt Shaker.

3. An homage to the influential radio classic *Inner Sanctum Mysteries*, occurs at the film's midpoint when the deranged Everest bids Jean goodnight with the classic line: "Pleasant dreams, Miss Lang."

4. There are several unintentionally funny moments in the film. The first occurs near the midpoint when Jean locates the book Everest has been searching for, *The Art of Poison*. Under the author's name it says, "We regret the unfortunate death of the author before the publication of this book."

5. Another humorous B movie moment occurs near the film's conclusion when the police send an all-points-bulletin teletype to their law enforcement colleagues in an effort to apprehend the mentally challenged Everest. Even by 1945 standards it's hard to believe the police would have referred to Everest in the following manner.

"Attention State Highway Patrol Division—Woodville—Urgent! Escaped homicidal maniac William Everest heading to Woodville with intention of killing local resident Edward Nesbitt—With him is Jean Lang, twenty-five-year-old girl unsuspecting of his identity—Block all roads—This man is dangerous."

6. One year after portraying the incredibly naïve heroine Jean Lang, versatile leading lady Janis Carter had an opportunity to offer her own interpretation of crazy as the cold-blooded sexual psychopath in the minor *noir* classic *Night Editor* (Columbia, 1946).

7. The best lines in *Power* are delivered by Jean's sister Francie and by the psychopath William Everest. The former comes at the beginning of the picture when trusting Jean follows a complete stranger out of the café then gets in a car with him.

FRANCIE: "She's got too much imagination for own good."

The latter is delivered at the end of the film as Everest climbs the ladder of the barn to murder Jean.

EVEREST: "I will keep you forever young. Time and life are your enemies; I am your friend."

My Take:

A well-made, tension-filled B shocker with an exceptional story idea, some great camera work, a bravura lead performance, and competent direction. The script is a minus, but the film is a winner.

The Power of the Whistler is far from a motion picture classic, but it certainly does have its moments. On the asset side of the ledger is the direction. One cannot help but wonder what the ingenious William Castle or the brilliant Alfred Hitchcock would have done with the story of *The Power of the Whistler*, but, as a whole, Lew Landers does a splendid job. One of the most prolific directors in all cinematic history, this film was definitely one of his achievements. Rising above script deficiencies he managed to build a fast-paced, attention-grabbing motion picture with excellent performances. Assisted by cinematographer L. W. O'Connell, Landers fashioned several effective sequences which established a dark mood while sustaining tension. The most memorable was perhaps *the* scariest in all eight pictures. It had the amnesiac Everest lying on the couch in Jean's apartment listening to sirens and the chirping of Jean's sister's parakeet. As the camera pans in for a close-up, the audience becomes fixated on Everett's eyes. As we come closer and closer, his quiescent, slightly confused, gaze turns into a deranged gleam. At that exact moment, the audience knows Everest has begun to recall who he is. A boffo scene!

Another great Landers contribution was *Power's* nail-biting conclusion, which reminds one of later suspense/horror classics like *Friday the 13th*. After a great chase sequence, the action ends with the knife-wielding Everest pursuing Jean in a barn. In a sweet, silky voice he says, "It won't do any good to hide, my little sweetheart, no good at all. There won't be any pain, my dear. One quick cut and it'll all be over. Your throat will be quiet for evermore." Attempting to escape, Jean climbs a ladder to the loft. As the wild-eyed mental patient follows, she picks up a pitchfork and thrusts it into his throat.

Like Castle, Landers efficiently utilized several gimmicks in the film; some were written in the script and some were not. One of the most imaginative inventions (which did not appear in the original Wisberg synopsis published by Columbia's publicity department in December 1944), involved Everest strangling three small animals (a kitten, parakeet, and a squirrel) during the course of the film. While animal lovers may rightly consider the contrivance distasteful, it is incredibly effective in creating tension and conveying the homicidal tendencies of the deceptively passive protagonist who cannot seem to control an instinct to kill.

Landers was aided by impressive performances. Dix is stunningly chilling as William Everest. In a demanding role requiring him to exhibit multiple personalities, the former western hero persuasively conveys the many facets of the villainous mental patient whose mild-mannered exterior masks dementia and evil. In the early scenes we witness his good side. Genuinely touched by Jean's kindness and concern, he attempts to pay her back by making breakfast for her and her sister. Attired in a frilly apron, he sets the table, cooks the eggs, and then says grace. Both Jean and Francie are surprised and touched by his kindness and domesticity. The mood changes abruptly, when Francie discovers her parakeet lying on the bottom of its cage.

Although the supporting cast of *The Power of the Whistler* is not as strong as its predecessors, there are several notable character performances which merit mention. Her unbelievable role notwithstanding, Miss Carter plays Jean with sincerity and conviction. Kudos also go to Jeff Donnell as Jean's smart, resourceful sister Francie, Loren Tindall as Francie's fiancé, and Tala Birell as the exotic ballerina. Great bits are contributed by Cy Kendall as an unethical druggist, John Abbott as a creepy bookstore owner, and talented Nina Mae MacKinney as Constantina's sassy maid.

The Power of the Whistler's minuses begin and end with the script. After conceiving a brilliant scenario featuring a captivatingly creepy lead character, scenarist Aubrey Wisberg squandered much potential by concocting a cacophony of loopholes and coincidences which strain credulity. Let me be clear: He does not destroy his script, but he does substantive damage; and it's a shame.

Most of the plot "holes" have to do with motivations and actions of the lead female character, Jean Lang. At first her innocent interest in helping the injured amnesiac appear understandable if a bit over-the-top, but as the story progresses and she learns more about her new "friend," Jean's naiveté seems unreal, delusional. For example, even if one accepts the fact that an attractive, respectable, intelligent young woman would willingly get into a car and go off with a middle-aged stranger suffering from amnesia without alerting a hospital or the authorities, it is impossible to believe she would let him sleep on her couch after learning he's been researching *The Art of Poison*. And what about the small animals who keep turning up dead in the man's vicinity? Unfortunately for Jean, and Wisberg's script, her trust and devotion appear positively unshakeable. Things become even more improbable near the film's conclusion but why pile on. Given all the above what is most remarkable is *The Power of the Whistler* remains a very scary, engrossing motion picture, and one of the best of the series.

RATING: 3

THE POWER OF THE WHISTLER PHOTO GALLERY:

Life is about to get very exciting for three young people having drinks and playing cards in a Greenwich Village café in The Power of the Whistler. From left to right: Janis Carter, Jeff Donnell, Loren Tindall.

Amnesiac William Everest (Dix) and his pretty companion Jean (Janis Carter) encounter a little girl and her kitten while searching for clues to his identity in *The Power of the Whistler*.

Lovely Jean (Carter) doesn't know it yet but she will soon learn some surprising information about her companion (Dix).

From left: Dix, Carter, Donnell.

VOICE OF THE WHISTLER (COLUMBIA–1945)

PRODUCTION DATES: July 23, 1945 – August 7, 1945
RELEASE DATE: October 30, 1945
RUNNING TIME: 60 minutes.
TAGLINES: "THE BRIDE MARRIED FOR GREED! THE GROOM MARRIED FOR SPITE! And The Whistler went on the honeymoon for MURDER!" "THEIR LIPS MET ... BUT THERE WAS MURDER IN THEIR HEARTS"

CREDITS: Rudolph C. Flothow (Producer), William Castle (Director), Chris Beute (Assistant Director), Wilfrid H. Pettit, William Castle (Screenplay), George Meehan (photography), Dwight Caldwell (editing), Wilbur Hatch (music), M. R. Bakaleinikoff (musical director).

CAST: Richard Dix (John Sinclair), Lynn Merrick (Joan Martin Sinclair), Rhys Williams (Ernie Sparrow), James Cardwell (Fred Graham), Tom Kennedy (Ferdinand), Egon Beecher (Dr. Rose), Gigi Perreau (Bobbie), Sam Ash (Gibson Motor Car Company Executive), Charles Coleman (Sinclair's Butler), Otto Forrest (The Whistler), Byron Foulger (Georgie), Martin Gallaraga (Tony, the Fruit Peddler), Stuart Holmes (Doctor), Wilbur Mack, (Sinclair Executive), Charles Marsh (Sinclair Executive), Harold Miller, (Sinclair Executive), Forbes Murray (Sinclair Executive), Clinton Rosemont (Train Porter), Frank Scannell (Druggist), Minerva Urecal (Georgie's Wife), Robert Williams (Pharmacist), Douglas Wood (Paul Kitridge, Attorney).

VOICE OF THE WHISTLER INTRODUCTION:

THE WHISTLER: Standard Recitation. "One of the greatest of these terrors is loneliness. In my wanderings I have seen the lonely people of the Earth. I have seen their drawn and haunted faces in a city of teaming millions; and I have seen them, too, in places that have been long deserted and forgotten. Gulfport Lighthouse was abandoned many years ago, but today a woman lives here all alone. She never leaves her forlorn and isolated home. Hers is a strange story. For she loved the bustling cities, the gay crowds, the laughter of pleasant company. Why then has she shut herself away in this desolation where no one ever comes to visit her?"

A sad-looking woman ascends a lighthouse stairway with a kerosene lamp in one hand and two kittens in the other.

THE WHISTLER: "Hers is a story of loneliness and greed. It began years ago in a big city when the great industrialist John Sinclair was rising from obscurity."

PLOT SUMMARY: Famed industrialist John Sinclair's (Richard Dix) ruthless, single-minded quest for business success has left him without love, friendship, and his health. Ordered by his doctor to take a long vacation, Sinclair opts to take a Great Lakes cruise and heads to Chicago. While in the Windy City, he collapses on the street outside Union Station and is rescued by a kindly cabbie, former boxer Ernie Sparrow (Rhys Williams), who takes him to his home to recover, then to a neighborhood clinic. There doctors give Sinclair six months to live and recommend he spend it taking in the healthy New England sea air. In the clinic Sinclair meets an attractive nurse, Joan Martin (Lynn Merrick), who shows him great compassion. Enamored of her, the lonely Sinclair proposes marriage as a business deal. In exchange for her care and companionship she will inherit his fortune. Although she doesn't love Sinclair, the financially-strapped, money-worshipping Joan agrees to the arrangement and breaks off her engagement to a young intern, Fred Graham (James Cardwell), who is bitterly disappointed. After the marriage, Sinclair, his new wife, and Ernie (who John invited to live with them) take up residence in a converted lighthouse on the coast of Maine.

As weeks pass, helped by the care and companionship of Joan and Ernie, Sinclair regains his health much to the chagrin of his young wife who is increasingly lonely and restless. When Fred suddenly appears on the scene and asks her to run away with him, Joan is torn between her love for money and security, and her feelings for Fred. Now in love with his wife, Sinclair overhears a conversation between the ex-lovers and plots revenge. After inviting Fred for an extended stay, the jealous Sinclair plants a murder scheme in his rival's mind (involving a sleepwalker who falls out a window) which he describes as the "perfect crime."

Taking the bait Fred informs Ernie he saw Sinclair sleepwalking and advises the former cabbie to buy locks for the windows to protect John from falling to his death. That night Fred places a sedative in Sinclair's dinner coffee and at 4 a.m. enters Sinclair's room with the intention of bludgeoning him to death. One step ahead of Fred, a waiting Sinclair fatally clubs Fred. Unable to open the window to dispose of the body, Sinclair is forced to drag it down several flights of stairs out to the rocky shore where he is observed by Ernie. His explanation that Fred fell out the window is rejected by Ernie who informs Sinclair he nailed the windows shut. Sinclair then admits he killed Fred, but says it was in self-defense. He tells Ernie he can prove it. As they reenter the lighthouse to check out Sinclair's story, they are met at the door by Joan, who accuses her husband of murder, and informs him she has summoned the police. Sinclair is apprehended and confesses. After her husband is executed for Fred's murder, Joan inherits his fortune, but at a price. Tormented by the circumstances of her lover's death, she spends the remainder of her life at the lighthouse in agony and isolation.

Voice of the Whistler epilogue:

The Whistler:	"Sparrow did what he could for his friend, but the jury didn't believe John Sinclair's story and he paid the extreme penalty for the murder of Fred Graham. Joan inherited the Sinclair millions and went away to the

life of luxury she had always craved, but constantly haunting her was the tragedy that cost the lives of a man she loved and a man she married. She traveled from city to city seeking forgetfulness but there was no escape from the past. She came back at last to live out a life of torment in the solitude and desolation of the lighthouse. I know because I am the Whistler."

Reviews for Voice of the Whistler:

Film Daily: "Top notch point in the series well directed by William Castle in a light absorbing style for thrills and action . . . Surrounded with interesting performances by lovely and capable Lynn Merrick and handsome James Cardwell, Dix is well girded for an engrossing role . . ."

Variety: "Its running time is short, and the story generates fair amount of interest to keep the customers satisfied. It starts out as a story on the dangers of loneliness but ends up as a murder melodrama as the principle characters run amuck. William Castle's direction of the Rudolph C. Flothow production manages considerable suspense at times and gives the characters good display . . . Dix does well by his lead role as does Lynn Merrick by her part of the nurse. Rhys Williams is the standout as the taxi driver . . ."

Council Bluffs Nonpareil: "The fourth and most thrilling of this series of psychological melodramas . . . Richard Dix excels and the successful unfolding of *Voice of the Whistler* is largely due to his crafty playing . . . Lynn Merrick, who has usually been seen in lighter roles, proves what she can give in this type of character. James Cardwell, a comparative newcomer, is definitely going places in the cinema world of leading men . . ."

Expert Opinions for Voice of the Whistler:

Leonard Maltin: "Haunting love story about an avaricious nurse who dumps her fiancé in order to marry a dying millionaire and finds herself a virtual prisoner. Not as suspenseful as the other Whistler entries, but just as gripping."

Robert Wise: "*Voice of the Whistler* with its haunting lighthouse setting (anticipating the climax of Dieterle's *Portrait of Jennie*), is as moody, atmospheric and unpredictable as a 1940s B film is likely to be, which means it's an absolute joy."

Interesting Facts/Trivia — Voice of the Whistler

1. The story on which this film was based, "Checkmate for Murder," penned by Allan Radar, was first broadcast as a *Whistler* radio episode on March 26, 1945.

2. Influenced by his friend Orson Welles' 1941 masterpiece, *Citizen Kane*, director William Castle began *Voice of the Whistler* with a newsreel chronicling the career accomplishments of industrialist John Sinclair.

3. In a distinct departure from the three previous entries *Voice* marks the debut of a more fiendish, ominous Whistler character. In addition to introducing and framing the story he plants devious, often malevolent thoughts in his characters' minds, and then goads them into action.

4. Although the precise location of shooting could not be determined, the lovely coastal scenes of Maine depicted in *Voice of the Whistler* were likely shot off the beautiful, rocky coast of California. These scenes are believed to constitute the one and only time the *Whistler* pictures were filmed outside the Darmour lot.

5. Although actor Donald Woods (one of the famed "Whistler's children" on radio) appears on several cast lists (including the

American Film Institutes') as portraying attorney Paul Kitridge in the movie, he does not appear in it. Actor Douglas Wood portrays Kitridge.

6. *Voice of the Whistler* marked the second *Whistler* appearance of two veteran character actors who contribute dandy bits: Minera Urecal (the cranky landlady in *The Mark of the Whistler* and bossy old biddy buying flowers in *Voice*) and Byron Foulger (the corrupt flophouse manager in *The Whistler*, the henpecked husband of Urecal in *Voice*). Foulger would appear a third time as a monument dealer in *The Secret of the Whistler* (1946).

7. Life has a tragic way of imitating art. Like his character Fred Graham, actor James Cardwell's life would be short, sad, and largely unfulfilled. For more consult his bio in Chapter 6.

My Take:

A highly unusual and effective entry, with striking visuals, a memorably haunting theme, top-drawer performances, and perceptive direction.

Greed = loneliness and ruination was the basic theme of the morality tale depicted in *Voice of the Whistler*, the fourth and most atypical entry of the Whistler series. Fresh from helming PRC's acclaimed B classic, *When Strangers Marry*, William Castle returned to direct and co-write this film, which reunited him with Dix and *The Mark of the Whistler* cinematographer George Meehan. The result was a highly unusual, expertly handled B which is praiseworthy in several respects despite a schizophrenic plot and various inconsistencies.

Based on Allan Radar's radio script, "Checkmate for Murder," Columbia scenarist Wilfred Pettit crafted an uncommon screenplay which chronicled a lonely, terminally ill millionaire's tragic quest to find companionship and meaning in his life by making an unfortunate bargain with a beautiful and greedy woman who agrees to marry him to inherit his fortune. Although Castle apparently liked Pettit's scenario, sources suggest he thought it too tame for the *Whistler* series and chose to rework the ending to add suspense. As a consequence the movie makes an abrupt detour about 2/3 of the way, from being an effective dramatic exploration of the tragic consequences of a man's single-minded pursuit of wealth and power, to a suspense thriller with a tension-filled climax. It works on both levels.

Once again director Castle is the primary reason the film succeeds. Realizing the necessity of making adjustments to his technique to better suit the storyline of *Voice*, he discarded the gimmicks and frenetic pace which had characterized his first two *Whistlers*. With a lighthouse as a backdrop (Pettit's evocative way of suggesting loneliness and isolation), Castle appropriately chose to unravel the tale in a more relaxed, low-key fashion, relying on strong character development. He picked up the pace and heightened the tension toward the end of the movie; but by that time he had managed to tell a surprisingly effective dramatic tale before ending it in a typical "Whistleresque" fashion.

Three excellent sequences illustrate Castle's contribution. The first is the impressive newsreel he assembled to showcase the background of his main character, industrialist James Sinclair (Dix). Although strikingly analogous to one in Welles' *Citizen Kane*, it is a well-mounted, visually effective way of introducing his protagonist without resorting to the timeworn flashback. The second is the tension-filled, wickedly entertaining murder scene near the film's conclusion which Castle both wrote and directed. In it we find the young doctor, Fred Graham (James Cardwell), sneaking into Sinclair's bedroom, grabbing a fireplace poker, and attempting to bludgeon his rival while he lies sleeping. When Fred realizes it is only pillows covered to resemble human form, he becomes agitated. With beads of sweat on his brow he cries,

FRED: "Where are you? I know you're in the room. I know you're here. Where are you?"

Increasingly panicked, his eyes canvas the darkened room.

FRED: "Where are you? Please, please, I wasn't going to…Sinclair, Sinclair, don't, don't!"

Fred wipes his brow, appears to regain his composure then turns to leave when an insane-looking Sinclair suddenly rises from the shadows and clubs him to death. As Sinclair hovers over Fred's body contemplating his next move, a sinister-voiced Whistler intervenes with advice.

THE WHISTLER: "You told Fred every step in your scheme and he helped you carry it out. Who would suspect that a murdered man would collaborate in his murderer's alibi? Hurry, John, hurry! The coroner may be able to determine that Fred was dead before his body struck the rocks!"

In the best *Whistler* tradition Sinclair's deadly plan ultimately fails and he gets his just desserts, but his young wife also gets hers. Castle ends the picture with yet another memorable scene which ties the disparate elements of the picture (both dramatic and melodramatic) together in a hauntingly ironic way. In it we find a somber, older-looking Joan at the top of the lighthouse with a lamp in her hand, two small kittens crawling on her shoulder. The Whistler's spooky, somber narration informs us her selfish quest for money has left her a tortured soul.

Of course, Castle did not work in a vacuum. His cast is uniformly superior. Dix is outstanding as the successful businessman whose immense wealth cannot buy him health and friendship. Again burdened with a cumbersome, near-impossible role requiring him to convey a complex, often inconsistent range of emotions, he appears up to the task. As the nurse who trades an uncomplicated life of love and hard work for money, charismatic Lynn Merrick also merits high marks. Although her character is hard, callous, unsympathetic, Merrick evokes pity and empathy for Joan, a woman whose poor and troubled childhood inspired her to pursue financial security over everything else. Rhys Williams and James Cardwell also distinguish themselves. The former is affecting as the ex-boxing champ-turned-cabbie with a heart of gold; and the latter is memorable as the young intern whose love for a ruthless woman leads him astray. Tom Kennedy, Byron Foulger, Minera Urecal, and four-year-old Gigi Perreau have nice bits.

Voice is also notable in the technical fields. Cinematographer George Meehan's beautiful coastal photography adds a rich atmospheric texture; and Dwight Caldwell's effective editing organizes both the dramatic and suspenseful elements of the picture, including stock footage and location shots. Of special note was the art direction and set design. For unknown reasons, Columbia chose not to credit the persons responsible for the very realistic lighthouse interior scenes which prove so pivotal to the plot. Although set designer Sidney Clifford and art director John Datu appear likely to have contributed, it could not be verified.

Like its immediate predecessor *Voice of the Whistler*'s main weaknesses have to do with the script, specifically the motivations of some of the characters, especially Sinclair and his rival Fred. After a remarkably effective mini-expose detailing the rehabilitation of the troubled Sinclair into a kindly, thoughtful human being, his abrupt transformation into a devious, cold-blooded murderer is not entirely credible. It is true he was a ruthless businessman; and he did love Joan and wanted to preserve his relationship with her, but it doesn't seem entirely logical he would resort to murder. Ditto Fred. Although love can inspire smart, sane individuals to do unconscionable things, it does appear farfetched that a man whose life has been heretofore devoted to healing and compassion would sacrifice everything for a woman who married another for his money. Near the film's conclusion Fred tells Joan, "You're not going to ruin my life," then immediately sets out to commit a murder because of her. This does fit comfortably with the *Whistler* theme of "everyday people" stepping into the shadows, but somehow doesn't make total sense.

Another small bit of B movie nonsense occurs early in the film when the kindly cabbie, Ernie Sparrow, opts to take the ill Sinclair to his home to recuperate after just meeting him. Like Jean Lang (who lets the psychotic William Everest sleep in her apartment in *The Power of the Whistler*), at times Sparrow seems a bit too naive and trusting to be true.

RATING: 5

VOICE OF THE WHISTLER PHOTO GALLERY

Terminally ill businessman John Sinclair (Dix) gets a new lease on life when fortune places him in the care of kindly Chicago cabbie Ernie Sparrow (Rhys Williams, back right). On their way to a local clinic they visit a fruit peddler (Martin Gallaraga) in *Voice of the Whistler*.

While being treated at a medical clinic Sinclair meets and becomes attracted to a money-hungry nurse, Joan Martin (Lynn Merrick).

In one of *Voice of the Whistler's* most exciting scenes, Doctor Fred Graham (James Cardwell) attempts to murder Sinclair in his bed.

CHAPTER FOUR: UNDER THE TRENCH COAT | 93

MYSTERIOUS INTRUDER (COLUMBIA – 1946)

PRODUCTION DATES: December 6, 1945 – December 20, 1945
RELEASE DATE: April 11, 1946
RUNNING TIME: 62 minutes.
TAGLINES: "A WOMAN SCREAMS! A KILLER STRIKES! AND 'THE WHISTLER' STALKS HIS PREY!"

CREDITS: Rudolph C. Flothow (Producer), William Castle (Director), Carl Hiecke (Assistant Director), Eric Taylor (story and screenplay) suggested by the radio series The Whistler created by J. Donald Wilson, Philip Tannura (photography), James Goss (second camera operator), Wilbur Hatch (music), Mischa Bakaleinikoff (musical director), Edwin Wetzel (music mixer), Dwight Caldwell (editing), Hans Radon (art direction), Robert Priestley (set decoration), Jack Haynes (sound recording), J. S. Westmoreland (sound mixer).

CAST: Richard Dix (Don Gale), Barton MacLane (Detective Taggart), Nina Vale (Joan Hill), Regis Toomey (James Summers), Helen Mowery (Freda Harrison), Mike Mazurki (Harry Pontos), Pamela Blake (Elora Lund), Charles Lane (Detective Burns), Paul Burns (Edward Stillwell), Kathleen Howard (Rose Denning), Harlan Briggs (Brown), Edith Evanson (Mrs. Ward), Dan Stowell, Donald Kerr (Reporters), Charles Jordan (Desk Clerk), Harry Strang (Desk sergeant), Jack Carrington (Bartender), Martin Garralaga (Detective), Joseph Palma (Doorman), Isabel Withers (P.B.X. operator), Selmer Jackson (Dr. Connell), Arthur Space (Davis), Stanley Blystone, Kernan Cripps (Policemen), Otto Forrest (The Whistler), Jessie Arnold (Woman in the Window), Eddy Chandler (Cop in the Squad Car).

MYSTERIOUS INTRUDER INTRODUCTION:

THE WHISTLER: Standard Recitation. "It is Edward Stillwell who walks alone. He is a kindly, unimportant little man, the type you pass on the street without noticing. Tonight, however, something will happen to him which changes everything; something to make his life important and exciting and dangerous."

PLOT SUMMARY: Kindly old music shopkeeper Edward Stillwell (Paul Burns) unknowingly attempts to engage a corrupt private investigator, Don Gale (Richard Dix), to help locate a young woman, Elora Lund, whom he knew seven years earlier. Her mother (now deceased) sold Stillwell several items to make ends meet, and now he wants to locate her daughter and return them. Gale is unmotivated to assist the elderly gentleman until Stillwell informs him if he finds Miss Lund she will make him "a wealthy man." Stillwell does not tell Gale the exact nature of the valuables, only that they're worth "tens of thousands."

In order to bilk the old man, Gale sends his partner, Freda Hanson (Helen Mowery), to the music shop to impersonate Lund. A menacing, scarred stranger, Harry Pontos (Mike Mazurki), waits outside as Frieda works her magic on the gullible Stillwell. Believing she is the real Elora, the old man gives Frieda a clipping which describes the valuables, then leaves the room. While Stillwell is on the telephone informing Gale he has found Miss Lund, Pontos sneaks into the shop, finds the storeroom, and takes a package addressed to Lund. When Stillwell returns, Pontos bursts in, stabs the old man to death, grabs Frieda, and flees the scene. Gale arrives a few minutes later, finds Stillwell's body, and alerts the police. Outside, Gale holds an impromptu press conference informing reporters he is certain the girl the old man identified as Elora Lund was an imposter. The police suspect Gale of being involved in Stillwell's murder.

To learn what information she may have obtained from Stillwell regarding his valuables, Gale visits Freda the next day. Frieda tells Gale at the time of Stillwell's murder she was blindfolded, gagged, and dragged to a house before being released. Gale is skeptical of her story. When they argue, Freda's landlord, Summers (Regis Toomey), orders Gale to leave the premises. Gale complies, but insists Freda accompany him on a mission to determine where she was taken the night before. From a scattering of clues they find the spot, an old house on a deserted street where Gale finds a drunken Pontos passed out. Before Gale can search the place, the police arrive. Pontos is killed in a shootout, but Gale escapes with Freda. Later, police detectives Taggart and Burns (Barton MacLane, Charles Lane), who saw Gale leave Pontos' house, arrest him for breaking and entering. While Gale is in jail, the real Elora (Pamela Blake) shows up and is enlisted by the police to help obtain information from him.

When Don is released he returns to Freda's apartment. Under pressure she admits she learned the nature of the valuables then attempted to double-cross him in partnership with Pontos. Before Gale can ascertain all the specifics, the doorbell rings. Thinking it's the police Gale hides in Freda's bedroom where he finds a newspaper clipping detailing the old man's treasure: two musical cylinders containing original recordings by famous "Swedish Nightingale" Jenny Lind. Freda is gone when Gale emerges from her bedroom. Gale returns to his office where he finds the real Elora waiting for him. Admitting he sent Freda to impersonate her, Gale makes a deal with Elora to claim 25% of the profits from the sale of the cylinders in return for locating them. To keep her away from the police and rivals Gale takes Elora to the home of Rose Denning (Kathleen Howard), a dipsomaniac who holds her prisoner. Elora eventually escapes through a kitchen window and heads to police headquarters. In the meantime, detectives Taggart and Burns receive word of the death of Frieda from her landlord, Summers, who says he found her strangled body in a closet. A hotel clerk identifies Gale as having visited Frieda around the time of her death. An intense manhunt is ordered to apprehend Gale for questioning.

After being warned by his faithful secretary, Joan (Nina Vale), to give himself up, a disguised Gale returns to the music shop to search for the cylinders. He plans to enter Stillwell's storeroom through the adjoining apartment owned by Stillwell's friend and fellow shopkeeper, Mr. Brown (Harlan Briggs). When Gale arrives at Brown's apartment, he finds him dead, and Summers and an accomplice, Davis (Arthur Space), searching through Stillwell's things in the downstairs' storeroom. As Gale hides in the shadows, Summers and Davis locate the treasure stored in a small tin box hidden in a large drum. Gale confronts them. A shootout ensues which ends in the deaths of both Summers and his henchman. With Elora's treasure in hand, Gale climbs the stairs to Brown's apartment. Intending to hand the treasure over to Miss Lund in order to prove he is innocent of the murders of Frieda and Stillwell, Gale telephones the police. As he hangs up he hears the sound of footsteps ascending the stairway. Thinking it's Summers, he panics, and begins firing at the person on the stairs. Gale is shot dead by Taggart and Burns, who are unaware the morally challenged private dick is innocent of the crimes. Ironically, during the gunplay, one of the bullets pierces the tin box and shatters both priceless cylinders.

MYSTERIOUS INTRUDER EPILOGUE:

THE WHISTLER: "And so after long years of balancing precariously on the borderline of the law Don Gale was trying at the end to do the right thing. But he made one fatal mistake. Thinking that one of the killers had come back to attack him, he fired blindly. Taggart and Burns will never know that Gale's shots were not meant for them."

REVIEWS FOR MYSTERIOUS INTRUDER:

Variety: "With its surprise ending, frequent plot twists, and generally excellent casting, *Mysterious Intruder* provides a consistently entertaining hour's performance . . . Dix, heading the cast, handles his part deftly with a pat touch of lightness that makes for a smooth portrayal. Net result is the creation of a hardboiled character who still is pleasant and casual enough for the audience to warm up to. Mike Mazurki, a reconstructed heavyweight wrestler, gives the right rough-hewn tone to his part. Helen Mowery, Nina Vale, Regis Toomey, and Barton MacLane are uniformly expert in supporting roles . . . . Direction of William Castle is nicely done. He keeps the action moving at a lively pace and the audience edged forward on their seats. Camera work and sound track obbligato are above par."

Film Daily: ". . . entertainment that melodrama fans will accept with little complaint . . . That the picture rates so well must be credited largely to director William Castle, who more than demonstrates his skill in building up a mood of suspense and sustaining it with little letdown right to the end. Under his guidance a commonplace murder yarn has been transformed into a melodrama which can be recommended with little reservation . . ."

The Independent Film Journal: "Except for a rather out-of-place ending, this latest in Columbia's Richard Dix 'Whistlers' is grim, realistic, and entertaining. Pic carries more believableness than most of its type and budget…"

The Hollywood Reporter: "William Castle has shown his accomplishments in handling serious melodrama and, in directing the Rudolph Flothow production of *Mysterious Intruder*, his skill is the deciding factor of a small entertainment that really entertains . . . Flothow's production is handsome in its bracket, and the alert photography by Philip Tannura records every value. Dix accounts for a strong portrayal of the double-crossing detective, and Barton MacLane is very good as his antagonist. The three women concerned are excellently played by the sultry Nina Vale, the appealing Pamela Blake, and interesting Helen Mowery . . ."

Expert Opinions for Mysterious Intruder:

Jon Tuska: "*Mysterious Intruder* directed by William Castle with story and screenplay by Eric Taylor may well be the best entry in the series. Nor am I alone in my affection for the picture. Don Miller, in an engaging essay titled, 'Private Eyes' for the English film magazine *Focus on Film*, Autumn, 1975, observed the Eric Taylor original had a fine gimmick, the quest for some rare Jenny Lind recordings, and some unforgettable characters, such as Mike Mazurki's brutish killer without dialogueue. Most haunting of all was the sleuth, Don Gale, as played by Richard Dix. 'I'm an unusual kind of detective,' says Dix early in the film, which is an understatement . . .' William Castle in his treatment of the story had certainly been influenced by what Edward Dmytryk had achieved in *Murder My Sweet* (RKO, 1944). The settings are musty old shops, and a dilapidated house where Mazurki is sleeping off a drunk. All the important action takes place in fitful lighting and heavy shadows. Dix's private detective is motivated by greed, as are most of the other characters. He proves himself smarter than the others but, ironically, in his haste makes a fatal mistake. I would go so far as to suggest that *Mysterious Intruder* is the best film Castle made at Columbia."

Motion Picture Guide: "Though routine in plot, this is a well paced film with some good moments of suspense. At one point Dix feels his way through a dark abandoned house searching for the killer. The direction keeps the audience on edge, with a good nervous laugh thrown in as well, while Dix gropes in the darkness. Though classically hardboiled, Dix's characterization has a soft spot, as well as providing some humor within the mystery. Some interesting camera work and a tightly plotted script make this a nifty programmer."

INTERESTING FACTS/TRIVIA FOR MYSTERIOUS INTRUDER:

1. Columbia scenarist Eric Taylor's script for this film, entitled "Murder is Unpredictable," was adapted from a novelette he penned, "Murder to Music," first published in the noted pulp-fiction magazine *Black Mask* in May 1936.

2. The Taylor screenplay includes several alterations from his original *Black Mask* story. The most important involved the persona of the main character, Don Gale, and the story's ending. In *Murder to Music*, Taylor's protagonist, Jess Arno, is more forthright, less cynical, and opportunistic. Although Arno was involved in various shady activities and consorted with criminals, in the end he battled the crooks in order to turn the cylinders over to Elora, and lived to tell the tale. The slippery con man, Gale, was not so ethical or lucky. According to various sources, Taylor made his protagonist unethical to fit the new postwar trend in crime films

we now refer to as *film noir*, and changed the ending of *Murder to Music* to satisfy Hollywood's Production Code which decreed crime could not pay.

3. Because he had already used the name Jess Arno as his main character in his script for the 1943 Columbia, mystery *No Place for a Lady*, Taylor was forced to invent a new character named Don Gale for the ethically challenged private investigator in *Mysterious Intruder*.

4. The best lines in the film are delivered by Gale to the elderly Stillwell when the latter attempts to hire him to find Elora. When the old man refuses to detail the contents of the valuables he is holding for Lund, Gale angrily upbraids him.

DON: "Let me tell you the success of this office depends on the mutual trust between my clients and myself. I may not be the greatest detective in the world but I am [*his voice softens*] the most unusual. If you want to put your confidence in me, I'll find Elora."

5. Curiously, the key character of shopkeeper, Mr. Brown (portrayed by Harlan Briggs), is not mentioned in the Taylor synopsis published by Columbia prior to the release of the film in the spring of 1946.

6. In a typical, unintentionally funny bit of B movie inconsistency filmgoers see New York's famous 59th Street Bridge from the window of Gale's shabby office. According to New York natives, that would place its location in the ultra-swank Sutton Place.

MY TAKE:

An action-packed, tension-filled, blood-spattered *noir*-ish extravaganza. William Castle's *Mysterious Intruder* is not only the best film of the *Whistler* series, it is one of the finest low-budget thrillers Columbia made during the postwar period; a great example of Castle's genius for storytelling combined with B unit craftsmanship.

To make the fifth series entry, Cohn, Briskin, and Flothow wisely assembled some of the most talented professionals from the previous four, including director Castle, scenarist Eric Taylor, cinematographer Phil Tannura, art director Hans Radon, and star Richard Dix. To that impressive roster they added a stalwart supporting cast of seasoned veterans and gifted newcomers. The result was rightly applauded by critics and audiences alike. *Mysterious Intruder* may not qualify as a great piece of art, but it is exceptional.

Its strengths begin with the script. Unlike three of its predecessors, and the three *Whistlers* which followed, Eric Taylor's screenplay for this film, which he entitled "Murder is Unpredictable," was more than a rough scenario. It was articulate and well-structured, with an unusually intriguing plot, memorable characters, good dialogue, and a hauntingly ironic climax. Adapted from his novelette, "Murder to Music" (about the unintended consequences of a dishonest private eye's quest to steal an innocent old man's valuables), Taylor transported the Whistler from the placid, low-key isolation of a deserted lighthouse back to the dark dangerous streets of New York, a shadowy, violent world of decadence and evil populated by scoundrels and fiends who prey like vampires on the weak and innocent.

Among the scoundrels is perhaps the most memorable character in all eight *Whistler* films: Taylor's anti-heroic protagonist, Don Gale (Dix), an unprincipled, avaricious, shifty-eyed gumshoe who has been skirting on the edges of the law for years. A consummate con man, whose slick, soft-spoken manner aids him in manipulating and feeding off the vulnerable, he is an individual with few redeeming qualities save an innate cunning, and a rather wry sense of humor. Taylor created several notable scenes with effective dialogue which illustrate Gale's fatally-flawed nature. The first occurs at the film's outset when the gentile old Mr. Stillwell (Paul Burns) attempts to procure Gale's services for $100. Despite Stillwell's apparent honesty and sincerity, Gale appears indifferent.

GALE: "A hundred dollars! Can't you dig deeper? Is there any way you can raise money? Then you're not very interested in locating her."

STILLWELL:	"I could mortgage my business and get a few hundred dollars."
GALE:	"I wouldn't do that to you. Why, a few hundred bucks would be gone like that."

After learning the old man has "tens of thousands" worth of valuables, Gale experiences a sudden change of heart. Taking the $100, he tells Stillwell, "I'll see what I can do." As the old gentleman leaves, Gale's all-knowing secretary, Joan (Nina Vale), confronts him.

JOAN:	"Are you really going to look for that girl?"

With a greedy gleam in his eye, Gale responds.

GALE: "Of course I am. What's more I'm going to find her."

Another illustrative scene occurs when the real Elora Lund shows up at Gale's office. Forced by necessity to be his conscience a worried Joan warns Gale not to take advantage.

JOAN:	"She's a sweet kid and she's been sick. I'm not going to stand by and see her robbed."
GALE:	"When have I ever robbed a client?"
JOAN:	"Whenever you've had the opportunity."

Taylor exposes yet another dimension of Gale's character near the film's midpoint when he confronts his double-crossing partner, Frieda. In a short scene we become aware the smooth-talking Don may have violent tendencies.

FRIEDA:	"You don't believe anything I say, so go ahead and tell the police about me. They won't do much to me, and it will cost you your license."

Enraged, Gale grabs her.

GALE: "It's not as simple as that. You and I have a lot to settle first."

Taylor keeps us guessing about Gale's intentions (regarding the valuable records) until the film's conclusion. Although he tells Joan he intends to confront Stillwell's killer, obtain the cylinders, hand them over to Lund, then give himself up, we are never quite sure he is capable of doing the right and moral thing until the film's final scene. In it Gale provides proof positive when he refuses to partner with the malevolent Summers (Regis Toomey) who has found the treasure. With gun in hand Gale confronts Summers.

GALE: "Right. I'm going to turn you over, and your friend here, and the records."

SUMMERS: "You're kidding; you wouldn't throw a fortune like this away."

GALE: "Oh, but I would. Someone's gonna hang for Frieda and Stillwell. If it isn't you I'm very much afraid, it might be me."

Taylor's compelling double-twist denouement served a dual purpose. The surprising death of Gale in the concluding scene not only communicated the "crime does not pay" moral of the tale, but was a hauntingly ironic, uniquely "Whistler" way of suggesting the unpredictability and unfairness of life: a prevalent theme of *film noir*.

An interesting analysis of *Mysterious Intruder* is found in David Wilt's informative volume *"Hardboiled in Hollywood"* (chronicling the lives and careers of five former *Black Mask* writers-turned-scenarists, including Eric Taylor). In it Wilt cites the film as, "One of the most interesting achievements of Taylor's career," and compares it to several noir classics, particularly *Kiss Me Deadly* (United Artists, 1955). "Both films concern a crooked, ruthless, private eye in search of an unknown valuable 'something,' in both cases the detective callously uses a female assistant to further his investigations, and in both films the protagonist dies after his chief rival for the valuable 'whatsit' is killed and the detective is apparently home free with the goods. Both films take place in seedy surroundings and dispense with traditional heroics and happy endings . . ."

The skilled direction of William Castle further refined, shaped, and enriched Taylor's melodramatic script by supplying an anxiety-filled atmosphere and exceptional detail. After discarding elements of his directorial arsenal in order to tell the low-key story featured in *Voice of the Whistler*, filmdom's P.T. Barnum again readjusted his approach to tell the hardboiled, doom-laden tale of *Mysterious Intruder*. Not only did he bring back the dim lighting, weird camera angles, and quickened pace of his early Whistlers, but utilized his trademark contrivances to create a sense of unease and anxiousness reminiscent of a Hammett or a Chandler yarn.

Castle's expert touch is felt in several key scenes beginning with the clever opener between the shameless shamus and Stillwell which approximates a psychiatric session. Another involved the shadowy murder of the sweet old Stillwell by the brutish, knife-wielding maniac, Pontos (Mike Mazurki). By using dim light and shadows, highlighted by a chilling full close-up of the deranged killer repeatedly stabbing his defenseless victim, Castle created a bloodcurdling image which added a thrilling dimension to the film even the cleverest scenarist could never have conjured on paper.

The sure hand of Castle is also felt in another top-drawer sequence which featured the drunken, demented Rose Denning (Kathleen Howard) hired by Gale to keep Elora from the police and others seeking the valuable recordings. When she first meets Rose, the innocent Lund believes her to be peculiar but benign; but as she learns more and more about her "hostess" she becomes increasingly uncomfortable and fearful. Castle cleverly crafts the scenes of Rose and Elora building tension gradually. With his audience on the edge of their seats he lowers the boom. As the two prepare to dine at the kitchen table the crazy Rose suddenly picks up a large knife and approaches Elora from behind. Instead of cutting her throat she cuts a slice of bread in front of the alarmed young girl. Great stuff!

Producer Rudolph Flothow assembled an outstanding cast and a topnotch group of technical experts to implement Taylor and Castle's visions. Dix outdoes himself as Don Gale. In one of his finest film portrayals he makes the slimy, money-grubbing predator a multi-dimensional human being who evokes sympathy. His three leading ladies, Vale, Mowery, and Blake, are standouts. Mowery, in particular, shines in the showy role of Frieda, the double-crossing *femme fatale*. Solid support is contributed by a large group of character players, including veterans Barton MacLane and Charles Lane as the detectives, Paul Burns as the tragic Stillwell, and Regis Toomey as the evil Summers. Of special note are the villainous performances of Mike Mazurki and Kathleen Howard. The former is mesmerizing as the silent, sadistic Pontos whose sinister face alone might have sufficed to scare old Stillwell to death. Miss Howard is fascinating as the matron who provides a safe house for Gale's "clients," hides a gin bottle in her sewing box, and seems uncomfortably adept with a kitchen knife. On the technical side, Philip Tannura's cinematography, Hans Radon's art direction, and Robert Priestley's sets were notable.

For all its admirable qualities the movie is occasionally marred by its humble origins (i.e. production values, time constraints, etc.), the complexity of its plot, illogical actions of characters, and instances of B movie balderdash. Like the original *Whistler* entry (also penned by Taylor), the film would surely have benefited from additional footage which could have been used to explain certain characters' motivations and clear up various loose ends. Adding a scene or two might have clarified the confusing details of Frieda's relationships with Pontos and Summers. Also in need of clarification was Elora's decision to let Gale take her to a "safe house" after police informed her he was a murder suspect.

The movie contains multiple examples of B movie nonsense. One occurs during the first half of the picture when an unidentified woman and her husband shoot at Gale as he escapes from Pontos' house. Although this bit of gimmickry enhanced Castle's exciting escape scene, it is a bit over-the-top even for a low-budget film. The world of *Mysterious Intruder* was undoubtedly a violent one, but was it so dangerous it was necessary for neighbors to indiscriminately shoot at passersby?

Another conspicuous bit rears its silly head near the end of the picture when the fugitive Gale, trying to avoid the cops and make his way to Stillwell's shop, goes "incognito" by wearing dark glasses and ensconcing himself in bandages. In an unintentionally hilarious 30-second scene he walks nonchalantly down the street and enters Brown's apartment (next to Stillwell's shop) in front of a policeman who never once appears suspicious of this mummy with sunglasses. A foolish, inane moment in a high-quality low-budget feature.

RATING: 1

Mysterious Intruder Photo Gallery:

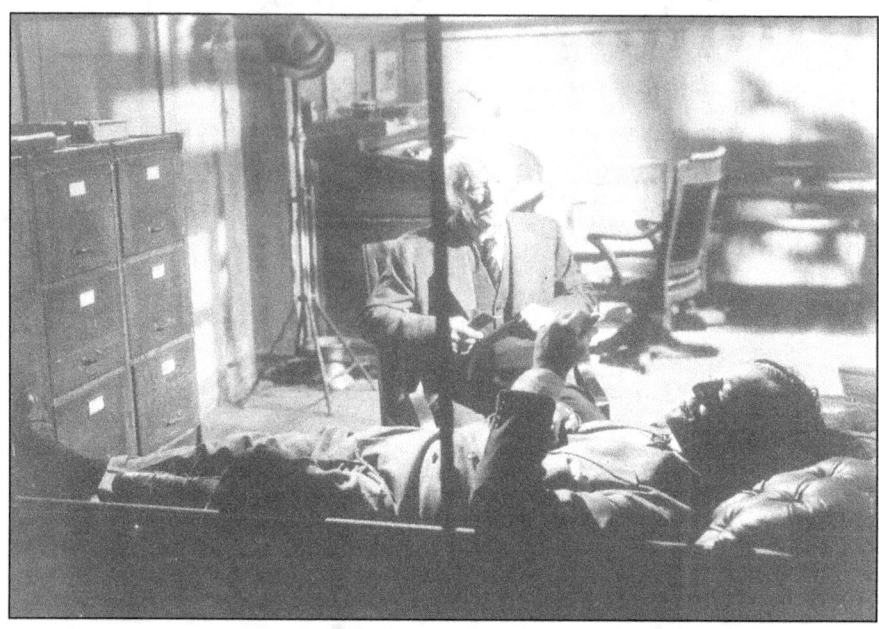

Kindly shopkeeper Edward Stillwell (Paul Burns, background) has a proposition for unscrupulous private eye Don Gale (Dix), one which has the potential to make him a rich man.

Naïve Mr. Stillwell (Paul Burns) thinks he's finally located the young girl he's been searching for when Freda Hanson (Helen Mowery) shows up at his shop. He is about to learn he should not have been so trusting.

Helen Mowery, and Barton MacLane (right) in a scene from *Mysterious Intruder*.

Dix and Nina Vale.

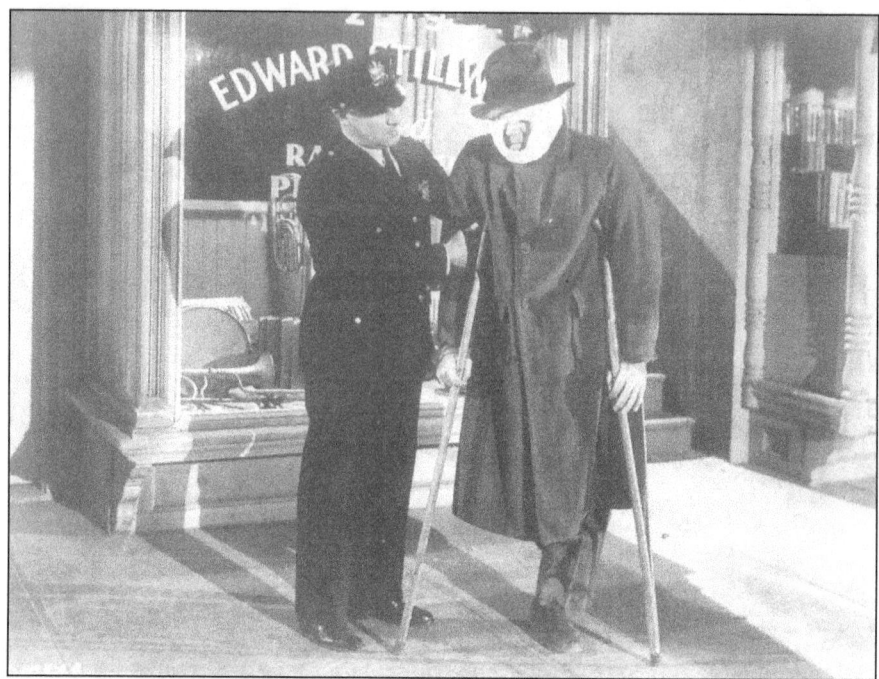

Richard Dix donned some hilariously over-the-top disguises in several of the *Whistlers*, including *Mysterious Intruder*.

Gale surprises the evil Summers (Regis Toomey) and his henchman before they can escape with the rare recordings in this exciting scene from *Mysterious Intruder*.

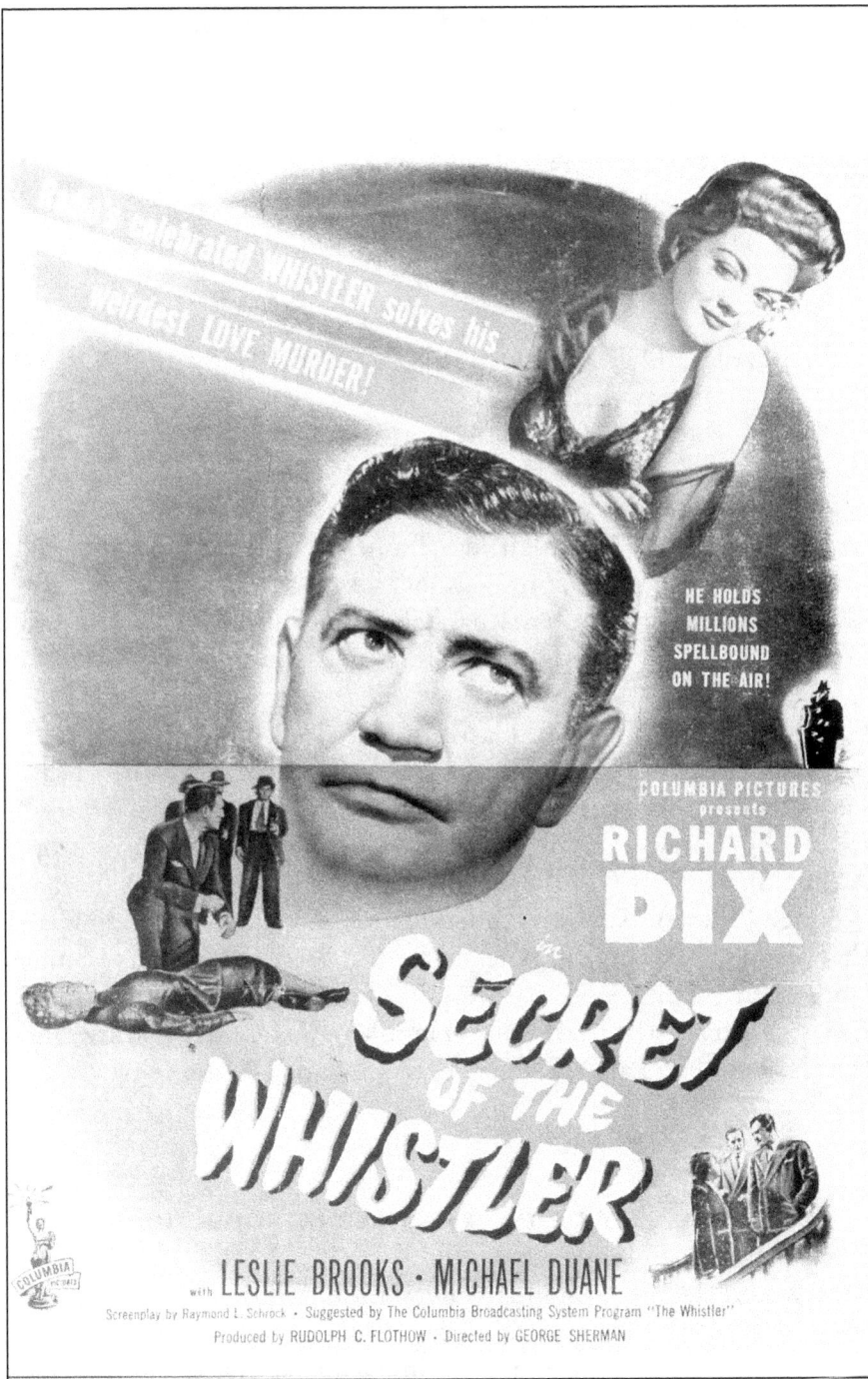

Poster for *The Secret of the Whistler*.

THE SECRET OF THE WHISTLER (Columbia–1946)

Production Dates: July 15, 1946 – August 1, 1946
Release Date: November 7, 1946
Running Time: 65 minutes.
Taglines: "THEY BEGAN BY KILLING FOR LOVE and ENDED BY LOVING TO KILL!"

"HE LEARNED TO KILL . . . IN TWO UNEASY LESSONS!"

Credits: Rudolph C. Flothow (Producer), George Sherman (Direction), Carter De Haven (Assistant Director), Raymond L. Schrock (screenplay), Richard H. Landau (story) based on the radio series, The Whistler by J. Donald Wilson, Allen Siegler (photography), Hans Radon (art direction), Robert Bradfield (set decoration), Wilbur Hatch (music), Mischa Bakaleinikoff (Musical Director), Dwight Caldwell (editing), Howard Fogetti (sound).

Cast: Richard Dix (Ralph Harrison), Leslie Brooks (Kay Morrell), Michael Duane (Jim Calhoun), Mary Currier (Edith Marie Harrison), Mona Barrie (Linda Vail), Ray Walker (Joe Conroy), Claire Du Brey (Laura), Charles Trowbridge (Dr. Winthrop), Arthur Space (Dr. Gunther), Jack Davis (Henry Loring), Barbara Woddell (Nurse), Nancy Saunders, Doris Houck (Girls), Snowflake (Harrison's servant), Baynes Barron (Artist), Byron Foulger (Jorgensen), Ernie Adams (George), Fred Amsel (Messenger Boy), Ernest Hilliard (Butler), John Hamilton (McLaren), Tony Shay (Detective), Pat Lane (Detective Lieutenant), Otto Forrest (The Whistler).

The Secret of the Whistler Introduction:

The Whistler: Standard Recitation. "And tonight in this obscure section of a large city, we find a woman shopping for an unusual item."

PLOT SUMMARY: Artist Ralph Harrison (Richard Dix) possesses little talent but has a wealthy benefactor: his sickly wife, who supplies him with a monthly allowance and pays for an expensive apartment he utilizes as a studio and as a place to conduct extramarital affairs. The story begins as his wife, Edith (Mary Currier), a terminally ill heart patient, purchases her gravestone as her husband hosts an elaborate party at his studio where he meets shapely blonde model Kay Morrell (Leslie Brooks).

After Edith suffers a second heart attack, is confined to bed, and given weeks to live, Ralph begins an illicit affair with gold-digging bombshell Kay, whom he hires as a model. Complications ensue when Edith unexpectedly regains her strength and decides to pay a visit to Ralph's studio to surprise him. While hiding in the backroom, she overhears him profess love for Kay. Heartbroken, on the verge of collapse, Edith returns home and records the event in her diary. Later, she confronts Ralph, orders him to move out, and informs him she intends to eliminate him from her will. She telephones her attorney to draw up the paperwork, but he is not in. Ralph listens to the conversation.

Shaken, Ralph opts to kill his wife before she can act. Thinking she is asleep, he sneaks into her room and pours a few drops of poison in one of her medicine bottles. Unbeknownst to him, Edith is awake. After recording the attempted murder in her diary, and hiding the incriminating medicine bottle so she can have it analyzed later, Edith suddenly dies of a heart attack. Assuming her death was due to the tainted medicine, and unaware of the headstone transaction, Ralph has his wife cremated to destroy the evidence.

Although tormented by conscience and fear he'll eventually be incriminated in Edith's death, Ralph marries Kay. The newlyweds decide to take up residence in Edith's newly remolded home. All seems well until a sensational murder case grabs newspaper headlines involving a husband poisoning his wife who left a diary incriminating him. Eerily similar to Ralph's own alleged crime, he becomes increasingly agitated and erratic, especially after he receives a bill for the monument Edith ordered. Kay notes his behavior and becomes suspicious. Her concern is heightened when Edith's loyal housekeeper, Laura (Claire Du Brey), tells Kay she believes the first Mrs. Harrison was murdered by Ralph, and informs her of the existence of Edith's diary and the missing bottle of medicine.

Fearing for her own safety, and seeing an opportunity to rid herself of Ralph, Kay locates the diary, reads the relevant passages, and tears out entries which document the attempted crime and prove her husband's innocence. Kay eventually locates the medicine bottle, and delivers it to her artist friend, Jim Calhoun (Michael Duane), who takes it to newspaper reporter/columnist Joe Conroy (Ray Walker) for analysis. When Joe telephones Kay to confirm the existence of poison in Edith's medicine, and informs her that the police have been summoned, Ralph overhears the conversation. Moments before authorities arrive to take him into custody, an enraged Ralph strangles Kay, unaware she possesses proof in the pocket of her dress (Edith's diary entries) that he did not kill his first wife. He is shot by the police while trying to escape, but Ralph survives and faces a murder rap, not for the death of Edith, but for killing Kay.

The Secret of the Whistler epilogue:

None

Reviews for The Secret of the Whistler:

Motion Picture Herald: "Best one of the Whistlers so far and that's saying plenty. They are all above average mysteries!"

The Hollywood Reporter: "Its cast, headed by Richard Dix, Leslie Brooks, and Michael Duane, lends '*The Secret of the Whistler*' class, and George Sherman puts pace in his direction of the Rudolph Flothow production. Most of the pictures based on the mystery radio program have followed a pattern of keeping an audience confused as long as possible. The screenplay by Raymond L. Schrock is a more than competent job, and it makes quite a bit of sense . . . Richard Dix gives a good account of the hero-murderer, and Miss Brooks is ultra attractive as the second wife. Duane plays a handsome portrait painter effectively, and Mary Currier leaves a strong impression with her performance of the murdered wife . . ."

Variety: "The shadow of 'The Whistler' falls across the screen for the sixth time, bringing its usual formula of melodrama, vengeance, and a touch of irony. *The Secret of the Whistler* concerns assorted high jinks in artistic circles . . . Dix goes through his paces with veteran ease. Mary Currier attracts considerable sympathy as the wronged first wife. Leslie Brooks' appearance is justified by that shot of her posing in a tight bathing suit, plus an all-around good performance as the model . . . Raymond L. Schrock's screenplay provides enough melodrama and plot twists to keep the audience in its seats until the main feature comes on screen . . ."

EXPERT OPINIONS FOR THE SECRET OF THE WHISTLER:

LEONARD MALTIN: "Nifty Whistler entry, with the customary ironic twist."

JON TUSKA: "*The Secret of the Whistler* was a letdown. None of the characters were sympathetic and there was no imagination in either the acting or the direction.

INTERESTING FACTS/TRIVIA — THE SECRET OF THE WHISTLER

1. For the first and only time during the series, the Whistler did not offer an epilogue, which traditionally served the dual purpose of foretelling the destiny of his main characters and tying up all the plot's loose ends. In *The Secret of the Whistler* he left the duty to a police officer who, after finding Kay's strangled body and pages from Edith's diary in her pocket, concludes, "This would have saved Harrison's neck, but it won't do him any good now." From this statement we assume Ralph will face the death penalty for murdering Kay.

2. The best lines in *Secret* are delivered by witty artist Jim Calhoun

(Michael Duane) to his friend and former model, Kay (Leslie Brooks), in two separate scenes. When Kay informs him the lustful Ralph (Dix) has been keeping her busy, posing her as a Mexican peasant, a Chinese girl, then a harem lady, he quips:

JIM: "Don't ever let him see you on a horse, or he'll want to paint you as Lady Godiva."

The acerbic Calhoun offers still more advice to Kay earlier in the film.

JIM: "If he gets fresh, threaten to tell his wife. That'll stop him quick. If he loses his meal ticket he'll have to go back to making sketches at the fairground."

3. Another bit of humor of the unintentional kind comes when the Whistler character refers to "the uncertainty of not knowing."

4. Ironically, actor Michael Duane, who persuasively played painter Calhoun, was a talented artist in real life. A few months after the debut of this film, a successful exhibition of his landscape paintings was held in Hollywood.

5. During the filming of *The Secret of the Whistler* Richard Dix had his first and only in-person meeting with the man who organized the worldwide, 5,000 strong Richard Dix Fan Club 21 years earlier. After a brief introduction to his idol, the Ottawa, Canada, native was invited to Dix's ranch near Topanga Canyon, and then taken on a personally guided tour of the film capital by the star.

My Take:

A very good thriller with an interesting plot, top-caliber performances and decent production values. Although the picture sometimes has the look and feel of an episode of TV's, *Alfred Hitchcock Presents*, it improves with repeated viewings, and is highly recommended.

If *The Secret of the Whistler* had been the first entry of the *Whistler* series, or had not followed *Mysterious Intruder* it might have appeared to better advantage. It is a very entertaining, sometimes compelling, low-budget melodrama with several meritorious elements. The problem is that it was the sixth *Whistler* film, and most of its predecessors had superior atmospherics, and more inspired direction. Now, don't get me wrong, director George Sherman was a fine B movie craftsman who helmed many superior low-to-medium-budget westerns and adventures in a long and distinguished career, but his direction here was uneven. He created some excellent scenes, but his leisure-like pace, and failure to address the script's weaknesses, was a letdown from past *Whistlers*, especially William Castle's tour-de-force, *Mysterious Intruder*.

To be fair, Sherman was hampered by a deficient screenplay. Although it had an exceedingly interesting storyline supplied by ace writer Richard H. Landau, Raymond L. Schrock's script generally lacked excitement, interesting settings, and assemblage of quirky minor characters which *Whistler* fans had come to associate with the series. Granted, the tale did not lend itself to exotic settings, but Schrock and Sherman did fail to exploit the story's full potential by relying on conversation rather than action to move the plot. This slowed the pace and weakened tension at several key points.

Another minus was the script's conclusion. While the double twist was exciting, and in keeping with the *Whistler's* trademark irony, Schrock's denouement was unnecessarily confusing. After relating a straightforward, uncomplicated story, he left filmgoers in the lurch by failing to answer a key question: Why did the gold-digging Kay hold on to the pages she tore from Edith's diary? If she was out to rid herself of Ralph and get his money by implicating him in the death of his first wife, why did she not immediately destroy the only evidence that exonerated him? Schrock and/or Sherman could easily have provided an explanation in the script or via a Whistler epilogue.

Despite the deficits, *Secret* is essentially an engrossing B movie which grows on you. It certainly merits 65 minutes of your time. Sherman deserves at least some of the credit, if for no other reason than for creating the boffo first scene which had Edith (Mary Currier) selecting her headstone from creepy monument dealer Jorgenson (Byron Foulger). Stylistically mounted and well played, it set in motion the chain of events chronicled in the psychological melodrama in a particularly eerie manner. Among the film's other plusses were the solid work of art director Hans Radon and set decorator Robert Bradfield, who constructed and designed realistic sets for Edith's mansion and Ralph's studio, and photographer Allen Siegler who lensed some interesting scenes containing unconventional camera angles which created an uncertain, off-center atmosphere.

The film's greatest asset was its distinguished cast. Once again Dix shines in a complex, essentially unsympathetic, role. He is totally believable as the debonair, untalented ne'er-do-well whose love for money and a beautiful blonde leads to violence and self-destruction. His excellence is equaled by his two screen wives, played memorably by Mary Currier and Leslie Brooks. Currier is heartbreaking as the cultured, soft-spoken Edith whom Ralph victimizes. She is especially fine in the scene in which she learns of her husband's infidelity. Watch the subtlety of her facial expressions as she listens to Ralph proclaiming love for another woman. Splendid! It is truly sad this exceptional actress was largely relegated to bits during her long career. Gorgeous Leslie Brooks does her one better as the fortune-hunting Kay Morell. Brooks' finely shaded performance not only conveys the hard, gold-digging aspects of her character, but the insecurities and fear as well. It is not an exaggeration to say, outside of Dix, and J. Carrol Naish's murderous turn in *The Whistler*, Brooks contributes the finest portrayal in all eight entries. The supporting performances of Michael Duane as the witty artist and Claire Du Brey as Edith's housekeeper (*Secret's* answer to Mrs. Danvers) are also very fine, as are Byron Foulger as the funeral home proprietor, Ray Walker as a newspaper columnist, and the always watchable Mona Barrie as Ralph's artist/friend.

RATING: 6

THE SECRET OF THE WHISTLER PHOTO GALLERY

Playboy artist Ralph Harrison meets shapely blonde model Kay Morell at a party he hosts from his studio. (From left to right: Michael Duane, Brooks and Dix.)

Harrison's terminally ill wife, Edith (Mary Currier), eventually learns of his infidelities and opts to disinherit him.

From left to right: Jack Davis, Claire Du Brey, Arthur Space, Richard Dix in a scene from *The Secret of the Whistler*.

Left to right: Leslie Brooks, Ray Walker, Michael Duane, Mona Barrie.

Richard Dix and Leslie Brooks relax in between takes during the filming of the sixth series entry, *The Secret of the Whistler*.

Poster for *The Thirteenth Hour*.

THE THIRTEENTH HOUR (Columbia–1947)

PRODUCTION DATES: October 3, 1946 – October 22, 1946
RELEASE: March 6, 1947
RUNNING TIME: 65 minutes.
TAGLINES: "MURDER ON A ONE-WAY HIGHWAY . . . TO THE GALLOWS!"

"THE NIGHT WAS MADE FOR LOVE . . . And MURDER when 'THE WHISTLER' WALKS THE EARTH AT THE THIRTEENTH HOUR"

CREDITS: Rudolph C. Flothow (Producer), William Clemens (Director), Carter De Haven (Assistant Director), Edward Bock, Raymond Schrock (screenplay), Leslie Edgley (story) based on the radio series, The Whistler by J. Donald Wilson, Vincent Farrar (photography), Hans Radon (art direction), Albert Rickerd (set decoration), Wilbur Hatch (music), Mischa Bakaleinikoff (musical direction), Dwight Caldwell (editing), Howard Fogetti (sound).

CAST: Richard Dix (Steve Reynolds), Karen Morley (Eileen Blair), John Kellogg (Charlie Cook), Jim Bannon (Jerry Mason), Regis Toomey (Don Parker), Bernadene Hayes (Mabel Sands), Mark Dennis (Tommy Blair), Anthony Warde (Radford), Ernie Adams (McCabe), Cliff Clark (Police Captain Linfield), Otto Forrest (The Whistler), Jack Carrington (Stack), Nancy Saunders (Donna), Lillian Wells (Secretary), Michael Towne (Driver), Stanley Blystone, Frank O'Connor, Pat O'Malley, Ralph Linn (Detectives), Robert Williams (Berger), George Lloyd, Hurley Breen (Waiters), Paul Campbell (Jimmy), Selmer Jackson (Judge), Charles Jordan (Bernie), Kernan Cripps (Policeman), Lou Davis, Brian O'Hara, Joe Palma, Eddie Parker, Wally Rose (Truck Drivers).

THE THIRTEENTH HOUR INTRODUCTION:

THE WHISTLER: Standard Recitation. "And tonight at this lonely spot on a highway near a small town we find an unusual birthday celebration in full swing."

Two short scenes follow. The first features a small group of truckers celebrating the birthday of diner proprietor Eileen Blair, newly engaged to trucker Steve Reynolds. Steve has one alcoholic drink to commemorate Eileen's birthday then leaves to finish a run. The second scene has Steve on the highway where he stops to pick up a hitchhiker.

THE WHISTLER: "Ordinarily, you don't pick up hitchhikers, Steve. But with a warming drink under your belt and the memory of Eileen's kiss on your lips you're feeling friendly toward everybody. It was only a moment's delay, but those sixty seconds are going to change the whole pattern of your life."

PLOT SUMMARY: Trucking firm owner Steve Reynolds (Richard Dix) celebrates the birthday of his sweetheart, Eileen Blair (Karen Morley), by gifting her with an engagement ring, and having a drink of alcoholic punch at a small gathering at the truck stop/diner she owns. While making a delivery that evening, Steve stops to pick up a hitchhiker, and is subsequently forced off the road by a reckless motorist who swerves into his path. To avoid a collision, Steve smashes his truck into McCabe's Gas Station, and is ticketed for drunk driving by motorcycle cop Don Parker, (Regis Toomey), a rival for Eileen's affections. In the meantime, the hitchhiker mysteriously disappears.

Convicted of driving under the influence, Steve's license is revoked for six months, forcing him to rely on other drivers to maintain his business. After turning down an offer by competitor Jerry Mason (Jim Bannon) to purchase his company, Steve violates the law by taking the wheel after one of his employees calls in sick. Steve's truck breaks down while on the road. When he attempts to repair it, he is rendered unconscious by a mysterious assailant who clubs him, loads his lifeless body in the front seat of the truck, and speeds away with the vehicle. When Steve's attacker is pulled over by

Parker for speeding, the attacker runs over the cop, crushing him, and then escapes leaving Steve with a murder rap and one clue: a lone glove which the assailant loses in a struggle with Steve.

Now wanted as a cop killer, Steve goes into hiding in order to locate the real culprit and clear his name. Suspecting Mason's involvement, he shadows his rival and discovers Mason is involved in a stolen car ring. Enlisting the assistance of his friend Charlie Cook (John Kellogg) who takes a job with Mason's firm to watch him, and Eileen, who hides the glove in her safe, Steve sets out to prove Mason was Don's murderer. Eileen's employee, waitress Mabel Sands (Bernadene Hayes), eavesdrops on conversations between Eileen and Steve.

When Charlie confirms Mason is receiving stolen property, Steve wants to go to the police, but Charlie persuades him that they can apprehend those responsible for Parker's murder themselves. Together Steve and Charlie proceed to Mason's garage. While Charlie waits outside, Steve enters his rival's office and finds Mason's dead body, and an empty safe. Before he can leave, he is knocked out momentarily by a shadowy intruder who escapes without detection. When Steve recovers and exits Mason's office, Charlie tells him he, too, was attacked and convinces his friend he should not give himself up. Steve returns to Eileen's apartment and learns she has discovered a cache of diamonds hidden in the glove. Eileen's son, Tommy (Mark Dennis), alerts Steve to the suspicious behavior of Mabel.

Convinced Mabel is involved in the killings, Steve places the diamonds in his tobacco pouch and follows Mabel to her apartment where he overhears her discussing Mason's death and stolen jewels on the telephone. Later, both Steve and Charlie return to Mabel's place in hopes they will find the killer. Shortly after entering, Charlie pulls a gun on Steve, admits he stole the diamonds then murdered the rogue cop for blackmailing him. Now a hostage, Steve is forced by Charlie and Mabel (who do not know he has the diamonds on him) to write a letter to Eileen demanding the jewels for his life. Charlie delivers the note to Eileen at the diner. Upon reading Steve's coded message, Eileen insists on accompanying Charlie to Mabel's apartment where she too becomes a hostage. The intelligent Tommy calls the police and supplies them with the license plate number of his mother's car. Things look bad for Steve and Eileen until the police arrive just in time to arrest the criminal duo and save their captives. Mabel turns states' evidence and Steve is cleared of the murder of Don. In recognition for his ordeal the police give Steve the reward offered for the return of the diamonds. With the money Steve is able to marry Eileen and return to the trucking business.

THE THIRTEENTH HOUR EPILOGUE:

THE WHISTLER: "Yes, Steve. You were lucky. Stopping for just sixty seconds to give a stranger a lift did change the whole pattern of your life. It might have ended in disgrace or even death, but fate was kind to you."

REVIEWS FOR THE THIRTEENTH HOUR:

Film Daily: "Effective thriller has fair story realism, and performances in its favor . . . The plot has action requirements and is set off to good advantage in the directorial handling . . ."

Daily Variety: "*The Thirteenth Hour* is a suspense chiller from Columbia's 'Whistler' hopper. Only occasionally does it have plot trouble, and lapses from credibility aren't enough to keep it from being strong support in double bills...Thesping by Dix, Karen Morley, John Kellogg, Bernadene Hayes and rest of the small cast is uniformly good . . . William Clemens' direction of the Rudolph Flothow production, Vincent Farrar's lensing, Dwight Caldwell's editing, and Mischa Bakaleinikoff's music are standout in technical credits . . ."

Motion Picture Herald: "Good mystery that holds interest throughout. One of the best of the Whistler series."

Interesting Facts/Trivia — The Thirteenth Hour:

1. The Leslie Edgley story on which this movie was based was titled *The Hunter is a Fugitive*. That title was retained for the film until Columbia's legal office determined it could not be used.

2. In a 1999 interview with this author, Karen Morley had few recollections of the 19-day production of *The Thirteenth Hour*, but expressed fond memories of her leading man, Richard Dix, with whom she was costarred in two films. Of Dix she said, "He was a very fine actor and a very thoughtful man. I always felt he was underappreciated. We worked very well together. The films we did were not memorable, but he was always a great pleasure to work with. He was quite ill during the *Whistler* picture and retired after it was completed. Sadly, it was his last film. I was saddened by news of his passing."

3. In publicity interviews published at the time he was filming his role as stalwart trucker Steve Reynolds Dix said he felt his *Whistler* roles were more substantive than many he'd played in his younger days. "This part is more dramatic than the ones I used to do at Goldwyn and Paramount. Then, I played devil-may-care, brassy boys who were strong on wisecracks; and back in some of those early films I made the jokes via printed titles."

4. During the filming of *The Thirteenth Hour* production was interrupted briefly when Princess Konnewe-ho of the Navajos visited the set to announce that star Richard Dix (who appeared as American Indians in *The Vanishing American, Redskin*, etc.) had been made an honorary chieftain of the tribe.

5. According to the pressbook for this film, Dix received a gift during production he'd long been coveting, a 16mm copy of his classic silent *The Christian*. It came from a fan whose father had managed a theatre and found it stored away.

6. Since there was no memorable dialogue in the film, we must settle for the unintentionally funniest lines delivered by lovers

Steve and Eileen (Dix and Morley) after the latter shows her boyfriend the contents of the glove (a tube full of diamonds) which Steve had inexplicably never discovered.

STEVE: "Am I stupid! I've been looking for a man with a missing thumb . . . ?"

EILEEN: "I guess you're not as curious as I am."

7. Sadly and ironically, *The Thirteenth Hour* would be the last film for both its star, Richard Dix, who would die in 1949, and director William Clemens, who retired from films after production wrapped in October 1946.

MY TAKE:

A fast-paced, action-packed crime meller. Not particularly original or distinguished, it is nevertheless worth your while. It contains some good scenes and is notable as the last screen appearance of the legendary Richard Dix.

The filmic series chronicling the tales of the Whistler took another serious creative hit with the release of the seventh entry, *The Thirteenth Hour*. Although the picture was a moderately entertaining B crime drama, it didn't measure up to the previous *Whistlers* in several creative categories, notably its screenplay which was insubstantial, intermittently incredible, and inconsistent with the overall theme of the series.

The film's redeeming elements include its direction. To his great credit William Clemens made a valiant attempt at making sense of an implausible story and script in order to make an exciting *Whistler* entry. His success is only modest, but he deserves kudos for some tightly structured, action-oriented scenes which lent the motion picture the majority of the substance and credibility it possessed. The best of these occurs approximately 40 minutes into the movie when, under cover of night, the protagonist Steve (Dix) sneaks into the business office of rival trucker Jerry Mason to determine if Mason is involved in murder. There he finds Mason's dead body, an empty safe, and a resolute killer determined to pin the crimes on him. In the best *Whistler* tradition Clemens cleverly constructed the scene; building tension and suspense gradually, aided by use of dim light and shadows, photographer Vincent Farrar's hand-held camera, which traced the intruder's footsteps, and a well-placed gimmick. (As Steve enters Mason's office, suddenly the telephone rings.)

The film's veteran cast also deserves credit for trying to cope with the ill-defined, stereotypical characters they were called on to play. For Richard Dix, portraying the protagonist Steve Reynolds in *The Thirteenth Hour* must have appeared something of a demotion from the complex characters he had previously essayed in the *Whistler* series. Although the part was the focus, it was largely an unchallenging one-dimensional heroic role Dix could have played in his sleep. With lines like, "Every dog has its day; mines' coming," and the classic, "I want you to keep your eyes open for a man with a missing thumb," the physically ill Dix probably wished he had skipped the film and retired after *The Secret of the Whistler*.

Unfortunately, Dix's leading lady, the talented and distinguished Karen Morley, fared even worse. You could almost see her gritting her teeth as she spoke her inane lines as the adoring, accommodating Eileen. The other cast members, which included the always interesting John Kellogg, Jim Bannon, Bernadene Hayes, and young Mark Dennis, also did their best, but their work suffered under the circumstances.

Those "circumstances" included a cluttered storyline which featured time-consuming subplots, underdeveloped characters, and various absurdities. Scenarists Ray Schrock and Edward Bock were talented writers who could have cleaned up some of the eccentricities of the Leslie Edgeley story but chose not to. The stolen diamonds subplot was particularly problematic. Hiding stolen gems in a glove might have been a creative idea for presentation in a pulp-fiction novel or a magazine article, but here it appears silly. Even if one accepts the idea a crook would hide jewels (approximately 15-20 diamonds in a small tube) in the thumbhole of a glove (Reynolds' only clue in the murder of Don Parker), it is inconceivable the intelligent Steve would not have found them.

The stolen car ring subplot is also confusing and distracting. It serves as a useful gimmick for keeping the audience focused on Jerry

Mason's possible involvement in murder, but it takes too much of the film's footage. Steve's miraculous recoveries from several significant blows to the head also strain credulity, as does the police captain's concluding speech (undoubtedly inspired by Hollywood's Production Code) extolling the virtues of "men in blue."

Even more importantly, the movie misses the mark thematically. With so many excellent *Whistler* radio stories and scripts to choose from it is perplexing why Rudy Flothow and associates opted to film Edgley's crime drama *The Hunter is a Fugitive* for the *Whistler* series. The basic plotline of a trucker framed for murdering a romantic rival may have been appropriate, if unoriginal, fodder for a B movie, but not particularly suitable as a *Whistler* "tale." The stories depicted by the mysterious Whistler (both on radio and in film) all involved momentous acts or decisions committed by main characters who consciously crossed lines of propriety and criminality. In *The Thirteenth Hour*, Steve Reynolds appeared more a victim of the evil acts of others than a perpetrator. Although one could argue he acted irresponsibly by taking a drink of alcoholic punch before driving, and by picking up a hitchhiker, in size and scope these decisions were simply not comparable to those of prior *Whistler* protagonists.

RATING: 7

THE THIRTEENTH HOUR PHOTO GALLERY:

Dix portrayed a trucker falsely suspected of committing two murders in *The Thirteenth Hour* costarring Karen Morley.

left to right: John Kellogg, Bernadene Hayes, Morley, and Dix.

Poster from *The Thirteenth Hour*.

THE RETURN ON THE WHISTLER (COLUMBIA – 1948)

PRODUCTION: October 13, 1947 – October 23, 1947
RELEASE: March 18, 1948
RUNNING TIME: 63 minutes.
TAGLINES: "THE BRIDE DISAPPEARS INTO A MAZE OF MYSTERY!" "Wedding Night whispers Turn to Shrieks of Terror!"

CREDITS: Rudolph C. Flothow (Producer), D. Ross Lederman (Director), Carl Hieckel (Assistant Director), Edward Bock, Maurice Tombragel (screenplay) based on the radio series, The Whistler created by J. Donald Wilson. Cornell Woolrich (story), Philip Tannura (photography), Joe Walters (still photography), Pat Sutherland (grip), George Brooks (art direction), James Crowe (set decoration), Wilbur Hatch (music), Mischa Bakaleinikoff (musical direction), Dwight Caldwell (film editing), Jack A Goodrich (sound), Helen Hunt (hair styling), Donna M. Norridge (script supervisor).

CAST: Michael Duane (Theodore "Ted" Nichols), Lenore Aubert (Alice Dupres Barkley), Richard Lane (Gaylord Traynor), James Cardwell (Charlie a.k.a. John Barkley), Ann Shoemaker (Mrs. Barkley), Sarah Padden (Mrs. Hulskamp), Wilton Graff (Dr. Grantland), Olin Howlin (Jeff Anderson), Eddy Waller (Sam the Gardener), Trevor Bardette (Arnold), Ann Doran (Sybil), Edgar Dearing (Captain Griggs), Fred Sears (Crandall), Abigail Adams (Secretary), William Newell (Painter), Jack Rice (Sawyer), Isabel Withers (Nurse), Harry Strang (Police Sergeant), Steve Benton, Kenner G. Kemp (Male Nurses), Dolores Castle (Nurse), Robert Emmett Keane (Hart-Hotel Manager).

THE RETURN OF THE WHISTLER INTRODUCTION:

THE WHISTLER: "Standard Recitation. "And here tonight driving through this rain-swept countryside are two young people about to embark on the greatest adventure of their lives.

Whether for better or for worse, only time will tell."

PLOT SUMMARY: Serious complications arise when engineer Ted Nichols (Michael Duane) and his French fiancée Alice Dupres Barkley (Lenore Aubert) attempt to tie the knot in a small town just outside of New York City, where Ted maintains an apartment. There's a nasty rainstorm; the justice of the peace is unavailable; and a mystery man is following them and tampering with their car.

Forced by car troubles to seek lodging in the small town of Marsden, Ted is forced to bribe the local hotel clerk, Anderson (Olin Howlin), to secure a room, only to be ordered out when the hotel management discovers the couple are not married. After spending the night in his car, Ted returns to Alice's room, but she is not there. Anderson tells Ted that Alice left of her own accord the night before. Ted does not believe him; and there's a dustup in the lobby. Upon being thrown out of the establishment, Ted meets private detective Gaylord Traynor (Richard Lane) who volunteers to help him find his missing fiancée. Unbeknownst to Ted, Traynor is working for Alice's former in-laws; and is the one who tampered with his car.

Traynor's inquiries lead Ted to reveal (via flashback) that he knows little about his future wife, only she met and married a transport pilot killed in France during World War II; and her husband's family treated her cruelly when she came to America after his death. Ted tells Traynor he first met Alice when she sprained her ankle near his vacation home while fleeing her husband's abusive family. She appeared so upset he let her stay with him; and they fell in love.

After Ted surrenders Alice's photo and original marriage license to Traynor (which reveals she married into the prominent Barkley family), the private eye knocks Ted unconscious and flees with the documents. A recovered Ted then visits the Barkley estate where the elder Mrs. Barkley (Ann Shoemaker), and her son Charlie (James Cardwell), who identifies himself as "John," inform him they persuaded Alice to leave the hotel and come "home." She is with them now. According to their story, she has mental problems and sometimes forgets she is married to "John."

When Ted verbally questions their story, the Barkleys allow him to see Alice who confirms she is "John's" wife. After Ted leaves, Traynor arrives at the Barkley residence and shares all the information he obtained, including the stolen marriage license. The scheming Mrs. Barkley, whose children "Charlie," Sybil (Ann Doran), and Arnold (Trevor Bardette) are really cousins of Alice's late husband by marriage, then telephones a psychiatrist to set her master plan in motion: to declare Alice insane, send her to an institution, and claim the fortune she inherited as her husband's widow.

Disheartened, Ted returns home and finds Alice's passport, which contradicts facts given him by Charlie. Now convinced the Barkleys are lying, Ted returns to their estate, but finds them gone. The gardener Sam (Eddy Waller) informs Ted that Alice has been taken to a sanitarium; and the family is planning to leave town. After locating the Woodland Sanitarium, Ted manages to get admitted as a patient. Later that evening, he sneaks into Alice's room and finds her in a straitjacket. He frees her but before the pair can escape, Charlie bursts in and the two men tussle. Ted knocks Charlie down the stairs, alarming the sanitarium staff who have two straitjackets ready for both Alice and Ted. Just when all seems lost Traynor, who was miffed the Barkleys had deceived him, suddenly arrives with the police to take Charlie, his family, and Dr. Grantland (the physician in charge) into custody. With their multitude of problems resolved Ted and Alice return to the justice of the peace to marry.

THE RETURN OF THE WHISTLER EPILOGUE:

THE WHISTLER: "You certainly were lucky, Ted. It might have ended differently with you and Alice worlds apart. But fate this time was on your side."

REVIEWS FOR THE RETURN OF THE WHISTLER:

The Hollywood Reporter: "*The Return of the Whistler* offers a somewhat incredible mystery yarn with some elements of action, but little in the way of suspense . . . The film is only a fair entry in the 'Whistler' series, and except where it is used for the lower spot of double bills it will merely get by on the strength of the title . . . Duane and Lenore Aubert do the best possible with the rather absurd characterizations handed them. Richard Lane fares better as the private detective. James Cardwell, Ann Shoemaker, and Sarah Padden register in supporting spots. The production by Rudolph Flothow is average for the budget, and the direction of D. Ross Lederman is handicapped by the weak script . . ."

Variety: "*The Return of the Whistler* misses because of obvious padding of an insufficient amount of story material. With some judicious editing, the film could have been a superior suspense thriller. However, there's an okay substitution of chase and fisticuffs to provide the picture with the normal quota of excitement. Fair dualer . . ."

EXPERT OPINIONS FOR THE RETURN OF THE WHISTLER:

Motion Picture Guide: "Loosely based on the CBS radio program, Duane is faced with a problem when the girl he is about to marry, Aubert, is missing . . . Shoddy script has a hard time holding any level of suspense."

ARTHUR LYONS: "The last and weakest of the Whistler series, this entry is of note primarily because it was based on a story by Cornell Woolrich, and also because it was the only film in the series that did not star Richard Dix."

INTERESTING FACTS/TRIVIA—THE RETURN OF THE WHISTLER:

1. *The Return of the Whistler* was loosely based on Cornell Woolrich's gothic romance "All at Once, No Alice," first published in *Argosy*, March 2, 1940.

2. The Edward Bock/Maurice Tombragel script for *Return* was a departure from the Woolrich story in several respects. In "All at

Once, No Alice," the protagonist, Cannon (the equivalent of Ted), is a lowly clerk who marries "Alice" whom he believes to be a penniless widow. Her real name is Alma Beresford and she's a wealthy heiress who changed her name and pretended to be poor so Cannon would not feel insecure.

3. The original story also contained psychological and horror elements not found in the film. In Woolrich's tale, Cannon's sanity becomes an issue when all witnesses to his marriage to Alma (including the justice of the peace, the hotel desk clerk, and bellhop) deny she ever existed. Cannon becomes so distraught he attempts suicide. Horror enters into the story when Cannon and Detective Ainslee (corresponding to Traynor) finally locate Alma's residence. When they arrive, they find her laid out in a coffin at her funeral. She is still breathing, but before they can help her escape from her tormenters, the pair is imprisoned by her legal guardian and his accomplice. Both miraculously escape as does their captive, Alma.

4. Character actors James Cardwell (*Voice of the Whistler*), Trevor Bardette (*The Whistler*), Edgar Dearing (*The Mark of the Whistler*), Robert Emmett Keane (*The Whistler*), and Isabel Withers (*Mysterious Intruder*) all made their second *Whistler* series appearances in this feature.

5. Surviving records reveal 62-year-old veteran actor Otto Kruger was originally slated to replace Richard Dix as star of the *Whistler* series. Plans changed when Columbia purchased the film rights to Cornell Woolrich's story "All at Once, No Alice," which required a much younger man to play the would-be bridegroom, Ted Nichols. Columbia contractee Duane's well-received performance as artist Jim Calhoun in *The Secret of the Whistler* apparently helped make him the ultimate choice.

6. Coincidentally, Marsden, the fictional small town which serves as the setting of the first few scenes of *The Return of the Whistler*, was strikingly similar to the name of the small village "Marsdenberg" which was the setting of the very first *Whistler* radio episode, "Retribution."

My Take:

Unfortunately, Columbia's attempt to carry on the *Whistler* series without Richard Dix falls flat. In spite of the sincere efforts of an attractive cast, a below-average script and dispassionate direction make *The Return of the Whistler* an inferior entry in the series.

Perhaps he was getting a little long in the tooth to stay up all night hiding in the shadows, or maybe he'd gotten tired of relating strange tales and describing nameless terrors; or just maybe he preferred to act on radio; whatever the reason even the ghostly Whistler appeared bored with his eighth and last filmic excursion, *The Return of the Whistler*. An uninspiring, unscary, affair, the film noses out *The Thirteenth Hour* for the title of the weakest *Whistler* film. It's a bit of a surprise given the talent and experience of those involved.

Records reveal the Cohns (Harry and Jack) and Flothow vigorously debated whether to continue the series after Dix's departure, but once a decision was made, went all out to make the project memorable. Flothow allotted the film a bigger budget, secured the rights to a dandy Cornell Woolrich story, and brought in a group of Columbia's best and brightest to breathe cinematic life into it. Lamentably, the film did not live up to expectations. The sincere effort was ultimately undermined by a poor screenplay and uninspired direction. The Edward Bock/Maurice Tombragel script totally missed the mark both in substance and mood. It contained little discernable suspense and memorable dialogue. Absent were the rich atmospheric settings and the ironic ending moviegoers had come to expect from a *Whistler* film. For unknown reasons the scenarists also chose to extricate the psychological and horror elements of the original Woolrich story to make their screenplay a traditional crime tale. In doing so they exorcized most of the yarn's originality and much of its entertainment value. What remained was overly talky and insubstantial. Even the normally spooky Whistler epilogue was pared down to a mundane, spiritless two-sentence restatement of the obvious: Ted *was* lucky, and fate *was* on his side.

To be fair, an undernourished script was not the sole problem with *Return*. B director D. Ross Lederman's indifferent, workmanlike attitude toward the picture also diminished it. Unlike the other four *Whistler* directors, Lederman seemed uncommitted to the atmospherics and theme of the *Whistler* series. Instead of attempting to infuse scenes with chills and suspense through the skillful use of photography, lighting, sets, etc., he appeared content to rely on timeworn flashbacks and fisticuffs to tell his tale. Even the climactic sanitarium escape scene was largely a ho-hum, unoriginal, affair which had Ted knocking his nemesis Charlie down a flight of stairs. It's safe to say the imaginative Bill Castle would never have exhibited such a cavalier attitude to the material or his audience.

Even with all its weaknesses this movie is still worth a look primarily because of its cast. Michael Duane, in particular, deserves enormous credit for his impressive portrayal of the bewildered Ted who cannot quite believe his lover is insane. Although filling the shoes of Richard Dix was an impossible task, Duane delivered a topnotch effort. He was ably supported by a truly exceptional group of supporting players headed by pretty Lenore Aubert, who is affecting and credible as his soft-spoken young bride, and Richard Lane's charismatic tough private eye. James Cardwell, Ann Shoemaker, Olin Howlin, and Eddy Waller also score in small roles. Msrs. Howlin and Waller earn special plaudits for noteworthy seriocomic bits. The former played a corrupt, cantankerous hotel clerk; and the latter a snoopy gardener.

RATING: 8

THE RETURN OF THE WHISTLER PHOTO GALLERY:

A young couple's (Lenore Aubert, Michael Duane) attempt to tie the knot leads to complications in *The Return of the Whistler*. On the right is Sarah Padden.

From left: James Cardwell, Lenore Aubert, Ann Doran, Trevor Bardette, Ann Shoemaker.

Eddy Waller (left), and Richard Lane.

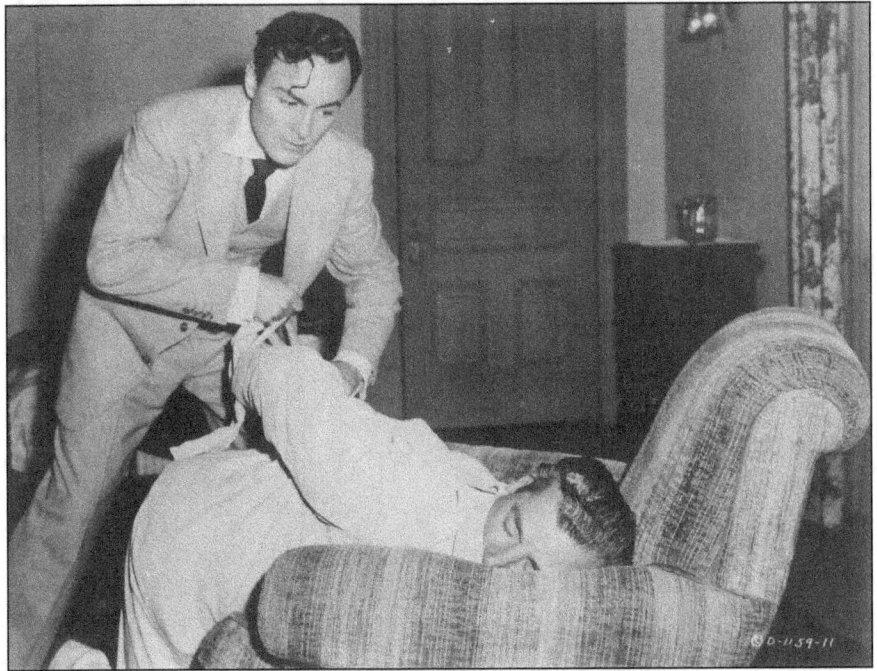

Brave Ted Nichols (Michael Duane) must perform several heroics to rescue his prospective bride in the climactic scenes of *The Return of the Whistler*.

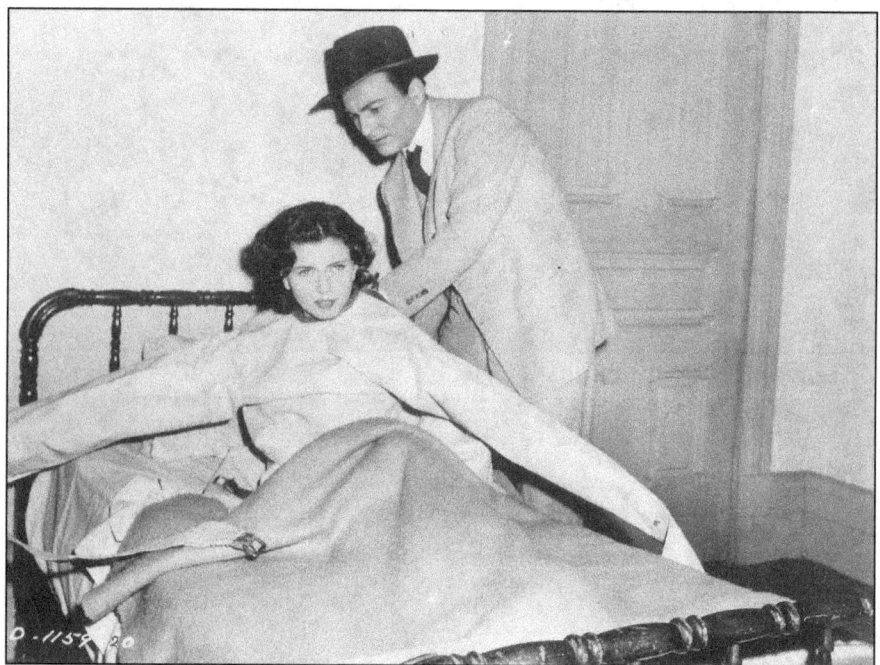
Ted (Michael Duane) releases his hospitalized fiancée Alice (Lenore Aubert) from a straitjacket.

CHAPTER FIVE
IN THE SHADOW OF THE WHISTLER
THE END OF THE SERIES AND BEYOND

By the latter 1940s a combination of events and irreversible trends spelled the end of the road for the motion picture Whistler. The cool reception (both critical and box office) which greeted the release of the seventh entry, *The Thirteenth Hour* (made in 1946, released in 1947), was the first indication the series might be running out of steam. The second blow came in the spring of 1947 when the series star Richard Dix officially retired due to ill health. Dix had always been the heart and soul of the *Whistler* films and his departure was devastating.

Cohn and Flothow seriously contemplated abandoning the series after Dix's retirement. Teletypes sent from Columbia's New York and California offices indicate the decision to continue was ultimately made because the studio owned film rights to the Whistler name. True to form the frugal Cohn brothers and company did not want to waste a penny. Once the decision was made teletypes also reveal there was a debate on the merits of replacing Dix with another actor. Otto Kruger was initially selected to star in a revamped series, but after Columbia acquired a Cornell Woolrich story which featured a young bridegroom as its main character, Kruger was cast aside for youthful Michael Duane. In the end all the difficult decisions were for naught. When *The Return of the Whistler* landed in theaters with a thud in March 1948, the film series was clearly on life support.

The fate of filmland's Whistler was officially sealed two months later in May 1948 when the U.S. Supreme Court handed down a landmark decision declaring the major studios guilty of monopolistic practices and restraint of competition. It ordered them to cease block booking, discriminatory pricing, and divest themselves of theater chains. Its impact was substantial and long lasting. While the Cohns owned no theaters, the decision initiated the demise of the double bill, dealing a body blow to B movies, Columbia's bread and butter. Harry was forced to change his entire production and distribution practices, and substantially trim his personnel and output as a result. Changing public tastes and the advent of television were also extremely important factors which helped to sound the death knell for the *Whistler* film series and other long-running fan favorites such as *Charlie Chan, The Falcon, Boston Blackie, The Lone Wolf, The Crime Doctor,* and *Blondie*. By 1951, all had disappeared.

Columbia's fate was a happier one. While other studios struggled to adapt and survive during this tumultuous period, Columbia made a remarkable, relatively seamless transition into the new era thanks to the inspired leadership of Harry Cohn and successors. Unlike many competitors Cohn was clever enough to realize change was a necessity not an option. Determined his beloved company would not be a casualty of the industry upheaval, he embraced the new medium of television, established a TV subsidiary, Screen Gems, headed by his nephew, Ralph, and began producing television programs. In response to the demands of an increasingly sophisticated film-going public, in the early 1950s Harry deemphasized his B pictures and began developing top box-office stars like Jack Lemmon and Judy Holliday, and producing more big-budget films such as *All the King's Men* (1949), *Born Yesterday* (1950), *From Here to Eternity* (1953), *The Caine Mutiny* (1954), and *The Bridge on the River Kwai* (1957). After Jack's and Harry's deaths in (1956 and 1958 respectively), their successors continued to profitably operate the company. Columbia changed hands several times in the following decades but survived. To this day it remains a vital force in the film industry under the rubric of Sony Pictures Entertainment.

Studio executives were not the only parties challenged by the changing landscape of the motion picture and radio industries. As studios restructured, costing cutting and roster trimming measures ended many creative careers and placed others in jeopardy. But as the old saying goes "when one door closes, another opens." The opening door was television. By the 1950s bringing visual entertainment into America's living rooms became *the* new and exciting challenge

Robert Hutton and Nancy Gates in "Dark Hour," an episode of TV's *The Whistler*.

Maureen O'Sullivan and Hal Gerard costar in "Trademark" from *The Whistler* TV series.

for many artists and ambitious entrepreneurs formally employed by radio and the movies.

With so many professionals migrating to TV, it was inevitable that many of film and radio's best-loved characters would find their way to the small screen. Among them was the Whistler. Although *The Whistler* radio program continued until 1955, some of the program's' movers and shakers began contemplating a *Whistler* TV series as early as 1950. Plans materialized in 1954 when *Whistler* scriptwriter Joel Malone joined forces with producer Lindsey Parsons to bring the "trench coated one" to television screens. To give their series a noteworthy sendoff, they hired an impressive list of professionals, including Whistler's "father" J. Donald Wilson to oversee, Malone's collaborator Harold Swanton to provide scripts, Will Jason, William F. Claxton, and Frank McDonald to direct, the unforgettable voices of Bill Forman and Dorothy Roberts to do the Whistler's voice and theme song, and some extraordinary film luminaries such as Miriam Hopkins, Lon Chaney Jr., Craig Stevens, Patric Knowles, Maureen O'Sullivan, and Richard Arlen to enact the tales.

Despite the talented roster and several atmospheric, well-produced episodes (many culled from old radio scripts), the series was a ratings failure and ceased production after only one year in July 1955, just two months before *The Whistler* radio program ended its 13-year run. The reasons were multiple. Certainly, the glut of new mystery/suspense TV series, such as *Lights Out* (1949–52), *Suspense* (1949–54), *The Adventures of Ellery Queen* (1950–52), *Climax!* (1954–58), *Lone Wolf* (1954), and many others made it more difficult for any new TV thriller to make an impact. The series' syndicated status also tended to limit viewership; but in the end the most crucial factor may have been the continuing evolution of public tastes. After 13 years, 692 radio episodes, eight feature films, and 40 television episodes, perhaps *The Whistler* had finally run its course.

The following is a list of all 40 episodes of *The Whistler* television series. Most include lead cast members. The first ten titles are listed in the order in which they were broadcast. The other episodes are listed randomly. Unfortunately, broadcast dates are unavailable.

1. "A Friendly Case of Scandal"— Cast Unknown.
2. "Search for the Unknown" — Barton MacLane, King Donovan.
3. "Backfire" — Lon Chaney Jr., Dorothy Green.
4. "Cup of Gold" — Tom Brown, Barbara Woodell.

5. "Stolen Chance" — Cast Unknown.
6. "Letter from Aaron Burr" — Howard Duff, Martha Vickers.
7. "Incident at Scully's Key" — Cast Unknown.
8. "A Trip to Aunt Sarah's" — Arthur Franz, Margaret Field.
9. "The Return" — Miriam Hopkins, Chick Chandler.
10. "Fatal Fraud" — Marie Windsor, Patric Knowles.

Other episodes include:

11. "Sleep My Pretty One" — Martha Vickers, Paul Langton.
12. "Kind Thought" — John Howard, Toni Gerry.
13. "The Big Jump" — John Ireland, Tina Carver, Robert Oesterloh.
14. "Lucky Night" — Irene Ryan, Byron Foulger.
15. "Cancelled Flight" — Richard Arlen, Walter Sande.
16. "Trademark — Maureen O'Sullivan, Fiona Hale.
17. "The Blank Wall" — Wallace Ford, Philip Van Zandt.
18. "Windfall" — Charles McGraw, Dorothy Green, Percy Helton.
19. "Lady in Waiting" — Craig Stevens, Nancy Gates, Taylor Holmes.
20. "Death Sentence" — Marshall Thompson, John Doucette.
21. "Grave Secret" — Miriam Hopkins, Pamela Duncan, Mervyn Vye.
22. "Marriage Contract" — Charles Winninger, Tom Brown.
23. "Borrowed Byline" — Arthur Franz, Philip Van Zandt.
24. "Other Hand" — John Howard, Angela Green, Dorothy Green.
25. "Favor for a Friend" — Robert Strauss, Hillary Brooke.
26. "First Years" — Craig Stevens, Virginia Field, Jonathan Hale.
27. "Friendly Case of Blackmail" — Paul Kelly, Ann Doran.
28. "A Case for Mr. Carrington" — Patric Knowles, Paul Dubov.
29. "Glass Dime" — Robert Hutton, Eve Miller.
30. "Pattern" — Robert Ellenstein, Ellen Corby, Milton Frome.
31. "Roark Island" — Tom Brown, Cathy Downs.
32. "Dark Hour" — Robert Hutton, Nancy Gates.
33. "Stranger in the House" — Virginia Field, Hugh Sanders.
34. "Lovely Look" — Mervyn Vye, Sheila Bromley, Pamela Duncan.

35. "Silent Partner" — Charles McGraw, Hugh Sanders.
36. "An Actor's Life" — Arthur Franz, Margaret Field, John Hubbard.
37. "Jubilee Earring" — Marguerite Chapman, Douglas Kennedy.
38. "Trigger Man" — Marshall Thompson, Hayden Rorke.
39. "Man Who Ran" — Cast Unknown.
40. "Meeting on Tenth Street" — Cast Unknown.

Even though the television series bearing his name was ultimately short lived, the influence of radio and filmland's *Whistler* was and remains considerable. On radio, his impact was felt in a whole host of new suspense anthologies, many featuring sinister hosts, which sprang up in the years immediately following *The Whistler's* successful debut. Among them were the great classic *Suspense* (1942–62), *The Mysterious Traveler* (1943–52), and *Quiet Please* (1947–49). During the mid-to-later 1940s, *The Whistler* was such a radio and film favorite its popularity transcended the suspense genre. In 1946, the program was parodied by both Jack Benny and Fred Allen. The former's send-up to the famous radio and film character was particularly memorable. Costarred with Mary Livingstone, Phil Harris, and Dennis Day, the incomparable Mr. Benny portrayed "The Fiddler" complete with a humorous recitation and the Whistler theme song hilariously scraped on his violin.

During the many years since he hung up his fedora countless important television and movie mystery suspense anthologies have been produced which trace their roots back to the Whistler's eerie tales of terror and spooky narration. The list is much too long for a complete rendering, but among the most prominent TV series examples were *Alfred Hitchcock Presents* (1955–1962), *The Alfred Hitchcock Hour* (1962–65), *The Twilight Zone* (1959–64), *Twilight Zone Revival* (1985–89), *Thriller* (1960–62), *The Outer Limits* (1963–65), *Night Gallery* (1970–73), *Tales from the Dark Side* (1983–88), *The Hitchhiker* (1983–91), *Are You Afraid of the Dark?* (Canadian, 1990–96), *Tales from the Crypt* (1989–96), *Goosebumps* (Canadian, 1995–98), and *Strange Frequency* (2001).

Notable film anthologies of the crime, mystery, horror genre include *Dead of Night* (British, Rank, 1945), *Tales of Terror* (Alta Vista, 1962), *Black Sabbath* (Italian, A.I., 1963), *Twice Told Tales*

(Admiral/United Artists, 1963), *Dr. Terror's House of Horrors* (Brit., Amicus, 1965), *Torture Garden* (British, Amicus, 1967), *Night Gallery* (TV, 1969), *Asylum* (British, Amicus, 1972), *Tales from the Crypt* (British, Amicus, 1972), *Tales That Witness Madness* (British, Amicus, 1973), *Trilogy of Terror* (TV, 1975), *The Uncanny* (British, Rank, 1977), *Creepshow* (Warner Brothers, 1982), *Twilight Zone, the Movie* (Warner Brothers, 1983), *Creepshow 2* (Laurel/New World, 1987), *Tales from the Darkside, the Movie* (Paramount, 1990), and many, many others.

Another potential legacy of the *Whistler* series is still being debated. The increasing popularity of *film noir* in recent decades has inspired innumerable discussions. Many center on a definition of *noir* and the classification of certain films. While there is no precise, agreed-upon definition of the term (which literally means dark or black film in French), most movie historians and experts agree it refers to a large group of postwar Hollywood crime films (mid-to-late 1940s to mid-1950s) which portray, according to Ephraim Katz's essential *Film Encyclopedia*, "a gloomy underworld of crime and corruption, films whose heroes as well as villains are cynical, disillusioned, and often insecure loners, inextricably bound to the past and unsure or apathetic about the future. In terms of style and technique, the film noir characteristically abounds with night scenes, both interior and exterior, with sets that suggest dingy realism, and with lighting that emphasizes deep shadows and accents the mood of fatalism. The dark tones and tense nervousness are further enhanced by the oblique choreography of the action and the doom-laden compositions and camera angles."

Many of the atmospheric, crime-themed *Whistlers* featured the aforementioned characteristics, yet are rarely cited in verbal and literary debates on *film noir*. Perhaps it is because experts do not feel they are noir. More likely it is professional snobbery. The *Whistlers* were low-budget series films; and for that reason are often dismissed or overlooked. This is beginning to change, however. In the last decade the *Whistlers* have been cited as early examples of *noir* in such well-respected volumes as Arthur Lyons' *Death on the Cheap* and Michael Keaney's *Film Noir Guide, 745 Films of the Classic Era* 1940–59.

In order to clear up this mini-controversy, expert opinions were sought. One distinguished authority is author Karen Burroughs

Hannsberry, whose critically acclaimed volumes, *Femme Noir* (1998) and *Bad Boys of Film Noir* (2003), and her monthly newsletter, *The Dark Pages*, are considered essential reading by *noir* scholars and enthusiasts. Recently, she took time to share her expertise and opinions on the *Whistlers* as *noir*, discussing the series in its entirety and each *Whistler* film in particular. Unsurprisingly, her conclusions are mixed.

Overview by Karen Burroughs Hannsberry:

Overall, I found the *Whistler* series contained a number of *noirish* elements: the films were always dark in tone, featured numerous shadowy scenes, and frequently had an underlying core of desperation, dread, and hopelessness. I would not categorize them as *film noir*, primarily because of the gimmicky nature of the Whistler character.

Although the character of the Whistler frequently serves the purpose of a voiceover, which is another characteristic in many *films noirs*, it is the Whistler's penchant for speaking directly to characters—sometimes serving as their conscience, in other cases acting as an all-seeing, all-knowing presence—that removes the films from the category of *noir* for me. Nonetheless, I think that the *Whistler* films were either strongly influenced by *film noir*, or clearly impacted by the circumstances that led to the rise of *film noir*. The following contains my thoughts on each film, along with highlights regarding *noir* features.

The Whistler

The opening scene of this film, in the waterfront bar, is very *nourish*—from the seedy setting to the shady character Earl Conrad pays to commit a murder. And the plot becomes even more *noirish* when we learn that Conrad has paid money to have himself killed.

This film offers up several offbeat, unusual, memorable characters—there's the deaf-mute who is obsessed with reading Superman comics, the hired killer who is obsessed with reading about necrophilia and has two pet mice, and the *femme fatale*-type character (Tony Vigran) who is cool and unflappable, even as she reveals her plan to kill herself and Earl Conrad because she believes he set up her husband for murder.

This feature also contains several visual *noir* elements, like the close-up on the shoes of Earl Conrad and his would-be killer as he "rough shadows" him.

The Mark of the Whistler

Lee Selfridge Nugent is a typical *noir* character—arrogant, cool, nerves of steel, yet capable of paranoia. Another is the owner of the men's clothing store (Joe Sorsby), who is avaricious, boorish, and dismissive. He isn't willing to give Nugent the time of day until he mentions the possibility of gaining a profit. He's also skeptical and mistrustful, insisting on accompanying Nugent to mail a letter and even taking a gun.

The story itself is *noirish*—full of fate and coincidences and cases of mistaken identity. There is a feeling of dread underlying almost every scene. Although Nugent manages to get the money, the viewer knows that no good will come of it.

The Power of the Whistler

The amnesia theme of this film is pure noir. Not much else is, though.

Voice of the Whistler

The beginning of the film describes the main character thusly: "Suspicion and distrust in his fellow man have driven John Sinclair to solitude." Suspicion and distrust are two typical *noir* characteristics. The description further notes the man's "ruthless drive for power and riches"—which is also a prime *noir* feature.

When Sinclair falls ill outside Union Station and the taxi driver takes him to his place, the flashing neon light outside of the window is strongly reminiscent of the opening scene in *Murder, My Sweet*, where Dick Powell sits in his darkened office.

Some of the dialogue in this feature is very *noirish*—for example, when Joan's fiancé Fred berates her for her plans to marry Sinclair: "You're doing it because you're selfish. Because you're not satisfied to wait and work hard like any normal, decent woman would do. I don't think you're being dishonest. I think you're rotten." Joan's rejoinder is equally dark: "Why shouldn't I have my chance . . . I've given you the chance to get ahead and you've failed. Now I'm going to do it my way."

This film also contains one of those juicy *noir*-like plot twists: Sinclair tells Fred his idea for getting away with murder, then Fred decides to put the plan into effect to kill Sinclair; and Sinclair winds up offing Fred. The final twist with Joan getting the Sinclair millions but winding up lonely and alone has a *noir* feel as well.

Mysterious Intruder

Mysterious Intruder, interestingly, featured several *noir* regulars—Barton MacLane, Regis Toomey, and Mike Mazurki. As in *Voice of the Whistler*, this film included a scene that reminded me of *Murder, My Sweet* (even more so here, in fact)—a guy goes into a PI's office looking for a woman, the room is dark, and the neon light is flashing outside the window.

Mysterious Intruder included a number of visual *noir* elements. In one scene, Pontos (Mike Mazurki) is lurking in the shadows, his face briefly illuminated by a lit match. In another, even more *noir*-like moment, Dix's character, Don Gale, goes to see a woman—when he opens the chain-locked door we see her in a mirror's reflection as she speaks to him through a cloud of cigarette smoke. Like no other scene in the series this was *film noir*.

Gale is a typical *noir* anti-hero—greedy, rude, cold, a user—a bit reminiscent of Mike Hammer. His hard-core secretary is also typical *noir*, as is the sweet-looking but tough-as-nails older woman (Mrs. Denning) who Gale asks to look after Elora. When Gale tries to pay her with a bill, she matter-of-factly takes the entire wad. She also has a bottle of booze hidden in her knitting basket.

The film's finale was *tres noir*, filled with irony and dumb luck, as Gale, for once trying to do something honorable, gets shot and killed, and the treasure that everyone wanted so desperately is destroyed. Of all the *Whistler* films this one was the most *noirish* and, interestingly, contained the least voiceovers from the Whistler. It is no surprise, as a result, that it is my favorite of all eight features.

The Secret of the Whistler

The opening of the film, with the woman purchasing a headstone for herself has a *noirish* feel as does the ironic twist at the end. In addition, the character of the second wife, Kay, is a *femme fatale* type—stealthy, calculating, and ruthless, willing to use every feminine wile at her disposal in order to snag the best catch. There aren't many other *noir* elements, though—no anti-heroes or shadowy rooms.

The Thirteenth Hour

This film also featured a couple of *noir* staples—Regis Toomey and the great John Kellogg.

One scene early in the film is pure *noir*, filled with one bad move after another. Dix's character, Steve, decides to deliver a load in his truck, even though his license has been suspended. During a stop to check the truck, Steve gets hijacked by a mysterious stranger who takes off in the vehicle. After being pulled over by Don Parker (Regis Toomey), the stranger runs him over with Steve's truck and escapes. When Steve sees a car coming, he drives off in the truck, winding up on the run for the remainder of the film. This coupling of fateful occurrences and bad decisions is classic *noir*.

The double-cross by Charlie Cook (John Kellogg) offers a nice twist, but the film's happy ending works against the *noir* feeling that was present for much of the feature.

The Return of the Whistler

This film, the only one without Richard Dix, is also the only one where the Whistler is walking in the rain. It contains flashback scenes, but there is little else that has a *noir* feeling.

* * *

The debate continues!

CHAPTER SIX
THE WHISTLER FAMILY ALBUM

THE STARS

RICHARD DIX (1893–1949)

Richard Dix

Earl Conrad in *The Whistler*
Lee Selfredge Nugent in *The Mark of the Whistler*
William Everest in *The Power of the Whistler*
John Sinclair in *Voice of the Whistler*
Don Gale in *Mysterious Intruder*
Ralph Harrison in *The Secret of the Whistler*
Steve Reynolds in *The Thirteenth Hour*

If one were given the task of constructing a prototype for a movie star, an ideal of what a movie star ought to be, the person would undoubtedly possess attributes such as talent, looks, charisma, humility, generosity, strength, and industry. They would be devoted to their craft and family, and wise enough to realize the importance of keeping both their bosses and their fans content. Actor Richard Dix possessed all the aforementioned characteristics in varying degrees. He was not a perfect person, but he was as close to a role model as any successful Hollywood star; the kind fans could look up to; someone people wanted to emulate. He was also adaptable, which explains the longevity of an acting career which spanned three decades and roughly 100 feature films. His relatively smooth transition from stage to screen, from matinee idol of silents, to sturdy hero of the 1930s, to character roles during the 1940s, demonstrated a versatility and a refreshingly realistic view of himself and his profession which were exceedingly rare.

Although he played many reckless, aimless young men in silent comedies and dramas, today Dix is best remembered for his heroic portrayals as pioneers and western heroes in 1930s adventure films. A stocky, well-built, square-jawed man with rugged features, he not only looked the part, but convincingly projected the necessary qualities. Bold, courageous, resourceful, two-fisted Dix's film hero was a man's man without excessive machismo, a tough guy who tempered his toughness with decency and gentility. On the rare occasions when a 1930s Hollywood script called on him to shed his veneer of tough nobility Dix could also persuasively play charming screen rogues or fallen heroes, displaying a vulnerability perfectly projected by his heavy-lidded sad eyes and gentle voice. His 1940s evolution into a character actor (often in overtly villainous roles) demonstrated yet another facet of his acting range. Off-screen, Richard Dix resembled his heroic impersonations. Although he displayed a fondness for drink, he was always a gentleman in every sense. A devoted husband, father, son, and friend, who treated his fans, coworkers, and employers with equal respect, he was extraordinarily popular both inside and outside Hollywood.

The actor affectionately known as "The Jaw" was born Ernest Carleton Brimmer, on July 18, 1893, in St. Paul, Minnesota, the second of three children born to Eli C. Brimmer (1858–193?) and his wife the former Josephine McKowan (1861–1932). The elder Brimmer's ancestors, John and Elizabeth Manchester Brimmer, were said to have come to America on the *Mayflower*, marrying two years after they landed on Plymouth Rock. Settling near Troy, New York, the Brimmer family became distinguished citizens.

Census records reveal Eli and Josephine Brimmer were married in Iowa in 1882, had a son, Archie, in 1883, and moved to the St. Paul, Minnesota, area sometime in the late 1880s. After renting various houses and farms, Eli, a soap salesman, purchased a home at 1208 Raymond Drive in St. Paul sometime in the early 1900s after the birth of Ernest and his younger sister, Josephine.

Little has been written on Ernest's childhood, but apparently it was a happy one. His parents were poor and times were hard but the family made do. Following his parents' wishes, older brother Archie enrolled in medical school and became a successful medical doctor and surgeon. Young Ernest was expected to follow his brother's lead but had interests which did not involve the medical profession or a higher education. A sturdy, muscular youth, Ernest loved hunting, fishing, woodcraft, baseball and football. In a 1932 interview he recalled working on railroad construction gangs and carrying cross ties, "just to toughen up so I'd play better football."

Ernest's other main interest was also non-academic, at least in the traditional sense. Unbeknownst to his parents, while in public school he attended drama classes two nights a week at the University of Minnesota. The robust Ernest literally kicked his way into amateur theatrics, winning a role as a football player in St. Paul's production of *The College Widow*. Buoyed by cheers from his high-school chums, and later by an $18-a-week offer from noted Shakespearean actor E. H. Sothern to join his touring company, the teenager made a life-altering decision to quit school and pursue a career in acting.

His parents would have none of it. His father, a religious man who considered the profession akin to "prostitution," insisted Ernest return to legitimate studies, and utilize his free time doing "respectable work" in a bank, or in an architect's office. Although the youngster temporarily obeyed his father it wasn't long before young Ernest quit school for good and joined a local St. Paul stock company.

Many reference books and short bios of Dix state he graduated from St. Paul Central High, and attended University of Minnesota Medical School. According to Richard's son, actor Robert Dix, this is untrue. "They [the biographers] get that mixed up. That was his brother, Archie. My father didn't have much of a formal education. He graduated, I think, from the eighth grade or something . . . He was self-educated."

With renewed confidence from his stock performances, financial assistance from brother Archie, and a new name, Richard Dix (which he took from a heroic buddy Ed Dix, a lifeguard who drowned trying to save a woman's life), in 1912 the dark brown haired, 6 ft., 180-pound budding actor headed to New York where he hoped to land a part on the "Great White Way." He was initially unsuccessful, but secured employment and valuable experience with a Pittsburgh stock company followed by work in Dallas and Montreal. In 1914 Dix returned to New York at the behest of impresario Arthur Hopkins to make his Broadway debut in *The Hawk* (1914), followed by an appearance in the dramatic *Song of Songs*, both starring William Faversham. While playing in the latter, flamboyant producer Oliver Morosco selected Dix over 40 other leading men to star in his production of *The Cinderella Man* staged at the Morosco Theatre in Los Angeles.

Dix became a West Coast resident after signing a contract with Morosco in the fall of 1916. For the next two years (1916–18), as part of the famed Morosco stock company, Dix developed and sharpened his acting skills essaying a broad spectrum of roles in a wide variety of plays. Supported by a loyal, primarily feminine coterie of fans, including influential *Los Angeles Times* columnist Grace Kingsley, Dix quickly rose in the ranks of the Morosco players, attracting the attention of the burgeoning film industry which desired stage-trained actors to work in motion pictures. According to son Robert, one of his father's admirers was film producer Jessie Lasky.

"My dad and Preston Foster were matinee idols at the Morosco Theater in L. A. Jessie Lasky saw one of his performances and came backstage and asked him if he ever thought of being in the movies. My dad said, 'What does it pay?' After he learned how much it paid, he told Lasky, 'I'm now in the movies.'"

Inspired by potential monetary rewards, in 1917 Dix made his feature film debut as a butler in the 50-minute dramatic non-entity *One of Many* (1917), and then made a screen test for noted DeMille scriptwriter Jeanie Macpherson. When Dix saw both the film and the test, he reportedly hated them so much he temporarily abandoned the notion of making motion pictures and headed back to New York where he was seen in producer Walter Hast's drama, *The Little Brother*, and three other Broadway plays: William LeBaron's farce *I Love You* (1919), the comic *First is Last*, and the Hopkins-produced drama *A Night's Lodging*.

Reinvigorated, in 1920 Dix returned to Los Angeles in hopes of breaking into the movies. While visiting old Morosco Theatre chums David Butler and Douglas MacLean on an Inceville film set, Butler made a suggestion which would change Dix's life. In a 1922 interview Dix recalled the incident. "The first thing he asked me when the hubbub of back slapping was over was what I was doing, and if I wasn't why hadn't I gone into pictures . . . And then he and his father Frederick Butler who was directing Dave for the screen, put me thru a camera test. Dave made me up. His father put me thru a few scenes. Of course it was comparatively easy going. With two old friends helping there was no danger of nervousness. But there were still a lot of ragged spots . . . Dave systematically cut them out until all we had left were the good parts . . . It was that test that convinced Sidney Franklin he wanted me for *Not Guilty*."

A routine film melodrama about mistaken identities, guilt, and sibling rivalry, *Not Guilty* (First National, 1921) was largely an unsuccessful venture save the two performances of its leading man. Dix's showy dual roles as identical twins (one good, one bad) won high praise and new film offers. One from producer Samuel Goldwyn proved too tempting for the 28-year-old to refuse.

Dix would work for Goldwyn for the next two years (1921–23) making nine films and establishing himself as a top film up-and-comer. In many of his early pictures (for Goldwyn and later Paramount),

The three phases of Rich. The carefree errant young man of the silent era, the stalwart hero of 1930s cinema, the character actor of the 1940s.

the dashing Dix portrayed reckless, errant young men saved from self-destruction by hard knocks and the redeeming love of a good woman. Although he appeared in comedies, *Dangerous Curves Ahead* (1921), *All's Fair in Love* (1921), *The Glorious Fool* (1922); dramadies, *Souls For Sale* (1923); and adventures, *Yellow Men and Gold* (1922); Dix's best films of the Goldwyn period were heavy dramas in which he played opposite some of Hollywood's most attractive young actresses. He was a selfish newlywed who sacrifices his wife's happiness in *The Poverty of Riches* (1921) with Leatrice Joy, a wayward young man who undergoes a life-altering transformation when he's trapped in a small-town saloon during a Mississippi River flood in director Frank Lloyd's *The Sin Flood* (1921) with Helene Chadwick, and a man of the cloth who falls in love with an actress (Mae Busch) in Maurice Tourneur's *The Christian* (1923).

The latter, partially filmed on location in England, was the second filmization of Sir Hall Caine's acclaimed novel and is notable as the motion picture which made Dix a top-ranked star. Much publicity surrounded its production and his selection for the coveted title role. His excellent reviews were the primary reasons Paramount chose to sign him to a term contract in January 1923 as an erstwhile replacement for Wallace Reid whose death from drug-related issues struck Hollywood like a lightning bolt. As writer Dewitt Bodeen stated in his insightful tribute to Dix published in *Films in Review* (October 1966), Paramount's selection of the young actor to replace Reid was odd. "What he [Dix] projected was not at all similar to the handsome, insouciant, daredevil image Reid had created. Dix was light-hearted, wholesome, completely masculine, and very American."

Dix's onscreen image was a natural reflection of his personal character. A sincere, self-effacing man who never forgot his family or his humble roots, who treated his bosses, coworkers, fans, and the press with respect, he quickly became a favorite of filmgoers and Hollywood insiders alike. A loyal friend and ardent admirer of genuine talent, Dix made a practice of assisting budding actors and craftsman he deemed worthy. Among those he helped during the 1920s and 1930s were such diverse talents as actors Ramon Novarro, Norma Shearer, Dolores Costello, and George O'Brien; character actors Edna May Oliver, Noah Beery; directors

Gregory La Cava, Frank Tuttle; scriptwriter J. Walter Ruben; and cinematographer Eddie Cronjager. Sometimes the assistance came in the form of a request for their appearance in his projects; other times it was more substantive. For instance, in 1928, the generous star gifted Mr. Cronjager, who lensed many of his silent films, including *Womanhandled* and *Warming Up*, with a beach lot property near Los Angeles. According to Robert Dix, the famed cameraman never forgot the kindness. "I met Mr. Cronjager when I was doing an episode of *Mike Hammer, Private Detective*. He was the director of photography on it. He came over and introduced himself after we'd worked on it. He said, 'I just want to tell you your dad was one of the greatest guys I ever met. He gave me my first break. I was a third cameraman and he made me a first. Then he'd ask for me on all his movies.'"

Also counted among Dix's admirers were members of the influential Hollywood press corps who were delighted by his humility and refreshing candor, and ceaselessly promoted him as one of the film capital's most talented performers, and "eligible bachelors." Breathless tales of chivalry and romance accompanied the release of each of his films which regularly cast him opposite beautiful bachelorettes like May Collins, Jacqueline Logan, Lois Wilson, and Bebe Daniels. There was some truth to the gossip regarding his popularity with his feminine costars, his fondness for drink and nights on the town, but many of the more colorful tales were born in the imaginative minds of studio publicity men. In typical Dix fashion, he bluntly dismissed them. "Do I look like a sheik, I ask you? Look at this funny nose of mine. Look at this mug! Could I be a lady-killer with this? All sorts of lies have been printed about me under the excuse of publicity. They weren't harmful, but I want people to get me straight . . ."

Dix made 33 pictures for Paramount in the period (1923–29), most made on location, or at the company's Astoria Studio in Long Island. Assisted by some of filmdom's best and brightest artists and craftsmen, he continued to develop his ability as a movie actor. His silent vehicles were varied and distinguished. Although, by the mid-1920s, he'd become renown as an action adventure star, it is important to note that Dix played notable leading roles in all genres during the silent era.

His memorable comedic parts included a bored millionaire who becomes a safecracker in "Hell's Kitchen" in *Manhattan* (1924), an effete, polo-playing easterner who attempts to impress his sweetheart by working on a southwestern ranch, in Gregory LaCava's scintillating *Womanhandled* (1926), a talented college footballer who moonlights as a milkman in *The Quarterback* (1926), a salesman mistaken for a millionaire in *Sporting Goods* (1928), and a rube baseball pitcher in love with the team owner's daughter in *Warming Up* (1928).

Dix also appeared in several significant Paramount dramas and melodramas. He was a ne'er-do-well who accidentally kills a man and allows another to take the rap in the John Galsworthy-penned *The Stranger* (1924), an offender who loves a New England spinster in *Icebound* (1924), a cashier who embezzles money to impress his best girl in *Men and Women* (1925). Dix's most famous 1920s drama was undoubtedly Cecil B. DeMille's 1.2 million-dollar spectacle *The Ten Commandments* (1923), an extravagant, all-star two-part epic which commenced with a recreation of the Jewish exodus, followed by a contemporary parable involving a Bible-toting woman (Edythe Chapman) and her two sons: one who follows the commandments (Dix) and the other who repudiates them (Rod LaRoque). Dix's portrayal of John McTavish, the sympathetic hardworking "good son" who rejects both his brother's hedonism and his mother's unbending fundamentalism, was widely praised.

Dix's other notable silents were adventures, three adapted from popular Zane Grey novels. Beautifully photographed on location in the American southwest, Victor Fleming's *Call of the Canyon* (1923) and *To the Last Man* (1923) costarred Dix with Lois Wilson. The latter had him as a half-Indian caught up in a destructive feud between two frontier families. Dix also played a Native American opposite Miss Wilson two years later in another Grey adaptation, the thought-provoking, heart-rending *The Vanishing American* (1925), a clash-of-cultures action drama about the inhumane treatment of the Indians by white invaders. Sumptuously filmed on location in the exquisite Monument Valley of Utah and Arizona's Grand Canyon National Park, the film is considered one of Dix's best. As the brave, ultimately tragic, Native American World War I hero Nophaie he was sensational. His restrained, affecting performance won deserved

Dix (center) contributed one of his finest film portrayals as Nophaie, the Native American World War I hero who returns to the poverty and degradation of the reservation in *The Vanishing American* (Paramount, 1925).

praise and a legion of new fans.

Paramount's 1927 decision to close its New York studios and move its film production to the West Coast initiated a tumultuous five-year period (1927–32) in the life and career of Richard Dix. Unhappy with the decision, the star made his opinions known to the studio brass and to the press. More disagreements followed when Paramount appeared reluctant to cast Dix in sound films; instead opting to cash in on his stardom by re-releasing *Quicksands*, a substandard actioner he had made in 1923. The growing enmity reached a fever pitch when the normally laid back star walked off the set of *The Gay Defender* in protest over the film's "inferior" script and his "miscasting" as Latin bandit Joaquin Murietta.

Dix eventually returned to work in 1928 with a salary increase ($4,500 a week—Paramount's highest paid star) and a promise of better vehicles, but things were never the same between star and studio. Paramount basically reneged on its promise of better material. Dix had a decent role as an Indian in the entertaining silent adventure drama *Redskin* (1928), but his other films of the period (1928–29)

One of Dix's last silent features was the comedy *Easy Come, Easy Go* (Paramount, 1928), which paired him with sparkling Nancy Carroll.

were routine or worse. Particularly disappointing were Dix's first two sound films: the stagy comedy *Nothing But the Truth* (1929) and the ludicrous romantic adventure *The Wheel of Life* (1929).

Dix's professional woes were compounded by personal and health issues. In April 1928 he was rushed to the hospital with an attack of appendicitis, and then stricken with lung complications and cystitis after an appendectomy. He hovered between life and death for a couple of days before rallying. One year later he underwent more surgery, for a hernia, and had another headline-making brush with death when he was forced to jump on the bumper of a speeding New York taxicab to avoid being hit by a car. In between illnesses and mishaps, Dix also made news when he lost most of his savings in the 1929 stock market crash; and in 1931 when he was charged by the U. S. government with two counts of tax evasion for the years 1927 and 1928. Although he was not at fault (his accountant was responsible), the actor was forced to pay back taxes, penalties, and fines amounting to almost $100,000, a huge sum at the time.

More challenges followed. After shooting wrapped on the silly comedy *The Love Doctor* (1929), Dix was summarily dropped from the Paramount roster, citing his lack of suitability for sound. The studio's abandonment was a severe blow to the intensely loyal Dix, fueling rumors his career might be over. In May 1929, Dix attempted to quell the gossip by signing a short-term pact with his old friend Bill LeBaron, the new head of production at the recently formed RKO studios (formally FBO). Since taking the helm, LeBaron had resurrected the career of another Paramount castoff, Bebe Daniels (who scored a triumph in the lavish 1929 musical *Rio Rita*), and was determined to work the same miracle for his chum and mentor.

Thirty-seven-year-old Richard Dix began the second phase of his acting career with a modestly successful remake of the George M. Cohan mystery comedy warhorse *Seven Keys to Baldpate* (1930), the first of 26 RKO films he would make in the next 11 years. Based on Earl Derr Biggers' novel, it chronicled the travails of an ace writer who must turn out a thriller novel in 24 hours while staying at a remote mountain inn full of kooky characters. Dix followed with two J. Walter Ruben-penned vehicles. In the comic *Lovin' the Ladies* (1930), based on Bill LeBaron's play *I Love You*, he reprised his Broadway role as a lowly electrician passed off as a gentleman as part of a wager, then played a crooked gambler who reforms in the melodramatic *Shooting Straight* (1930). *Lovin' the Ladies* was notable as the sixth and final pairing of Dix with pretty Lois Wilson with whom he had been romantically linked for years. According to Robert Dix, there *was* respect and affection between the two, but the rumored romantic love was strictly one-sided. "She was in love with Dad and never married. She was brokenhearted for the balance of her life because he wouldn't marry her. He married my mom instead. But Lois and Dad, needless to say, were very close. They worked together several times."

In the spring of 1930, LeBaron seized an opportunity to reenergize the Dix career, spending the princely sum of $125,000 to purchase the screen rights to Edna Ferber's sweeping historical novel *Cimarron*, which had as its main character the flamboyant Yancy Cravat, a former gunslinger-turned-renaissance man, who, with his loyal wife Sabra, helps settle Oklahoma. Cravat assists in founding and developing the city of Osage as a newspaperman, lawyer, and preacher, before abandoning his family for adventure in the Cherokee Strip. Determined to make an epic western on the grandest of scales, LeBaron engaged the services of an impressive group of professionals headed by scriptwriter Howard Estabrook, director Wesley Ruggles, cinematographer Eddie Cronjager, composer Max Steiner, and a superb cast of thousands headed by his old pal Rich as Yancy, Broadway musical star Irene Dunne (recommended by Dix) as Sabra, and stage veterans Nance O'Neil, Estelle Taylor, and Edna May Oliver. At a professional low point Dix was ecstatic when he received the news he would play Cravat. "I'm in love with this part, and I'll give it everything in me that I've got to give . . . I want to get into the spirit of this man. I want to BE Yancy Cravat in spirit as well as in appearance. This is the picture which is going to make or break me. I want to put my heart and soul into this interpretation."

In order to capture the "essence" of his character Dix ordered his costume two months before shooting began, let his hair grow, special ordered two pearl-handled pistols, practiced walking in long, swift strides to mimic Yancy, and even had drops put in his eyes so the whites would be whiter to resemble "Indian's eyes."

Filming on *Cimarron* (which covered a span of forty years in the Oklahoma Territory from 1889 to 1929) began in August 1930 and lasted through the remainder of the year. No expense was spared. The film's most spectacular scene, a recreation of the famous

Oklahoma Land Rush, was shot at the Jasmin Quinn Ranch near Bakersfield in seven days, employing one of the largest camera crews in film history, and approximately 5,000 extras, including Nino Cochise the grandson of the famed Chiricahua chief. In addition, three separate replicas of the town of Osage were constructed with interiors to represent the three distinct eras depicted: 1889, 1895, and 1907. Employing over 50 actors in speaking roles the total cost was a staggering 1.4 million.

Although it garnered mainly superlative reviews, seven Academy Award nominations, and three wins, including Best Picture, *Cimarron* was controversial. Depression-era filmgoers were mesmerized by it, but not enough to compensate for the film's humungous price tag. Netting red ink to the tune of $565,000, the epic rocked the newly-minted RKO back on its heels and sent its boss into the doghouse (LeBaron would be forced from his position in 1932). There was also some grumbling from reviewers regarding the film's 126-minute length, its "tacked on ending," and "overripe" performances. Today, the movie is still being critiqued for its sentimentality, and its stereotypical depiction of minorities; yet it remains a timeless classic, one of the first great early sound epics. Containing spectacular scenes, superlative period detail, vigorous action, memorable characters and performances, it captures the American pioneer spirit.

Dix was unforgettable as Cravat. It *is* true he played the part in a grand manner, but the grandiosity was perfectly in keeping with the larger-than-life character of Yancy. Utilizing a booming voice, and extravagant gestures, Dix captured the essence of a true American original: a dynamic frontiersman and champion of the downtrodden; a renaissance man as handy with a gun and his fists, as a Bible or a printing press. His best scenes: conducting Osage's first church service in a saloon aided by a ready pistol, defending the devious harlot Dixie Lee accused of "public nuisance," and expressing sympathy for racial and social minorities, reflected the duality of Cravat whose egocentricities, violent tendencies, and wanderlust are mitigated by courage and compassion.

The role not only brought Dix his first and only Oscar nomination (he would lose to two actors: Wallace Beery in *The Champ* and Fredric March in *Dr. Jekyll and Mr. Hyde*), but reinvigorated his career at a critical juncture. He would eventually grow tired of playing adventure

Richard won a well-deserved Oscar nomination for his bigger-than-life portrait of adventurer Yancy Cravat in *Cimarron* (RKO, 1931), costarring Irene Dunne.

From left: Dix, Dunne, and Stanley Fields in *Cimarron*.

heroes, but Richard Dix would always be grateful to have had the opportunity to play Yancy. Robert Dix put it this way: "Dad was thrilled with *Cimarron*. He made no bones about it. He knew if he would get that part it would put him up in the super-star category. I would say the role of Yancy in *Cimarron* affected his life for at least 15 years afterward. It kept him in star status."

In June 1931, a reenergized Richard had every right to be optimistic as he affixed his name to a long-term RKO pact which paid him $50,000 per picture, five pictures per year, with 12 1/2% of the net proceeds. His name topped several movie popularity polls; and his employer was promising grade A-level vehicles. But things did not go as planned. With the exception of 1932's *The Conquerors*, RKO was unable or unwilling to provide Dix with a *Cimarron*-quality project again; and his career would suffer a slow, steady decline. The reasons were not entirely clear-cut. Certainly, RKO's financial situation was a factor, but Dix's advancing age may have had the greatest affect. At 37, he was simply becoming too old to believably play the young dynamic starring roles which might have maintained his position atop Hollywood.

Despite declining fortunes Dix accomplished a great deal during the remainder of the 1930s and 1940s. In fact, he made more than a few notable films, some distinguished in multiple respects. In 1931–32 he added seven more film appearances. He was a gangster who reforms after adopting an orphan in *Young Donovan's Kid*, a Yankee officer who seeks information behind enemy lines in the Civil War drama *Secret Service*, a boozy riverboat captain battling a bloodthirsty Chinese bandit in the campy actioner *Roar of the Dragon*, and a former intelligence officer who becomes a moral burglar known as "The Reckoner" in the mystery melodrama *The Public Defender* (1931).

The most prestigious film of Dix's post-*Cimarron* RKO career was undoubtedly 1932's *The Conquerors*, an attempt to duplicate the look and feel of its predecessor by tracing the ups and downs of a banking family from the 1870s to the stock market crash of the 1920s. Expensively produced by RKO's new head of production, David O. Selznick, with an extraordinary director William Wellman, a script from *Cimarron's* Howard Easterbrook, montages from the master Slavko Vorkapich, and a first-rate cast, including Ann Harding

From left: Joel McCrea, Dorothy Jordan, and Dix in *The Lost Squadron* (RKO, 1932).

and Edna May Oliver, the movie had enormous potential, but it just didn't work. It contained compelling sequences, but lacked subtlety and attempted to cover too much ground. Overlong and uneven, it was simply too ambitious for its own good.

More successful for Dix and RKO, both on commercial and artistic levels, were two medium budgeters: *Hell's Highway* and *The Lost Squadron*. The former, a hard-hitting pre-*I Am a Fugitive from a Chain Gang* drama (released two months before the LeRoy/Muni classic), boasted effective social commentary and superb acting from Dix as a put-upon chain gang convict. The latter, an absorbing melodrama, showcased another fine Dix performance as a World War I flyer forced by financial difficulties to do dangerous aerial movie stunts.

On October 20, 1931, Dix surprised fans and Hollywood insiders by eloping with San Francisco socialite/model Winifred Coe, whom he'd met at a party hosted by his brother. After a brief honeymoon, the couple took up residence at Dix's hideaway, called "The Haven," a 165-acre ranch in the Santa Monica Mountains with a Spanish

American-style home, a six-car garage, tennis court, barn, tack room, and chicken houses. Gossip columns and movie mags had a field day with the news; painting the courtship and marriage with typical superficial flourish. Things were not as idyllic as they appeared, however. All too soon, Dix began to regret his impulsive marriage to the spoiled Winifred who resented her husband's long work hours and missed her family and friends. The couple's disagreements were temporarily set aside when Winifred gave birth to Martha Mary Ellen Brimmer, on January 25, 1933, but the couple separated and divorced a few months later (September 1933). Winifred received a financial settlement and custody of little Mary Ellen. In 1934, the former Mrs. Dix decided she had not received her fair share of community property and filed suit, asking the couple's Mexican divorce and property settlement be set aside. An out-of-court pact was eventually reached, and Winifred moved on to husband #2, a successful Los Angeles surgeon.

By the time his "ex" filed her second suit Rich, too, had found love again; this time for keeps. On June 29, 1934, he wed his secretary, Virginia Webster, in a small ceremony in Jersey City, New Jersey, after a short courtship. A native of Santa Monica, California, the attractive blue-eyed, chestnut-haired Virginia was a masters-degreed teacher whom Dix met after she secured a position as his secretary/script supervisor over 600 other applicants.* After a honeymoon excursion through the Panama Canal, the newlyweds returned to California where they settled in Dix's custom-built, sixteen-room Pennsylvania Dutch mansion on Crescent Drive in Beverly Hills. The marriage would be a long, happy one lasting until Rich's death. Dix admired his wife's education and respected her opinions and abilities; and Virginia reciprocated by accepting her husband's long hours, his fondness for drinking, and "boy's night out." After their marriage Virginia resigned her position and became the head of the Dix household. On May 8, 1935, the couple welcomed twin boys, Richard and Robert. Seven years later in 1942, they adopted a daughter Sara Sue.

---

* For charming stories of Dix's first meetings and courtship and other important details of his father's life, please consult Robert Dix's inspirational autobiography *Out of Hollywood*, published in 2009.

Dix made a dozen feature films during the next three years 1933–36. Ten were medium-budget RKO features with decent production values, competent direction, fair-to-good scripts, and technical expertise. All featured excellent acting, especially by their star who had the opportunity to play a broad range of characters. He was an alcoholic advertising man in *No Marriage Ties* (1933), a young husband jailed for embezzling money to pay for his wife's extravagance in *Day of Reckoning* (1933, on loan to MGM), a sculptor/pacifist who becomes a bloodthirsty World War I fighter pilot in the beautifully photographed *Ace of Aces* (1933), a mustachioed bandit who steals the heart of a young opera singer in director William Wellman's *Stingaree* (1934), a professional gambler who executes a daring prison escape to rescue his young daughter from her abusive mother in the moving *His Greatest Gamble* (1934), and an unethical attorney who goes to work for the FBI in *Special Investigator* (1936). Dix also returned to the old west to hero in three films: as a honest cowboy who helps a rancher and his "daughter" in Zane Grey's *West of the Pecos* (1934), a marshal who cleans up a rowdy, crime-ridden 1880s western town in *The Arizonian* (1935), and a gold miner who goes undercover to clear his name in *Yellow Dust* (1936).

In reference to the Dix career two films of the period were standouts. *The Great Jasper* (1933), a charming 1890s comic drama, gave him one of his most unusual roles as a womanizing trolley car operator who becomes a successful fortune teller on Atlantic City's Boardwalk. As the happy-go-lucky rogue Jasper Horne, who cannot seem to manage his irresponsible impulses (including an uncontrollable wink when he's lying), Dix contributed one of his finest performances. Directed by pal J. Walter Ruben, lensed by the great Leo Tover, with a supporting cast populated by the likes of Florence Eldredge as Horne's domineering wife, and the one and only Edna May Oliver as an alcoholic astrologer, Madame Talma, *The Great Jasper* was an unadulterated delight.

Another unique Dix gem was *Transatlantic Tunnel*, a.k.a. *The Tunnel* (Gaumont, 1935), a fascinating British-made action drama about the construction of an undersea tunnel between England and the United States. Set in the future, the film focuses on the physical and psychological challenges faced by the project's creators particularly its designer (Dix), who becomes so preoccupied he neglects his family.

The seriocomic abilities of Dix were never better utilized than as the ne'er do well who becomes a fortune teller in *The Great Jasper* (RKO, 1933). Pictured with Dix are Walter Walker and Wera Engels.

A driven designer's quest to build an undersea tunnel between England and America has tragic consequences in the well-made British disaster movie *The Tunnel* (Gaumont, 1935). Seen with Dix is Jimmy Hanley.

A granddaddy of today's disaster picture, the movie contains several electrifying scenes involving hazards encountered in construction, notably the eruption of a subterranean volcano which causes the death of scores, including the designer's own son. Superbly produced by Michael Balcon (grandfather of actor Daniel Day Lewis), with an intelligent script by Kurt Siodmak, boffo photography/special effects, and a great cast lead by Dix, memorable as the driven McAllen, *The Tunnel* is a forgotten film to remember.

After the expiration of his second RKO contract in 1935, Dix surprised the Hollywood establishment by declining to renew it. No longer content with being "bound," he inked a short-term pact with Harry Cohn's Columbia, who gave him leads in four entertaining Bs: *It Happened in Hollywood* (1937), in which he affectingly impersonated a has-been cowboy star, and his famed "Devil's Trio" which included action dramas: *Devil's Squadron* (1936), *The Devil's Playground* (1937), and the drama *The Devil is Driving* (1937). Perhaps the best of the three was the latter which featured Dix as an attorney who successfully defends a wealthy, young man from a drunk driving rap despite knowledge of his guilt. Cast as a victim in the picture was a young brunette actress named Ann Rutherford, who had recently scored her first important break in the movies playing feminine leads in John Wayne and Gene Autry westerns. In a 2008 interview with the author Miss Rutherford recalled her admiration for Dix, but said he inadvertently caused her some frustration during the production of *The Devil is Driving*. "I had fallen in love with him when I saw *Cimarron*. I just thought he was wonderful. He was lovely to work with and a very nice man. He was always professional, hit his mark, came equipped, always knew his dialogueue . . . I thought he was a natural actor. I have absolutely no knowledge of whether he did the theater or not, but he listened well. As an actor he listened to the other people when they were talking and you could see it in his face. Acting is listening; it's reacting really . . . I had not completely finished my part when I had been cast by MGM to be in the first Hardy film. Then Richard Dix tripped over a cable and broke his arm, and held up the company so I was not in the first Hardy picture. A little girl named Margaret Marquis, the daughter of a wardrobe woman, played Polly Benedict and Lionel Barrymore was the father. I did the other Hardy pictures."

Richard Dix returned to RKO in November 1938. Published reports stated he negotiated a two-year, "two-way contract," which called for him to both act and direct, and allowed him freedom to work for other studios. For unknown reasons the opportunity to direct never materialized, but RKO and two other studios kept the star employed through the remainder of the 1930s in nine movies. All save one were medium to low budgeters.

The RKO productions included three Lew Landers' B adventure thrillers which teamed Dix with a talented costar. With super canine Ace the Wonder Dog, he made the well-paced thriller *Blind Alibi* (1938); with Chester Morris he filmed the exciting actioner *Sky Giant* (1938); and with Lucille Ball he made the nifty crime melodrama *Twelve Crowded Hours* (1938). In 1939 he portrayed an alcoholic reporter saved from ruination by the son he never knew in the emotional drama *Here I Am a Stranger* (Twentieth Century Fox, 1939), an attorney who helps establish the famed Nevada city in *Reno* (1939), a pilot in *The Marines Fly High* (1940), and an alcoholic stunt flyer who rehabilitates himself in *Men Against the Sky* (1940).

Dix's last great role in a quality production came in 1939, not at RKO but at the economically-minded Republic heretofore known for producing low-budget westerns. In a bid for respectability, Republic pulled out all the budgetary stops to bring the story of the life and times of legendary Sam Houston to the silver screen. One of their wisest decisions was to hire Richard Dix for the title role in *Man of Conquest*, an action drama which traced the history of the frontier fighter/politician from his young adulthood with the Cherokee Indians in Tennessee to his involvement in Texas' fight for freedom and statehood. As produced by Sol Siegel, with Academy Award-nominated technical work, and a spirited supporting cast headed by Edward Ellis as General Andrew Jackson and ace villain C. Henry Gordon as Mexican General Santa Ana, *Man of Conquest* is a classic.

Rightly sensing this might be one of his last opportunities to demonstrate the depth of his artistic talent in a top flight project 45-year-old Richard Dix gave his titled portrayal an extra oomph. The result was his finest screen acting since *Cimarron*. His multi- layered performance as Houston was strikingly similar to

Lucille Ball and Dix.

Dix played several historical figures in the 1930s and 1940s, including the legendary Sam Houston in Republic's excellent grade-A action drama *Man of Conquest* (1939). From left: George "Gabby" Hayes, Dix, and Max Terhune.

his Yancy Cravat. At once restrained and dynamic, Dix effectively communicated the multi-faceted nature of Houston's character: a fascinatingly complex combination of brashness, bravado, humility, and compassion. Dix's dedication to the role literally caused him pain. While filming a wrestling scene, he fractured two bones forcing a week's delay in production. He was rewarded with his best reviews in years.

In declining health the hard-working Rich began the last decade of his life by turning increasingly toward family, friends, and hobbies to find joy and personal satisfaction. Although he continued making movies until 1946 his focus appeared to transition away from his career to those he loved, and the things he loved to do. According to Robert, his father was a man of varied tastes and multiple hobbies. "One of the things my dad respected most was education. He loved to read, and was self-educated. He had a library in the Beverly Hills home and at the ranch with medical books, history books, etc. And he read all that stuff. That's one of the reasons he was able to give so much dimension to the period characters he portrayed. He also loved to play bridge. He'd have his buddies come over and they played bridge together . . .

"My dad was a dedicated husband and father. My mother and father had a very loving relationship. It was modeled to us as kids. They were always, like lovers, very affectionate. We were a very kissing, hugging family . . . My mom had a master's degree and was a teacher. He enjoyed the company of her collegiate friends and sorority sisters and their husbands. Those were the people who mainly came into our home. Duke Wayne, Gregory LaCava, and Randolph Scott came over to play bridge, but most of the Hollywood people were not invited into our home. Dad would meet them elsewhere and tip a few . . .

"There were times when he was working he wasn't home very much, but when he was we did a lot of things together. We'd ride horseback for a half day or longer together. There was a place called Saddle Peak at the top of Topanga Canyon on the edge of the property he owned. We'd ride to the top of that. From the very top of that plateau you could see Los Angeles, San Fernando Valley, Santa Monica, Pacific Ocean, everything. He taught me how to fire a rifle. Every kid wants his first .22. I got mine when I was about 12. Of course, I had to do chores around the ranch. I had to clean up the chicken coops. We had 180 chickens . . .

"Dad was also a shrewd investor. One day during a visit to the dentist he bought a piece of Sunset Boulevard! While the dentist had him in the chair, he told Dad he would sell him a 110 ft. piece of frontage on Sunset Boulevard for $60,000. It was leased to Union Oil and sublet to Ben and Frank's, which was a restaurant chain. When it was sold years after my father's death, it went for 2.4 million . . ."

The success of *Man of Conquest* turned out to be a double-edged sword for the veteran star who preferred to work in a variety of film genres. It reenergized his career, but led to his typecasting as western heroes. For the next three years (1940–43) Dix worked mainly in highly-polished B westerns, often portraying famed historical figures. For his old employer, Paramount, Dix made three pictures. He was the new marshal of a lawless Oklahoma town named Goliath in *Cherokee Strip*, an upright rancher whose wedding is marred by the appearance of his bride-to-be's roguish old flame (played by Dix's Morosco Players buddy Preston Foster) in *The Roundup* (1941), and the legendary Wyatt Earp who dispenses of graft and villainy in the titled Arizona town in *Tombstone the Town Too Tough to Die* (1942). For both United Artists and Universal he made three B plussers. At UA, he was a cattle breeder who fights off insider corruption to establish a vast cattle ranch in *American Empire* (1942), a gunfighter who joins forces with the Missouri Central Railroad to battle criminals in the well-produced *The Kansan* (1943), and a hired gun who routs the James Gang and the crooked city officials who employed him in *Buckskin Frontier* (1943). At Universal, the movie veteran was a police chief with a past in *Eyes of the Underworld* (1943), the father of Donald O'Connor in the musical *Top Man* (1943), and the famed frontiersman Wild Bill Hickok in the superior star-studded western *Badlands of Dakota* (1941).

The latter was particularly memorable to Robert, who visited the set and recalled his father's intense preparation for the role. "Dad practiced his craft like a painter with his paintbrush. He told me he studied all his characters, but particularly if they'd been real people. He liked to give a character an 'inner life.' A trick he used that I have used in my acting career is when you get the information on a character from the screenplay you build a life for him. And I think the best way you know if you've done your job well is if, to some extent, you become that character on the set. It's dangerous because when you walk off you're no longer Frank James! . . . Dad really got into the characters he played. I remember one time in the hallway of our Beverly Hills home he was telling me about how deadly Wild Bill Hickok was with a pistol. He put me on one end of the hallway and stood at the other end. And he had on these six-guns. Of course, they were empty. Anyway, he whipped one out and clicked it like he fired it, and then told me, 'At this distance Hickok would have split the third button on the man's shirt.'"

A combination of factors precipitated Dix's 1943 decision to abandon the western genre and begin the final phase of his acting career. His deteriorating health (high blood pressure and heart problems) was definitely an issue which necessitated a change from the physically demanding action pictures to more sedentary assignments; but even more importantly, Dix's decision was motivated by a desire to flex his acting muscles, to expand his artistic horizons. After years of playing noble westerners he longed to break out of the professional straitjacket and meet a new challenge. He voiced his desires to friends and family, including his eight-year-old son. "Dad was a dimensional actor. He wanted to show the world he could play various parts. Lots of people thought of him only as a western star. He wasn't. As you know he came from the theater where he played a variety of roles. When he was playing at the Morosco in Los Angeles, he was doing a different play every week. When he began in silent pictures, he played in comedies, deep dramas, and the various genres. After *Cimarron* he got stuck with a cowboy hat on . . . He used to say he rode the crest of *Cimarron* for fifteen years. They kept putting him in westerns where he'd have two lines and shoot a guy. Many were good pictures which paid a lot of money but as far as his craft was concerned they weren't satisfying. He once told me, 'I hope I never see another horse's rosette!'"

Dix's desire for a change of pace was fulfilled when he accepted the role of a psychotic sea captain who terrorizes his youthful third officer in legendary producer Val Lewton's acclaimed atmospheric chiller *The Ghost Ship* (RKO), the first of eight offbeat roles Dix would play during the remainder of his acting career. His rich, realistic

The famous action hero of the 1930s essentially became a character player during the 1940s, beginning with his turn as the sadistic sea captain Will Stone in the melodramatic *The Ghost Ship* (RKO, 1943).

portrayal of the sadistic Captain Will Stone surprised even his most ardent fans. Harry Cohn was sufficiently impressed to offer the veteran star another chance to play suspense, this time as a wealthy man who changes his mind about suicide in *The Whistler* (1944), based on the mega-hit radio anthology series. Dix's exceptional work in the picture won him more raves and an offer from Columbia of a starring role in a new *Whistler* series. By the summer of 1944, Dix had signed on and was already at work on a second installment, *The Mark of the Whistler* (1944), about a drifter who becomes so desperate he turns to a life of crime. Despite their status as B pictures, Robert Dix says his father jumped at the opportunity to do the *Whistler* series and to work for Harry Cohn. "He took the *Whistlers* as a challenge. It took some courage because he didn't know if the audience was going to accept him with these mystery stories. An actor can never really be better than the screenplay. The *Whistlers* were well written and gave him a lot of opportunities to show his range. Dad wanted to use all of his talent, not just a portion. He was especially proud of the Whistlers because it was a different tack for him . . . My father liked Harry Cohn and Mr. Cohn had a high regard for him. I can't tell you why he got along with Cohn. Most people hated him. Perhaps it was because they were staunch individualists . . . My dad was a personality star. People came to see the *Whistler* series because they liked Richard Dix. Cohn recognized that. The few times I met him he was most courteous and kind."

Dix would make two *Whistlers* per year between 1943–46, playing an array of anti-heroes: a psychotic killer in *The Power of the Whistler* (1945), a jealous husband who resorts to murder in *Voice of the Whistler* (1945), a sleazy private eye who gets mixed up in homicide in *Mysterious Intruder* (1946), and a shiftless, philandering artist who decides to off his rich wife in *The Secret of the Whistler* (1946). Aided by excellent directors, fascinating stories, and committed supporting casts, Dix pulled out all the stops to make his *Whistler* performances both affecting and unsettling. His understated acting, and soft, gentle manner added complexity to the characterizations, often making him a decidedly cunning and dangerous villain.

Critics and audiences stood up and took note. In 1944, Dix's new-found success in character-type roles prompted columnist Erskine Johnson to ask the actor the secret of his longevity as a film star. His response showed a refreshing candor and a savvy realism which succinctly explained why his career had survived when so many others had not.

"Making movies is a business. Sure, some of the pictures stink. But you gotta play ball with the producers. You gotta work in the stinkers. That's where a lot of youngsters make their mistake. One good picture puts you back on the top of the pile."

After shooting wrapped on the most physically taxing of the seven *Whistlers, The Thirteenth Hour*, in late fall 1946, Dix suffered his first major heart attack in the company of Robert. "We sold our home in Beverly Hills when I was about eight or nine and moved to the ranch in Topanga Canyon. We had a tennis court on the grounds. We'd play tennis together and he always beat me. He was a much better player than I was. On this particular day I was beating him. I thought to myself, 'Boy, am I getting good!' Suddenly, I realized he wasn't moving like he usually did. Finally, he said, 'Hey, I think we've got to quit.' As we're walking up the road to the main ranch house I said, 'What is it, Dad?' I could see he was blue around the lips. He said, 'I feel like I swallowed a piano.' My mother got him to the hospital. That was his first heart attack in 1946. He survived that one."

Forced by his worsening condition to abandon acting, and sell his beloved ranch (due to the 2,000 ft. altitude) Dix spent the remainder of his days in semi-retirement in a home he purchased at 220 North Bristol in Brentwood, formerly owned by Clark Gable. He continued to see his family and friends, read, and played bridge. In the fall of 1948, he fell and fractured his hip, and suffered his second heart attack which necessitated his convalescence at a Monrovia California sanitarium. Upon his return home, he seemed resigned to the inevitable.

"My fondest memories of my dad were our man-to-man talks in the library when he was dying . . . He had this big leather chair. It was *his* chair. Well, he put me in that chair and he would sit opposite me sucking on oxygen. And we would have these man-to-man talks. And he would say things to me like, 'For God's sake, Son, don't ever lose your sense of humor,' 'Don't take yourself too seriously,' 'Don't worry about what they say about you as long as they spell your name right.' That's the advice he would give. To him being an actor was a craft, a profession that you honed as you would if you were a banker, an accountant, or a stock salesman. He accepted the responsibility of being an American movie star. When he left the house, he had the suit, the matching hat and so forth to go to Beverly Hills because he was going to meet John Q. Public. He was beholden to them. He respected the fact that people went to see his movies and was terribly worried about some of the images that were being presented to the world on behalf of our way of life."

In the summer of 1949, a gravely ill Richard Dix received permission from his doctors to take his family (wife and two sons, his daughter stayed behind) on a European vacation. All went well until the group entered the high altitudes of the Swiss Alps, where the ailing actor experienced problems breathing. Temporarily abandoning the tour to recoup in Nice, an ill-looking Dix eventually rejoined his family in France before boarding the *Queen Mary* in

Cherbourg for the trip home. During the journey across the Atlantic, Dix apparently had another serious heart attack, but continued on. His medical condition worsened on the train trip from New York to Chicago forcing him off the *20th Century Limited*, and into Chicago's Presbyterian Hospital. Unable to travel, he remained in the Windy City for four weeks before his physician agreed to let him come home. On September 8, he flew to the West Coast and was hospitalized at Hollywood Presbyterian.

Los Angeles newspapers provided daily updates on his condition, noting his "courageous battle" and slow improvement. The noted actor was still battling the morning of September 21, 1949, when he suffered cardiac collapse and died one hour later with Mrs. Dix holding his hand. According to the *Los Angeles Times*, "He was conscious to the last spasm, a gamester who wanted to live." His physician, Dr. Berg, made a brief statement complimenting his patient's courage and citing the actor's physically taxing roles and "disdain for doubles" as contributing factors to his overall health problems.

Services were held on September 22, 1949, at the Little Chapel of the Flowers, at Forest Lawn Memorial Park in Glendale where Dix was interred (Lot 2387 in Whispering Pines section). Among the large contingent of mourners present to bid adieu to their beloved friend, colleague, and champion were many Hollywood celebrities, including Bill LeBaron, Gregory LaCava, Irene Dunne, and Preston Foster.

Surviving were Dix's wife, Virginia, his twin sons, two daughters and his sister, Mrs. Josephine Compton. According to published accounts, his estate was split between his wife and children. Mrs. Virginia Dix (1910–2005) would marry three more times after Dix's passing. All would predecease her. Her second husband was Walter Van de Kamp, the head of a Southern California chain of bakeries. Richard Dix Jr. would marry at sixteen, have a son, and die tragically on August 31, 1953, the result of a logging accident. He is buried next to his father. Daughter Sara Sue remains in California as does Robert Dix who followed his father's lead, and carved his own niche in the entertainment industry as a film and television actor, producer, and writer. A former MGM contract player, Robert's credits include *Forbidden Planet* (MGM, 1956),

Forty Guns (Fox, 1957), *Screaming Eagles* (Allied Artists, 1956), and *The Little Shepherd of Kingdom Come* (Fox, 1961). In 2009, Mr. Dix published an autobiography, *Out of Hollywood*, an articulate, heartfelt account of his early years with his father in Hollywood, his own successful show-business career, and his inspirational struggle and triumph over addiction. When asked in 2008 for an assessment of his famous father, and for his opinion on how his dad would have liked to be remembered, Robert replied, "I was proud of my father not only for his work but for the man he was. I saw his relationships with other people. I saw how he treated folks. And let's face it; it's the example not the word that affects our lives as we're growing up . . . I was fourteen years old when my dad passed but of course during my life with him I heard wonderful stories about him. He had a wonderful sense of humor and was a real man's man. I have never heard a negative word about my father and his work or his relationship to the crew, costars, etc., and that's wonderful to hear . . . If I had to say how he would like to be remembered I would say as an American actor. He was really proud to be an American. He underscored that in our lives."

On the day of Dix's funeral columnist Jimmy Starr paid tribute to his friend by relating the touching story of one of the countless good deeds the veteran actor had done during his 56 years. The story involved one of Starr's coworkers, a newsboy who was hit by a truck and severely injured. Too poor to handle the exorbitant medical expenses, his family became desperate. When Dix learned of the young man's plight, he told Starr to tell the family not to worry. He would take care of everything as long as Starr did not publicize it. When the newsboy recovered, he and his pals took up a collection and purchased an engraved plaque for the star on which they expressed their thanks. Although it contained their own particular sentiments, it could just as easily have been written by any one who knew and admired Richard Dix.

It read:

"TO A SWELL FELLOW AND A GUY WE'LL NEVER FORGET."

MICHAEL DUANE (1914–1963)

Michael Duane.

JIM CALHOUN in *The Secret of the Whistler*
TED NICHOLS in *The Return of the Whistler*

Debonair, boyishly handsome stage and screen actor, art director, artist Michael Duane enjoyed a disappointingly short career in the movies during the mid- to late 1940s. Signed by Columbia in 1943, the former interior designer-turned-thespian seemed headed for major stardom when the studio cast him in a lead role in his first film and announced their intention to give him a "big buildup." Instead, they ushered the personable young actor into lackluster romantic leads in low-budgeters and inconsequential supporting parts in B+ features which squandered his acting ability, easygoing all-American charm, and screen charisma. In 1948 a disillusioned Duane simply gave up and returned to a highly successful career in art and design, winning acclaim and an Emmy nomination in the 1950s as an art director on television.

Whistler's second "son" was born Duane Peterson McKinney, on April 12, 1914, in Dunkirk, Indiana, the only child of businessman Arthur L. McKinney and his wife, the former Lena Peterson. Joint owner of Dunkirk's famed McKinney Department Store, renown for being "Indiana's greatest country store," Duane's father was a patron of the arts and a songwriter who encouraged his son's interest in performing. By the time he was in grade school Duane was already staging plays and organizing his own mini-circus in the McKinney home. In 1921, the family moved to Harrisburg, Pennsylvania; and Duane became enrolled in the Harrisburg Academy. Later, the McKinneys settled in Indianapolis where Duane attended school, took up the trombone, and played in the John Robison Circus Band.

In 1928, 14-year-old Duane made his formal acting debut carrying a spear in a stock company play starring Mrs. Leslie Carter and Guy Bates Post. After graduating from the Culver Military Academy in Culver, Indiana, he enrolled in the John Harron Art School taking courses in art and scenic design. His talent as an artist/designer and interest in acting eventually landed him a position at The John Goodman Theater (part of the Chicago Institute of Art) where he remained for a three-year apprenticeship.

In 1934 Duane moved to New York and started his own interior design business which quickly flourished. Among his clients were Bonwit Teller, Saks Fifth Avenue, Encore Club, and the famed Algonquin Supper Club. During the summers, he pursued his passion for acting, appearing in stock productions across the northeast with such noted stage stars as Cecilia Loftus, Kenneth McKenna, and Josephine Hull. In the latter 1930s McKinney toured in *Night Must Fall*, and then spent two years in the touring company of *You Can't Take it With You*.

While working in stock Duane became reacquainted with stage actress Phyllis Ellerman whom he met at the Chicago Art Institute. They were married in 1940. One year later, the budding stage star, billed as Duane McKinney, made his Broadway debut at the Forest Theater in the drama *Walk Into My Parlor*, starring Nicholas Conte and Joseph De Santis. When the play flopped, the determined Duane resumed his work as a designer, returned to summer stock, and began acting on radio. Among his radio credits were roles on several serials, including *Stella Dallas, John's Other Wife*, and *Second Husband* costarring Helen Menken.

While in New York, the handsome, 6 ft. tall, brown-haired, hazel-eyed McKinney was approached by a Hollywood talent agent who suggested he try his hand at the movies. In 1942, the McKinneys moved to California where fortune soon smiled on the 28-year-old. Because there were so many male movie stars serving in the military, work for aspiring film actors was plentiful. Within weeks Duane secured his first film role: a male lead opposite lovely Linda Darnell in Columbia's low-budget melodrama, *City Without Men* (1943), about a group of women living in a boarding house adjacent to a prison where their men are serving time. Billed as Michael Duane, the young actor's performance as a ship's pilot falsely convicted of aiding the Japanese and sentenced to a five-year prison term won critical favor.

His excellent reviews prompted Columbia to sign Duane to a long-term contract and proclaim him their next star. His name appeared in several influential columns at the time. Hedda Hopper cited him as "a major find" who Columbia intended to give a "big buildup." At this critical juncture Duane had reason to believe he would be promoted to A-level pictures, but his optimism was unfounded. Instead, the studio immediately placed him in four programmers which did little for his career. Among them were *Redhead from Manhattan* (1943), a minor mistaken identity comedy which cast him as a sax player in love with one of two look-alike cousins portrayed by Lupe Velez, and *Is Everybody Happy?* (1943), a Ted Lewis musical vehicle with Duane in a flashback as Lewis as a young man.

Michael was set to play the role of John Ainsley (eventually played by Roland Varno) in Columbia's memorable *Return of the Vampire*, starring Bela Lugosi, when he was inducted into the military on

September 1, 1943. While serving in the Army Air Corps, his experience as an actor/performer worked to his personal and professional advantage when he was selected to appear in writer-director Moss Hart's moving tribute to Army Air Force flyers, *Winged Victory*, which opened on Broadway to rave reviews and packed audiences in November 1943. The musical drama was such a success inspiring Americans to buy war bonds the entire company eventually toured the U. S. and Europe, and then made a movie of the production for Twentieth Century-Fox. After the show broke up Duane was assigned to one of the many Army entertainment groups. He was stationed in Miami until his honorable discharge on November 1, 1945.

With high hopes Duane resumed filmmaking in February 1946, but nothing had changed. Although his "comeback" film, *The Devil's Mask* (1946), the second installment of Columbia's short-lived *I Love a Mystery* series, was an exciting suspenser which featured thieves, murderers, and shrunken heads, it was decidedly low-budget; and his heroic role hardly a challenge. Sadly, none of Duane's follow-up films did much for him either. He demonstrated a unique combination of grit, sensitivity, and charm as the police lieutenant in the melodramatic *Shadowed* (1946), the older brother of a boy with a problem burro in the kiddie-oriented *Personality Kid* (1946), a detective who suspects a kindly old man of being a jewel thief in *Alias Mr. Twilight* (1946), and as two troubled artists in *The Secret of the Whistler* (1946) and *Keeper of the Bees* (1947), but the motion pictures simply did not have the heft to propel his career. More successful were his real-life efforts as a painter. In the fall of 1947 a highly-acclaimed exhibition of his oils (primarily landscapes) was held in Hollywood.

Things remained unimproved during the period, 1947–48. Dapper Michael appeared in six films which would prove to be his last. Three of them, *The Swordsman* (1948), *The Prince of Thieves* (1948), and *The Gallant Blade* (1948), were colorful, well-produced B+ swashbucklers which might have aided his career if his supporting roles had been larger, more substantive. Unfortunately, Duane's better parts came in programmers. The best of them, by far, was *The Return of the Whistler*, the 8th and final installment of the famed series in which Duane had the unenviable task of filling the unfillable shoes of ailing *Whistler* star Richard Dix. Prior to the film's release,

Publicity shot from *The Return of the Whistler* (1948).]

Michael Duane played a supporting role in the Robin Hood swashbuckler *The Prince of Thieves* (Columbia, 1948) starring Jon Hall, Patricia Morison, and beautiful Adele Jergens (seen here).

newspapers reported Columbia's interest in a rejuvenated *Whistler* series with Duane as star; but enthusiasm dissipated when the film received mixed reviews and flopped at the box office. It was too bad as Duane's lead performance as a bridegroom whose betrothed disappears on the night of their nuptials was superb.

After appearing in 17 motion pictures, the disillusioned actor made no effort to continue making movies when Columbia did not renew his contract in 1949. Tired of the Hollywood rat race, Michael, Phyllis, and young son Nicholas (born in 1947) returned to the East Coast where the former artistic prodigy resumed being Duane McKinney and settled in Wilton, Connecticut. In the years immediately following his move back east McKinney acted in regional theater, did a few live television roles, and directed an episode of TV's *Colgate Theatre*, "Mr. and Mrs. North"; but by the early 1950s was concentrating his creative energies on art and design. One of his last television acting credits was *Kraft Television Theatre's* 1954 production of "Dark Victory" costarring Viola Dana.

By 1955 McKinney was beginning to make a name for himself as an art director on the small screen. In a 2009 interview with the author, Duane's son Nicholas recalled his father's many interests and accomplishments. "My father's greatest love in the world was to paint. We spent many summers on Cape Cod and Block Island where seascapes and people were his great love . . . He became the art director for NBC's *Kraft Television Theatre*. He worked for J. Walter Thompson doing all the live *Kraft* shows in the fifties prior to the invention of videotape. Among his producers was George Roy Hill. My father was nominated for an Emmy and won the Sylvania award for his staging of 'A Night to Remember' (1957—produced by Hill) on live television. Using three entire NBC stages he built the *Titanic* then flooded it with water . . . His other accomplishments included the movie *Patterns* (originally a *Kraft Theatre* production) and the *DuPont Shows of the Month* (CBS, 1957–62) that followed the demise of *Kraft* in the late 1950s . . . Along with Ralph Alswang, my father designed Central Park's 'Theatre in the Round,' where Shakespearian plays are still staged today."

Mr. McKinney's last notable TV art directing credit came in 1959 when he won acclaim for his work on NBC's adaptation of the

Agatha Christie classic "Ten Little Indians" starring his old Columbia pal Nina Foch.

The talented, creative Duane McKinney, a.k.a. Michael Duane, continued to chalk up accomplishments in art and interior design until March 26, 1963 when he collapsed and died of a heart attack at New York's Grand Central Station while on his way home from work. He was only 47 years old. Duane's wife, Phyllis, eventually became a school librarian at the Wilton Elementary School and Driscoll School. She died in September 1990 at the family home in Wilton. Son Nicholas became a quality assurance testing manager for software engineering and lives in Rhode Island. He has three very gifted grown children.

THE LEADING LADIES

LENORE AUBERT (1918–1993)

Lenore Aubert.

ALICE DUPRES BARKLEY in *The Return of the Whistler*.

Tall, dark, and lovely Lenore Aubert (pronounced "Oh-bear") was a Yugoslavian-born actress who came to the United States during the early 1940s to escape the scourge of Hitler and to make a name for herself on the American stage and screen. After appearing in some well-received West Coast theatrical productions, in 1943 she seemed poised to achieve major cinematic success when famed producer Samuel Goldwyn signed her to a movie contract and promised to promote her. Unfortunately, there were strings attached; when Lenore failed to cooperate, Goldwyn successfully sabotaged her career. For a time the articulate, bronze-haired, continental beauty found work in supporting roles and minor films as exotics, notably as the glamorous scientist under the evil spell of Dracula in the hilarious *Bud Abbott and Lou Costello Meet Frankenstein* (1948), but she never came close to becoming a top star. Disappointed, but undefeated, in 1949, Lenore left the film capital. Later, she became a philanthropist and a patron of the arts.

The daughter of an Austrian army general, Lenore was born Eleanore Maria Leisner on April 18, 1918 (1913–1920?) in the Yugoslavian city of Celje (pronounced "Cilli") in what is now Slovenia. Raised in Vienna and educated in convent schools, she became interested in an acting career as a teenager. Her parents were unhappy with her vocational choice, but Eleanore persevered. Eventually, she found work as an extra in several Austrian films, and made her American film debut in 1937 when a crew shooting background shots in Austria for Ernst Lubitsch's comedy *Bluebeard's Eighth Wife* hired her because she resembled star Claudette Colbert from a distance.

In 1938, Eleanore married budding actor Julius Altman, who was Jewish. Hitler's march across Europe necessitated the young couple's migration to Paris, then Marseilles, and Portugal. In 1941, they sailed to New York, where both hoped to find acting work. Flat broke, they took whatever employment they could find. The svelte 5 ft. 7½ in. tall, blue-gray-eyed Eleanore landed a job as a dress model. When she was offered the part of Lorraine Sheldon in *The Man Who Came to Dinner* at San Diego's famed La Jolla Theater, the Altmans boarded a bus for the West Coast. Eleanore enrolled in acting classes while playing in various Los Angeles-area community theater productions. In 1942 a talent scout for Sam Goldwyn spotted her at the Bliss Hayden Theater and asked her to do a screen test.

Saluting her "tantalizing accent, waltz-like walk, and TNT charm," in the spring of 1943 Goldwyn signed the 25-year-old actress, renamed her Lenore Aubert, and then cast her in a substantive supporting role as a Mata Hari-like spy opposite Bob Hope and Dorothy Lamour in the comedy *They Got Me Covered*. Thrilled with her first big break in the movies, which she hoped would lead to a long and fruitful "Hedy Lamarr-type" movie career, Aubert's optimism soon turned to disgust when she learned Goldwyn expected her to become his mistress in exchange for promoting her. When she flatly refused, the mogul reportedly informed her she would be allowed to make films but, "you will never ever be a star for me or anyone else."

True to his word, Goldwyn spitefully declined MGM's offer to buy Aubert's contract in 1943, but agreed to sell it to the less-prestigious RKO one year later. During the period, 1944–45, RKO utilized Aubert in three films: as a French freedom fighter in Nazi-occupied Paris in the entertaining comic/drama *Passport to Destiny* (1944), a glamorous magician's assistant in the mystery-comedy *Having Wonderful Crime* (1945), and an Arab girl in the well-mounted spy melodrama *Action in Arabia* (1944). Although all were decent roles, the films were minor productions, which did not increase Aubert's reputation. What they *did* do was establish a screen persona for the dark-haired beauty with the European accent which was not to her liking: as a low-budget exotic and/or *femme fatale*.

Hoping to escape typecasting and play more substantive dramatic parts, in 1945 Aubert left RKO and began freelancing, but little changed. She was tested for several important roles, including the French vixen Clio in *Saratoga Trunk* (1945), Georges Sand in Columbia's Chopin biopic *A Song to Remember* (1945), and the gypsy Lydia in Paramount's *Golden Earrings* (1947), but lost the parts to more established actresses. The roles she won, feminine leads in *The Wife of Monte Cristo* (PRC, 1946) and *Catman of Paris* (Republic, 1946), etc., were strictly minor league.

Still hopeful, Lenore continued to make motion pictures for the remainder of the decade. During her peak filmmaking period, 1947–49, she appeared in seven movies, five of which were among her most memorable. She was fine as international entertainer Fritzi Barrington (her personal favorite role) in the lush musical *I Wonder Who's Kissing Her Now* (Fox, 1947), a young woman whose family is massacred in the newly opened Louisiana Purchase Territory in the frontier adventure, *The Prairie* (Screen Guild, 1947), and as an

Lenore in a scene from *Bud Abbott and Lou Costello Meet Frankenstein*.

unfortunate widow kidnapped and held hostage by her in-laws in *The Return of the Whistler* (Columbia, 1948).

In 1948, Lenore made her most famous film, *Bud Abbott and Lou Costello Meet Frankenstein* (Universal International), opposite the famed comic duo. The tale of two dimwitted railway porters-turned-freight handlers who get mixed up with crooks and Universal's famed monsters, Dracula, Wolf Man, and Frankenstein (Bela Lugosi, Lon Chaney Jr., and Glen Strange), the movie was a laugh riot and a box-office mega-hit. As Sandra Mornay, a beautiful researcher under the hypnotic evil of Dracula who seduces Costello to steal his brain, Aubert won acclaim and new fans. The film was so popular the comic duo requested Lenore for their next film, *Abbott and Costello Meet the Killer, Boris Karloff* (Universal International, 1949). It, too, was a success, but not the type elegant, aristocratic Aubert wished to be associated with. *Killer* turned out to be the actress' last Hollywood film.

In 1949, Lenore's husband Julius insisted the couple return to New York where he hoped to open a garment business. Disenchanted with her film career, Aubert acquiesced. In New York, she made a handful of television appearances in 1949–50, including an episode of *Suspense*. When her marriage to Altman ended in 1951, Lenore returned to live in Europe for a time. During 1951–52 she appeared in two foreign-language films, *Falschmunzer Am Werk* (Germany, 1951) and *Une File Sur La Route* (France, 1952), then retired from show business.

While living in Europe, Aubert met wealthy businessman Milton Greene, became his wife, and moved back to America in 1959. For the next fifteen years the Greenes divided their time between a Manhattan penthouse and a luxurious home in Florida. As Mrs. Greene, the former actress volunteered her time with a variety of charitable organizations, and served on the staff of the United Nations Activities and Housing Section. When her second marriage ended in divorce in 1979, Lenore remained in New York and continued her charity work. In 1983, she suffered the first of several strokes which left her memory impaired. Four years later she did her last interview, with Canadian journalist Jim McPherson, one of only two she'd granted since she left Hollywood. In it she expressed appreciation for her film career and said she was delighted so many movie fans still remembered her. She stated her only regret was she did not get the opportunity to appear in better films. Lenore Aubert died at age 75, on July 31, 1993, at her home in Great Neck, Long Island, New York.

PAMELA BLAKE (1915–2009)

ELORA LUND in *Mysterious Intruder.*

Pamela Blake was an able American actress who decorated over fifty feature films in the mid-1930s to the early 1950s. A petite, improbably pretty brunette with beautifully expressive hazel eyes, a sunny smile, eye-catching dimples, and a pleasant-speaking voice, she projected warmth and likeability which made her an ideal screen heroine. Although she played a range of roles in all genres, she is

Pamela Blake.

best remembered as a gentle lady in B westerns and adventures, including four cliffhanger serials.

Born Adele Pearce in Oakland, California, on August 6, 1915 (1918?), her father was an employee of the Pacific Gas & Electric Company of San Francisco. When her mother died at age three, Adele was sent to live with an aunt and uncle who also resided in the Bay area. During her formative years as a student at Galileo High School, the youngster joined the dramatic club and appeared in various school productions.

In 1934 the attractive, 19-year-old, 5 ft. tall aspiring actress auditioned for a role in Paramount's *Eight Girls in a Boat*. After interviews, she was selected over hundreds of girls for the coveted bit. Upon completion of her film debut, Adele returned to San Francisco where she studied dramatics, acted in a theater group at the Paramount Hotel, and on radio in various playlets. When opportunities presented themselves, she returned to Hollywood for three more tiny parts in *One in a Million* (Twentieth Century-Fox, 1936), *Stage Door* (RKO, 1937), and *Island in the Sky* (Twentieth Century-Fox, 1938).

Adele's first significant break in the movies came in 1938 when she was tapped by Grand National to play Tex Ritter's best girl in the low-budget singing western *The Utah Trail*. In spite of the film's dismal reviews, charismatic Adele was seen to advantage and received good notices. Recognizing her potential, director John Farrow cast Pearce as a young college girl who longs to enter an exclusive sorority in RKO's sentimental drama *Sorority House* (1939) starring Anne Shirley. Impressed with Adele's moving performance, Farrow utilized her again in the melodramatic *Full Confession* (1939), and recommended her for a part in RKO's remake of 1933's *Sweepings* entitled *Three Sons* (1939). In between RKO gigs the freelancing Adele supported singer/actress Movita in Monogram's *The Girl from the Rio* (1939), and provided the romantic interest for John Wayne in Republic's low-budget western *Wyoming Outlaw* (1939). In 1939, she wed B western actor Bud McTaggart, with whom she had conducted an onscreen romance in *Full Confession*. The marriage ended after only a few months (August 1940).

In 1940, Farrow helped Adele secure a term contract with RKO, where she would make 11 films in the span of just one year. Regrettably, none advanced her career. She had bit parts in two of the studio's bigger-budget pictures, *Too Many Girls* (1940) and Hitchcock's charming *Mr. and Mrs. Smith* (1940), but the majority of her RKO assignments were juvenile leads in second features hampered by modest production values and script deficiencies. The best of the lot was the Leon Errol slapstick comedy *Pop Always Pays* (1940), in which Adele gave a charming performance as the love-struck daughter of a businessman.

After leaving RKO in 1941, Adele was selected by director Frank Tuttle for a key supporting role in Paramount's crime drama *This Gun for Hire* (1942). At the studio's request she changed her name to Pamela Blake, a combination of her favorite novelist's first name and one she pulled out of a telephone book. As Annie, the abused girlfriend of a cold-blooded assassin (Alan Ladd), Blake was impressive. Her part was substantially trimmed prior to release, but enough remained to inspire a contract offer from the "Cadillac" of studios, Metro-Goldwyn-Mayer.

Blake was initially ecstatic when she affixed her name to a MGM contract in 1942, but her enthusiasm was short-lived. After a promising start as the girlfriend of Red Skelton in the charming Ann Sothern series' vehicle *Maisie Gets Her Man* (1942) and a feminine lead opposite James Craig in the western *The Omaha Trail* (1942), MGM seemed to lose interest. They gave her another Maisie assignment and two other Bs in 1943, and loaned her to Monogram for the mystery meller *The Unknown Guest* (1943), but largely ignored her potential.

MGM seized an opportunity to cancel Pamela's contract when she wed former radio announcer-turned-Air Cadet Michael Stokey in Laguna Beach, California, on Christmas Day, 1942, then left the area to be with him prior to deployment overseas. Her pact stipulated she could not leave town without studio permission. The Stokeys' six-year union would produce two children: Michael Stokey Jr., in 1946, and Barbara Ann, in 1947. After their divorce (November, 1948) Mike Stokey became a successful television producer best known for his famous *Pantomime Quiz* (1950–63) and *Stump the Stars*.

Now a freelance actress, Pamela began her most prolific filmmaking period (1945–50), in which she appeared in over 20 low-budget features. No longer concerned with attaining Grade-A stardom she took whatever work was offered and enjoyed modest success as a B movie actress in the employ of several studios. Her beauty, vulnerability, and charm made her a natural screen heroine; and although she played a few borderline bad girls, she was almost always found on the right side of the law, in the arms of the hero at the fadeout. Most of her post-Metro movies were melodramatic adventures or westerns dominated by male leads, such as *Highway 13* (Screen

Guild, 1948) with Robert Lowery, *Sky Liner* (Screen Guild, 1949) with Richard Travis, *Federal Man* (Eagle Lion, 1950) with William Henry, *Sons of God's Country* (Republic, 1948) with Monte Hale, *Gun Fire* (Lippert, 1950), and *Border Rangers* (Lippert, 1950) starring Don "Red" Barry. Her excellent turn as the put-upon young heiress manipulated by a sleazy attorney in the *Whistler* thriller *Mysterious Intruder* (Columbia, 1946) was a critical highlight, and stands as one of her best.

Of all Pamela's B movies perhaps the most fondly remembered are the four cliffhanger serials she completed in the latter 1940s: *Chick Carter, Detective* (Columbia, 1946), in which she portrayed a private investigator who helps detective Nick Carter's son, Chick (Lyle Talbot), catch jewel thieves; *The Mysterious Mr. M* (Universal, 1946), which cast her as an insurance investigator assisting a local detective (Dennis Moore) find a traitor; the tropical adventure *The Sea Hound* (Columbia, 1947), in which she aided a noble sea captain (Buster Crabbe) fight off pirates, kidnappers, and deadly natives; and *Ghost of Zorro* (Republic, 1949) a cowboydized version of the classic story with Pamela as a telegraph company owner who wards off outlaws with the assistance of a surveying engineer (Clayton Moore) who dons the mask of his grandfather Zorro.

When her film career waned in the early 1950s, Blake made several appearances on television on such popular series as *The Cisco Kid* (three episodes in 1950), *Front Page Detective* (1951), *Boston Blackie* (1951), and *The Range Rider* (three episodes from 1952–53), before retiring in 1954 so she could spend more time with her children. Her last two films were westerns: *Waco* (Monogram, 1952) with Bill Elliott and *Adventures of the Texas Kid: Border Ambush* (Franklin, 1954) costarring Hugh Hooker.

During the remainder of her life Miss Blake lived in Las Vegas. In an interview published in the Boyd Magers and Michael Fitzgerald's book *Westerns Women* (1999) she explained the reason why she moved to Sin City: "I wasn't seeing the children enough. Actually, when I divorced Mike, I came out to Las Vegas. I had to stay for six weeks, so I met quite a few people. I liked it and just wanted to be with the kids. I only intended to stay a couple of months or so, but I found a house here and brought the children up."

Pamela was married for a third time in 1983 to John Canavan, who served as chief master sergeant at Nellis Air Force Base and was a former U.S. Army POW in World War II. They remained together until Canavan's death in 1996. Pamela Blake died of natural causes at a Las Vegas nursing facility on October 6, 2009, age 94. She was survived by her two children, and laid to rest next to Canavan at the Southern Nevada Veterans Memorial Cemetery. Pamela's son, Michael Stokey Jr., is also in show business. A former marine awarded the bronze star for valor while a combat correspondent attached to the 1st Marine Division Informational Services in Vietnam, Stokey became involved in filmmaking as a Military Technical Advisor. His credits include such noted films as *The Thin Red Line* (1998), *Born on the Fourth of July* (1989), *Heaven and Earth* (1993), and *Tropic Thunder* (2008).

LESLIE BROOKS (1922–)

KAY MORRELL HARRISON in *The Secret of the Whistler*.

Nebraska-born actress, dancer, model Leslie Brooks can best be described in one word: WOW! A beautiful, shapely blonde with striking catlike features, a pleasant singing voice, acting ability, poise, and sex appeal, she had the makings of a big star. Sadly, the fates and Harry Cohn decreed otherwise; and her potential would remain largely untapped. Although she proved herself a superb actress in a handful of memorable A-level supporting performances, Leslie's primary employer, Columbia, chose to waste her gifts in low-budgeters in which she often portrayed unsympathetic tormentors; elegant, yet dangerous women with evil intentions. To be fair, Leslie was a spectacular B movie bitch, but the films were beneath her. After the expiration of her Columbia contract in 1947, Brooks and Hollywood seemed to lose interest in one another. When negative personal headlines surfaced one year later Leslie's short movie career (1941–48) came to an end.

Born Virginia Leslie Gettman, on July 13, 1922, in Lincoln, Nebraska, she was the youngest of two daughters of Paul and Fern Cottle Gettman. The future star's interest in show business appears

Leslie Brooks.

to have been inherited from her father who was an amateur violinist and a successful radio engineer and technician. His career on the airwaves necessitated multiple moves during Virginia's youth. At one time or another, the family lived in Lincoln, Omaha, Chicago, and Fort Wayne, Indiana. For several years Virginia took up residence with her grandparents who owned a small hotel in Crofton, Nebraska. It was there the youngster made her first baby steps toward movie stardom by acting and singing in multiple grade school and junior high productions.

In 1937, her parents moved to Southern California and Virginia accompanied them. Enrolling in the renowned Hollywood High School she majored in algebra and English, dabbled in oil painting, played on the girl's basketball team, and sang with the glee club. By then the young miss was blossoming into a stunningly attractive beauty who turned heads. During her senior year she gained the attention of noted fashion photographer Tom Kelly who asked her to pose for a series of fashion photos. When one turned up in Stage magazine in 1940, offers began pouring in. Suddenly, the statuesque, 5 ft. 5 in. tall, blue-eyed redhead (now billed as Lorraine Gettman) was in demand as a model. After posing for noted photographer Paul Hesse, her lovely face and curvaceous figure adorned many magazine covers especially those of the mystery-detective genre. "My usual prop," she laughingly recalled in a 1945 interview, "was a jeweled dagger, dripping with blood that came out of a catsup bottle."

Her modeling successes soon attracted the attention of film talent scouts. In 1941, after a brief screen test, Metro-Goldwyn-Mayer selected Lorraine over 500 other competitors for an uncredited bit as a "Ziegfeld girl" in the film of the same name. She was then signed by Warners who instructed her to bleach her hair blonde. During the period of 1941–42, as Lorraine Gettman, she sang and danced as 1/6 of the "Navy Blues Sextette" in *Navy Blues* (1941) and *You're In the Army Now* (1941), and played uncredited bits as a bridesmaid in *The Body Disappears* (1941), a "Hollywood blonde" in *The Man Who Came to Dinner* (1942), and a chorus girl in *Yankee Doodle Dandy* (1942).

The "alarmingly pretty" 20-year-old had high hopes of scoring major success in the movies when Columbia purchased her contract and changed her name to Leslie Brooks in 1942. It was not to be. Cohn gave her a few decent grade-A assignments in support of his golden girl, Rita Hayworth, including the younger sister role in *You Were Never Lovelier* (1942) and as a dancer in a war-torn London Music Hall in *Tonight and Every Night* (1945), but mainly the Brooks name appeared on the bottom half of the double bill. More successful were her efforts as a model for various top companies, and as a pin-up girl for American forces in World War II.

Leslie made a total of 17 movies during her Columbia years

Charming candid of Leslie Brooks on the set of *Cigarette Girl*.

(1942–47) all but four low-budgeters in which she had feminine leads or second leads. Although she played sympathetic heroines in action adventures such as *Overland to Deadwood* (1942), *Underground Agent* (1942) and musicals like *Two Senoritas from Chicago* (1943), *I Love a Bandleader* (1945), *It's Great to Be Young* (1946), and *Cigarette Girl* (1947), Brooks became best known for portraying conniving, manipulative, and spiteful seductresses in melodramas and mystery thrillers. Her catlike features, graceful carriage, clipped delivery, and heavy-lidded "Bette Davis eyes" projected an icy yet alluring demeanor which made her perfect for villainous roles like the unfaithful spouse of a prisoner in *City Without Men* (1943), or the sexy, gold-digging wife of a murderous artist in *The Secret of the Whistler* (1946).

For obvious reasons Miss Brooks was a popular pin-up model.

Brooks' two best Columbia films cast her in largely unsympathetic characterizations, as the sarcastic sorority sister/murder suspect in the underrated mystery/comedy thriller *Nine Girls* (1944) and as the devious, scheming Maurine, the erstwhile friend and rival of dancer Rita Hayworth, in Charles Vidor's grade-A musical drama, *Cover Girl* (1944). The latter afforded the underrated actress an opportunity to sing, dance, and look magnificently bitchy in Technicolor.

In 1947, after playing a small role in support of George Brent and Joan Blondell in the intriguing comic thriller *The Corpse Came C.O.D.*, Leslie completed her initial Columbia contract. To the surprise of many, the studio chose not to renew it. Forced by monetary difficulties to take whatever work she could find, Leslie signed a short pact with low-budget studio Eagle-Lion for which she appeared in three pictures. One of them, *Blonde Ice* (1948), won her unexpected praise, and a place in Hollywood history. Although the film was an inferior production with chintzy production values and plot absurdities, Leslie's fascinatingly ruthless lead performance, as a cold-blooded black widow who marries then callously dispenses with her husbands, riveted critics and continues to fascinate film enthusiasts as one of the wickedest women of 1940s cinema.

Increasingly disenchanted with her status as a B movie queen, by the mid-1940s Brooks began focusing on her personal life. On January 6, 1945, she wed former actor and ex-Marine hero Donald Anthony Shay in a quiet ceremony at the office of a Beverly Hills police judge. Ten months later, on November 8, 1945, the newlyweds welcomed a baby girl, Leslie Victoria. Newspaper and movie magazines featured pictures of a radiant Leslie and her beautiful baby replete with interviews extolling the virtues of motherhood and marriage; but things were not nearly as idyllic as they appeared.

Rumors of trouble in the Shays' marriage began surfacing in 1947. By the time *Blonde Ice* premiered in theaters in May 1948, the couple had separated, a suit of divorce had been filed, and a battle royal was underway for custody of their young daughter. Throughout the summer of 1948 the dispute became uglier and uglier, generating headline-making charges and counter charges almost on a weekly basis. Shay accused his wife of being "an absentee mother." Leslie countered, charging Shay with physical abuse, and of being a deadbeat dad. She testified that Shay demanded she find him acting work at Columbia and insisted they turn their home "into a gambling resort, with my movie friends as customers." According to Brooks, she lost her contract with Columbia as a result.

In July 1948 Leslie's trauma entered a new phase. She won legal custody over the youngster who had been temporarily placed in the care of her paternal grandmother; but when she arrived to pick up the 2½-year-old, Shay had fled with the child. He was reportedly spotted in several states and countries, including New Zealand, during the next months. Bench warrants were issued, but Leslie's young daughter was never returned to her distraught mother.

The entire ordeal left personal and professional scars which would endure. In the midst of all the psychological stress Leslie fell in love with actor and real estate developer Russ Vincent whom she'd met on the set of *Blonde Ice*. The couple was married in 1950, and Leslie retired from show business to raise their three daughters: Dorena Maria, Gina L., and Darla R.

For understandable reasons Miss Brooks chose to steer clear of the limelight after her retirement; but when her husband became president of Hollywood's Mount Olympus Development, she surfaced briefly (along with her young daughters) to do a series of commercials for him. In 1970 she reemerged to make a filmic appearance, along with Russ, Mary Beth Hughes, John Agar, and Grant Williams, in the sexy melodrama *How's Your Love Life* (Independent), which Vincent wrote, directed, and produced. After Russ Vincent's death on January 30, 2001, the intensely private Miss Brooks was thought to have resided in Hawaii. Today, she lives in Southern California; a lovely setting for one of Hollywood's loveliest stars, and most underrated actresses.

Janis Carter (1913–1994)

Patricia Henley in *The Mark of the Whistler*.
Jean Lang in *The Power of the Whistler*.

Statuesque, blue-eyed, blonde actress and singer Janis Carter appeared to have a bright future as a musical stage star in 1941 when Twentieth Century-Fox lured her from Broadway with promises of fame and fortune in the movies. An intelligent, articulate, charismatic young beauty, Janis had a winning smile, acting ability, and a trained singing voice which could have been utilized to maximum effect in

Janis Carter.

the cinema. All she needed were proper vehicles; but that turned out to be the rub. After keeping her waiting for eight months for an initial film assignment, the studio shunted Janis into leads in low-budgeters, second leads, supporting roles, and bits in As. Her fortunes remained unimproved when she moved to Columbia and later to RKO. Although she persuasively played a wide range of characters, from sunny heroines to evil *femme fatales*, in over 30 features, neither the parts nor the films were substantial enough to make her a major star. In the early 1950s, Carter deserted the movies for a successful career as a hostess and pitchwoman on television.

Born Janis Ella Carter Dremann, on October 10, 1913, in Cleveland Ohio, the future B movie star was the only child of a businessman and his stay-at-home wife. Her parents were artistically-oriented; her father, John Henry Dremann, dabbled in painting and photography and her mother Grace was a singer and musician. When Janis was four, her father died suddenly (1918) leaving his widow to run his dry cleaning business which employed over 300 workers. Mrs. Dremann successfully operated the company until she remarried in 1924.

Following in the footsteps of her mother and grandmother, both singers, young Janis set her sights on a musical career. At age 10, she began vocal lessons while attending Chambers Grammar School, and then Shaw High School in Cleveland. After obtaining her high-school diploma in 1931, she enrolled in Western Reserve University (now Case Western Reserve University) where she continued her musical studies. While working as hostess and model at Higbee's department store and restaurant she studied voice under former Metropolitan Opera contralto Lila Robeson and became active in various collegiate activities. As a member of the University Players and choir Janis starred in three Noel Coward plays and sang opposite future film star John Howard in the opera *Dido and Aeneas*. The highlight of her college artistic efforts came in 1935 when she performed on radio as a soloist with the Cleveland Symphony Orchestra.

After graduating from Western in 1935 with dual degrees in English and music, Janis moved to New York where she hoped to find work as a singer. Changing her name to Janis Carter (her grandmother's maiden name), she worked as a hostess at Schrafts and earned extra cash as a church soloist while studying voice under the tutelage of noted vocal coach Edwin Swain. When she failed her dream audition with the Metropolitan Opera and was unable to find work singing on the radio, the intelligent, industrious young beauty took a job at an advertising agency, worked as a model for the well-known Powers and Conover Company (posing for cigarette, hosiery, soap, and fashion ads), and wrote radio scripts for such programs as *We the People* and *Gangbusters*.

Carter finally achieved a show-business breakthrough in 1938 when she won a small musical comedy part in the Broadway production of *I Married an Angel*. The following year she was selected by producer Buddy DeSylva (who referred to her as the "Dish") for a role in support of Ethel Merman and Bert Lahr in the popular musical comedy *DuBarry Was a Lady* (1939–40). In 1940 Carter had a role and a solo song in DeSylva's musical *Panama Hattie*. Prior to the show's opening, she married musician and dance band arranger Carl Prager on September 29, 1940 in New York.

While appearing in *Panama Hattie*, Carter was spotted by Darryl Zanuck who persuaded the photogenic young beauty to do a screen test at Twentieth Century-Fox's New York office. Her blonde good looks, dramatic, and musical abilities inspired the studio to offer her a contract. In February 1941, the Pragers headed for Hollywood in hopes Carter would have the opportunity to realize her potential as a film actress/singer; but Janis would soon regret her decision to abandon the stage. After keeping her waiting eight months for her first movie assignment (a loan to MGM to reprise her stage role in the studio's lavish adaptation of *I Married an Angel*), Zanuck all but squandered Carter's film potential by subsequently assigning her supporting roles in six medium-to-low-budget Fox features; non-entities like *Who is Hope Schuyler* (1942), *Just Off Broadway* (1942), and *Girl Trouble* (1942). In 1943, Janis' husband Carl helped negotiate the sale of her T.C.F. contract to Harry Cohn.

Columbia would be Janis Carter's home for the next seven years (1944–51). Like Zanuck, Cohn appeared content to cast his attractive employee in Bs and small featured parts which did nothing for her career. She was given a couple of interesting supporting roles in medium-budget productions, as a publicist in the screwball farce *A Woman of Distinction* (1950) with Rosalind Russell and as Randolph Scott's best girl in the action adventure *Santa Fe* (1951), but the remainder of Carter's Columbia features were minor leaguers in which she was most often seen as intrepid reporters and career girls: *The Mark of the Whistler* (1944), *One Mysterious Night*, (1944); or as scheming, predatory dames: *I Love Trouble* (1948), *Miss Grant Takes Richmond* (1949), *And Baby Makes Three* (1949), and *The Woman on Pier 13* a.k.a. *I Married a Communist* (on loan to RKO –1949).

Highlights of Carter's "Columbian" period included two minor *noirs* which cast her as sinister *femme fatales*. She was terrific as a remorseless murderer and blackmailer in the extremely interesting, but little-seen, thriller *Night Editor* (Columbia, 1946) and as a scheming, murderous woman who victimizes a down-on-his luck mining engineer in Richard Wallace's taut melodrama Framed (Columbia, 1947). Her performance in the latter was widely hailed and considered her finest on film.

In 1947, in between second-string villainous assignments, Cohn gave the former operatic singer what she thought would be a real opportunity, the singing part of Musetta, in Columbia's version of *La Boheme: Addio Mimi*, a.k.a. *Her Wonderful Lie*. Filmed in Italy, the operatic musical, which starred Metropolitan veterans Marta Eggerth and Jan Kiepura, had the potential to establish Carter as a film singer. Janis was ecstatic with the assignment until the studio decided to incorporate her aria into Eggerth's role.

In the late 1940s, the frustrated Janis began making headlines, but not ones which pertained to her career. In 1950, she was named correspondent in divorce proceedings between Howard Hughes' right-hand man Noah Dietrich and his wife Carol. Miss Carter denied the affair, but the publicity damaged her reputation and her decade-long marriage, which ended in 1951.

According to Janis, it was her love of music that prompted her to leave Hollywood and return to the East Coast after her Columbia contract expired in 1950. In a 1951, interview with reporter John L. Scott, published in the *Los Angeles Times*, she explained, "A singer who doesn't sing is very apt to lose her touch. I went into seclusion there [New York], found a good voice coach, and started studying again. Then the TV offers started rolling in. That meant learning a great many pages of dialogue and business for one shot performances. When you do three TV shows a week, you don't have much time for anything else . . ."

After a few months in New York doing singing gigs and appearing on television, RKO head Howard Hughes lured Carter back to films by promising to feature her in A-level pictures and allow her a chance to showcase her musical abilities. The result was three modestly successful films (1951–52) which gave her decent parts but did not reinvigorate her flagging movie career. Among them were Nicholas Ray's *Flying Leathernecks* (1951), which cast her as the loving wife of brave marine fighter pilot (John Wayne), and the western *The Half Breed* (1952), in which she sang and danced as a vocalist who operates a traveling all-girl revue. In 1954, Carter made what would be her last two theatrical films in Europe, the comedy

The Sergeant and the Spy and the melodramatic *Double Face*. Both had limited releases in America.

By the time her final films were produced, Carter was already being seen frequently on television, working as a pitchwoman for Revlon Cosmetics, and as a guest star on such noted comedy, drama, and variety series as *Suspense* (1953), *Center Stage* (1954), and *The Elgin Hour* (1955). In 1954 the vivacious blonde joined Bud Collyer for a two-year stint as co-host of the NBC quiz show *Feather Your Nest* and achieved a career highlight in 1955 when she recreated her Broadway performance in Panama Hattie for a television special.

On December 26, 1956, Carter gave up show business to marry New York lumber and shipping tycoon Julius Stulman in Houston, Texas. After her retirement the warm, outgoing Janis and her husband traveled the world and became active in various civic and charitable causes. In 1974 they moved to Longboat Key, Florida, near Sarasota, where Janis became a movie critic on radio. She also served as director of the Ringling Brothers Museum, and became an executive of the Asolo Center for the Performing Arts, and the Asolo Opera Guild. During the 1970s she appeared as an extra in two TV movies filmed in Sarasota. One of them, *The Great Wallendas* (1978), starred her old Columbia chum Lloyd Bridges.

By the late 1980s the Stulmans were dividing their time between homes in Florida and Durham, North Carolina. The still lovely Janis continued her patronage of the arts in both locations until her sudden death of a heart attack on July 30, 1994, at her home in Durham near Duke University. She was 80 years old. After her death her husband Julius and stepchildren established the Janis Carter Stulman Cultural Fund in her memory at Duke Medical Center. On October 10, 1994 (her birthday), a celebration of her life was held at her beloved Asolo Center.

In a revealing 1952 magazine interview with entertainment journalist Louis Berg, Miss Carter summarized her film career perfectly when she referred to herself as "a siren in Bs and a heel in As." She told Berg during her many years at Columbia she was often sent out as a "goodwill ambassadoress" visiting over 500 cities, and logging over 200,000 miles to promote pictures in which she never appeared. At the end of the interview, she added, "I have the finest collection of keys to various cities of any star. Not one key opened any Hollywood door!"

Lynn Merrick (1919–2007)

Joan Martin Sinclair in *Voice of the Whistler.*

One of filmdom's most attractive leading ladies, sultry, Texas-born Lynn Merrick made 40+ films in a 15-year movie career. A shapely, blue-eyed blonde with a dazzling smile and a quick wit, she had much in common with fellow Columbia contractees and *Whistler* alumnus Janis Carter and Leslie Brooks. All were talented, ambitious, and photogenic ex-models who began their careers on the stage. All were brought to Hollywood during the early 1940s, given a few A-level opportunities, but were mainly seen in low-budgeters often in unsympathetic characterizations as other women or *femme fatales*. Sadly, all became the subject of negative publicity during their Hollywood years which took a personal and professional toll.

Born Marilyn Llewelling, on November 19, 1919 (1921?), in Fort Worth, the future star was the daughter of a businessman. Her grandfather on her mother's side was Samuel Hugh McClure, a descendant of a prominent Fort Worth family and chief engineer at Hotel Texas. Her aunts were actresses Gladys McClure and Adrienne Ames. During Marilyn's formative years, the family moved several times. Although she attended grammar school at the Rose Haven Seminary in New Jersey, by the late 1930s the Llewellings were living on the West Coast where the youngster became enrolled at Beverly Hills High and the Westlake School for Girls. Even at the tender age of eight Marilyn knew she wanted to act. In a 1943 interview, she recalled one of her grade school teachers asking what she wanted to do with her life. According to Lynn, she replied, "'I want to be another Katharine Cornell. I want to be the greatest actress on earth!'"

Upon graduating from high school in 1937, the exceedingly attractive, 5 ft. 4 in. tall Merrick tried her hand at radio, worked as a model, and studied drama at the Max Reinhardt School while appearing in several musical and dramatic stage productions at the Bliss Hayden and Guy Bates Post Theaters in Los Angeles. In 1939,

Lynn Merrick.

a Warner Brothers talent scout signed her to a term contract. Little came of it except a couple of uncredited bits under the name Marilyn Merrick in *'Til We Meet Again* (Warners, 1940) and *Flight Angels* (Warners, 1940). When her Warners' pact expired, Marilyn worked for RKO, Universal, and Republic playing small roles in low-budgeters such as *Dr. Christian Meets the Women* (RKO, 1940) and *Ragtime Cowboy Joe* (Universal, 1940, notable as her first western). In 1941 Marilyn took a new name, Lynn Merrick, played her first lead feminine role, in the Republic western *Two Gun Sheriff*, and acquired a screen partner, up-and-coming cowboy star Don "Red" Barry.

After being named one of thirteen "Baby Stars of 1940" by the Motion Picture Publicist's Association, Merrick inked a two-year pact with Republic, which began in March 1941 and ended in March 1943. With the exception of the frothy, low-grade musical *Youth on Parade* (1942), in which she portrayed a college student, all of Lynn's Republic appearances were B westerns costarring Barry. Legend has it the diminutive Don was difficult to work with, but he and Merrick got on splendidly, and had great screen chemistry. All in all they would make 16 low-budget westerns, and in the process, become one of the most enduring B western romantic duos in cinematic history. Their pictures, which included *Desert Bandit* (1941), *Kansas Cyclones* (1941), *Arizona Terrors* (1942), *The Cyclone Kid* (1942), and *The Sombrero Kid* (1942), were smartly produced, excellently directed by George Sherman, and enthusiastically enacted. They were great examples of B genre filmmaking, but hardly the quality of material Merrick needed to establish her as a film actress of substance. A reviewer for *Variety* said it best when commenting on Merrick's performance in *Stagecoach Express* (1942): "Lynn Merrick looks helpless and pretty which is par for a western heroine."

Hoping to escape the sagebrush and saddle sores, in April 1943 Lynn left Republic and signed a long-term pact with Columbia where she would spend the remainder of her short filmmaking career. Unfortunately, her situation did not improve at her new home. If she harbored any illusions of improving her status, they were dashed when she was immediately cast in a long series of program pictures (16 in all), mostly musicals and whodunits, which doomed any prospects of superstardom. Although she looked sensational, and made the most of the limited acting opportunities afforded her as juvenile leading ladies in B musicals such as *Doughboys in Ireland* (1943), *Swing Out With the Blues* (1944), *Stars On Parade* (1944), *The Blonde from Brooklyn* (1945), or as unsympathetic schemers in second-string mystery/suspense films like *Boston Blackie Booked on Suspicion* (1945), *A Close Call For Boston Blackie* (1946), and especially *Voice of the Whistler* (1945), the projects were largely ignored by Hollywood's movers and shakers.

The one instance in which Merrick came close to scoring a breakthrough came in 1944 as the sarcastic drama student in Columbia's starlet-studded comic mystery, *Nine Girls* (1944). A whodunit

At the outset of her movie career Lynn appeared in 16 Republic B westerns starring Don "Red" Barry.

about a group of sorority sisters and their teacher who are detained at a vacation retreat while two inept policemen investigate the murder of a hated fellow student, it was full of gags, funny lines, and real suspense. As Eva Sharon, a pseudo-intellectual who imitates a Bryn Mawr/Katharine Hepburn accent, Merrick had a smart, sassy role she could sink her teeth in. After playing so many boring, one-dimensional heroines it must have been a treat for Lynn to have a decent storyline and humorous dialogue. Her delightful performance proved what an excellent actress she could be given the proper material.

By 1945, 24-year-old Lynn was becoming disenchanted with her movie career. Mired in Bs and distracted by a headline-making romance and marriage (1945) to 48-year-old veteran actor Conrad Nagel, she seemed to lose all interest. After making three undistinguished film appearances for Columbia, as a lady lawyer in the minor musical comedy *Dangerous Business* (1946), a muse in the lavish Rita Hayworth vehicle *Down to Earth* (uncredited bit, 1947), and a politician's wife with a sordid past in the melodramatic *I Love Trouble* (1948), she quietly completed her studio contract and told reporters she intended to end her filmmaking career.

Unlike many actors who retire, Merrick did not disappear from view. Quite the contrary. As her film career cooled her private life heated up. Less than one year after she wed the middle-aged Nagel the couple went through a very public separation and divorce (1948). When asked why the marriage had not succeeded, Nagel chalked the failure up to "the difference in our ages." Lynn was not as diplomatic. At her divorce hearing she stated Nagel had "been a bachelor too long," and "had no room in his life for a wife." After the break up Merrick became the subject of much romantic speculation when she was photographed at Hollywood nightspots with several rich, eligible bachelors, including golfer-turned-movie actor Joe Kirkwood Jr, Stuart Barthelmess, and John Ringling North, president of the Ringling Brothers & Barnum and Bailey Circus. In 1949, Lynn met former musician, would-be filmmaker Robert Goelet Jr., the playboy son and heir of one of America's richest men. After a whirlwind courtship, the two wed in Paris on October 25, 1949. A second marriage for both, it would be a match made in hell.

Four days after the nuptials, Goelet's Italian mother, the Duchess de Villarosa, was reportedly so distraught over the union she disinherited her son. On March 26, 1950, four months after the couple returned to America and set up housekeeping in West Los Angeles, the Goelets again made headlines when Lynn attempted suicide by ingesting ten Phenobarbital tablets after a domestic dispute. According to breathless press reports, Goelet summoned an ambulance, which spirited the actress to a Santa Monica hospital in time to save her life. Two days later the Goelets again made the papers when they were charged with assaulting a photographer who attempted to take a picture of Merrick as she left the hospital. Charges were eventually dropped against Lynn, but Robert was convicted of battery in April, 1950 and paid a fine. The couple divorced in 1956.

Lynn's disastrous marriages and the bad publicity associated with them had negative ramifications both on a personal and professional level. After emerging from her self-imposed retirement to do some television work in Europe, a few summer theater appearances, and a poorly received film, the low-budget indie thriller *Flugten Til Danmark* a. k. a. *Escape From Terror* (1955), Merrick decided to call it quits for good. For a time the former film actress continued to attract journalistic attention with a succession of wealthy suitors like European film producer Henry Lester and interior designer Paul Manno, but she never married again. In the 1960s, Merrick moved to New York and worked in the fashion industry. Between 1967 and 1974 she served as an executive field director for the Barbizon School of Modeling. Later, she took jobs at department stores in California and Florida. During the last decade of her life Lynn resided at a retirement village in West Palm Beach, Florida, where she died quietly in her sleep at age 87 on March 25, 2007. She had no children.

In a newspaper account published at time of Miss Merrick's death, her closest relative Phil Schoen told a reporter his second cousin had always been reluctant to talk about her Hollywood career, but toward the end of her life changed her attitude. He said, "I think she came to grips with it. You might as well enjoy it. She actually kept a small supply of pictures under her bed. If someone came over and asked for one, she'd sign it and give it to them."

Classic film fans are glad the ever-lovely Lynn Merrick finally came to appreciate her movie career. We sure did!

Karen Morley (1909–2003)

Eileen Blair in *The Thirteenth Hour.*

The most accomplished actress of all the leading ladies of the *Whistler* was surely Karen Morley. A thin, blonde leading lady with high cheekbones, hooded eyes, unlimited poise, a well-modulated

Karen Morley.

speaking voice, and abundant acting ability, she brought an intelligence and intensity to her film acting which remained evident throughout her two-decade-long, 40+ movie career. Entering films as an MGM contract player in 1930, early on Karen seemed destined for greatness after scoring several important film successes opposite some of Hollywood's most illustrious stars; but her potential would remain unfulfilled. An intellectual and a natural rebel, Morley sabotaged her career by taking controversial political stands, defying her studio bosses, and resisting some of the responsibilities of movie stardom. By the end of the 1930s her stature had diminished; and she was being relegated to lackluster character roles and low-budgeters. A decade later when her name turned up on Hollywood's infamous blacklist, the Morley film career came to an official end.

The third and youngest child of a poor farm family, the future star was born on December 12, 1909, in Ottumwa, a small factory town in southeastern Iowa. At age three she was adopted by prosperous realtor Walter Linton and his wife Elizabeth who named her Mildred. The youngster appeared born to be a performer. She recalled her youth in a 2002 interview with the author. "I had designs on a career in acting from a very early age, perhaps when I began grade school. It was at this time I appeared in my first play. It was community theater in Ottumwa, Iowa. I performed throughout my formative years, seventeen plays I believe, until we moved to Los Angeles when I was sixteen."

In 1925, the intelligent Mildred became a student at Hollywood High School where she graduated class valedictorian in 1927. After a year at U.C.L.A. studying drama and medicine one of her professors, noted actor/film director Irving Pichel, encouraged her to seek work in the movies. She left school, changed her name to Karen Morley, and started haunting casting offices. When her initial attempts to enter films proved unsuccessful, she played small roles, walk-ons, and served as a part-time usher at the famous Pasadena Community Playhouse. During her stage apprenticeship the brown-haired, reed-thin young woman honed her acting and vocal skills and made valuable contacts.

In 1929, Karen scored her first break in the movies when a talent agent caught her lead performance in PCP's production of *Fata Morgana*, and arranged an interview with Metro-Goldwyn-Mayer. Legend has it on the day of the appointment Robert Montgomery was on the Metro lot testing for the male lead in the Greta Garbo drama *Inspiration* (MGM, 1931), and requested a female to read lines to him. Karen was the girl at hand. Impressed by her poise and resonant voice, the film's director, Clarence Brown, reportedly hired the thin brunette on the spot for the key supporting role of Liane, the 18-year-old mistress of an aging playboy. Her performance was so good MGM signed her to a contract before the film's premiere.

Insisting she become a blonde, the studio introduced the starlet in a series of small, mostly undistinguished roles as jilted fiancées and long-suffering wives in such films as *Daybreak* (1931), *The Cuban Love Song* (1931), and *Never the Twain Shall Meet* (1931). Again luck intervened on Morley's behalf when independent producer Howard Hughes happened to see one her films and asked if he could test her for a key role in a gangster melodrama he was planning loosely based on the life of crime baron Al Capone. The result would be a melodramatic classic which contains Morley's most famous film characterization.

A sensational expose on the rise and fall of a notorious gangster, *Scarface, The Shame of a Nation* (United Artists, 1932) was an acclaimed landmark production which made stars of its four lead players: Paul Muni, Ann Dvorak, George Raft, and Karen Morley. As Poppy, the sexy, power-mad mistress of underworld kingpin Tony Camonte (Muni), Karen was a revelation. Her performance not only netted her rave reviews but changed her screen persona entirely. Gone were the naïve heroines which had marked her early film work and in their place intelligent, worldly, no-nonsense women. The role of Poppy (which remained Karen's favorite) also initiated the all-too-brief peak period of her career (1932–35) in which she landed several strong parts in top-drawer productions opposite many of Hollywood's most prestigious talents.

During her heyday Karen proved the depth of her ability in a wide variety of MGM films. She was especially fine as a swindler recruited by a veteran police detective to pose as a Russian countess in the lighthearted Barrymore brothers' melodrama *Arsene Lupin* (1932), the gold-digging wife of a Lincolnesque politician (Lionel Barrymore) in the dramatic *Washington Masquerade* (1932), a vamp who winds up dead in the murder/mystery *Phantom of Crestwood* (1932), the errant wife of German wrestler Wallace Beery in the drama *Flesh* (1933), an assistant to a highly unusual President of the U.S. (Walter Huston) in the mega-hit allegory *Gabriel Over the White House* (1933), and the wronged wife of a doctor (Edmund Lowe) in producer David O. Selznick's witty classic *Dinner At Eight* (1933).

At the height of her prestige and popularity Karen appeared to undermine her movie career by establishing an uncooperative

Karen and Wallace Beery in *Flesh* (MGM, 1932).

relationship with her home studio, and by being standoffish with the influential Hollywood press. A nonconformist who valued her privacy, and viewed the "trappings" and responsibilities of stardom with skepticism, Karen soon gained a reputation as ungrateful and contrary. She made matters worse by becoming attached to several left-leaning political organizations, and by defying Metro's "King" Louis B. Mayer by secretly marrying Hungarian director Charles Vidor on November 5, 1932, then giving birth to a son, Michael Karoly Vidor, on August 26, 1933. Years later Morley admitted her defiance had cost her. "After my marriage, Mayer loaned me out on contract to make several bad movies. He held a grudge."

In 1934, Karen chose not to renew her Metro contract and tried her hand freelancing. She had three more good opportunities: as an unhappy wife whose divorce wreaks havoc on her young son in the B+ feature *Wednesday's Child* (RKO, 1934), a communal farmer in King Vidor's memorable Depression-era drama, *Our Daily Bread*

(Independent, 1934), and a young woman torn between love for a poor coal miner and her yearning for a better life in Michael Curtiz's stark drama *Black Fury* (Warners, 1935), but her career declined as the decade progressed.

Her diminished status became apparent after she signed with Twentieth Century-Fox in 1935, then Paramount in 1937. Both studios gave Morley small A-level supporting parts, such as Shirley Temple's ill-fated mother in *The Littlest Rebel* (Fox, 1935) and as an Irish widow in the moving drama *Beloved Enemy* (Goldwyn, on loan from Paramount, 1936), but mainly utilized her in low-budgeters like *Thunder In the Night* (1935, Fox), *Last Train to Madrid* (Paramount, 1937), and *The Girl from Scotland Yard* (Paramount, 1937). Karen capped the decade with tiny supporting parts in two important films, *Kentucky* (Fox, 1938) and *Pride and Prejudice* (MGM, 1940).

Hoping to find greener pastures on the New York stage, Morley left Hollywood in 1941. Although she won critical favor in three Broadway plays, all were unsuccessful. By November, 1942 she was back on the West Coast trying to save her crumbling marriage and find film work. In January 1943, she divorced Vidor; and two years later, returned to the silver screen as a charming murderess in Republic's ultra-low-budget melodrama *Jealousy* (1945). In 1946, Karen signed a pact with Columbia where she made three B movies, the best of which was the gothic murder mystery *The Unknown* (1946), which cast her in the role of a psychotic traumatized by the murder of her betrothed. After leaving Columbia in 1947, Morley made only three more motion pictures. Her last was the sub-par western *Born to the Saddle* (Astor, 1953).

As her career waned during the mid-1940s Morley's interest and involvement in politics intensified. Encouraged by the new man in her life, gifted, politically active actor Lloyd Gough, she accelerated her activities in support of leftist causes, most involving civil rights and union organizing. Eventually, her activism placed her in the crosshairs of the increasingly powerful House UnAmerican Activities Committee who began investigating Communist influence in Hollywood following the end of World War II. After her name surfaced in Committee testimony Karen was blacklisted by the film industry who vowed not to employ alleged Communists or sympathizers. To be removed from the list and be employable required testifying before the committee and supplying names of purported Communists.

Miss Morley refused to implicate friends and colleagues when called to testify before the H.U.A.C. on November 13, 1952. Accompanied by her attorney, former Congressman Vito Marcantonio, the poised, dignified star smiled at the committee and gently cited her Fifth Amendment right against self-incrimination. "The idea that being blacklisted is heroic—forget it!" she recalled years later. "It was very ugly. It was terrible to see people fold." By failing to name names Karen officially ended a movie career which started so promisingly two decades before.

The end of her film career was not the end of the world for the indefatigable Miss Morley. By autumn 1952, she was back on Broadway appearing with Gough in the comedy *The Banker's Daughter*. In 1954, she resumed her political activities as the American Labor Party candidate for New York Lieutenant Governor, garnering 45,000 votes. When the blacklist ended in the 1960s, Karen and Lloyd, now husband and wife, returned to the West Coast where Lloyd became a featured player on television and his wife pursued other interests including aiding in the research and development of alternative medicines for cancer patients.

During the 1970s Morley was tempted out of semi-retirement to guest star on television in such popular series as *Kung Fu* (1973), *Kojak* (1973), and *Police Woman* (1975). After Lloyd Gough died of an aortic aneurysm in 1984, Karen limited her public appearances to occasional retrospectives on *Scarface* and *Pride and Prejudice*, videotaped commentary for Turner Classic Movies Archival project, and filmed segments for biographies on the lives of the Barrymores and Garbo. In 1999, the San Francisco International Film Festival saluted the veteran actress as part of their ongoing series honoring "filmmakers who have faced repression and censorship." Miss Morley died of pneumonia at age 93 on March 8, 2003, at the Motion Picture Country Home in Woodland Hills, California. She was survived by three extremely gifted grandchildren: business consultant M.C. Vidor, commercial director, screenwriter, actor John Vidor; and still life artist Molly Vidor.

GLORIA STUART (1910–2010)

Gloria Stuart.

ALICE WALKER in *The Whistler*.

Today, most film fans remember stage and screen actress Gloria Stuart for her remarkable Oscar-nominated comeback performance as 101-year-old Rose in the acclaimed mega-hit disaster film *Titanic* (1997), and for a handful of motion pictures she made afterward. Too few are aware of the lovely and talented young Gloria who arrived in Hollywood in 1931 and graced the silver screen for the next fifteen years appearing in over 40 motion pictures. Despite her stunning patrician beauty, driving ambition and genuine skill, Gloria was never able to ascend to the top rank of stardom on her first try. She had a handful of decent supporting opportunities in A-level pictures, but was mainly seen in decorative leading lady parts and second features which did not show her to advantage. By the mid-1940s, she became so unhappy with her movie career she abandoned filmmaking to pursue other artistic avenues. Lucky for us Gloria never gave up on the movies for good. In 1996, producer-director James Cameron lured the 86-year-old out of semi-retirement to play Rose and the rest is history.

Born Gloria Frances Stewart, on July 4, 1910, in Santa Monica, California, the future star was eldest of three children born to attorney Frank Stewart and his wife Alice, a former postal clerk. An intelligent, precocious child, Gloria harbored ambitions of doing something "big and great" with her life at an early age. Upon graduation from Santa Monica High School in 1927, she entered the University of Southern California at Berkeley majoring in Greek philosophy. There she developed an intense interest in acting as a part of the Berkeley Players, and met sculptor Gordon Newell. They were married in 1930 and moved to Carmel, a haven for artists, writers, and musicians.

In Carmel (1930–31) Gloria honed her acting skills, making several appearances at the prestigious Theater of the Golden Bough where she attracted the attention of actor-director Morris Ankrum who cast her as Olivia in his production of Shakespeare's *Twelfth Night* at Gilmor Brown's famed Pasadena Playhouse. In 1931, Ankrum returned to Carmel to direct Gloria as Masha in the Bough's acclaimed production of Chekhov's *The Seagull*, and then asked her to reprise the role at Brown's private theater, The Bank Box. On the night of her debut performance she received offers of film work from Paramount and Universal studios. Financially challenged and inexperienced, she signed both contracts.

A protracted dispute between the studios for Gloria's services was finally settled by the flip of a coin. Much to her eventual regret Universal won the toss. Armed with high hopes, and Universal's extravagant promises to showcase her talent in topnotch projects, the lovely 5 ft. 5 in. tall, hazel-eyed blonde Gloria Stuart (her name shortened to better fit a theater marquee) began a seven-year contract in 1932. In the period 1932–35 she would appear in 23 motion pictures for Universal or on loan. Her appealing performances and good looks caught the eye of filmgoers, but her career at Universal never took off. The studio gave Stuart a handful of substantive supporting assignments in good films, and loaned her to other studios for some decent leading lady parts, but mainly wasted her in nondescript roles (as adoring wives and girlfriends), or in Bs which failed to exploit her proven dramatic ability.

Her notable supporting credits included two James Whale horror classics, *The Old Dark House* (1932) and *The Invisible Man* (1933). The former cast her as an upper-crust young wife who must spend the night in a sinister Wales estate inhabited by a bizarre family; and the latter had her as a bewildered young woman engaged to a reckless scientist whose experiments transform him into a megalomaniacal murderer. Her other notable roles of the Universal period were: a school teacher in love with a brave air mail pilot in the John Ford actioner *Air Mail* (1932), the daughter of the master of a sinister castle in the eerie B murder mystery *Secret of the Blue Room* (1933), and an errant wife murdered by her Austrian doctor husband in James Whale's melodramatic *A Kiss Before the Mirror* (1933).

On loan Stuart had three showy leading lady roles. For Warners she was James Cagney's main squeeze in the Oscar-nominated *Here Comes the Navy* (1934) and Dick Powell's best girl in Busby Berkeley's lavish musical *Gold Diggers of 1935*. For Goldwyn she was an enslaved princess in the million-dollar musical comedy *Roman Scandals* (1934). Unfortunately for Gloria the parts she didn't get were more impressive than those she played. They included leads in two critically acclaimed Universal dramas, *Only Yesterday* (1934) and *Little Man, What Now?* (1935), both went to Margaret Sullavan, and the prize role of Hermia in Max Reinhardt's 1934 stage production of *A Midsummer Night's Dream* eventually played by Olivia de Havilland when Universal refused to allow Stuart to do it. In 1933, Gloria became one of the founding members of the new Screen Actors Guild, the first of several important political associations she would have in her life.

While working on *Roman Scandals*, Gloria fell in love with

scriptwriter Arthur Sheekman (*Duck Soup, Monkey Business, Kid Millions*, etc.). She divorced Newell in May 1934 and married Sheekman two months later (July 29, 1934). The happy Sheekmans would remain husband and wife for the next 44 years until Arthur's death. They would have one daughter, Sylvia, born on June 10, 1935.

In the summer 1935 Arthur helped the frustrated Gloria extricate herself from Universal. In October she signed a four-year pact (1935–39) with Twentieth Century-Fox, who treated her with similar indifference. After a promising start as the young countess in the Freddie Bartholomew/Victor McLaglen adventure *Professional Soldier* (1936) and as the devoted wife of famed Dr. Samuel Mudd in John Ford's splendid drama *Prisoner of Shark Island* (1936), the studio followed Universal's lead and cast Stuart in routine character roles in As and a long series of feminine leads in Bs. Although she performed admirably in support of Shirley Temple and the zany Ritz Brothers in such films as *Poor Little Rich Girl* (1936), *Rebecca of Sunnybrook Farm* (1937), and *The Three Musketeers* (1939), and in a whole host of entertaining, fast-paced programmers like *Three Hours to Kill* (1936), *The Crime of Dr. Forbes* (1936), *Change of Heart* (1937), and *Time Out for Murder* (1938), none advanced her career in the slightest.

Hoping to make her mark on Broadway, Gloria left Hollywood in 1939. When that did not pan out in 1941, she found work in radio and regional theater before reentering films in 1943. After five low-budgeters (including her excellent turn as Alice in Columbia's *The Whistler*), Stuart decided to give up the movies and turned her creative energies in new directions, including gourmet cooking, decoupage, and oil painting. In the mid- to late 1940s the multi-talented Gloria became one of Hollywood's most prominent hostesses, then purchased a small antique shop on Hollywood's La Cienega Boulevard where she displayed and sold her renown decoupage and other art objects. In 1961, 42 of her oil paintings were displayed in a highly successful one-woman show at the prestigious Hammer Galleries in New York.

Following her husband's death in 1978, Gloria resumed acting in character roles both on the big and small screens. Her assignments ranged from bits to small, inconsequential supporting roles in theatrical releases like *My Favorite Year* (MGM, 1982), *Mass Appeal* (Universal, 1984), and *Wildcats* (Warners, 1986); made-for-television movies such as *Irwin Allen's Adventures of a Queen* (1975), *In the Glitter Palace* (1977), *Merlene of the Movies* (1981); and the TV series *The Waltons* (1975) and *Murder, She Wrote* (1987). In 1983, along with her companion, famed master printer, graphic designer Ward Ritchie Gloria, she became involved in designing, illustrating, and printing handmade collector's books of poetry and art. Purchasing her own printing press she turned out several important works eventually housed in the Victoria and Albert Museum in London, the Getty Center in Brentwood, California, and the Library of Congress.

Four months after Ritchie's death in 1996, 86-year-old Gloria Stuart was again lured back to films by producer-director James Cameron, who hired her for the coveted supporting role of Old Rose in the star-studded *Titanic*. The lavish epic became the most successful box-office film of all time and won multiple Academy Award nominations, including one for Gloria's sensitive performance. Although she lost the Oscar, Miss Stuart won several honors for her role in *Titanic*, including the coveted Screen Actors Guild Award for best supporting actress. Most importantly, the octogenarian won the respect of the film industry, and realized her lifelong dream of doing something "big and great."

In demand, Gloria continued to work in film and television well into her 90s. Among her latter portrayals were the eccentric grandmother in *The Love Letter* (DreamWorks, 1999), the profane bag lady in Wim Wenders' *noir* thriller *The Million Dollar Hotel* (Lions Gate, 2000), and the mother of a C.I.A. agent in the TV comedy *My Mother the Spy* (2000). Her last film to date was a small role in Wenders' evocative drama *Land of Plenty* (Emotion, 2004). In 1999, Gloria, aided by her talented daughter Sylvia Sheekman Thompson (the author of multiple bestselling cookbooks), shared her exceptional life story in a witty, irreverent autobiography appropriately titled *I Just Kept Hoping*.

On July 4, 2010, acclaimed actress, oil painter, gourmet cook, book designer, printer, pioneer social activist, and world-class dreamer Gloria Stuart added yet another amazing accomplishment to her impressive resume when she celebrated a century of life. She passed away less than three months later, on September 26, 2010, at her

Claude Rains and Gloria Stuart in James Whale's *The Invisible Man* (Universal, 1933).

From left to right: Bill Paxton, Gloria, and Suzy Amis in James Cameron's *Titanic* (Paramount, 1997).

home in West Hollywood. She was survived by her daughter, four grandchildren, 12 great grandchildren, and millions of fans and admirers who were entertained and inspired by her life and work.

THE CHARACTER PLAYERS:

JIM BANNON (1911–1984)

Jim Bannon.

JERRY MASON in *The Thirteenth Hour*.

Tall, dark-haired, pleasant-looking Jim Bannon was a leading man and character actor who appeared in over 50 feature films, primarily Bs, from 1944–65. Born on April 9, 1911, in Kansas City, Missouri, the lanky, resonant-voiced Jim was a star athlete at Rockhurst College before entering radio as a sportscaster at KCKN in Kansas City, then later KNOX in St. Louis. In 1938, he landed in California where he found success as an announcer, narrator, and actor on several notable radio programs. To make extra money the well-built young man worked as a movie stuntman. In 1944, he was asked to do a screen test for Columbia, who signed him to a term contract.

During 1944–47 Bannon played leads, second leads, and character parts (as both heroes and villains) in 16 Columbia motion pictures all save one Bs. His most notable early starring role was as private detective Jack Packard in the short-lived, radio-inspired *I Love a Mystery* series, which consisted of three films: *I Love a Mystery* (1945), *The Devil's Mask* (1946), and *The Unknown* (1946). He was also memorable as an aggressive reporter trying to unravel a baffling murder case in *The Missing Juror* (1944), a brave submarine commander killed in a World War II kamikaze raid in the actioner *Out of the Depths* (1945), a freight company proprietor falsely accused of crimes in the Charles Starrett "Durango Kid" oater *Trail of Laredo* (1948), and a crooked cop in two films, the B+ *noir* thriller *Johnny O'Clock* (1947) and the comic melodrama *The Corpse Came C.O.D.* (1947).

After his departure from Columbia Jim appeared as Christopher Royal, a Canadian Mountie battling a criminal gang, in the 12-episode Republic serial *Dangers of the Canadian Mounted* (1948), then dyed his hair red to play what would be his most famous part, the comic book western hero "Red Ryder" in a four-film series produced by poverty row's Eagle-Lion. As a result of his well-received Red Ryder appearances, Bannon became effectively typecast as a western actor.

During the early to mid-1950s Jim played leads, second leads, and featured roles in a variety of second-string westerns. Among them were *Sierra Passage* (Monogram, 1951), *The Great Missouri Raid* (Paramount, 1951), *Rodeo* (Monogram, 1952), *The Great Jessie James Raid* (Lippert, 1953), *Jack Slade* (Allied Artists, 1953), and *War Arrow* (Universal International, 1953). When movie offers dwindled, the resilient star began working as a character player on TV, primarily in westerns and adventures. In 1955 he had a costarring role as the uncle of a young boy who keeps a wild horse as his companion in the Gene Autry-produced kiddie series Adventures of Champion. He continued to work in television and films, primarily in tiny supporting roles and bits, until 1965.

During his later years Bannon resided in Plano, Texas and Scottsdale, Arizona. In 1975 he penned an autobiography (largely consisting of correspondence) entitled *The Son That Rose in the West*. He moved back to California prior to his death in Ventura on July 28, 1984, of emphysema-related problems. Jim Bannon was married twice. His first wife, actress Bea Benaderet (1938–50), bore him two children. The eldest, John "Jack" Bannon, is an actor.

TREVOR BARDETTE (1902–1977)

THE BUM IN THE NEXT BED in *The Whistler*.
ARNOLD in *The Return of the Whistler*.

With a birth name like Abraham Lincoln one might logically presume Arkansas-born, California-bred character actor Trevor Bardette would have played brave heroic types on the silver screen. Of course, that would be wrong, very wrong. Although there were more than a few sympathetic characterizations in Bardette's 200+ film resume (even a part as President Lincoln's cousin) his main claim to fame was as a film bad guy. His darkly chiseled features, heavy brows, and prominent nose made him look shifty, sinister, and Hollywood capitalized. Bardette's list of credits is something akin to a hall of shame chockfull of malefactors of all shapes and variations from treacherous counterfeiters, to sadistic sea captains, from vengeful ranchers, and worthless cowpokes, to dishonest businessmen, venomous sheiks to Mexican bandits, and other assorted convicts, henchmen, and agitators.

Bardette was born on November 19, 1902, in Nashville, Arkansas. Not much is known about his early life. Apparently his family moved to the West Coast when he was a youngster; and it was there he became involved in stage work. Taking the name Trevor Bardette he began appearing in small character roles and bits in both A- and B-level movies in the latter 1930s. Early on, he became established as a cinematic blackheart. Notable early roles included the vengeful brother of a murdered student in the dramatic *They Won't Forget*

Trevor Bardette.

(Warners, 1937), a murderous medium's servant killed by his boss in the whodunit *Charlie Chan at Treasure Island* (Twentieth Century-Fox, 1939), a warring Huron chieftain in the adventure *The Deerslayer* (Cardinal, 1943), a treacherous extortionist in *Dick Tracy* (RKO, 1945), head of a counterfeiting ring in the crime thriller *Secret Service Investigator* (Republic, 1948), and an honorable Indian in the oater *Apache Chief* (Lippert, 1949). Other memorable Bardette parts included innumerable turns (mostly villainous) in B westerns starring Allan "Rocky" Lane, Charles Starrett, Roy Rogers, Monte Hale, Gene Autry, and Rex Allen.

Bardette also had small parts in several memorable high end features during the late 1940s and early 1950s such as *The Big Sleep* (Warners, 1946), *The Sea of Grass* (MGM, 1947), *Lone Star* (MGM, 1952), *Macao* (RKO, 1952), *Johnny Guitar* (Republic, 1954), *Run for Cover* (Paramount, 1955), and *The Rack* (MGM, 1956). His last film appearance was an uncredited bit in the western *Mackenna's Gold* (Columbia, 1969). Beginning in 1952, this classic movie knave took his treachery to the small screen; and continued to appear on TV for the next two decades mostly in western and adventure series. Trevor Bardette died at age 75 in Los Angeles on November 28, 1977.

MONA BARRIE (1908–1964)

LINDA VAIL in *The Secret of the Whistler.*

Elegant, soulful-eyed actress and singer Mona Barrie became a noted movie character player after an unsuccessful try as a leading lady. Signed by Fox in 1933, the British-born, Australian-educated, stage-trained brunette was originally groomed to be a feminine star in the mold of Kay Francis whom she resembled. Cast in second leads in As and leads in Bs often as refined, aristocratic wives and/or "other women," she won raves but somehow failed to click with the public. Despite her obvious gifts (in both drama and comedy), pleasant speaking voice, and camera-friendly good looks, Fox dropped her in 1936. Barrie tried freelancing, but her movie career suffered a steady decline. By the end of the 1930s she was working exclusively in Bs and character parts. She continued to descend on cast lists throughout the 1940s until her early retirement in 1953.

Born Mona Barlee Smith in London, on December 14, 1908 (1909?), her mother, Jessie Barlee was a light opera singer/actress who gained a following in London around the turn of the century. Although records of Barrie's early life are sketchy, a clipping stated the family moved to Sydney, Australia, when Mona was in her early teens. By then the attractive youngster was already studying voice, piano, and dance in hopes of following in her mother's footsteps. At 16, she made her professional debut as a ballet dancer and adopted the name Mona Barrie.

Mona Barrie.

Mona continued to perform as a solo dancer while appearing in multiple plays and musicals in Australia and in London in the late 1920s to early 1930s. Among her stage credits were leads in the comedies *Hay Fever, Let Us Be Gay,* and *Private Lives*; a drama, *Autumn Crocus*; and a Noel Coward operetta, *Bitter Sweet* (1929). In 1933, while en route to London to appear in a play, Mona made a fateful stop in New York to see friends. During her stay, she met a Fox studio executive who arranged a screen test. Before her ship sailed for England 25-year-old Mona had affixed her name to a Fox movie contract.

During the next two years Fox groomed the 5 ft. 5 in. tall, 114-pound, hazel-eyed Barrie for stardom, utilizing her as second leads in several notable medium-to-high-end productions while giving her leads in lesser films. Possessed with an innate elegance and sophistication Mona contributed convincing performances in a wide range of assignments. Her best roles at Fox cast her as "other women." She was excellent as a rich girl whose dowry is used by an impoverished southern plantation family to restore their faded grandeur in the post–Civil War drama *Carolina* (Fox, 1934), an aristocratic Englishwoman who marries a World War I vet only to find he loves someone else in the drama *All Men Are Enemies* (Fox, 1934), the fiancée of a murdered inventor in the entertaining mystery *Charlie Chan in London* (Fox, 1934), a beautiful but destructive opera student who victimizes a Broadway producer in the musical drama *King of Burlesque* (Fox, 1935), the ex-flame of a voice coach who competes with his star pupil for his affections in the musical biopic *One Night of Love* (on loan to Columbia, 1934), and a jewel thief posing as a archeologist's daughter in the comic melodrama *Here Comes Trouble* (Twentieth Century-Fox, 1936).

As a way of determining if Mona could "carry" a picture, Fox also placed the budding movie actress in several B features in starring and costarring roles. She had top billing as a snoopy London-based newspaperwoman who becomes involved in a murder case in *Ladies Love Danger* (1935) and as a desperate wife attempting to locate documents proving her husband's innocence in the international intrigue programmer *Mystery Woman* (1935). On loan to Universal, Mona was costarred with stalwart action hero Jack Holt in three entertaining dualers, the best of which was the aerial adventure *Storm Over the Andes* (1935) in which she portrayed an officer's wife living in Bolivia who becomes the object of an American flyer's affection. A favorite of critics, a typical Barrie review was offered by *Variety* who panned *Storm Over the Andes* and its male star, but reserved praise for its leading lady who "doesn't have so much to do, but looks well doing it." Unfortunately, none of Mona's excellent notices seemed to help her career.

Oblivious to her potential and critical nods, Fox dropped Barrie from its roster in 1936. The reasons were unclear. Some felt she was not glamorous enough, or distinctive enough to be the Kay Francis-type star Fox envisioned. Others thought her secret 1933 marriage to Canadian investor Paul Macklin Bolton was the deciding factor. Apparently, the intensely private young starlet never bothered to inform her employer or the nosy Hollywood press she was married. The Bolton/Barrie union would last over 30 years until Mona's death. The couple had no children.

In spite of Fox's disinterest the demand for the freelancing Mona's services remained strong for the next few years. During the period 1936–42 she would make 25 motion pictures of all genres and budgets for most of the major and minor studios. Although she was costarred in a handful of Bs the vast majority of her parts were supporting assignments often as intelligent socialites whose sophistication was a mask for corruption and villainy. Her notable roles of the period included a phony baroness/spy who chases an heiress and a reporter across Europe in search of a valuable map in the A-level comedy *Love On the Run* (MGM, 1936), the sophisticated wife of a young man pursuing another woman in the comic *I Met Him in Paris* (Paramount, 1937), a famed actress linked to a young married dancer in the musical *Something to Sing About* (Grand National, 1937), a glamorous troublemaker who breaks up a marriage in *Love, Honor, and Behave* (Warners, 1938), and a bewildered producer's wife forced to listen to a bumbling scriptwriter's crazy ideas in the W.C. Field's Hollywood spoof *Never Give a Sucker an Even Break* (Universal, 1941).

By 1940, Mona was appearing almost exclusively in programmers. Her descent into Bs did nothing for her career but did provide a few interesting parts which she infused with her unique blend of class and commitment. She had showy murder suspect roles in several entertaining B mysteries during the early 1940s. Among them were *Who Killed Aunt Maggie?* (Republic, 1940), *Murder Among Friends* (Twentieth Century-Fox, 1941), *Ellery Queen and the Murder Ring* (Columbia, 1941), *A Tragedy at Midnight* (Republic, 1942), and *The Strange Case of Dr. Rx* (Universal, 1942). Mona's other significant B roles included: the wife of a murdered businessman who helps clear an innocent chap accused in his death in *Today I Hang* (PRC, 1942), a pioneer wife who loses her husband on the road west in Buck Jones' last adventure film *Dawn on the Great Divide* (Monogram, 1942), and, memorably, as a gangster moll in the crime comedy *Love, Honor, and Oh Baby* (Universal, 1940). Barrie was reportedly delighted with her role in the latter which afforded her an opportunity to sing "Wasn't It You." In a 1940, interview the witty star commented on her profession and the unusual role. "Let's face it, chum. What intelligent woman can't endure leg art in the morning, machine gun massacres in the afternoon, and small talk and smoky Scotch in the evening! None that I'd care to know."

In between film assignments busy Mona made time for her first love, the stage. In 1937 she made her Broadway debut at the Center Theater in the romantic musical *Virginia* (60 performances), toured Australia and New Zealand in several plays (1939–40), then returned to Broadway briefly in 1943 to play the feminine lead opposite Leon Ames in the unsuccessful farce *Slightly Married*.

Mona continued to play featured roles in motion pictures (mainly Columbia Bs) throughout the remainder of the 1940s and into the 1950s. Five of her last 12 features were entertaining entries in the *Lone Wolf*, *Crime Doctor*, *I Love a Mystery*, *Whistler*, and *Rusty* series. Barrie's other significant credits included the spy thriller *Storm Over Lisbon* (Republic, 1944), the grade-A drama, *Cass Timberlane* (MGM, 1947), and the domestic comedy *The First Time* (Columbia, 1952). Perhaps the most interesting role Barrie played toward the end of her film career was as a patroness who withdraws support for a pianist when he weds a troublemaking dancer in producer/actor Hugo Haas' melodrama *Strange Fascination* (Columbia, 1952). Mona's last film appearance was a bit role as a tourist in the minor Glenn Ford adventure *Plunder of the Sun* (Warners, 1953).

Barrie chose to retire from show business during the 1950s and devote her time to traveling and social activities. During the latter 1950s, ill health plagued her. A clipping reported the Boltons' move from the East to West Coast in 1963; and on June 27, 1964, Mona died in Los Angeles of cancer. She was 55 years old. She was buried in the Bolton family plot in Knox United Church Cemetery in Agincourt, Ontario, Canada. Her husband, Paul (1899–1966), joined her two years later. Although she never won significant awards during her lifetime Mona Barrie was eventually honored with a star on the Hollywood Walk of Fame (6140 Hollywood Boulevard), an overdue tribute to a lovely and talented actress who dazzled the critics and continues to entertain classic film connoisseurs with her consummate skill intermingled with wit, elegance, and charm.

TALA BIRELL (1907–1958)

Tala Birell.

CONSTANTINA IVANESKA in *The Power of the Whistler.*

For those forever lamenting the current spate of sequels and celebrity clones meet Tala Birell, a glamorous blonde Romanian-born, stage-trained actress, one of several Garbo look-alikes brought to

Hollywood in the early 1930s to capitalize on the popularity of the legendary star. Like the others she ultimately failed to click but unlike most she did have authentic ability which she demonstrated in character roles in both high- and low-end productions.

The youngest of five children of a Serbian businessman and a Polish baroness Tala was born Nathalie Bierl on September 10, 1907 (1908?) in Bucharest. Educated in Berlin, she began appearing on the stage while attending school. Her beauty and acting ability eventually attracted the attention of Max Reinhardt who engaged her as an understudy to Marlene Dietrich in his hit play *es Leight in der Luft* (*The Light in the Sky*). When Dietrich left the production, Bierl took the play to Vienna. As a protégé of Reinhardt, Miss Bierl played a variety of stage roles across Europe, and made four German-language films (as Thala Birell) beginning in 1926.

Universal brought "Thala" to Hollywood, renamed her Tala Birell, and signed her to a term contract in 1930. Dubbed as "the new Garbo," the 5 ft. 5 in. tall, blue-eyed, fair-haired actress was given a star buildup then cast in two films. When the last of them, the ludicrous jungle programmer, *Nagana* (1933), flopped she was summarily dropped from the Universal roster; but turned up one year later in a 9th billed character role as a temperamental film actress in the mildly diverting musical *Let's Fall in Love* (Columbia, 1933). Birell's humorous homage to her own Garboesque screen image in the latter delighted critics and won her a Columbia contract (1934–35).

The elegant, charismatic Birell played foreigners and exotics for the next fifteen years in both major and minor productions. Her roles ranged from tiny featured parts to leads and second leads. Among her more memorable 1930s assignments were the loyal girlfriend of an alcoholic newspaperman who tries to keep him sober in *The Captain Hates the Sea* (Columbia, 1934), a beautiful pickpocket who almost fries in the electric chair when she's framed for murder in *She's Dangerous* (Universal, 1937), and a glamorous gold-digger in the romantic comedy *Josette* (Twentieth Century-Fox, 1938).

In 1939, Tala temporarily ceased making films and turned her attention to the theater. After making her second Broadway appearance, in *My Dear Children* (1939–40) starring John Barrymore (her first was *Order Please* in 1934), she remained on the East Coast for the next two years appearing in various stage productions and becoming a U.S. citizen.

Returning to Hollywood in 1942 an older looking Birell appeared in tiny parts in a few A-class films such as *The Song of Bernadette* (Twentieth Century-Fox, 1943), *Mrs. Parkington* (MGM, 1944), and *Song of Love* (MGM, 1947), but was mainly seen in supporting roles in low-graders like the espionage meller *Seven Miles from Alcatraz* (RKO, 1942), the *Lone Wolf* mystery *One Dangerous Night* (Columbia, 1943), and the adventure serial *Jungle Queen* (Universal, 1945). Birell's best 1940s parts came in three programmers: as a mad scientist's assistant who helps put an end to his evil experiments in PRC's horror *The Monster Maker* (1944), a woman who awaits execution for mistakenly killing a detective in the prison melodrama *Girls of the Big House* (Republic, 1945), and a starring role as a captive forced to "entertain" Japanese and Nazi officers in the World War II melodrama *Women in the Night* (Film Classics, 1948).

In 1948, Birell left Hollywood and took up residence with her mother in Munich. In 1951, she was appointed by the U. S. Army to organize theatrical productions for G.I's serving in Europe. She also appeared occasionally in European stage productions and on German television in the 1950s. In 1955, she acted in two television series which would air in America, *The Orient Express* and an episode of *Flash Gordon*, both filmed in Berlin.

Tala Birell was diagnosed with terminal cancer in 1957 and died on February 17, 1958 in the U. S. military hospital at Landstuhl, Germany. She was survived by her mother, siblings, and a few nieces and nephews. She is buried in the Bierl family plot in Marquartstein in Bavaria.

JOHN CALVERT (1911–)

EDDIE DONNELLY in *The Mark of the Whistler.*

Dark and distinguished John Calvert cut a dashing figure in over a dozen Hollywood motion pictures during the 1940s, but film acting was not his overriding interest or his main claim to fame. One of the world's foremost magicians/illusionists, Calvert's magic

John Calvert.

shows are the stuff of legends thrilling and baffling audiences around the world for over seven decades and counting. His career as a moviemaker: (thespian, director, writer, and producer) pales in comparison, but classic film fans still remember this "magic man" as a versatile actor, adept at playing both sophisticated heroes and dastardly villains.

Madren Elbern "John" Calvert was born in New Trenton, Indiana, on August 5, 1911, the son of Elbern F. and Naomi P. Calvert. A natural entertainer, he began doing magic tricks at age eight after his father took him to see famed magician Howard Thurston in Cincinnati. By the time he graduated from high school John had been doing illusions for almost a decade and was determined to combine his love for performing with gainful employment. While attending college he approached a local auto dealer in Connersville, Indiana, with an idea for increasing his sales: magic tricks. The results were multiple highly publicized stunts, the most spectacular of which was a "blindfolded" Calvert driving around town in a Chevrolet. By the early 1930s the young illusionist had gained fame throughout Indiana and Kentucky, and was dreaming of bringing his magic act to an even greater audience. That dream became a reality after John landed in Hollywood in 1939.

Calvert recalled his initial experiences in the film capital in a 1998 interview with film historian Robert Kendall published in *Classic Images*. He said while performing at Hollywood's Masquer's Club he was approached by famed hostess Elsa Maxwell who wanted him to entertain at a private party. Three days after turning her down, he was contacted by columnists Louella Parsons and Hedda Hopper who promised to promote his career if he played the movie land party circuit. Calvert eventually relented. His debut event was attended by many influentials who offered him work in and out of the movies. After headlining at Hollywood's Las Palmas Theater, Calvert fulfilled one of his fondest ambitions to perform on Broadway.

John's first film appearance came in 1941 when he was paid $600 a day as a hand double for Clark Gable in the adventure *Honky Tonk* (MGM, 1941). During the early 1940s Calvert had tiny roles as a thief in *Ali Baba and the Forty Thieves* (Universal, 1944) and a magician in two films: the World War II actioner *Bombardier* (RKO, 1943) and the juvenile delinquent drama *Are These Our Parents?* (Monogram, 1944). Tall, distinguished, and supremely confident, Calvert exuded an innate poise and charisma which made him a natural for the movies. With his sparkling eyes and easy smile he could be believably cast in both heroic and villainous parts.

Recognizing his potential as an actor, Harry Cohn signed the entertainer to a term contract in 1944. For the next two years, Columbia provided Calvert with steady work beginning with the acclaimed melodrama *The Mark of the Whistler*, a tale of crime's unintended consequences, directed stylishly by young William Castle. As Eddie Donnelly, a man consumed with hatred and vengeance for wrongs perpetrated on his family, Calvert was terrific. Critics and industry types stood up and took note. *Film Daily* called Calvert's work "convincing." *The Hollywood Reporter* said he came off "like a veteran with his first try." Among those singing his praises was 50+ year-old columnist Hedda Hopper whom John reportedly dated.

Eager to capitalize on his good reviews Cohn placed Calvert in supporting roles in four more B films in 1945. In all but one he played heavies. He was a sleazy saloon proprietor in *The Return of the Durango Kid*, an evil western town boss in *Lawless Empire*, and a shifty dance club operator in *Ten Cents a Dance*. In the drama *Youth On Trial* Calvert also portrayed a nightclub operator, this time one with ethics which cost him his life.

Calvert left Columbia in 1946 and returned to performing his increasingly elaborate magic act in stage shows across the United States and abroad. As his fame grew Hollywood took note again. In 1947, he was approached by independent producer Philip Krasne to play the lead in a revised series of movies based on Michael Arlen's famed private detective known as the Falcon. A fan of the original RKO George Sanders/Tom Conway series which was discontinued in 1946, Calvert accepted the offer and returned to the film capital to play bon vivant crime solver Michael Waring.

Under the banner of Falcon Pictures (released by Film Classics) production began on the first of three films in December 1947. Although not in the same league as their predecessors, all three, *The Devil's Cargo* (1948), *Appointment With Murder* (1948), and *Search For Danger* (1949), were well-paced, modestly entertaining low-budget mysteries with decent production values, respectable if unremarkable plots, and some standout acting especially by their star whose intelligence and charm were on full display. In the 1998 Kendall interview, John recalled his experiences playing the Falcon which he likened to doing his magic shows. "The more immersed I became in the Falcon series the more closely I realized that the experience paralleled my life on the magic show circuit in one basic respect. When you put on a good magic show and seek to attract interested audiences throughout the world, you'd better be sure you're always propelling those audience members to the point where they're begging for more. You do one magic trick, and you'd better be sure that the next one intrigues and entertains them at least as much. The same yardstick applies to performing in an adventure series like the Falcon. Each fast moving action sequence must be as intriguing and entertaining to the audience as the one before it."

After the series ended magician Calvert returned to his shows, purchasing the first of several airplanes to shuttle his equipment. In 1947 his first big plane, *Mystic Lady*, crashed near Nashville, Tennessee. Calvert was unharmed but wasn't so fortunate in January 1948 when another of his planes, a DC-2, crash landed in a Burbank, California, vacant lot. This time Calvert and a passenger sustained critical injuries including skull fractures but "magically" escaped with their lives.

In 1954, Calvert was again lured back to the film capital by an opportunity to co-direct (with Victor Saville) Warners' religious epic *The Silver Chalice* and to produce and star in the action-packed Monogram-released B western *Gold Fever*, which paired him with his second wife, lovely blonde Ann Cornell, whom he married shortly after the two filmed *Search for Danger* in 1949. The Calvert/Cornell union lasted a decade and produced a son, John. Calvert had a daughter, Mandrien, by his first marriage to Jessie McCormack during the 1930s.

In the mid-1950s Calvert acquired a 100 ft. yacht from the Ford family to haul his show around the world. He loved sailing and became quite the adventurer. His daring exploits on the high seas while traveling to and from such exotic locations as Japan, Singapore, the Philippines, and Australia were legendary. In the summer of 1959, John experienced the most spectacular of his nautical "adventures" when his yacht *Sea Fox* with John, his pet monkey Jimmy, and eight others aboard encountered problems while sailing in the Arafura Sea off the coast of Australia. In a distress call to Australian RAAF officials Calvert reported high winds had ripped away the main sail causing the craft to take on water. When he was unable to provide accurate position, Australian officials initiated a headline-making sea search. Eventually, they located the vessel, assisted it to shore, and saved Calvert's valuable equipment; but the *Sea Fox* was wrecked after it toppled over while beached near Darwin. Controversy swirled around the incident. Calvert blamed the Australians for his loss; and they insinuated the incident was a hoax. Lawsuits were threatened, but none materialized.

In 1956 Calvert, billed as John Trevlac (Calvert spelled backwards), made what would be his last film to date; producing, directing, writing, and starring in (along with John Carradine and Miss Cornell) *Dark Venture*, a story of an explorer in pursuit of elephants in darkest Africa. Partially shot on location the documentary-style movie remained unfinished until the late 1990s.

The extraordinary Mr. Calvert has remained in the public eye in the decades since he made his last film. In 1967 he married his lovely Portuguese assistant, Barbara de Melo, whom he calls "Tammy." Together they travel the world doing magic shows and conducting lectures. The handsome couple resides in Bowling Green, Kentucky, near both John's children. In 1987, Calvert's colorful life was the subject of an affectionate biography by noted magic buff William V. Rauscher entitled *John Calvert — Magic and Adventures Around the World*.

Today at 99 years, young the suave, still-youthful-looking John Calvert continues to astonish and inspire his countless fans and admirers with his breathtaking illusions, positive attitude, and long life. Although he suffered a minor stroke in April 2009, he bounced back and is now believed to be planning the next big milestone in his extraordinary life, an engagement at the London Palladium booked for August 5, 2011, the hundredth anniversary of his birth. Considering the life and accomplishments of this illusionist, inventor, actor, producer, director, adventurer, it promises to be a great show.

JAMES CARDWELL (1921–1954)

FRED GRAHAM in *Voice of the Whistler*.
CHARLIE BARKLEY in *The Return of the Whistler*.

Earnest, boyish, black-haired actor James Cardwell played leads,

James Cardwell.

second leads, and supporting roles in an abbreviated film career almost entirely confined to low-budgeters. A former shipping department employee, the Camden, New Jersey, native came out of nowhere to win a major role as one of five ill-fated brothers in the acclaimed 1944 war drama *The Sullivans* (Twentieth Century-Fox). His persuasive performance netted him rave reviews and a Fox contract. For a brief moment in time young Cardwell appeared poised to be Hollywood's new golden boy, but destiny got in the way. He had a few more decent supporting parts in As immediately following *The Sullivans*; but by 1946 was mired in B quicksand which destroyed his promise and swallowed his career. At the time of his sad, desperate death in 1954 he was out of work and out of hope.

Born Albert Paine Cardwell, on November 21, 1921, in Camden, New Jersey, he was the son of gas station employee Raymond Cardwell and his stay-at-home wife, the former Elizabeth "Bessie" McCarroll. Young Mr. Cardwell grew up around show people. His uncle and namesake James was stage manager for Camden's Stanley Theatre where vaudeville acts performed weekly. Although "Al" initially professed a desire for a writing career and became heavily involved in athletics while a student at Camden's Albert Cranmer Junior High School and Woodrow Wilson High, he seemed perpetually drawn to performing, frequently writing sketches about meeting such noted entertainers as Sophie Tucker and Duke Ellington.

When he sustained a severe ankle injury in a football game necessitating three surgeries, the teenaged Cardwell gave up sports and joined the dramatic and debate clubs. A natural actor and a fine public speaker, he excelled in high-school plays and became the president of the high-school dramatic club while serving as a narrator of pageants for the University of Pennsylvania. Cardwell continued to act after graduating in 1940. While employed in the shipping department of RCA Victor, he appeared in area theatrical productions with the Camden Drama Guild, the Merchantville Players, and the Hedgerow Theater Group in Moylan, Pennsylvania. In June 1942, he married fellow RCA employee Esther Borton. Cardwell's young wife did not share his enthusiasm for the arts and the marriage ended after only two years.

Fortune smiled on the good-looking, 6 ft. tall, 170-pound, brown-eyed Cardwell for a time in 1943. While working in the Hedgerow Theater parking lot, he was spotted by a Paramount talent agent who arranged a screen test. Although no offers were forthcoming the experience apparently whet Cardwell's appetite for an acting career. A few months later Al packed his bags and headed to New York looking for work and representation. It was a case of being in the right place at the right time. With so many established stars serving in the military several movie studios were actively scouting out fresh talent. Twentieth Century-Fox was looking for new faces to star in its upcoming grade-A, wartime drama *The Sullivans*. After another screen test Cardwell won a coveted role. By September 1943 the young wannabe (now known as James Cardwell) was in Hollywood filming his first motion picture.

Based on the tragic true story of five Waterloo, Iowa, brothers who served together on the cruiser *Juneau* and were killed at Guadalcanal, *The Sullivans* was a sentimental, patriotic tribute to bravery and simple American values. Produced by Sam Jaffe, directed by Lloyd Bacon, and enacted by a spirited cast made up largely of unknowns, the film captivated wartime audiences and charmed critics. As the eldest brother George young Cardwell had several key scenes and handled them well. He was rewarded with a long-term contract with TCF and a lead role as a trombone player who lets success go to his head in the modestly entertaining Benny Goodman musical *Sweet and Low Down* (1944). Although the latter engendered mixed reviews, it established Cardwell as a young actor on the rise.

Cardwell's surprising Hollywood success was enthusiastically shared by the community of Camden who turned out in droves to view the premiere of *The Sullivans* at a local theater. A program was organized which featured speeches by teachers, fellow students, and associates paying tribute to their hometown hero. In honor of Cardwell's success Camden's mayor proclaimed the week of the premiere, "Jimmie Cardwell week."

The eager, ambitious 23-year-old James was on top of the world during the summer of 1945. In just a few months time he had acquired the status of idol, been named one of the top new talents by influential critics and columnists, and completed his third major motion picture, the affecting wartime drama *A Walk in the Sun* (TCF, 1946), in which he had a showy supporting role as a young sergeant wounded during an attack by a U.S. battalion on a Nazi hideout in Salerno, Italy. His euphoria would be short-lived. By the time *Sun* premiered in January 1946, Jimmy Cardwell's streak of good luck had run out.

The end of World War II precipitated the return of several key American actors from active military service crowding out many rising stars, including Cardwell who was dropped by Twentieth Century-Fox in 1946. The disappointed but determined young film actor was left with two unattractive choices. He could quit the business or accept work in low-budgeters. He chose the latter course, but it came at a price. Although the program pictures in which he appeared (mainly for Columbia, Republic, Monogram) were not without merit, they provided few opportunities; and once an actor became associated with them it was virtually impossible to rise from the ashes.

The freelancing James would have leads, second leads, featured roles, and bits in 23 motion pictures during the latter 1940s. With the exception of tiny uncredited parts in two Grade-A features, the western adventure *Canyon Passage* (Universal-International, 1946), and the drama *Tokyo Joe* (Columbia, 1949), all were in programmers, heavy on action, light on substance. A few of Cardwell's better B assignments gave him interesting characters which he played admirably. Notable roles included: a private detective/murder suspect in the Charlie Chan mystery *The Shanghai Cobra* (Monogram, 1945), a young doctor inspired to commit murder by an amoral nurse and her jealous husband in *Voice of the Whistler* (Columbia, 1946), a blackmailing columnist in the Shadow series entry *Behind the Mask* (Monogram, 1946), a heroic Navy flyer in the teenage social drama *The Devil on Wheels* (PRC, 1947), a henchman involved in a parole-fixing racket in *Parole Inc.* (Eagle Lion, 1948), and a Robin Hood thief in the action-packed Monte Hale western *San Antone Ambush* (Republic, 1949).

Undoubtedly the best opportunity of Cardwell's post-TCF movie career came in Eagle-Lion's *He Walked By Night* (1949), a semi-documentary-style *noir* said to be the inspiration for Jack Webb's radio series *Dragnet*. Chronicling the dogged efforts of the L.A.P.D to capture a cop killer, the film was an exciting, action-packed nail biter with a literate script, superb direction from Alfred Werker (assisted by Anthony Mann), and first-rate performances. As Chuck Jones, a dedicated police sergeant who tracks down the culprit but is paralyzed in a shootout, Cardwell was impressive. His performance was widely hailed and might well have led to better opportunities had it not been for the simultaneous release of his follow-up film, *Daughter of the Jungle* (Republic, 1949), a ludicrous, Z-grade female Tarzan adventure.

Things began to seriously unravel for Jimmy shortly after the premiere of *Daughter of the Jungle*. He had a fifth-billed part as a crook in Republic's Rex Allen western *The Arizona Cowboy* (1950), but no film offers followed. While looking for work, the financially challenged Cardwell began taking pre-med courses at U.C.L A. To make ends meet in 1950 he became part of comedian Joe E. Brown's vaudeville tour; then joined the Coleano Troupe, a circus comedy acrobatic act. In 1953, Cardwell traveled to New York in hopes of finding work on television. Despite two brief appearances on Rod Cameron's crime drama series *City Detective* (1953) his attempt to break into TV was unsuccessful.

Determined he was "going to be an actor or nothing" the 32-year-old Cardwell returned to the West Coast in the winter of 1953, but things did not get better. All the elites whose extravagant praise had inflated the young man's hopes now seemed content to discard him. After a bit appearance as an army officer in the sci-fi thriller *Them!* (Warners, 1954) Jimmy was again out of work. With debts mounting he became increasingly disheartened. On the evening of January 31, 1954, he apparently decided he'd had enough. He borrowed a friend's car, drove it to a parking lot two blocks from his rented two-bedroom bungalow in West Hollywood, pulled out a .45-calibre pistol, put it up to his right temple, and pulled the trigger. His body, slumped over the steering wheel was found by a concerned neighbor a few hours later. Police found no suicide note in the car, only a letter from a real estate agent demanding payment of back rent, and a Screen Actors Guild card which was several months in arrears on its dues.

Just ten years after the city of Camden celebrated Cardwell's amazing success came the inevitable obit printed in the *Camden Courier Post* which read, "Jimmy Cardwell Found Shot to Death in Auto." The article recounted the sad, grizzly details of the young actor's death, but in contrast to most obituaries published in the Los Angeles papers included many career highlights and various honors he'd received. To his hometown, Jimmy was more than just another Hollywood casualty he was a neighbor, friend, and idol. Services were held at the Murray Funeral Home in Camden on February 6, 1954. Interment was in Harleigh Cemetery. Cardwell was survived by his parents and by a proud community who'd bid their hometown boy adieu to pursue his dreams, but now welcomed him home to stay.

MARY CURRIER (1904–1997)

Mary Currier.

EDITH MARIE HARRISON in *The Secret of the Whistler.*

Cultured, soft-voiced, dark-haired Mary Currier was one of many gifted thespians whom the movies never seemed to know what to do with. Although she possessed intelligence and genuine talent and proved it in a range of parts, Hollywood never saw fit to reward this worthy actress with roles commensurate with her abilities. Instead, the film industry seemed shamefully content to waste her in Bs and bits.

Born in Tennessee, on August 9, 1904, and raised in California, Mary played in stage productions before making her Hollywood movie debut in the 1934 Warners' B comedy *Merry Wives of Reno.* An exceptional player and a real trooper, she stayed in the film capital for the next 15 years (1934–49) playing second leads, featured roles, and more than a few uncredited bits in over 70 motion pictures. Currier could never quite disguise her natural intellect and innate grace so apparent in her acclaimed supporting performance as Edith in *The Secret of the Whistler* (Columbia, 1946), but during her Hollywood years she played every type of character on the silver screen from lowly sales clerks to lady judges, from secretaries, nurses, and librarians to a Countess from Luxembourg.

Her credits include both high- and low-enders. In big-budget films like *Dark Victory* (Warners, 1939), *Kitty Foyle* (RKO, 1940), *Here Comes Mr. Jordan* (Columbia, 1941), *The Valley of Decision* (MGM, 1945), *The Razor's Edge* (Twentieth Century-Fox, 1946), and *Joan of Arc* (RKO, 1948) she was relegated to bits and tiny supporting roles. She fared better in second features, but apparently was not deemed good enough to be promoted. Among her better parts were the proprietor of a private school in the family drama *The Five Little Peppers in Trouble* (Columbia, 1940), a compassionate woman who takes in a handicapped orphan and her brother in the dramatic *Nobody's Children* (Columbia, 1940), the mother of a dedicated nurse in the espionage meller *The Unwritten Code* (Columbia, 1944), a suspicious acting desk clerk in the mystery *The Falcon in Mexico* (RKO, 1944), and a lady judge with a problem daughter in *Youth on Trial* (Columbia, 1945). Miss Currier retired from the screen in 1949 and spent her last years in a small town in Idaho. She died at age 92, on March 25, 1997, in Coeur d'Alene, Idaho.

ALAN DINEHART (1889–1944)

GORMAN in *The Whistler.*

Tall, round-faced, distinguished-looking Alan Dinehart was an American-born stage and screen actor, stage manager, director, and writer who landed in Hollywood in the early 1930s after establishing

Alan Dinehart.

himself on Broadway. From 1931–44 he enjoyed an extremely successful movie acting career playing leads, second leads, and mainly featured roles in both A and B productions often as sophisticated rogues.

Born on October 3, 1889, in St. Paul, Minnesota, Dinehart began acting in various stage productions as a teen. In 1918, he found his way to the Broadway stage; and by the early 1920s had established a significant acting resume as a lead, and character player in such hit plays as *The Mirage* (1921), *Lawful Larceny* (1922), and *Two Fellows and a Girl* (1923). In 1925 he branched out into stage managing: *The Patsy* (1925–26), *Merry-Go-Round* (1927); and stage directing, *Americana* (1926–27), before heading to Hollywood in 1930.

Although he occasionally portrayed romantic leads and other sympathetic characters, Dinehart's ability to play charmingly deceptive screen villains was so impressive he quickly became typecast as a screen heavy. Specializing in crooked businessman, underhanded politicians, slick confidence men, or difficult, demanding Broadway producers, he exuded a combination of ruthlessness, insecurity, treachery, and urbane refinement which made his characterizations credible and memorable. During the next 13 years he would make over 80 film appearances. At one time or another he worked for almost all the major and minor studios, but was most often employed by Fox (later Twentieth Century-Fox).

Dinehart's best roles were largely confined to programmers and mid-range productions. He was memorable as a married architect whose affair with a renown dress designer causes unforeseen heartache in the dramatic *Street of Women* (Warners, 1932), a conniving lawyer who frames an innocent for murder to collect a fortune in *As the Devil Commands* (Columbia, 1932), a refined confidence man in the comic drama *Jimmy the Gent* (Warners, 1934), an "ethical" gangster in the Joe E. Brown comedy *A Very Honorable Guy* (Warners, 1934), an internationally known sportsman who resorts to murder in *Charlie Chan at the Race Track* (Twentieth Century-Fox, 1936), the aggressive manager of a musical comedy star in *Sweet Rosie O'Grady* (Twentieth Century-Fox, 1943), and a wealthy playboy who leads two girls astray in *Seven Days Ashore* (RKO, 1944).

Other significant Dinehart credits were *Girls About Town* (Paramount, 1931), *Lawyer Man* (Warners, 1932), *A Study in Scarlet* (KBS, 1933), *The World Changes* (Warners, 1933), *Baby Take a Bow* (Fox, 1934), *The Cat's Paw* (Fox, 1934), *Dante's Inferno* (Fox, 1935), *Born to Dance* (MGM, 1936), *Ali Baba Goes to Town* (Twentieth Century-Fox, 1937), *This is My Affair* (Twentieth Century-Fox, 1937), *Rebecca of Sunnybrook Farm* (Twentieth Century-Fox, 1938), *Second Fiddle* (Twentieth Century-Fox, 1939), *Slightly Honorable* (United Artists, 1940), *The Heat's On* (Columbia, 1943), and *Moon Over Las Vegas* (Universal, 1944).

During his years in Hollywood the veteran star returned to Broadway three times. In 1940–41 he wrote, stage managed, and starred in the hit comedy *Separate Rooms*, costarring Glenda Farrell and Lyle Talbot (613 performances). Alan Dinehart died on

July 17, 1944, at age 54. He was survived by his second wife, actress Mozelle Britton (1912–53), and three children. He was buried at Forest Lawn Memorial Park in Glendale, California. One of his sons was television actor Alan Dinehart Jr. (1918–92). His grandson, Alan Dinehart III (1936–) is also a film and television actor.

JEFF DONNELL (1921-1988)

FRANCIE LANG in *The Power of the Whistler.*

Pert, charming, button-nosed Jeff Donnell was a versatile and talented stage and screen actress first brought to Hollywood by Columbia Pictures in the early 1940s ostensibly to play leads and second leads. Instead, she was quickly ushered into featured roles as sincere ingénues, best friends, and matrons in low-budget musical comedies, mysteries, and westerns. In the 1950s, she made a name for herself on television.

The daughter of a prison administrator and a schoolteacher, Jean Marie Donnell was born July 10, 1921, at the South Windham Boy's Reformatory in Maine where her father Harold was superintendent. When she was two, the family moved to Towson, Maryland. It was at this time she was dubbed "Jeff" by her favorite Uncle Phineas because she loved the characters Mutt and Jeff. During her youth, the artistically inclined Jeff began taking piano and voice lessons and attending stage performances. After graduating from Towson High School in 1938, she attended the Leland Powers School of the Theatre in Boston. One of her professors, William R. Anderson, became her husband on December 21, 1940.

In 1941, while she attended Yale Drama School, Anderson helped establish the budding actress by setting her up in her own little theater, the Farragut Playhouse, at Rye Beach, New Hampshire. Not long afterward she was discovered by Columbia talent scout Max Arnow and brought to New York to make a screen test for Harry Cohn. Even though she displayed natural ability and a unique, wholesome charm, the tall, excessively thin, flat-chested girl with the enormous brown hair, huge brown eyes, and a button nose was

Jeff Donnell.

no glamour girl. After cruelly critiquing her looks, Cohn sent her home.

Much to Jeff's surprise, one month later she was offered a long-term Columbia pact at $100 a week which she signed shortly before discovering she was pregnant. After giving birth to son Michael Phineas on January 21, 1942, Jeff, husband William (who became a dialogue director at Columbia), and bundle boarded a train to Hollywood. The Andersons would adopt a daughter, Sarah Jane, "Sally," in 1948.

"Miss Jeff Donnell," as she was initially billed to make sure audiences knew her sex, would remain under contract to Columbia for the next six years. Her career began auspiciously with three showy supporting roles: as the wife of a pro-footballer referred to as "The Wreck" in the acclaimed Grade-A comedy *My Sister Eileen* (1942), a newlywed who discovers suspicious doings at the decaying New England Inn she and her husband purchased in the horror comedy *The Boogieman Will Get You* (1942), and a young married who resides in an apartment house where a murder was committed in the B-mystery comedy *Night to Remember* (1942). Sadly, it was all downhill after that. Donnell was attractive in a perky, unpretentious way, but she did not look like a typical leading lady; and her career suffered for it. Columbia and other studios would give her a handful of decent parts during her career; but her natural ability, charm, and exuberance were largely wasted in lightweight musical comedies, westerns, and mysteries in which she often portrayed supporting roles as bobbysoxers, ingénues, young wives, or spunky girlfriends.

Notable early Donnell parts cast her as an Irish lass who becomes the object of a singing G.I.'s affection in the wartime musical *Doughboys in Ireland* (Columbia, 1943), the daughter of a failed businessman in Sol Lesser's warm comedy *3 Is a Family* (on loan—United Artists, 1944), the younger sister of a woman mixed up with a psychopath in the mystery/thriller The Power of the Whistler (Columbia, 1945), and the unsophisticated wife of a homicide detective infatuated with an evil *femme fatale* in *Night Editor* (Columbia, 1946). B western fans also fondly recall Donnell as a cowboy sweetheart in five B-musical oaters featuring future *Gunsmoke* star Ken Curtis.

Donnell's finest role at Columbia and her own personal favorite was the sorority sister/murder suspect Butch Hendricks in the entertaining comic murder mystery *Nine Girls* (1944). As the shirt-and-jeans-clad physical fitness enthusiast who lacks athletic ability but knows how to deliver a comic quip, Jeff shined. One of her funniest lines comes after klutzy police investigator Walter Cummings (William Demarest) finishes a meal after spilling much of it on himself.

WALTER: "That was certainly a good meal."

BUTCH: "Yeah, and on you it looks good."

Hoping to boost her status Donnell left Columbia and signed a pact with RKO in 1947, then worked for Republic and Monogram; but nothing changed. By 1950, she was back at her old home studio decorating the grade Z western *Hoedown* with Jock Mahoney, trading funny lines with Lucille Ball in the B comedy *The Fuller Brush Girl*, and appearing all to briefly as the frightened wife of a policeman in Nicholas Ray's *noir* classic *In A Lonely Place*.

The Donnell career declined still further in the 1950s. The ebullient star soldiered on, landing a leading lady role as Scheherazade in Columbia's colorful, Arabian nights action adventure *Thief of Damascus* (1952), and a few supporting parts in fair to middling pictures like *Skirts Ahoy!* (MGM, 1952), *The Blue Gardenia* (Warners, 1953), and *So This is Love* (Warners, 1953), but by 1953, her hopes of being a major motion picture star were over. Refusing to give up acting, Jeff turned her attentions to television. In 1953, she appeared as Ann Rutledge in the *Cavalcade of America* production of "The New Salem Story" and had a role on *Hallmark Hall of Fame's* "The Courtship of Miles Standish."

In 1952, Jeff divorced William Anderson after a long estrangement. Two years later, on September 30, 1954, she married husky, blond up-and-coming actor Aldo Ray after an off-again, on-again courtship. Lamentably, the marriage never really got off the ground. According to Donnell, Aldo expressed regret over the union shortly after the nuptials, and was frequently absent for days at a time. The Rays separated and reconciled several times before Jeff accepted the inevitable and sought a divorce in July 1956. During her short, stormy second marriage, she carved a new acting niche for herself as a television star, playing the recurring role of George Gobel's wife, "spooky old Alice," in sketches on his popular NBC comedy/variety series (1954–58). The warm public response to her work on the Gobel show surprised and delighted Donnell.

From 1957 through the 1970s Jeff continued to play small supporting roles in feature films. She was the loving wife of brave test pilot in *Destination 60,000* (Allied Artists, 1957), Molly the maid in the unsuccessful remake of *My Man Godfrey* (Universal, 1957), the secretary of a sleazy press agent (Tony Curtis) in the searing drama *Sweet Smell of Success* (United Artists, 1957), the mother in two Gidget vehicles, *Gidget Goes Hawaiian* (Columbia,

1961) and *Gidget Goes to Rome* (Columbia, 1963), and a lady pilot in the World War II action/drama *Tora! Tora! Tora!* (Twentieth Century-Fox, 1970). TV credits included multiple made-for television movies and series episodes. Among them were *Perry Mason* (2 episodes, 1962–64), *Dr. Kildare* (5 episodes, 1966), *The Partridge Family* (1972), *The F.B.I.* (2 episodes, 1969–72), *Marcus Welby M.D.* (1974), *Kolchak: The Night Stalker* (1975), and *Fantasy Island* (1979). In 1975, Donnell had a continuing role as Ethel the telephone operator on the adventure series *Matt Helm*.

On September 1, 1958, Jeff married for a third time, to advertising executive John Bricker, whom she met while working on the Gobel show. For a time Jeff lived quietly with her husband in Manhattan where he became a successful dairy executive, but the call of acting was strong; and by the early 1960s she was back on the West Coast. The Brickers divorced in 1963. Donnell embarked on a fourth marriage, to Radcliffe Bealey, in 1974, but it too ended in divorce one year later.

Jeff scaled back her artistic activities during the final years of her life due to multiple health issues. Suffering from Addison's disease, a disorder of the adrenal system, she experienced muscle weakness and fatigue which became progressively more severe even after she underwent surgery to remove her adrenal glands in the 1960s. Despite her deteriorating condition in 1980, she accepted the small recurring role of Stella Fields, the quirky housekeeper of the wealthy Quartermaine family, on the popular daytime drama *General Hospital*. She would appear sporadically on the hit program for next eight years (1980–88).

On the morning of April 11, 1988, Jeff Donnell died of a heart attack in her sleep at the West Hollywood home she shared with her tortoiseshell cat "Lily." She was 66 years old. Her son, Michael, "Mickey Finn," and daughter Sally Durham survived her. A memorial service was held on April 15 at Pierce Brothers Mortuary in West Los Angeles. In attendance were several of Donnell's friends and admirers, including Barbara Hale, Marie Windsor, Edith Fellows, and a wheelchair-bound George Gobel, who stood up at the end of the service in honor of his beloved costar. On the day of her funeral, *Hollywood Reporter* columnist Hank Grant paid a long overdue tribute to the unique actress, one with which classic film lovers would heartily concur: "The sudden death of actress Jeff Donnell was a personal blow to me…Jeff had a long string of second and third banana, co-starring roles but never a complaint to me. For my money, she had more charm and sex appeal than the film queens she supported and had a warm cheery voice that always made my day. I among many others will sorely miss her."

CLAIRE DU BREY (1892–1993)

Claire Du Brey.

LAURA in *The Secret of the Whistler*.

Stern-looking American-born Claire Du Brey appeared in well over 200 films in a five-decade-long acting career which began in 1916 and lasted until 1959. Although she played occasional leads and second leads in silents (often as vamps and other women), today the versatile Du Brey is best known for featured roles and bits she played in the 1930s and 1940s as matrons, housekeepers, nurses, librarians, saleladies, townspeople, with an occasional murder suspect and/or collaborator thrown in for good measure. Her specialty was straight-laced, prim and proper types whose rigidity was oftentimes a veneer for corruption.

Born Clara Violet Dubreyovich, on August 31, 1892, in Bonner's Ferry Idaho, the future actress moved to California as a teen and was educated in a convent school. In 1916, billed as Claire Du Brey, she made her motion picture debut as the best friend of Billie Burke in the comedy *Peggy* and continued to find work in the movies throughout the remainder of the silent era. Appearing in over 70 silent features for all the major and minor studios she essayed a wide variety of roles from vamps to virginal heroines. Notable silent credits included westerns: *The Drifter* (Bison, 1917), *The Fighting Gringo* (Universal, 1917); adventures: *Prisoner of the Pines* (Paralta, 1917), *To Have and to Hold* (Paramount, 1922), Frank Lloyd's *The Sea Hawk* (Frank Lloyd Productions, 1924); comedies: *Follow That Girl* (Universal, 1917), *Miss Nobody* (First National, 1926); dramas: *The Rescue* (Blue, 1917), *The Old Maid's Baby* (Pathé, 1919), *The Bronze Bell* (Paramount, 1921), von Sternberg's *Exquisite Sinner* (MGM, 1926); and thrillers: *Brace Up* (Universal, 1918), *The Green Flame* (Brunton/Hodkinson, 1920).

When film work became scarce during the early 1930s, Du Brey took a job as personal assistant/secretary to her close friend and confidante Marie Dressler whose career was experiencing a renaissance. Claire handled the star's fan mail, appeared in tiny roles in Dressler's films and other MGM productions, and even nursed the aging star after she became ill with cancer. The two parted company in 1932 when rumors began circulating regarding their relationship. They were still estranged at the time of Marie's death on July 28, 1934. When she received nothing in Dressler's will, Claire submitted a bill for $25,000 to the estate for secretarial and personal nursing services, but was granted only $3,000.

By 1936 the distinguished, 5 ft. 6½ in. tall, brown-eyed, 40+ year-old screen veteran had begun the second, highly productive, phase of her movie career as a character actress and bit player in high- and low-budget productions. Frequently confined to unimportant, incidental characters as stern maids, housekeepers, dowagers, etc., she still managed to stand out. When a rare substantive opportunity presented itself (mostly in Bs), Claire made the most of it. Among Du Brey's memorable characterizations were the insane Bertha Rochester in Monogram's unsuccessful version of Bronte's *Jane Eyre* (1935), the wife of Bob Ford who murdered the titled "hero" in the western *Jesse James* (Twentieth Century-Fox, 1939), a puritanical murder suspect in *Charlie Chan's Murder Cruise* (Twentieth Century-Fox, 1940), a struggling wild west show proprietor in the entertaining Gene Autry oater *Bells of Capistrano* (Republic, 1942), the loyal, yet sinister, housekeeper of a woman believed murdered in *The Secret of the Whistler* (Columbia, 1946), and the mother of a young innocent mixed up with gangsters in *Destination Big House* (Republic, 1950).

Du Brey's other credits included an assortment of small roles and bits in several high-profile productions, including *Juarez* (Warners, 1939), *Blossoms in the Dust* (MGM, 1941), *Now, Voyager* (Warners, 1942), *The Best Years of Our Lives* (Goldwyn/RKO, 1946); and *Unconquered* (Paramount, 1947). Claire also made multiple stage appearances and did feature roles on television during the 1940s and 1950s. Her television credits included *Four Star Playhouse* (1954), *Cavalcade of America* (2 episodes, 1954–55), *Dragnet* (1956), *Private Secretary* (1956), *Adventures of Superman* (1957), and *Richard Diamond, Private Detective* (1960).

Du Brey retired from acting in 1958 at age 66 and spent the remainder of her long life out of the limelight. An accomplished athlete and sports fan, she indulged in various hobbies including golf and horticulture. During her final years, she was cared for by her longtime friend, actor John Phillip Law, who served as conservator of her estate. Claire Du Brey died in Los Angeles on August 1, 1993, one month shy of her 101st birthday. Although she married briefly during the 1920s, she left no survivors. In a rare interview conducted after her retirement she expressed her life philosophy which had served her well in the toughest times. She said, "I learned early in life to do things for myself, by myself. If I expected my life to be a happy one I always knew that I had to carve a world of my own."

Paul Guilfoyle (1902–1961)

Limpy Smith in *The Mark of the Whistler.*

With over 80 feature films, over a dozen Broadway plays, innumerable television series and specials on his resume, it is more than ironic stage, screen, and television actor, director, casting agent Paul Guilfoyle is best known today for a small uncredited role he played in 1949 as hood Roy Parker in Warners' *noir* thriller *White Heat.* In a memorable scene the treacherous Parker is shoved into the trunk of a car and peppered with bullets by crazed killer Cody Jarrett (James Cagney).

The unhappy ending suffered by Parker was a fate shared by many of the characters played by the diminutive, dark-haired Guilfoyle, who for two decades was one of Hollywood's busiest bad guys. His wiry build, weak chin, and furtive, close-set features made him a perfect fit for character roles as ruthless gangsters, henchmen, weak-willed informers, shifty con men, or mental and physical cripples. Although he became bored playing villains, Guilfoyle managed to infuse his characterizations with depth and realism born out of an overriding commitment to do good work. In the 1950s, he branched out into casting and directing feature films and television.

The son of John and Sarah Moran Guilfoyle, Paul was born on July 14, 1902, in Jersey City, New Jersey. Although he expressed an interest in the arts as a child, he did not begin acting until he was a teenager. During the early 1920s, he won a scholarship to attend the New York School for the Theatre and became one of its star pupils. Eventually he was chosen by Shakespearean actor Walter Hampden to join his company. Guilfoyle made his Broadway debut in 1923 in a small role in the comedy *The Jolly Roger*, the first of 16 appearances he would make on the "Great White Way." In 1925, the young actor scored his first major theatrical success as the "sniveling

Paul Guilfoyle.

invert," Gerald March, in the drama *The Green Hat*, starring Katharine Cornell and Leslie Howard. From then on Guilfoyle became typecast as disturbed, alienated individuals.

Hoping to be given more diverse acting assignments in the cinema, Paul moved to Hollywood in 1935. After playing several small parts in assorted productions, he was signed by RKO, who gave him a major supporting role in *Winterset* (1936), a powerful drama based on the acclaimed Maxwell Anderson play about injustice and the search for truth. As the haunted, remorseful gangster Garth Esdras, who witnessed a murder and allowed an innocent man to be executed, Guilfoyle contributed a powerful portrayal, one which netted him superlative reviews. The tough *New York Times* called his performance, "a miracle of casting . . . one of the film's finer things . . ." Unfortunately, Garth turned out to be a mixed blessing for Guilfoyle. Like his role in *The Green Hat* it increased his visibility, but became the first of countless film roles he would play as morally and ethically challenged individuals who exhibit instability or cowardice.

For the next 24 years Paul portrayed many variations of the tortured Garth for both major and minor studios. Although he was occasionally seen in tiny featured parts in prestige pictures like *The Grapes of Wrath* (Twentieth Century-Fox, 1940), *The North Star* (RKO, 1943), *The Seventh Cross* (MGM, 1944), *Julius Caesar* (MGM, 1953), and *Torch Song* (MGM, 1953), most of his work was done in "bottom fillers"; nonentities such as *Roaming Lady* (Columbia, 1936), *Millionaires in Prison* (RKO, 1940), *The Corpse Vanishes* (PRC, 1945), and *Why Girls Leave Home* (PRC, 1945).

Guilfoyle's better opportunities allowed him to shed the villainous straitjacket and/or use it to comic effect. He was entertaining and admirable as an Indian who competes with a zany city slicker in a bareback riding contest in the comic *I'm From the City* (RKO, 1938), an understanding chauffer and best friend of a playboy in the drama *Wildcat Bus* (RKO, 1940), a physically challenged peddler who saves the life of the man who stole his fortune in *The Mark of the Whistler* (Columbia, 1944), and the greedy, irresponsible uncle of a young newlywed who wins an expensive fur in the comedy *Miss Mink of 1949* (Twentieth Century-Fox, 1949).

Guilfoyle's finest post-*Winterset* role was largely played for laughs. It came in the fifth entry of RKO's entertaining *Saint* series, *The Saint Takes Over* (1940). As the reformed pickpocket, safecracker Clarence "Pearly" Gates, who attempts to assist dashing criminologist Simon Templar (George Sanders) solve a complex murder case involving a horse race fixing ring, Guilfoyle was delightful. So delightful he was asked to reprise the role in the sixth entry, *The Saint in Palm Springs* (1941), all about a hunt for killers and rare postage stamps.

During the 1950s Guilfoyle expanded his professional repertoire to include casting agent and director. As an actor he frequently appeared on television in such series as *Space Patrol* (2 episodes, 1952–53), *Schlitz Playhouse of Stars* (1953), *Climax!* (1954), *Sea Hunt* (2 episodes, 1958–59), and *Gunsmoke* (1960). His directorial credits included theatrical films *Captain Scarface* (Astor, 1953), *Tess of Storm Country* (Twentieth Century-Fox, 1961) and over 60 television series' episodes, among them *Dr Christian* (1956–57), *Highway Patrol* (1955–57), *Science Fiction Theatre* (1955–57), *Sugarfoot* (1959), and *Lawman* (1959–60).

Guilfoyle remained a busy TV and feature film director and actor until his sudden death of a heart attack on June 27, 1961, age 58. He was buried at Forest Lawn Memorial Park in Glendale. He was survived by his wife, musical theater actress Kathleen Mulqueen (1899–1990), and a son, Anthony. Certain bios published in recent years have alleged Mr. Guilfoyle's death was a suicide, but official obits state otherwise. Some short summaries of his career list contemporary film and television actor Paul Guilfoyle as his son. They are not related.

PORTER HALL (1888–1953)

JOE SORSBY in *The Mark of the Whistler*.

During filmdom's "golden age" when Hollywood needed an actor to play a mean-spirited businessman, a dishonest politician, bigot, judgmental agitator, cowardly killer, or cold-hearted penny pincher, they frequently turned to shifty-looking, beady-eyed, mustachioed Porter Hall. One of the busiest, most reliable character players of his day, the Ohio-born, former itinerant Shakespearian actor had a long and distinguished stage resume prior to migrating to the film capital at age 43. He stayed in Hollywood between 1934 and '54 and made 75 feature films.

Clifford Porter Hall was born in Cincinnati, on September 19, 1888. Educated in the city's public school system and at the University of Cincinnati, Hall began acting in local stage productions while working in a steel mill. After acquiring experience in various

Porter Hall.

repertory companies, and appearing in several productions of Shakespearean plays, Hall eventually landed roles on Broadway in the mid-1920s. In 1931, he came to Hollywood to try his hand at film acting. Although he began his movie career as a drunk in the drama *Secrets of a Secretary* (Paramount, 1931), it was not until 1934 he made his character playing mark as the embezzling murderer of an inventor in the hit mystery comedy *The Thin Man* (MGM). The role appeared to fit the short, dark-haired, sour-faced-looking actor like a glove, and would be the first in a very long line of knaves he would portray.

Between 1935–40 Hall made over 30 pictures, essaying varying shades of nasty from unethical and judgmental to cold-blooded murder. His notable roles of the period included a blackmailer who ends up dead in the comedy *The Princess Comes Across* (Paramount, 1936), the assassin Jack McCall who shoots Wild Bill Hickok in the back in *The Plainsman* (Paramount, 1936), an avaricious American in league with a power-hungry warlord in *The General Died at Dawn* (Paramount, 1936), an unscrupulous prison overseer who takes a bribe in *Prison Farm* (Paramount, 1938), a killer running a crooked mail order operation in *Scandal Sheet* (Paramount, 1938), and an ethically-challenged senator in Frank Capra's legendary political drama *Mr. Smith Goes to Washington* (Columbia, 1939).

Hall's filmic corruption and moral turpitude continued unabated throughout the 1940s into the 1950s in grade-A films like *His Girl Friday* (Columbia, 1940), *Going My Way* (Paramount, 1944), *Double Indemnity* (Paramount, 1944), C.B. DeMille's *Unconquered* (Paramount, 1947), and many, many Bs, including *Trail of the Vigilantes* (Universal, 1940), *The Mark of the Whistler* (Columbia, 1944), and *Bring On the Girls* (Paramount, 1945). During the early 1940s Hall became associated with director and screenwriter Preston Sturges, appearing in three of his classic comedy dramas: *Sullivan's Travels* (Paramount, 1941), *The Miracle at Morgan's Creek* (Paramount, 1944), and *The Great Moment* (Paramount, 1944).

Other Hall highlights included both comedies and heavy dramas. He was especially fine as the eccentric patriarch of a murderous hillbilly family in the raucous comedy *Murder He Says* (Paramount, 1945), a small-town southern bigot in the racially-charged drama *Intruder in the Dust* (MGM, 1949), a publisher who hires an amoral reporter in the searing drama *The Big Carnival* a.k.a. *Ace in the Hole*, (Paramount, 1951), and an adulterous undertaker who witnesses a cop killing in the melodramatic *Vice Squad* (United Artists, 1953). Perhaps no part typified Hall's screen image more than his role in the sentimental drama *Miracle on 34th Street* (Twentieth Century-Fox, 1947), which cast him as a Macy's personnel manager who attempts to have saintly Kris Kringle committed to Bellevue mental institution.

Hall had just completed his role as a corrupt archeologist in the adventure *Return to Treasure Island* (Paramount, 1954) when he died of a heart attack in Los Angeles on October 6, 1953, age 65. He was buried in Forest Lawn Memorial Park in Hollywood Hills. Ironically, the man who film fans loved to hate was a devoted father and husband and a much beloved church deacon and community leader. He was survived by his wife Geraldine (1905–70), and two children, David and Sarah Jane.

In addition to his films, Porter Hall also appeared in theatrical productions, both amateur and professional, throughout his life. He trodded the boards on Broadway nine times, notably supporting James Rennie and Florence Eldredge in *The Great Gatsby* (1926). Between 1950 and 1953 Hall appeared three times on live television.

BERNADENE HAYES (1903–1987)

MABEL SANDS in *The Thirteenth Hour.*

Blonde, Missouri-born stage, screen, and radio actress and singer Bernadene Hayes had a two-decade-long, 50-feature-film career in the 1930s and 1940s as a B movie bad girl. While she could and did play sympathetic film roles on occasion, notably as western heroines in three Hopalong Cassidy oaters, Bernadene's face had a certain "lived-in" look which made her perfect for parts as molls, dancers, saloon singers, cheating girlfriends, and assorted gold-diggers, troublemakers, and cheap floozies.

Born May 4, 1912, in St. Louis, the future film actress attended public schools and enrolled in Washington University. An accomplished vocalist, Bernadene left college when she was hired as a singer on KMOX in St. Louis. Eventually, her vocal prowess landed her on Broadway and then in Hollywood. In 1934, Hayes made her film debut in Universal's quickie comedy *The Human Side*. By 1935, she had settled in to a familiar groove, playing small supporting roles in Bs as tough dames. Although her lovely face and figure had previously won her the title of "most beautiful woman on radio," Bernadene exuded an earthy quality which soon typed her as a toughie in such entertaining, but forgettable, second features as *Absolute Quiet*

Bernadene Hayes.

(MGM, 1936), *Great Guy* (Grand National, 1937), *That's My Story* (Universal, 1937), *Panama Lady* (RKO, 1939), *Don't Gamble With Strangers* (Monogram, 1946), *Dick Tracy's Dilemma* (RKO, 1947), and *Bunco Squad* (RKO, 1950).

Even when she portrayed more likeable, morally upright characters, as in *North of the Great Divide* (Republic, 1937), *Prison Nurse* (Republic, 1937), *Trouble at Midnight* (Universal, 1938), and *Idiot's Delight* (MGM, 1939), in which she memorably danced with Clark Gable in his famous "Puttin On the Ritz" number, Bernadene looked and acted as if she'd been around. After making a handful of appearances on series TV, Hayes retired from acting in 1956. She died in her sleep of a heart attack in Los Angeles on August 29, 1987, age 84. Her sister, Lorraine Randall, also had a brief career as a B movie actress in the latter 1930s.

KATHLEEN HOWARD (1879–1956)

ROSE DENNING in *Mysterious Intruder.*

Distinguished looking, sweet-faced, Canadian-born singer and actress Kathleen Howard took an unusual route to character acting fame in Hollywood. An accomplished operatic contralto, who performed for the crowned heads of Europe, a star of the Metropolitan Opera, then a fashion editor for *Harper's Bazaar*, she arrived in the film capital in 1933 with an impressive resume. Well into her fifties, Howard utilized her stage training and formidable presence to make her mark as sharp-tongued society matrons, snobbish mothers, grandmas, aunts, assorted grand dames, and shrews in over 50 features of both the A and B varieties. Her abilities were never better utilized than in the mid-1930s when she was paired opposite W. C. Fields, sparring with the great comedian in three of his best-loved motion picture comedies.

Born Kathleen Howard, on July 27, 1879 (1884?), in Clifton, Ontario, Canada (later known as Niagara Falls), she was one of four children of an Englishman and his Canadian-born wife. When she was a small child, the family moved to Buffalo where Kathleen grew up. Her father's love for music was passed on to each of his children. In her articulate, heartfelt memoir entitled *Confessions of an Opera Singer* (1918), Howard recalled her father's dedication to the arts and the development of her singing ability. "My father's greatest joy in life was music, and he always played imaginative musical games

Kathleen Howard.

with us in the evening. The earliest one I remember was when we were tiny tots . . . I had always been able to sing, but the sudden growth of my voice was a surprise. One day in school we were asked to write a composition on our favorite wish. All the other girls said they wished for curly hair, for pretty dresses, for as much candy as they could eat, for any frivolous thing that came into their heads. But I took it seriously and told my dearest wish in all the world— a great voice, a voice with which I could make audiences cry or laugh at my will. And strangely enough, from that time my girlish voice began to grow stronger and stronger, until I could proudly make more noise with it than any other girl in school . . ."

The intelligent, ambitious Kathleen moved back to Canada to pursue a performing career around the turn of the century. Her first major job came in 1903 when she toured as a soloist with the Coldstream Guard Band in Toronto. She eventually studied voice under such noted instructors as Oscar Saenger in New York and Jacques Bouhy in Paris. She began her operatic career as a chorus singer; and in 1907 made her debut as a featured vocalist in Metz, Germany. Later, she won accolades as the principal contralto with the Court Opera of Darmstadt, Germany, and sang at the Royal Opera in England's Covent Gardens.

Her prestige and fame as a singer grew during the period 1910–16, during which she performed with New York's Central Opera and did concerts throughout England and northern Europe. In Russia Czar Nicholas II presented her with the Imperial Crown Brooch. Kathleen's greatest musical achievement came in 1916, when she began the first of a dozen successful seasons at New York's Metropolitan Opera performing such noted roles as Zita in Puccini's *Gianni Schicchi*.

When her voice began to deteriorate in the latter 1920s, Kathleen was forced to give up singing. A sophisticated, well-dressed woman and an excellent writer, she was hired by *Harper's Bazaar* as a fashion editor in 1928. She remained in the position until 1933 when she moved to the West Coast to become an editor for *Photoplay*. While in Hollywood, she was approached by Paramount to play a supporting role as the grande dame Princess Maria in the romantic fantasy drama *Death Takes a Holiday* (1934). Kathleen's first film acting venture netted her excellent reviews and more offers. Her natural charisma, trained voice, and imposing presence worked to her advantage for the next 16 years when she would appear in over four dozen major and minor motion pictures in substantive supporting roles, minor parts, and uncredited bits frequently as society snobs, nagging matrons, or puritanical spinsters.

Howard's best-loved movie roles came early in her career (1934–35) as W.C. Fields' foil/nemesis in three of his hilariously inane comedies. Although the films were at best Bs with flimsy plots and silly situations, the genius of Bill Fields doing many of his best-loved routines, supported by some of the cinema's most talented character players, made them classics. Howard's snooty, shrewish characterizations were a major asset which won her acclaim and scores of fans, not the least of which was her costar who never tired of singing her praises. In *You're Telling Me* (Paramount, 1934) she was a small-town "sophisticate" who refuses to let her son marry a poor amateur inventor's (Fields) daughter until she learns he is a friend of a princess. She was Fields' overbearing wife in two other motion pictures, *It's a Gift* (Paramount, 1934) and *Man On the Flying Trapeze* (Paramount, 1935). Many consider *Gift* to be the classic comedian's best film in no small part due to the chemistry and hilarious back-and-forth between put-upon shopkeeper Harold Bissonnette and his eternally nagging spouse Amelia. Their classic exchanges are often cited by film historians as some of the cinema's funniest.

AMELIA: Seems pretty strange someone would call you from a maternity hospital in the middle of the night.

HAROLD: They didn't call me from a maternity hospital. They called thinking this was the maternity hospital.

AMELIA: Why were you sitting there like a stone image when those men were insulting me?

HAROLD: I was just waiting for one of 'em to say something to me.

As a freelance player, Kathleen continued to portray variations on Amelia in multiple films. Among them were *Hit Parade of 1937* (Republic), *Young People* (Twentieth Century-Fox, 1940), *Sweetheart of the Campus* (Columbia, 1941), *Blossoms in the Dust* (MGM, 1941), *Miss Polly* (Hal Roach, 1941), and *Ball of Fire* (Goldwyn, 1941). The latter, a much-beloved comedy starring Gary Cooper and Barbara Stanwyck, cast the former operatic diva as Miss Bragg, a prudish housekeeper who threatens to summon the police when her boarders (including linguist Cooper) allow a sexy entertainer (Stanwyck) to move in with them. The picture would turn out to be memorable for Howard in two ways. It won her excellent reviews, but also landed her in the hospital with a fractured jaw when Miss Stanwyck accidentally struck her in the face while filming a scene.

Kathleen's best parts of the post-Fields period tended to be the most atypical. They included the sympathetic teacher who runs a school for girls in the Deanna Durbin musical drama *First Love* (Universal, 1939), the wry judge in the musical comedy *One Night in the Tropics* (Universal, 1940), a cranky but lovable dowager in the Jane Withers comic drama *The Mad Martindales* (Twentieth Century-Fox, 1942), the wife of a meddlesome dime store king in the entertaining B youth comedy *Reckless Age* (Universal, 1944); and a wealthy widow who attracts the attention of a cardsharp in the crime comedy *Shady Lady* (Universal, 1945);

Howard began playing a wider variety of characters in the latter 1940s, but by then her career was in decline, and she was being relegated to tiny speaking roles and bits. She was a wealthy patroness' cook in the *noir* classic *Laura* (Twentieth Century-Fox, 1944), the gin-soaked crony of a corrupt attorney out to bilk his client in *Mysterious Intruder* (Columbia, 1946), a maid for a class-conscious Boston family in the gentle satire *The Late George Apley* (Twentieth Century-Fox, 1947), a small-town doctor's nurse in the youth-oriented romantic comedy Cynthia (MGM, 1947), and the mother of a nurse attending a cold-blooded killer in the *noir* thriller *Cry of the City* (Twentieth Century-Fox, 1948).

Kathleen curtailed her acting career during the early 1950s due to ill health. Her final filmic roles came in 1950: as a college professor in the musical comedy *The Petty Girl* (Columbia) and as a society matron/fundraiser in the drama *Born to be Bad* (RKO). In 1951 she made her live TV debut in *Bigelow Theatre's* production of the comedy "Make Your Bed" starring Bonita Granville and Bill Williams. Sadly, it would be her one and only television appearance; and the last significant performing credit of her career.

Kathleen Howard died after an unspecified "long illness," on April 15, 1956, in Hollywood, age 76. Survived by two brothers and her sister, Marjorie, she was buried in Forest Lawn Cemetery in Buffalo, New York, near other family members. In an affectionate tribute to her published in the *Toronto Sun* entitled "W.C. Fields' Funny Foil," writer Jim McPherson quoted a letter Miss Howard wrote to Canadian singer Eva Gauthier in 1948. In it she expressed her gratitude for her film career, but said she'd lived a "very lonely life" in Hollywood. "But don't think I am complaining. I am only too grateful that I have been able to find a niche and earn a living in this rather grim place—especially when I realized that colleagues of mine, much greater artists than I was, have not had that luck. If much of me died with my singing career, I was extremely lucky to find work elsewhere . . ."

JOHN KELLOGG (1916–2000)

CHARLIE COOK in *The Thirteenth Hour.*

Lean, intense, wavy-haired stage and screen actor John Kellogg played supporting roles and bits usually as smart-alecky hoods, cowardly bandits, or tough-talking military men in over 60 feature films and countless television movies and series in a 50-year career. A former stage actor who came to Hollywood in 1940 in hopes of becoming a movie star in the John Garfield mold, Kellogg worked earnestly throughout the 1940s and 1950s in a variety of productions both A and B. Despite consuming ambition, obvious potential, a few memorable supporting parts in acclaimed crime dramas, and adventure films, he ultimately failed to ascend the last rung in the ladder of success. The reasons were multiple, but his controversial private life did not help. He eventually settled down and won acclaim as a stage actor, but his film potential remained unfulfilled.

The son of a stage actress Giles Vernon Kellogg Jr. was born in Hollywood, California, on June 3, 1916. Unlike most future movie stars he expressed no interest in acting early in his life. While attending Beverly Hills High School, he followed a business curriculum. Upon graduation in 1933 Kellogg worked as a filling station attendant while job hunting. During the mid-1930s, on a whim, he began attending drama school where he caught the acting bug.

After a brief unsuccessful attempt at breaking into films, with $90 in his pocket Kellogg hitchhiked to New York where he also met with rejection. Out of luck and funds, he and his friend, future film actor Tom Drake, reportedly slept in Central Park and often went hungry. Eventually, young Giles hitchhiked to Cohasset,

John Kellogg.

Massachusetts, where he found work with the South Shore Players. In 1937, a Shubert scout saw him and brought him to New York to appear in the drama *Honor Bright*. The play flopped, but Kellogg found stage work in two more dramas, *Dance Night*, and *Escape By Night*. The latter opened on Broadway April 22, 1938. One year later the aspiring actor landed the male lead in the road show version of the service comedy *Brother Rat*.

In 1940, Kellogg decided to give films another try. Now billed as John Kellogg (the "John" from his idol, John Garfield), he succeeded in winning a few tiny supporting parts and uncredited bits mainly as soldiers, flyers, and/or reporters in 14 Hollywood features. When World War II erupted, Kellogg enlisted in the U. S. Marine Corps and served two years. After an honorable discharge due to physical disability in 1944, he returned to California and resumed his quest for cinematic stardom. In 1945, he secured his first substantive film part as a tough-talking American infantryman in wartime Italy in the psychological drama *A Walk in the Sun* (Twentieth Century-Fox). Although the role was not large Kellogg's talent and dedication impressed *Sun*'s director Lewis Milestone who hired the 29-year-old actor for his next film, the melodramatic *The Strange Love of Martha Ivers* (Paramount, 1946), in which Kellogg portrayed a private detective.

John's breakthrough role came in 1946 when he was cast as the bodyguard/valet of a crooked casino proprietor (Dick Powell) in the *film noir* thriller *Johnny O'Clock* (Columbia). His excellent performance as Charlie, who betrays his friend/boss out of fear and jealousy, proved to be a benchmark in the Kellogg career. It not only won him critical plaudits and a Columbia contract, but became the first of many film roles he would play (often in *noirs*) as morally challenged toughs and killers who exhibit cowardice and/or disloyalty.

Unfortunately, nothing much came of Kellogg's Columbia contract except another part as a guy who betrays his best friend in the *Whistler* entry *The Thirteenth Hour* (1947). Hoping to break out of the bad boy mold in 1947, Kellogg tried freelancing but more crooks and cowards followed in crime films such as *The Gangster* (Allied Artists, 1947), *Secret Service Investigator* (Republic, 1948), *Port of New York* (Eagle-Lion, 1949), and in westerns like Autry's *Robin Hood of Texas* (Republic, 1947) and *Bad Men of Tombstone* (United Artists, 1949).

In 1949, Kellogg signed with Twentieth Century-Fox and achieved another career highlight as Major Joe Cobb, a brave combat commander of a B-17 squadron shot down over Germany, in the Academy Award-winning wartime drama *Twelve O'Clock High*. His acclaimed supporting performance initiated the most productive phase of his film career (1949–54) in which he was cast in 18 motion pictures, mostly crime dramas and westerns.

Just when his film career appeared to take off Kellogg's private life veered out of control. Known as a partier and a "ladies man," the 5 ft. 10 in. tall, 180-pound, wavy-brown-haired, craggily handsome actor surprised many in August 1946 by eloping with dancer Laura Stevens, a fellow *Johnny O'Clock* cast member. The headline-making marriage ended in days. A few weeks later Kellogg wed wife #2, beautiful, red-haired film actress Linda Brent. In February 1947, Kellogg attracted more unwanted publicity when he was booked on a felony charge of wife beating after the Beverly Hills Police were summoned to the couple's apartment and found Mrs. Kellogg with lacerations and puffed eyes. The charges were later dismissed, but the notoriety was damaging.

Kellogg's reputation took still another hit two years later in 1949 when he obtained a quickie Mexican divorce and wed wife #3, Helen Shirley Togan. The actor's third marriage, which produced a daughter, Cheryl Ann (born December 2, 1949), would also end after only a few months, but not without more controversy. In 1950, Kellogg was hauled back to court by two of his wives. Miss Brent claimed her break with Kellogg was not legal, and Miss Togan sued for divorce charging verbal and physical abuse, alcoholism, and neglect. Everything was eventually sorted out in July 1952, but only after the actor spent five days in jail for non payment of alimony and child support. Kellogg would marry for a fourth time during the 1950s, have another daughter, Sharon Lee, and an adopted son, Steven.

In the midst of the turmoil which ultimately harmed his image and movie career John played some significant motion picture supporting roles. Although he could effectively portray heroic types Hollywood preferred him as villains and blackguards. During a five-year period (1950–55) Kellogg cut a cinematic swath of death and destruction across a wide range from the busy streets of New York to the old west, from an African safari to a circus big top. His memorable roles included a henchman involved in a phony fortune-telling racket in *Bunco Squad* (RKO, 1950), a vicious anti-Quantrill guerilla leader in the historically inaccurate Audie Murphy western *Kansas Raiders* (Universal International, 1950), a reporter on the trail of a notorious couple involved in murder in *Tomorrow Is Another Day* (Warners, 1951), a murderous elephant poacher in the Bomba adventure *Elephant Stampede* (Monogram, 1951), a vengeful crook who helps orchestrate a catastrophic circus train robbery in Cecil B. DeMille's Oscar-winning epic *The Greatest Show on Earth* (Paramount, 1952), and a carnival barker/murder victim in the nifty 3-D Panoramic thriller *Gorilla at Large* (Twentieth Century-Fox, 1954).

As early as 1949 Kellogg was also taking his treacheries to America's living rooms via the small screen, showing up frequently as a guest star on TV. Among his series credits were *The Lone Ranger* (1949), *Boston Blackie* (3 episodes, 1952–53), *Adventures of Superman* (3 episodes, 1952–53), *One Step Beyond* (2 episodes, 1960), *The Untouchables* (memorable as gangster Lucky Quinn for 3 episodes, 1962), *Bonanza* (5 episodes, 1963–68), *The Virginian* (4 episodes, 1964–69), *Gunsmoke* (6 episodes, 1962–69), *Kojak* (1977), *St Elsewhere* (4 episodes, 1987), and, notably, a recurring role as lunatic uncle Jack Chandler on multiple episodes of the primetime soap *Peyton Place* (1966–67). John also appeared in several made-for-television movies. Among them were Rod Serling's *The Doomsday Flight* (1966), the slasher western *Night Slaves* (1970), and two dramas, *The Silence* (1975) and *Blind Justice* (1986).

Although Kellogg worked in both film and television throughout the remainder of his career, by the latter 1950s, he was focusing much of his creative energies on the stage. A charter member of Hollywood's Theater Alliance (which became the Actors Lab), Kellogg's passionate quest to develop his acting talent and demonstrate his range via theatrical appearances began paying dividends when he wowed critics with his titled performance in Chekhov's *Uncle Vanya* at the Fourth Street Theater. During the 1960s and 1970s, John continued to impress, essaying a wide variety of stage roles in Hugh Leonard's *Da*, Thomas Babe's *Fathers and Sons* at the New York's Public Theater, and the dramatic *Memphis is Gone* (1977) at the St. Clements. The latter won Kellogg the best notices of his career. In a review critic Norman Charles called his performance "highly dedicated craftsmanship carried to a transcendental level."

John's final motion picture credits included small roles in the La Traviata-based drama *Go Naked in the World* (MGM, 1961), the prison melodrama *Convicts 4* (Allied Artists, 1962), the slasher western *A Knife for the Ladies* (Warners, 1974), and the gangster napping drama *Orphans* (Lorimar, 1987). His portrayal of the tough-talking yet tender father of a young woman (Sissy Spacek) trying to rekindle an old romance in Columbia's 1986 drama *Violets Are Blue* was highly regarded.

John Kellogg was forced to abandon acting in the 1990s when he was diagnosed with Alzheimer's disease. At the end of his life he was cared for by his daughter Sharon. He died at the Cedars Sinai Medical Center in Los Angeles on February 22, 2000 age 83. After a private memorial service on Malibu Beach, Kellogg was cremated. He was survived by Sharon, adopted son Steven Wilson, and daughter Cheryl Ann Kellogg Phillips who penned an article about her famous father published in *L.A. Times' West Magazine* in September 2006. It was appropriately titled "The Untouchable" and chronicled Phillips' distant, often nonexistent, relationship with her dad. In a poignant, yet often bitter, piece she recalled coming to know her parent through "the soft glow of a 19-inch black-and-white zenith." Many classic film and TV fans also got to know John Kellogg on our black-and-white "zeniths" and we liked him.

RICHARD LANE (1899–1982)

Gaylord Traynor in *The Return of the Whistler.*

Broad-shouldered, square-jawed, fast-talking Richard Lane was one of the cinema's busiest and most underrated supporting players of the 1930s and 1940s, an actor who enlivened many a dull B movie script with his enthusiastic approach and the sheer force of his dynamic personality. Lane played all types of characters during a five-decade-long acting career which extended beyond the cinema to vaudeville, legitimate theater, radio and television, but in the movies he was most often found in a uniform or a business suit as tough military men, police detectives, or as slick businessmen and/or reporters. Lane made a whopping 170 feature films in Hollywood, but his greatest claim to fame was not as a film actor but as a pioneer sportscaster, newsman, and pitchman on television. His work in the formative years of Los Angeles TV, and his 25+

Richard Lane.

year stint broadcasting professional wrestling and roller derby from the Olympic Auditorium in Los Angeles earned him the status of a legend.

The son of a chemist, Lane was born on May 2, 1899, in Rice Lake, Wisconsin, a rural community 49 miles northwest of Eau Claire. A natural "show-off," he became interested in theatricals during grade school. When he was a teenager, Richard joined a local theater company and soon hit the road as an actor/performer in tent shows, road shows, vaudeville, and stock throughout the Midwest. He even toured Europe as part of a circus troupe, doing an "iron jaw" routine which required him to hang by his teeth. After a two-year stint in the U. S. Army in World War I, serving with the 32nd Division A.E.F. in France, Lane scoured New York for work in the entertainment world. Despite never having lifted a drum stick, he eventually landed a job as a drummer for entertainer Trixie Friganza, and then went on tour with the legendary Texas Guinan.

By the end of the 1920s, the young performer had chalked up an impressive entertainment resume. He'd played the Palace (the top booking in vaudeville), worked with Al Jolson in *Big Boy* at the Winter Garden, made his Broadway debut (155 performances) in the musical comedy *Present Arms* (1928–29), and toured in two hit shows, *30 Million Frenchmen* and *Irene*. He'd also met and married (June 7, 1929) the love of his life, dancer/actress Esther Lloyd. The two would remain wed for over 50 years. During the 1940s they adopted two children, Barry Michael and Victoria Ann.

In the early 1930s, Lane appeared as an actor/performer in various venues and began working as a radio announcer. In 1930, he landed on the "Great White Way" again in *The Vanderbilt Revue* and in the hit musical revue *George White's Scandals* (1935–36). While appearing in *Scandals* at the Biltmore Theater in Los Angeles, Lane was spotted by RKO who signed him to a short-term movie contract.

Wise enough to realize he did not have the looks or physical stature to be a movie leading man, the 5 ft. 11 in. tall, 175-pound, brown-haired, blue-eyed Richard Lane accepted character assignments of all shapes and sizes from the outset. His only stipulation was that he be paid for two weeks work no matter how small the part and how long it took to complete. Hollywood enthusiastically acceded to Lane's demands, and made him one of the busiest, most-sought-after film character players of his day.

During his first three years in Hollywood (1937–40), Lane, who acquired the sobriquet "Seabiscuit of the Spielers" (because he could exhale 411 words of dialogue in 51 seconds), would be seen in over 50 films. He worked for most of the major and minor studios, but primarily appeared in low-budget musicals, comedies, or mysteries. While he could convincingly portray a range of characters, he was particularly adept playing urban types: military men, police officials, reporters, businessmen, bookies, and gangsters who talked fast and acted forcefully. Many were humorless conventionalists or crooked connivers whose main purpose was to be "straight men" for comic leads.

Lane began his film career in the atypical role of a desperado in the RKO western drama *Outcasts of Poker Flat* (1937), but by his second and third film he was settling into familiar territory as a police detective in the melodramatic *You Can't Buy Luck* (1937) and a newspaperman in the screwball comedy *There Goes My Girl* (1937). Other memorable early roles included an eccentric movie mogul in the satirical comedy *Crashing Hollywood* (RKO, 1937), a killer who assumed the identity of a police detective in the whodunit *Charlie Chan in Honolulu* (Fox, 1938), and a crusading reporter in the mystery *Sued for Libel* (RKO, 1939). Also notable were Lane's "straight man" appearances opposite RKO comedian Joe Penner in five wacky comedies, including *The Life of the Party* (1937), *I'm from the City* (1938), and *Mr. Doodle Kicks Off* (1938).

The 1940s would be an incredibly productive decade for the hyperactive Lane who continued to astound with the sheer number of his film credits (18 in 1941 alone!). Sadly, most were Bs, or gave him all-too-familiar assignments as military men: *I Wanted Wings* (Paramount, 1941), *Navy Blues* (Warners, 1941), *To the Shores of Tripoli* (Twentieth Century-Fox, 1942), *Arabian Nights* (Universal, 1942), *Air Force* (Warners, 1943), *Corvette K225* (Universal, 1943), *Gung Ho!* (Universal, 1943), *Mr. Winkle Goes to War* (Columbia, 1944), *Devil Ship* (Columbia, 1947); reporters and editors: *Sunny* (RKO, 1941), *Tight Shoes* (Universal, 1941), *Two O' Clock Courage* (RKO, 1945); police detectives and law enforcement officials: *The Penalty* (MGM, 1941), *Dr. Broadway* (Paramount, 1942), *Time to Kill* (Twentieth Century-Fox, 1942), *Bermuda Mystery* (Twentieth Century-Fox, 1944), *Out of the Blue* (EL, 1947), *The Creeper*

(Twentieth Century-Fox, 1948); or crooks and gangsters: *Brother Orchid* (Warners, 1940), *Butch Minds the Baby* (Universal, 1942), *It Ain't Hay* (Universal, 1943), *Crazy House* (Universal, 1943), *Louisiana Hayride* (Columbia, 1944), and *The Bullfighters* (Twentieth Century-Fox, 1945).

Sandwiched in between standard assignments Richard managed to contribute a handful of blue ribbon performances in atypical parts: as a dog breeder who learns valuable lessons in life from his son and dog in the touching drama *The Biscuit Eater* (Paramount, 1940), a Boston Braves coach who helps train a legend in *The Babe Ruth Story* (Allied Artists, 1948), baseball manager Clay Hopper in *The Jackie Robinson Story* (EL, 1950), and, famously, as the intractable, perpetually suspicious, inevitably frustrated police detective Inspector Faraday on the trail of a reformed jewel thief named Boston Blackie in 14 entries of the classic Columbia series (1941–49).

During the 1940s Lane also worked on several popular radio shows, became a businessman and entrepreneur, and, late in the decade, a television newscaster and pitchman for the infant KTLA in Los Angeles. In the latter capacity, Lane gained notoriety for his aggressive, advertising promotions (beating on used cars) on *The Spade Cooley Show*, his colorful coverage of early telecasts of Pasadena's *Tournament of Roses Parade*, and his weekly broadcasts of professional wrestling, later roller derby, from L.A's Olympic Auditorium. Lane would eventually come to be known as the voice of professional wrestling thanks to his colorful commentary and his signature exposition, "Whoa, Nellie!" Lane was nominated for an Emmy as "Most Outstanding Personality" in 1951.

Increasingly preoccupied with television, other business and artistic endeavors, Lane scaled back his film work beginning in the early 1950s. Among his latter credits were supporting parts as a police detective in the Mickey Rooney crime drama *Quicksand* (United Artists, 1950), a fight promoter in the comedy *The Admiral Was a Lady* (United Artists, 1950), a fashion industry executive in the dramatic *I Can Get it for You Wholesale* (Twentieth Century-Fox, 1951), and tiny cameos (as commentators) in the 1976 roller derby epic *Kansas City Bomber* (MGM) and Disney's *The Shaggy D.A.* (1976). Lane's last film appearance was a bit in the wrestling dramady *The One and Only* (Paramount, 1978). He also made a handful of appearances on series television, notably as an announcer in an episode of *The Munsters* (1965).

In order to devote more time to family and business interests the veteran actor/ television broadcaster retired from show business during the late 1970s. Richard Lane died on September 5, 1982, at his home in Newport Beach, California. He was 83 years old. Surviving were his wife Esther, a son, daughter, and a granddaughter. Five years before his passing Lane summed up his rich and rewarding life in and out of the performing arts this way: "I never got rich in this business but I'm very comfortable. I have a lovely wife, a lovely home down in Newport Beach close to my son, daughter, and granddaughter. In fact I would say I'm probably the luckiest actor I ever knew."

BARTON MACLANE (1902–1969)

DETECTIVE TAGGART in *Mysterious Intruder.*

Large-framed, squinty-eyed, purse-lipped, red-haired character actor Barton MacLane looked like a tough guy and Hollywood cast him as such in over 140 motion pictures. Although he played some softer sympathetic roles and had a few leads (in Bs) during four decades on the silver screen, MacLane was almost exclusively cast in featured parts as uncouth gangsters, brutish gunmen, desperadoes, convicts, assorted thugs and bullies, or as hard-nosed cops, and western lawmen (both of the honest and crooked varieties). MacLane was also seen frequently on television.

The son of a mental institution superintendent, Barton MacLane was born on December 25, 1902, in Columbia, South Carolina. A rugged, muscular youth, he was a renown high-school athlete before attending Wesleyan University in Connecticut where he became a headline-making pigskin star. His prowess on the football field eventually landed him an invitation from Paramount Studios to do an uncredited bit as a footballer in the Richard Dix comedy *The Quarterback* (1926). MacLane enjoyed the experience so much he studied at the American Academy of Dramatic Arts, and then joined a Brooklyn stock company. In 1927, he took the first of eight

Barton MacLane.

Broadway bows in the small role of an assistant district attorney in the melodramatic *The Trial of Mary Dugan* starring Ann Harding.

While appearing on Broadway in the drama *Hangman's Whip*, MacLane was brought to Hollywood and signed by Paramount Pictures who featured him in bits and small roles in several films. Among them were *His Woman* (1931), *The Thundering Herd* (notable as his first bad guy part), and *Tillie and Gus* (1933). In 1932, MacLane surprised many insiders by penning a melodramatic play, *Rendezvous*, which turned up on Broadway. Warner Brothers noted his potential and signed him in 1934.

Although WB gave MacLane an occasional opportunity to play sympathetic, heroic types in minor leaguers like *Man of Iron* (1935), *Bengal Tiger* (1936), *Draegerman Courage* (1937), *The Kid Comes Back* (1938), and a costarring role as hapless cop Steve McBride in the entertaining *Torchy Blane* series, his imposing physical presence, loud, raspy voice, and ability to project villainy ultimately won out. During the period 1934-39 the burly actor won high praise in supporting roles as mean, vicious gangsters, brutal henchman, and thugs in many A- and B-level Warners' films, including *Black Fury* (1935), *Stranded* (1935), *Dr. Socrates* (1935), *Bullets or Ballots* (1936), *San Quentin* (1937), and *The Prince and the Pauper* (1937).

MacLane's career reached its zenith in the early 1940s with several high-profile tough guy supporting parts in acclaimed films helmed by distinguished directors. He was dogged police Lieutenant Dundy out to solve murders associated with the pursuit of a valuable artifact in John Huston's *The Maltese Falcon* (Warner Brothers, 1941), an ex-cop-turned-ruthless mobster in Raoul Walsh's crime classic *High Sierra* (Warners, 1941), a bank robbing killer out to stop the construction of an Omaha telegraph line in Fritz Lang's *Western Union* (Twentieth Century-Fox, 1941), and an abusive nightclub owner who cripples his singing girlfriend in Irving Reis' melodrama *The Big Street* (RKO, 1942).

MacLane played leads, second leads, and featured roles as crooks, knaves, hard-as- nails cops, or rugged military men in low-to-medium budgeters of all genres for the next three decades. Among his film credits were crime dramas: *Hit the Road* (Universal, 1941), *Highway By Night* (RKO, 1942), *Kiss Tomorrow Goodbye* (Warners, 1950); horrors: *Cry of the Werewolf* (Columbia, 1944) and *The Mummy's Ghost* (Universal, 1944); war dramas: *Bombardier* (RKO, 1943) and *Marine Raiders* (RKO, 1944); swashbucklers: *The Spanish Main* (RKO, 1945); westerns: *Cheyenne* (Warners, 1947), *Silver River* (Warners, 1948), *Relentless* (Columbia, 1948), *Best of the Badmen* (RKO, 1951); series' mysteries: *Crime Doctor's Strangest Case* (Columbia, 1943) and *Mysterious Intruder* (Columbia, 1946); and jungle adventures: *Nabonga* (PRC, 1944), *Tarzan and the Amazons* (RKO, 1945), and *Tarzan and the Huntress* (RKO, 1947). Perhaps MacLane's best remembered late 1940s screen appearance was as a con man contractor beaten to a pulp by two employees in the western classic *Treasure of the Sierra Madre* (Warners, 1948). MacLane's last significant film credits were tiny supporting roles as a straight-laced army major in the zany Jerry Lewis comedy *The Geisha Boy* (Paramount, 1958), a police commissioner in Frank Capra's comic drama *Pocketful of Miracles* (United Artists, 1961), and a crooked sheriff in *Arizona Bushwhackers* (Paramount, 1968).

Beginning in 1953 MacLane was often seen on the small screen, guest starring on 30+ television series. Among them were such diverse programs as *The Whistler* (1954), *Four Star Playhouse* (2 episodes, 1955), *Kraft Television Theatre* (1958), *77 Sunset Strip* (1958), *Disney's Wonderful World* (3 episodes, 1959–60), *Perry Mason* (4 episodes, 1959–64), and *Gunsmoke* (2 episodes, 1966–67). He had recurring roles on two NBC series: as a dedicated marshal who helps track down wanted fugitives in the Oklahoma Territory in *The Outlaws* (1960–62) and as the blustery General Peterson on the fondly remembered comedy *I Dream of Jeannie* (1965–69).

MacLane was still filming *I Dream of Jeannie* when he died at age 66 of double pneumonia in Santa Monica, California, on January 1, 1969. He was survived by his second wife, actress Charlotte Wynters (1899–1991), a son William, and a daughter Marlene. He was buried in Pierce Brothers Valhalla Memorial Park in North Hollywood.

Mike Mazurki (1907–1990)

Harry Pontos in *Mysterious Intruder*.

Six ft. five in., 240-pound, fearsome-looking Mike Mazurki menaced his way through 90+ movies in a career which began in 1941 and spanned almost five decades. His size and intimidating looks (a scarred, pock-marked face with small eyes and a hook nose) quickly typed him as one-dimensional toughs, thugs, gangsters, maniacal killers, or dumb clucks. Occasionally, he would have a more complex part which hinted there was genuine talent behind the hulking façade, but Hollywood seemed content to cast the former pro football, basketball, and wrestling star as brutish villains. In life, Mazurki was very different from his screen persona. Film devotees are often

Mike Mazurki.

surprised to learn that movieland's bloodthirsty barbarian was a genial, well-read, immaculately dressed, college-educated gentleman who was saddened so many people were put off by his appearance.

Of Ukrainian heritage, Mike was born Mikhail Mazurski (some sources list Mazurkiewicz), on December 25, 1907, in Tarnpol, Galacia, Austria-Hungary (now Ternopil, Ukraine). In 1913 his parents, Julius and Anna, emigrated to the United States and settled on a farm in Cohoes, New York, near Albany. A large, well-built youth, Mikhail, known as "Mike," was educated at the Cohoes grammar school then the LaSalle Institute in Troy, a Christian brothers military academy. A good student and a superb athlete, Mike received academic and athletic scholarships to Manhattan College where he graduated in the top 10% of his class in 1930 with multiple letters in football, basketball, wrestling, and track. Afterward, he attended law school and worked on Wall Street making $30 a week as an assistant to an auditor.

In 1931 a chance meeting with a friend led to a tryout with the Brooklyn Visitations professional basketball team, and a spot as the team's forward earning $100 per week. Later, young Mazurski played professional football for Staten Island's Stapleton Team before accepting a promoter's lucrative offer of work as a pro wrestler. In a 1976 interview with writer William Hare, published in *Hollywood Studio*, Mike remembered his first wrestling bout. "I won my first match in five minutes. The next day they came around and paid me $500. I said to myself, 'This is great. $500 for a five-minute match.' I asked where I would get booked and they told me Boston. So I headed for Boston. Before I knew it I was wrestling all around the east, and finally all over the country."

During the next 15 years Mazurski, known as "Iron Mike," became one of the wrestling sport's most renowned performers, competing with many of the best in the business. In the process, he managed to break almost every bone in his body. His "Alcatraz face" and slurred speech were but a few of the permanent aftereffects of his wrestling days.

In 1933 Mike moved to the West Coast. In between wrestling matches, he moonlighted as a bodyguard for actress/comedienne Mae West and played bits in films, including Mae's comedy *Belle of the Nineties* (Paramount, 1934). Mike had been living in the Los Angeles area for years when film director Josef von Sternberg officially "discovered" him in 1940 after attending one of his wrestling matches in the Olympic Auditorium. In the midst of casting *The*

Shanghai Gesture (United Artists, 1941), von Sternberg was looking for a big brawny fellow to play a Russian peasant. When he learned Mike was Ukrainian and spoke Russian, he offered him the 11th-billed part. Although both the film (an early example of *film noir*) and Mazurki (the actor dropped the "s" in his name.) earned plaudits, box-office receipts were tepid; and no substantive movie offers followed. The best the budding actor could do was secure bits in approximately 20 movies as wrestlers, thugs, henchmen, and morons.

Mike did not play a significant film role again until 1944, when he was chosen to portray the ex-con Moose Malloy in the *film noir* classic *Murder, My Sweet* (RKO). Mazurki was perfection in the role of the menacing, lovelorn killer determined to find the sweetheart he'd left behind when he entered prison. His performance not only won him raves, and scores of fans, but new offers. Most historians cite Moose as the most memorable role of Mazurki's long career. The actor told William Hare he almost didn't get the part. "Despite all the coaxing, the film's director, Edward Dmytryk, was against me having the part. He kept telling me that I just didn't fit it. But fortunately for me he was overruled by Charlie Koerner who was head of the studio at the time. Koerner saw me in the commissary and thought that I was right for the part. That part along with the von Sternberg film got me my start in pictures. The von Sternberg film provided me with a debut, but this was a much bigger part."

During the mid-1940s Mike gave up wrestling for a career on the silver screen. His acclaimed role in *Murder, My Sweet* initiated the peak period of his career as a Hollywood supporting actor (1945–50), in which he appeared in 25 motion pictures of both the A and B varieties, including many fondly remembered *film noirs*. His size and looks tended to limit his assignments to violent, muscle-bound brutes, or simpleminded lugs, but Mazurki managed to infuse many of his characters with depth and humanity. Highlights included his roles as "Splitface" in RKO's nifty melodramatic adaptation of Chester Gould's famous comic strip hero *Dick Tracy* (1945), the humorous sidekick of a book salesman in the mystery comedy *The French Key* (Republic, 1946), a sympathetic simpleton who works for smugglers in the minor-league melodrama *The Devil's Henchmen* (Columbia, 1949), the psychopathic brother of a vet duped by gamblers in

Dark City (Paramount, 1949), and the violent wrestler appropriately named "The Strangler" in the underrated *noir Night and the City* (Twentieth Century-Fox, 1950). Perhaps Mazurki's best post-Moose role was as Bruno the Strongman who defends the honor of his beautiful young assistant from the immoral intentions of a sleazy carnival roustabout in Edmund Goulding's *Nightmare Alley* (Twentieth Century-Fox, 1947).

If the former wrestler-turned-actor appeared all thumbs and muscles on celluloid, in life he was anything but. Witty and intelligent, the well-dressed, soft-spoken, college-educated Mazurki was known around Hollywood as a ladies man who could hold his own conversing with the highest of highbrows. On June 30, 1945, he married Glendale socialite Jeanette Briggs. Their union would last five years, until September 1950, and produced two daughters, Manette, born in 1947, and Michele, in 1948. In 1968 Mike married agent Sylvia Weinblatt (1916–97).

Although his parts became progressively smaller Mazurki continued to appear in the movies for the remainder of his life. During the 1950s and 1960s, he had the honor of working with many directorial greats in top-drawer productions. Among his better parts were the caring bodyguard of a shady defense attorney in *Criminal Lawyer* (Columbia, 1951), a crook who turns snitch in the *noir* melodrama *New York Confidential* (Warners, 1955), a sympathetic Polish cavalry sergeant in John Ford's all-star frontier epic *Cheyenne Autumn* (Warners, 1964), and the comically dumb "Mountain Ox" in Disney's entertaining *The Adventures of Bullwhip Griffin* (1967). Mazurki was also seen in William Wellman's *Blood Alley* (Warners, 1955), DeMille's *The Buccaneer* (Paramount, 1958), Billy Wilder's *Some Like It Hot* (United Artists, 1959), Capra's *Pocketful of Miracles* (United Artists, 1961), Stanley Kramer's *It's a Mad, Mad, Mad, Mad World* (United Artists, 1963), and two more John Ford films, *Donovan's Reef* (Paramount, 1963) and *Seven Women* (MGM, 1966).

Beginning in 1951 Mazurki appeared frequently on television and on the stage. He had a regular role on two TV sitcoms: as the dim-witted lackey of a conniving caveman in *It's About Time* (1966) and as a gangster in the short-lived *The Chicago Teddy Bears* (1971). Other TV credits included guest appearances on *Have Gun—Will*

Travel (3 episodes, 1958–62), *Wagon Train* (1964), *Perry Mason* (2 episodes, 1963–64), *The Munsters* (1964), *Batman* (1967), *The Beverly Hillbillies* (1968), and *Bonanza* (2 episodes, 1968–69), etc. Mazurki also made numerous stage appearances in stock productions of *Guys and Dolls*, *Lil' Abner*, Steinbeck's *Of Mice and Men*, and in 1965 co-founded the Cauliflower Alley Club, an association of retired pro-wrestlers and boxers who gathered weekly to socialize, exchange "war stories," and support worthy causes.

Mike's final screen credits consisted mainly of tiny supporting roles and bits in theatrical films: *The Centerfold Girls* (General Film, 1974), *The Magic of Lassie* (International, 1978), *Dick Tracy* (Touchstone, 1990); and the TV movies *Mad Bull* (1976) and *The Adventures of Huckleberry Finn* (1981). The one exception came in 1972 when he achieved a career highlight, playing the lead in the children's wildlife adventure film, *Challenge To Be Free* (Pacific International Enterprises), the story of a trapper and his half-wolf dog pursued by Mounties across the frozen North Alaskan wilderness. Directed by veteran Tay Garnett and shot on location, the film lived up to its title, requiring the 65-year-old actor to endure the harshest conditions imaginable, and to do some of his own stunts.

Mike Mazurki acted up until his death at age 83 on December 9, 1990 at the Glendale Adventist Hospital. A hospital spokesman said the actor suffered "numerous health problems in recent years." Services were held on December 19, 1990, at the Ukrainian Orthodox Church of St. Vladimir in Los Angeles with interment at Forest Lawn Cemetery in Glendale. Mazurki was survived by his wife Sylvia, two daughters, and scores of admirers. In a brief 1971 interview with writer/critic Vernon Scott, Mazurki summed up his career and revealed he was often taken aback when strangers recoiled at the sight of him. "Nobody was ever more typecast than me . . . Producers were convinced I could play two roles—a comedy moron and a killer . . . I didn't always look like this. But maybe I wouldn't have worked as often otherwise."

HELEN MOWERY (1922–??)

Bruce Cabot (left), Helen Mowery, and Roscoe Karns (far right) in *Avalanche* (PRC).

FREDA HANSON in *Mysterious Intruder*.

Attractive blonde Helen Mowery was a B movie leading lady, character actress, and bit player who enjoyed an all-too-brief career in the movies during the latter half of the 1940s into the early 1950s. Mainly in the employ of Columbia and PRC, she portrayed bombshells or cowboy sweethearts in over a dozen features. Her best roles were feminine leads opposite Charles Starrett in three "Durango Kid" westerns, as a hostess of an exclusive ski lodge in the murder mystery *Avalanche* (1946), and memorably as the conniving accomplice of a thief and killer in search of valuable Jenny Lind recordings in *Mysterious Intruder* (1946).

The Wyoming-born Mowery also played tiny uncredited roles and bits in multiple medium-to-high-budget productions, including the adventure drama *Tap Roots* (Universal, 1948), the crime thriller *Knock On Any Door* (Columbia, 1949), the musical biopic *Jolson*

Sings Again (Columbia, 1949), the soap operatic *No Man of Her Own* (Paramount, 1950), the prison melodrama *Caged* (Warners, 1950), and the classic drama *All About Eve* (Twentieth Century-Fox, 1950).

When her movie career fizzled in the early 1950s, Helen began guesting on TV. Her small screen credits included episodes of such popular series as *Schlitz Playhouse of Stars* (1953), *Science Fiction Theatre* (1956), Perry Mason (1957), and *Sea Hunt* (1960). She retired from acting in 1960 then disappeared from view.

J. CARROL NAISH (1897–1973)

THE KILLER in *The Whistler.*

One of the most respected featured actors of his generation, stage, screen, radio, and television star J. Carrol Naish portrayed an astonishing array of roles in a 40-year career which encompassed 170 feature films. Although he occasionally played leads and second leads, the versatile, dark-haired, dark-complexioned Naish was primarily seen in ethnic character parts. A master of dialects and disguises, he portrayed every possible race and nationality in the movies from Native Americans, African Americans, to Europeans, South Asians, East Asians, and many Latinos.

Of Irish heritage, Joseph Patrick Carrol Naish was born January 21, 1897, in New York City, the second of seven children born to Catherine Moran and Patrick Sarsfield. His father, an Irish scholar, emigrated to the U.S. in the 1890s and worked as a streetcar operator before becoming employed by a life insurance company. Young Carrol grew up on the tough streets of New York's Yorkville/East Harlem neighborhood where he learned how to fight and survive. Possessed with a fine soprano voice, he became a minstrel at St. Cecilia's Academy, but was kicked out of Commerce High School at 14 when he threw a classmate into the river following a dustup. After an unsuccessful attempt at selling insurance, the ambitious teenager utilized his singing ability as a song plugger for Irving Berlin, and then joined the Gus Edwards child vaudeville troupe. At 17, he enlisted in the Navy and served in the Army Signal Corps. During World War I, he saw action in France and Italy, and

J. Carrol Naish.

received two medals despite incidents of fighting and misbehavior.

While waiting in Brest for transportation home after the armistice, Naish and two buddies decided to form a song-and-dance act. They were so good they received several job offers, including one from American actress/entertainer Elsie Janis in Paris entertaining U.S. troops. Naish *sans* buddies joined her show. Then he was hired by famed French musical comedy star Gaby Deslys for a prominent role in her production *Frou Frou*. The restless Naish remained in Europe for the next few years doing odd jobs in and out of the entertainment industry while absorbing several cultures, languages, and dialects.

In 1926, he was offered a job singing in a club in Shanghai, China. Anxious to see more of the world, he boarded an oil tanker out of Hamburg. As fate would have it four hundred miles off the California coast the tanker ran into a typhoon and was forced to put in at San Pedro. Intrigued by the climate and the burgeoning film industry, Naish decided to remain. He did extra work and stunts in several films; and as J. Carrol Naish was seen briefly as a soldier in the Victor McLaglen classic *What Price Glory?* (Fox, 1926), before securing his first major acting job in an L.A. stage production of Pirandello's *The Pleasure of Honesty*. In 1927, he was hired to understudy the role of the Japanese prince in the road company version of the Broadway hit *The Shanghai Gesture*. In the cast was a pretty young Irish American actress named Gladys Heaney with whom Naish became smitten. When the tour reached New York in 1929, the couple was married in St. Patrick's Cathedral. They would remain wed for 45 years until Naish's death. The couple had one child, Elaine, born in 1932.

Long before he became a married man, "Carrol" decided acting was his life's calling. As was his custom he poured his heart and soul into the effort. In 1929, he appeared in several unsuccessful New York stage productions, including the short-lived Broadway farce *The Crook's Convention* (1929). An opportunity to reenter films presented itself in 1930, when Naish learned that movie executive William Fox was in a New York hospital following an auto accident. The ever-gregarious, resourceful Naish rushed to the hospital and volunteered as a blood donor. Placed on a bed next to Fox, the two became fast friends. When Fox recovered, he sent for Naish and signed him to a Fox contract. Unfortunately for Carrol, his mentor was in the midst of a power struggle at the studio which he would soon lose. After only three small parts the young actor was again out of a job; but not for long.

The 5 ft. 9 in. tall, black-haired, brown-eyed, 160-pound dynamo freelanced for the next five years (1932–37) appearing in over 70 features which ran the gamut from grades A through Z. His parts ranged from uncredited bits, to miniscule speaking parts, to more substantive supporting roles. Although he was occasionally cast as sympathetic and/or heroic individuals, his dark hair, swarthy complexion, heavy brows, and mastery of dialects quickly typed him as a screen foreigner or villain.

Often seen in elaborate make-up and disguises, Naish's most memorable 1930s characterizations constituted a virtual United Nations of treachery. He was an aging Chinese merchant murdered by his best friend during San Francisco's Tong wars in *The Hatchet Man* (First National, 1932), the blackmailing boyfriend of Ginger Rogers in *Upper World* (Warner Brothers, 1934), a Grand Vizier in colonial India in the Gary Cooper actioner *The Lives of a Bengal Lancer* (Paramount, 1935), an Arab slave trader in *The Crusades* (Paramount, 1935), an Indian major involved in the Crimean War in *Charge of the Light Brigade* (Warners, 1936), a cold-blooded killer dressed as an ape in *Charlie Chan at the Circus* (Twentieth Century-Fox, 1936), a French army officer in *Anthony Adverse* (Warners, 1936), and a homicidal, three-fingered, Mexican bandit in *Robin Hood of El Dorado* (MGM, 1936).

In 1937, Naish received a promotion of sorts when he inked a three-year pact with Paramount, joining ace character players Akim Tamiroff, Lynne Overman, and Lloyd Nolan as stars of the studio's new B+ unit. The results were several superior crime-related programmers lifted by decent production values, good scripts, and excellent acting. Most of the Naish vehicles featured him in lead roles as vicious mobsters or cruel miscreants. He was a Capone-like beer baron in *King of Alcatraz* (1938); gangsters in *Illegal Traffic* (1938), *Persons in Hiding* (1939), and *Queen of the Mob* (1940); a physician and an attorney who serve the mob in *Undercover Doctor* (1939) and *Hunted Men* (1938); and the cruel proprietor of a jungle labor camp in *Island of Lost Men* (1939). In between low-budgeters, J. Carrol appeared in a few grade-A Paramount productions, notably as a thief and informer in the studio's lavish action adventure *Beau Geste* (1939).

By 1940, Naish was widely hailed as one of the cinema's preeminent featured players, one who could portray any type of character in any genre. Throughout the 1940s into the early 1950s, he lived up to his reputation by contributing an astonishing variety of stellar supporting performances, some in atypical sympathetic roles. Highlights included: a washed-up matador reduced to begging in *Blood and Sand* (TCF, 1941), a diplomat who forces his son to join the Japanese army in World War II in Edward Dmytryk's *Behind the*

Rising Sun (RKO, 1943), an ape-turned-semi-human by evildoers in *Dr. Renault's Secret* (TCF, 1942), a tough marine lieutenant involved in World War II's famed Makin raid in *Gung Ho!* (Universal, 1943), the proud father of a violinist in the affecting drama *Humoresque* (Warners, 1946), a Latin papa in *That Midnight Kiss* (MGM, 1948), an Italian American police inspector in the excellent melodrama *Black Hand* (MGM, 1950), and Chief Sitting Bull in two films, the lavish musical *Annie Get Your Gun* (MGM, 1950) and the western *Sitting Bull* (United Artists, 1954).

Naish's two most famous 1940s characterizations won him Academy Award nominations for best supporting actor. The first came in 1943 for his memorable portrayal of Giuseppe, an Italian soldier who comes to see the evil of Hitler as an Allied prisoner in the Libyan desert in the stirring World War II classic *Sahara* (Columbia, 1943). Two years later Naish's career reached its pinnacle when he gave what many consider his best screen performance, as a the proud Latin American father of a troublemaking youngster who becomes a posthumous war hero in *A Medal For Benny* (Paramount, 1945). He lost the Oscar both times, but won the Golden Globe and many other accolades for *Benny*.

In the years following *Benny's* release, Naish granted several interviews in which he discussed his work and approach to it. One of the best was published in 1951 by the *Chicago Sunday Tribune Magazine*. In it he spoke at length about his career, theory of acting, and the specific techniques he employed to effectively "inhabit" a character. "I am convinced that no actor knows exactly what makes him click. But I think that a true definition of acting is this: the subjugation of one's own personality, the finding, psychologically and physically of the real nature of the character he is to portray and the losing oneself in the creation of the role . . . Getting a true concept of the character he is to play is 80 per cent of the actor's job. I never worry about outward mannerisms, such as a way of speaking or walking. Once you've established the character within yourself, his incidental traits come naturally . . ."

The demand for Naish's services in the movies declined slightly in the late 1940s. To find acting work he turned increasingly to other media. In 1948, he accepted the starring role in *Life with Luigi*, a radio comedy/drama series which chronicled the struggles of a newly arrived Italian immigrant to adjust to his adopted country. Created by Cy Howard, the long-running show (1948–53) provided listeners with a half hour of gentle humor tinged with pathos, and its star a unique showcase for his singular gifts. In 1952, an attempt was made to bring the series to television, but the project failed.

After *Luigi's* demise the hyperactive Naish managed to find work in several venues. He returned to the Broadway stage in Arthur Miller's affecting drama *A View From the Bridge* (149 performances 1955–56), did TV specials, including a critically acclaimed turn as Murillo in Alcoa Theater's production of "Key Largo," and took the title role in the short-lived 30-minute syndicated TV mystery series *The New Adventures of Charlie Chan* (1957). Naish also guest starred on multiple TV series, including *Wanted: Dead or Alive* (1958), *The Untouchables* (1960), *Wagon Train* (1959–60), and played character parts in eleven motion pictures, mostly westerns and crime dramas.

Naish remained busy throughout the sixties, beginning with a regular role as "Chief Hawkeye" on the western comedy series *Guestward Ho!* (1960–61). He returned to feature filmmaking in 1961 as the wise father of a dimwitted jock in *Force of Impulse* (Independent, 1961), appeared in a television movie, *The Hanged Man*, in 1964, followed by TV guest shots on multiple series, including *I Dream of Jeannie* (1965), *The Man from U.N.C.L.E.* (1966), *Green Acres* (1967), *Bonanza* (1968), and *Get Smart* (1968).

After a small featured part in the John Gavin TV western movie *Cutter's Trail* (1970), 73-year-old Naish decided to call it quits. Suffering from emphysema, he was confined to a wheelchair one year later when producer Al Adamson coaxed him out of retirement to appear as Dr. Durea, a.k.a. Dr. Frankenstein, in the low-budget horror *Dracula vs. Frankenstein* (1971). An ill-advised, absurdly entertaining, grade-Z shocker, the film paired veteran Naish with another former movie great, Lon Chaney Jr. It would be the last film for both.

On January 24, 1973, J. Carrol Naish died of emphysema-related complications at Scripps Memorial Hospital in La Jolla where he had been a patient for a week. He was 76 years old. His wife Gladys and daughter Elaine Sheridan survived him. Naish was buried in Calvary Cemetery. In a sad bit of irony Naish passed two days before his friend Edward G. Robinson who threw the fateful hatchet in *The Hatchet Man*, the film which effectively launched Naish's career.

Many attempts have been made through the years to summarize the colorful life and unique gifts of Naish, but no one put it better than an unnamed producer in the 1940s. When a journalist asked him why he kept casting Naish over and over in his features, the producer replied, "I put stars in my pictures to be sure people come into the theater. I put J. Carrol Naish in to be sure they don't walk out."

REGIS TOOMEY (1898–1991)

JAMES SUMMERS in *Mysterious Intruder*.
DON PARKER in *The Thirteenth Hour*.

Light-haired, smiling-faced, slightly-built Regis Toomey was an all-purpose actor who Hollywood could easily cast in a variety of film roles from morally tough soldiers, cops, detectives, to determined reporters and editors; from scheming weaklings to hardened criminals; humorless eager beavers to cynical sidekicks. A leading man of the early sound era, Toomey transitioned into supporting parts to salvage his acting career after making several undistinguished appearances in mediocre movies opposite dominant feminine stars. By the early 1940s, he had become one of filmdom's most reliable and successful featured players. In the 1950s he also became a popular television star.

Of Irish descent John Regis Toomey was born in the Lawrenceville district of Pittsburgh on August 13, 1898, one of four children of Francis X. and Mary Ellen Toomey. His father was the superintendent of a large steel mill. Although the Toomeys were not wealthy they were comfortable enough to provide their children with good educations. John Regis contemplated a career in law while attending Peabody High School, but changed his mind prior to graduation. Possessing a fine baritone voice, he opted to pursue a career as a concert and light opera performer before enrolling in the University of Pittsburgh where he appeared in college theatricals as a member of

Regis Toomey.

the Cap and Gown Club. Later, he played in stock at Pittsburgh's Empire Theater and then worked in a local steel mill to earn enough money to study drama at Carnegie Institute of Technology. In 1924, he quit his job and went to New York.

One of the first people he met in the city was Kathryn Scott, a choreographer for Oscar Hammerstein II currently casting the musical *Rose Marie*. Scott encouraged Toomey to tryout. Four days later the brash 26-year-old walked into the theater, auditioned for Hammerstein's musical director, and, amazingly, won the role of understudy to star Dennis King. On January 14, 1925, Toomey married Kathryn in St. Patrick's Cathedral. The marriage lasted 56 years.

Days after the nuptials Kathryn sailed for England to do choreographic work. At first opportunity her husband followed. While in Britain Toomey played the juvenile lead in George M. Cohan's musical *Little Nelly Kelly* and a supporting role in the musical comedy *Is Zat So*. Both were hits and the young actor toured the provinces, but the strain ruptured something in his voice. When a doctor advised him to give up singing for five years or face surgery, Toomey was forced to quit vocalizing and become a full-time actor.

His misfortune was short-lived. Upon his return to America Toomey was immediately signed for the road companies of *Twinkle, Twinkle* with Joe E. Brown and *Hit the Deck*. The latter brought him to Los Angeles and to the attention of producer/director Roland West who cast him (as Regis Toomey) in *Alibi* (Paramount, 1929), a hard-hitting crime drama about a ruthless gangster (Chester Morris) and the corrupt police who pursue him. As the undercover homicide cop Danny McGann, Regis had a showy role and a famous death scene which charmed the critics and inspired Paramount to sign him to a term contract. Alibi proved a benchmark for Toomey. The film not only initiated his 50-year movie career, but the role of Danny would be the first of countless characters he would play who met a tragic end.

In the first six years of his Hollywood career (1929–35) Toomey played leads, second leads, and substantive supporting parts in 46 films for Paramount and other studios. Donning a toupee, early on he was seen in several overblown dramas opposite some of Hollywood's most illustrious leading ladies, including Stanwyck, Bennett, Bow, and Astor in such films as *Rich People* (Pathé–1929), *Other Men's Women* (Warners–1931), *Kick In* (Paramount, 1931), and *Shopworn* (Columbia, 1932). This might have proved advantageous to Toomey if the films had been better made and his roles as loyal husbands, jilted fiancés, or poor boys who make good not so bland. Toomey fared better in character type assignments as cops and intrepid reporters in B crime dramas, mysteries, and adventures such as *Murder By the Clock* (Paramount, 1931), *The Finger Points* (Warners, 1931), and *Shadow of a Doubt* (MGM, 1935). Among Toomey's best early roles were the jealous gangster husband of a nightclub singer in *24 Hours* (Paramount, 1931), the doomed friend/sidekick of FBI agent Jimmy Cagney in *"G"Men* (Warners, 1935), and a young boxer who gets mixed up with crooks in *They Never Come Back* (Weiss Brothers, 1932). The latter was one of many films Regis made for minor studios like Monogram, PRC, Mascot, Mayfair, Tower, and Allied. Initially hesitant to appear in poverty row projects, the financially needy actor acquiesced when his agent convinced him no one would see the pictures.

His agent was right. Nobody *did* see the pictures, but that became problematic. By the latter half of the 1930s the once ascendant young star had fallen in stature to tiny roles and uncredited bits. By decade's end Toomey realized if he wanted to continue making movies he would have to become a full-time character player; but that, too, presented a problem. In a 1952 interview with columnist Howard McClay, published in the *L.A. Daily News*, Toomey explained. "I know it sounds silly but it happened to me too. For a long time producers told me I was too old for romantic leads and too young for character parts. This was a ridiculous situation at my age to say the least . . . I've got one of those Irish kissers and I've always looked younger than my age. It was a help at first but later turned out to be a disadvantage. Although I managed to keep working, it cost me several good character roles . . ."

Regis' fortunes began turning around in 1939 when Cecil B. DeMille selected him to play a small role in his lavish epic adventure Union Pacific (Paramount). He followed with a string of small parts in top-drawer films, as cops, soldiers, or reporters in *His Girl Friday* (Columbia, 1940), *'Til We Meet Again* (Warners, 1940), *Arizona* (Columbia, 1940), *They Died With Their Boots On* (Warners, 1940), and *Spellbound* (Selznick-UA, 1945). Especially notable was his role as a soda jerk in *Meet John Doe* (Warners, 1941), which gave him a great scene and a memorable speech.

As Toomey's stock rose, the freelancing actor (*sans* "rug") received offers of more substantive supporting roles in both high- and low-budgeters. Warner Brothers gave him some showy character parts: as a cop who helps a reporter identify a killer in the thrilling *A Shot in the Dark* (1941), a navy flyer who dies due to pilot fatigue in the action adventure *Dive Bomber* (1941), a doctor held hostage by gangsters in the crime drama *Bullet Scars* (1942), and an army officer in love with a colonel's daughter in the comedy *You're In the Army Now* (1941). Toomey made Hollywood history in the latter taking part (with Jane Wyman) in the longest screen kiss, 185 seconds! Other notable credits included *The Forest Rangers* (Paramount, 1942), *Tennessee Johnson* (MGM, 1942), *Strange Illusion* (PRC, 1945), and two Universal serials, *Adventures of the Flying Cadets* (1943) and *Raiders of Ghost City* (1944).

Toomey added 20 more motion pictures to his resume in the latter half of the 1940s. Most featured him in familiar roles as law or military officers, ministers or sympathetic fathers, but the angelic-looking Regis also began turning up on the wrong side of the law as crooks and killers in films such as *Mysterious Intruder* (Columbia, 1946), *The Thirteenth Hour* (Columbia, 1947), and *The Devil's Henchmen* (Columbia, 1949).

Toomey's movie career reached its zenith in the 1950s. By then he was dividing his time between making movies, doing television, and charity work, but still managed to contribute several finely etched characterizations which exhibited a depth, maturity, and humor sometimes missing from his earlier work. His most memorable portrayals were: the tough ethical Police Detective Cobb in the clever *noir* thriller *Cry Danger* (RKO, 1951), a police captain combating big city crime in *The Human Jungle* (Allied Artists, 1954), and a whisky-soaked minstrel man in the western *Dakota Incident* (Republic, 1956). Toomey was particularly fine as the uncle of do-gooder Jean Simmons in Joseph L. Mankiewicz's lavish musical *Guys and Dolls* (MGM, 1955) and as a compassionate man who becomes an unwitting victim of four juvenile toughs in the ultra-low-budget thriller/drama *Joy Ride* (Allied Artists, 1958). The Metro musical gave the former stage singer his first opportunity to perform a song on film, Frank Loesser's "More I Cannot Wish You." Unfortunately, it was cut from the final print.

Toomey's love affair with television began during the late 1940s and continued for three decades. Small screen credits included recurring roles on *Hey Mulligan*, a.k.a. *The Mickey Rooney Show* (1954–55 as Rooney's father), *Richard Diamond, Private Detective* (1957, as Lieutenant McGouh, L.A.P.D.), *Burke's Law* (1963–65, as Detective Sergeant Lester Hart), and *Petticoat Junction* (1968–69 as Doc Stuart), as well as countless guest star turns on series and specials. Among them were *Cavalcade of America* (1954), *December Bride* (3 episodes, 1955), *Four Star Playhouse* (8 episodes, 1952–56), *Zane Grey Theater* (2 episodes, 1957–58), *Rawhide* (2 episodes, 1959–60), *Death Valley Days* (1961), *Cheyenne* (4 episodes, 1956–62), *Perry Mason* (2 episodes, 1960–65), *Green Acres* (1966), *The Doris Day Show* (1972), *Adam 12* (1973), and *Fantasy Island* (1978).

Since arriving in Hollywood in 1929, Regis and Kathryn Toomey had been active in support of multiple charities in the Southern California area. In 1943, Regis became secretary, then later president, of the Permanent Charities Committee which raised millions for various causes, was on the board of directors of the Sister Kenny Foundation and the Screen Actors Guild, and was active in the Los Angeles Community Chest. Kathryn was a member of the Assistance League, American Women's Voluntary Service, and the Flower Guild.

Toomey's final screen roles were largely small and inconsequential. He was a medical doctor aboard the atomic submarine "Sea View" in the sci-fi fantasy *Voyage to the Bottom of the Sea* (Fox, 1961), a ranch manager in Robert Aldrich's western *The Last Sunset* (Universal, 1961), and the supervisor of a fishing tournament in the comedy *Man's Favorite Sport* (Universal, 1964). Other credits included *The Errand Boy* (Paramount, 1961), *The Out of Towners* (Paramount, 1970), and *The Carey Treatment* (MGM, 1972).

After Kathryn Toomey's death from a stroke in June 1981, 80+ year-old Regis made only two more acting appearances, one on TV: an episode of the comedy *It's a Living*; and one on film: the ludicrous zombie horror *Evil Town* (New World Pictures, 1987). He remained active in charity work during the 1980s while residing at the Motion Picture Country Home and Hospital in Woodland Hills, California. He died there of natural causes at 93 on October 12, 1991. Shortly before his death, he was visited by longtime friends former President Ronald Reagan and Nancy. A memorial service was held on October 18, at St. Mel's Catholic Church in Woodland Hills. Mr. Toomey was cremated and his ashes scattered at sea. He was survived by one brother, two nieces, three nephews, and film fans who mourned the passing of one of filmdom's foremost character stars and all-around good guys.

NINA VALE

Nina Vale.

JOAN HILL in *Mysterious Intruder.*

Multi-talented, raven-haired, Boston-born Nina Vale, a.k.a. Anne Hunter, found her way to the film capital during the early 1940s after gaining success as a ballet dancer and as an actress/dancer on the New York stage. Sadly, her career in the cinema would be exceedingly short, ending almost before it began leaving her substantive potential unfulfilled. All in all she is believed to have appeared in only four films: as the fiancée of the famous filmic sleuth in *The Gay Falcon* (RKO, 1941), a dancer in the musical comedy *Hi Diddle Diddle* (United Artists, 1943), a Nazi sympathizer in *Cornered* (RKO, 1945), and as the faithful secretary of an unscrupulous private eye in *Mysterious Intruder* (Columbia, 1946).

When she failed to make a go of it in the movies, the svelte, 5 ft. 5½ in. tall, brown-eyed Nina returned to dancing in the late 1940s then disappeared from movie radar screens. Her Broadway stage credits included Claire Booth Luce's comic smash *The Women* (1936–38) and the musical *The Girl from Wyoming* (1938–39). Vale was also in the cast of the road show version of *Doughgirls* (1939), understudied for a role in the stage version of *The Philadelphia Story*, was featured in Leonard Stillman's *New Faces* revues, and appeared in the operetta *Bittersweet* (1942). She had several important ballet roles in the 1940s, including *Aurora* at the Los Angeles Philharmonic Auditorium (1944). For unknown reasons some sources incorrectly list the credits of 1940s juvenile actress Nita Hunter under Vale's name.

RHYS WILLIAMS (1897–1969)

ERNIE SPARROW in *Voice of the Whistler*

Stocky, balding, round-faced, cheerful-looking Rhys Williams was a Welsh-born, stage, screen, and television actor who didn't become involved in filmmaking until 1941 when at age 44 he was hired as a dialogue coach for the Oscar-winning drama *How Green Was My Valley*. Director John Ford was so impressed with the stage veteran, he cast him in a small but significant role in the film thereby launching one of the cinema's most distinguished character acting careers spanning 30 years and roughly 70 films. Williams portrayed a surprising number of crooks, spies, and other villains in the movies, but is best known for his sympathetic portrayals. His smiling eyes, smooth silky voice, and affable demeanor made him perfect as jovial priests, storekeepers, doctors, farmers, other workmen. Apparently, the kind, friendly impersonations mirrored his own personal character. A thoughtful, amiable family man, Williams was proud of

Rhys Williams.

his roots and grateful he was able to make a decent living in a profession he so loved and admired.

Rhys Williams was born on New Year's Eve, 1897, in the Welsh village of Clydach-Cwm-Tawe. At age three, the family of seven moved to America, settling in a community of Welsh immigrants in Newcastle, Pennsylvania, where the elder Mr. Williams became employed at a steel mill. Rhys would spend the first 20 years of his life in Newcastle. While attending public school he began acting in various Welsh festivals and productions. By the time he was a teenager, he knew he wanted to perform. The problem was he needed to make a living.

Taking off cross-country 21-year-old Williams looked for acting gigs while working in various menial jobs. According to Rhys the going was tough but the experiences priceless. He did minstrel shows, worked in department stores, served as a concert manager for the San Carlos Opera, read lines for the Sue Hastings' puppets, and won a hog calling contest in Dallas, Texas. By the mid-1920s the budding actor was in New York doing voices for the Tony Sarg marionettes while searching for stage work. Eventually he joined the Globe Theatre Players (headed by Maurice Evans) and toured in 14 Shakespearean plays. During the late 1930s, he wed stage actress Elsie Dvorak, who would remain his wife for three decades. They would have two sons, Evan and Tudor.

In February 1937, Williams made his Broadway debut in the Globe's production of Shakespeare's *King Richard II* at the St. James Theatre. The acclaimed revival ran 171 performances and was the first of several Shakespearean histories and tragedies Williams would do on Broadway during the next three years. Among them were *Hamlet* (1938–39), (1939–40), *King Henry IV* (1939), and another revival of *King Richard II* (1940).

In 1940 the 5 ft. 10½ in. tall, 172-pound actor scored a career breakthrough when he was chosen for the key supporting role of minister John Goronwy Jones who assists a devoted English schoolteacher to educate and inspire children in a poor Welsh mining town in the Emlyn Williams play *The Corn is Green*. Starring Ethel Barrymore, the affecting drama won superlative reviews and garnered mass audience approval (477 performances).

Apparently, someone at Twentieth Century-Fox saw the production, became aware of Williams' heritage, and recommended him as a technical advisor for their upcoming film adaptation of Richard Llewellyn's bestselling novel of the joys and heartaches of life in an impoverished Welsh mining community, *How Green Was My Valley*. Directed by the legendary John Ford, filmed completely in California's San Fernando Valley and on the TCF lot, Rhys served as a dialogue coach and authenticator for the production. So impressed was director Ford he cast the veteran stage actor in a small supporting role, and initially hired him to narrate the film (as the grownup Huw Morgan). Williams had completed the narration when the meticulous director changed his mind (apparently because Rhys played a role in the film) and hired actor Irving Pichel to do the voiceover. It has been said the Williams version exists and was used in England, but it has not been confirmed.

Despite the loss of the choice assignment, Rhys Williams scored heavily in his film debut. As Dai Bando, the ex-prizefighter called on to teach young Huw (Roddy McDowell) the art of boxing, and later to help locate patriarch Willum Morgan (Donald Crisp) trapped after a mine collapse, Williams was memorable. It would remain his favorite role and the one most associated with him.

Williams' work in the Oscar-winning best picture inspired a demand for his services. He would have nine releases in 1942 alone; mainly high-end productions for a variety of studios. Highlights included turns in three patriotic wartime dramas: as a family friend in MGM's Oscar-winning *Mrs. Miniver*, an R.A.F. officer in the flag-waving *Eagle Squadron* (Universal), and cast against type as a Nazi spy in the action-oriented *Remember Pearl Harbor* (Republic). Other notable roles were the English boxing instructor in Warners' biopic *Gentleman Jim* and the manager of a troupe of entertainers in the award-winning drama *Random Harvest* (MGM).

After one year in Hollywood, Williams returned to Broadway in two unsuccessful dramas, Emlyn Williams' *The North Star* (1942) and producer Gilbert Miller's *Lifeline*, before striking pay dirt as Calvin Stowe in *Harriet*, an Elia Kazan-staged dramatization of the life of *Uncle Tom's Cabin's* author Harriet Beecher Stowe. Williams would trod the boards on Broadway three more times during the mid- to latter 1940s in the comic drama *Chicken Every Sunday* (1944–45) and two comedies, *Mr. Peebles and Mr. Hooker* (1946) and *The Biggest Thief in Town* (1949).

After the close of *Chicken Every Sunday*, Rhys was summoned back to the film capital to reprise his famed Broadway role in Warner's adaptation of *The Corn is Green* (1945) starring Bette Davis. The picture would initiate his most productive period on the silver screen (1945–55) in which he played supporting roles in over four dozen motion pictures of all types for both major and minor studios. Although benevolent, agreeable impersonations were his specialty, it is important to note the versatile Williams played a surprising number of rogues and blackguards. In fact, for every compassionate kindly character he played, such as the gentle ex-boxer/cabbie in *Voice of the Whistler* (Columbia, 1945), the supportive doctor in *The Bells of St. Marys* (RKO, 1945), the sympathetic priest who talks a gambler out of a coma in *Easy Come Easy Go* (Paramount, 1947), or the crusading police detective in the film noir *The Crooked Way* (United Artists, 1949), there were as many villains, like the traitorous reporter on the payroll of the Japanese government in the suspense drama *Blood on the Sun* (United Artists, 1945), the crook hired by a politician to ruin the reputation of an opponent in *The Farmer's Daughter* (RKO, 1947), the henchman for a 15th-century murderer in the adventure *The Black Arrow* (Columbia, 1948), and the cold-blooded sheep herder who punishes Lassie in the drama *The Hills of Home* (MGM, 1948).

Other notable film roles included a blind newspaper vendor in *Tenth Avenue Angel* (MGM, 1948), a crooked businessman trying to fleece the Mayflower pilgrims in *Plymouth Adventure* (MGM, 1952), and the trusted caretaker of a disgraced knight's children in the swashbuckling *Black Shield of Falworth* (Universal, 1954). Williams' one and only starring role in a motion picture came in 1950 in producer Sam Katzman's *Tyrant of the Sea* (Columbia), a B-adventure which cast him as a brilliant yet overly severe British naval commander combating Napoleon's forces in 1803.

In 1952, the 55-year-old veteran actor began a very successful career in television with a starring appearance on the dramatic anthology *Studio One*. During the next two decades, he would be seen frequently on the small screen as a guest star on innumerable series episodes. Among them were *Four Star Playhouse* (6 episodes, 1952–55), *The Loretta Young Show* (1956), *Alfred Hitchcock Presents* (1957), *Wagon Train* (1958), *The Donna Reed Show* (1958), *Maverick* (1960), *The Rifleman* (6 episodes in the recurring role of Doc Burrage, 1959–60), *General Electric Theatre* (5 episodes, 1956–61), *Dr. Kildare* (1963), *Mission Impossible* (1967), *The Andy Griffith Show* (1967), and *Mannix* (1969).

Williams' busy schedule on television limited his motion picture appearances in later years. After 1955, he would make only eleven more movies, mostly in small to miniscule roles. He was a tavern keeper in the pre-revolutionary action adventure *Mohawk* (Twentieth Century-Fox, 1956), a deputy sheriff on the trail of a hypnotic killer in the expressionistic thriller *Nightmare* (United Artists, 1956), and a cuckolded husband in Metro's Civil War epic *Raintree County* (1957). Other significant credits included the John Wayne western *The Sons of Katie Elder* (Paramount, 1965), Fox's Bondian spoof, *Our Man Flint* (1966), and the unintentionally funny Burt Reynolds adventure *Skullduggery* (Universal, 1970).

Williams continued to work up until shortly before his death of "natural causes" at age 71 on May 28, 1969, at St. Johns Hospital in Santa Monica, California. He had recently undergone an operation to relieve a painful hip and never recovered. A memorial service was held at the Good Shepherd Chapel in North Hollywood. Interment was in Forest Lawn Memorial Park in Hollywood Hills. He was survived by his wife Elsie (1908–94), two sons, two brothers, and two sisters. One of his brothers, Tom Emlyn Williams, was also an actor who appeared on Broadway five times during the 1940s.

Weeks before his death the veteran actor recounted some of the highlights of his successful character playing career in a conversation with Canadian writer/journalist Jim McPherson. At the end of the session the ever-gracious, humble Mr. Williams expressed gratitude for his life. "I've enjoyed myself in this business, but I never live in the past. I want for nothing. I have a happy family life, and this to me is a great thing. I've had a good time. No regrets at all."

JOAN WOODBURY (1915–1989)

ANTOINETTE "TONY" VIGRAN in *The Whistler.*

Sultry, alluring Joan Woodbury was an accomplished dancer who came to Hollywood in the mid-1930s hoping to make a name for herself as a lead actress/dancer in the cinema, a 1930s version of Ann Miller or Cyd Charisse. Instead, the shapely brunette became one of the queens of Bs, playing leads, second leads, character roles, and uncredited bits in a range of second features which ran the gamut from grades B through Z. Although she was often cast as foreign-born exotics (primarily Latinas) who were not always on the up and up, Joan could also be found playing all-American good girls, western sweeties, damsels in distress, and spunky serial heroines. When her interest in filmmaking waned in the 1950s, the

Joan Woodbury.

multi-talented Woodbury continued to entertain, impress, and inspire by founding the Palm Springs-based Valley Players Guild which staged plays featuring talented newcomers and veteran performers.

Interestingly, one of B movies' favorite senoritas had no Spanish blood. Of Danish, English, and Indian descent, she was born Joan Elmer Woodbury, on December 17, 1915, in Los Angeles, the daughter of hotel owner Elmer C. Woodbury and his wife, Joan Haden, a noted stage actress who had the distinction of being the third queen of Pasadena's Tournament of Roses Parade. Joan's grandmother was a prominent actress in the Danish Art Theatre.

Educated at the Notre Dame Academy in San Francisco, Joan knew she wanted to follow in her mother's footsteps after seeing Cornelia Otis Skinner in a San Francisco stage production. At 15 she began studying dramatics and dance, and performing in various stage shows and local functions. In 1933, her mother took her to Hollywood to look for work in motion pictures. A gifted dancer possessed with stunning looks, singular poise, and good singing and speaking voices, she obtained various jobs performing in local night spots and cafes while completing her education at Hollywood High School.

In 1934–35 the enthusiastic Miss W. began appearing in movies, doing uncredited bits as singers, show girls, school girls, etc. in such films as *Eight Girls in a Boat* (Paramount, 1934), *Folies Bergere* (Fox, 1935) and *The Call of the Wild* (Fox, 1935). She made such an impression in the tiny role of a "half-caste girl" in Mervyn LeRoy's award-winning dramatic epic *Anthony Adverse* (1936), actor Francis Lederer invited her to be part of his East Coast vaudeville tour. This led to several acclaimed dance appearances at the Agua Caliente Casino in Mexico and a Hollywood screen test.

In 1935, Joan scored her first significant cinematic break when she won a small role as a Spanish senorita and a featured song in the Hopalong Cassidy western *The Eagle's Brood* (Paramount). She followed with feminine leads in several poverty row productions. She was the love interest of Tim McCoy in two oaters, *Bulldog Courage* (Puritan, 1935) and *Lion's Den* (Puritan, 1936), the daughter of a police chief in the crime drama *The Fighting Coward* (Victory, 1935), and a murder suspect in the entertaining low-grade mystery *Rogue's Tavern* (Mercury, 1936). In between film assignments Joan pursued her dancing career. In May 1936, she was chosen premiere ballerina for the Corps de Ballet's performances of Opera Under the Stars at the prestigious Hollywood Bowl Grand Opera Festival.

In the fall of 1936, Grand National chose her as Tex Ritter's leading lady for his debut western musical, *Song of the Gringo*, which featured one of multitalented Woodbury's musical compositions, a song entitled "You Are Reality." More film offers followed, both leads and supporting. Most featured the 5 ft. 4½ in. tall, blue-eyed brunette as tough girl singers and dancers (mostly Latin) with checkered pasts. The best of these was undoubtedly the Fox series whodunit *Charlie Chan on Broadway* (1937), in which Joan had a showy featured role and an attention-grabbing dance number as a racketeer's girlfriend. In its review of the film *Variety* cited Woodbury as a girl who "shows possibilities" with "a combo of looks and acting ability." After Joan won high praise as a nightclub entertainer in her follow-up film, the mystery/comedy *There Goes My Girl* (RKO, 1937), RKO signed her to a term contract.

Woodbury seemed on the precipice of bigger and better things in 1937. At RKO, she would make five minor but memorable films. All featured her in substantive supporting roles, and all but one gave her a chance to perform. She had welcome comic parts in two entertaining satires, as a jealous sausage heiress in RKO's remake of *Rafter Romance* entitled *Living On Love* (1937) and as an aspiring film actress in the farce *Crashing Hollywood* (1938). Other RKO/Woodbury highlights included the Hildegarde Withers mystery *Forty Naughty Girls* (1937) and the crime comedy *Night Spot* (1938).

Despite glowing reviews and a rapidly increasing fan base, RKO chose not to renew the young star's contract in 1938. The freelancing Joan attempted to rebound by accepting multiple film offers in low-budgeters. This kept her in the public eye, but inevitably damaged her chances of becoming a first-ranked star. Although she did managed to land a small yet significant part, as the native girl Aicha, in Walter Wanger's acclaimed, atmospheric Casbah thriller *Algiers* (United Artists, 1938), her follow-ups, Fox's comedy *Passport Husband* (1938), Grand National's spy melodrama *Cipher Bureau* (1938), and Universal's *Crime Club* suspenser *Mystery of the White Room* (1939), were at best minor efforts which did nothing for her.

The budding B movie queen took solace in her private life. While filming the convoluted "Camera Devil" adventure *Chasing Danger* (Twentieth Century-Fox, 1938), costar Lynn Bari introduced Joan to fellow supporting cast member British actor Henry Wilcoxon who had found fame through his association with producer Cecil B. DeMille. Sparks flew on and off screen. By the end of the month the couple was engaged, and formalizing their wedding plans. On Joan's 23rd birthday, December 17, 1938, she and Wilcoxon wed. The union would be a long and stormy one (with several real and rumored separations) lasting over 20 years and producing three daughters, Wendy Joan (1939), Heather Ann (1947), and Cecilia Dawn (1950). Joan and Henry divorced during the 1960s.

Woodbury's most productive years on the silver screen began shortly after her marriage. During the period (1941–45) she would play leads, second leads, small supporting roles, and bits in 28 low-budget motion pictures. She continued to play foreign-born singers and dancers, gangster molls, and various toughies, but was also seen as demure all-American types in minor leaguers of all genres for Monogram, PRC, and Columbia. The majority were fast-paced and entertaining. There were musical comedies: *Two Latins from Manhattan* (Columbia, 1941), *Sweetheart of the Fleet* (Columbia, 1942); musical westerns: *In Old Cheyenne* (Republic, 1941), *Sunset Serenade* (Republic, 1942); adventures: *A Yank in Libya* (PRC, 1942); crime dramas: *I'll Sell My Life* (Select, 1941), *Dr. Broadway* (Paramount, 1942); mysteries: *I Killed That Man* (Monogram, 1941), *Confessions of Boston Blackie* (Columbia, 1941), *Phantom Killer* (Monogram, 1942), *The Chinese Cat* (Monogram, 1944); suspense thrillers: *The Whistler* (Columbia, 1944); and horrors: *King of the Zombies* (Monogram, 1941), and *The Living Ghost* (Monogram, 1942).

Underrated Woodbury's best early 1940s roles demonstrated her range. She was a lady racketeer bent on revenge in the nifty crime meller *Paper Bullets* a.k.a. *Gangs Inc.* (PRC, 1941), a penniless young girl who helps a hotshot reporter avoid a criminal syndicate in the crime comedy *Man from Headquarters* (Monogram, 1942), a hard-bitten entertainer who shares a song and her heart with a notorious gunslinger in the Johnny Mack Brown western *Flame of the West* (Monogram, 1945), and, notably, the irrepressible comic book heroine in the 13-chapter serial *Brenda Starr, Reporter* (Columbia, 1945). Fans often cite the latter as Woodbury's best. It was most definitely her favorite. In latter-day interviews she fondly recalled filming *Brenda* and the standing ovation she received from the crew when she performed a complicated scene in a single take to save money. She also told interviewers she preferred Bs because they rarely required retakes which bored her.

In the midst of all the film work and raising children Joan still found time for dance, theater, and charitable work. In January 1944, while Henry was in the Coast Guard, she opened her own dancing school; and in 1950 she and her husband organized a theater group, The Wilcoxon Group Players, which put on scaled-down versions of musicals and plays. The Wilcoxons also became heavily involved in various charities. In 1949, they organized a square dancing group composed of film stars who entertained at hospital wards, and raised monies for the Lou Gehrig Foundation and other worthy causes.

Although Woodbury's film appearances became rarer toward the end of the 1940s, she still managed to contribute some first-rate performances in second-rate movies. She was terrific in the 11th billed part of an actress murdered by an evil nightclub owner in the psychological *film noir The Arnello Affair* (MGM, 1947), a sheriff's daughter in the western comedy *Yankee Fakir* (Republic, 1947), a glamorous jewel smuggler in *Boston Blackie's Chinese Venture* (Columbia, 1949), and as the double-crossing burlesque queen Bubbles LaRue in producer Hal Roach's delightful slapstick comedy *Here Comes Trouble* (United Artists, 1948).

For all intents and purposes Woodbury's film career, which lasted 15 years and 78 motion pictures, ended in 1949. She appeared in three more films during the 1950s and early 1960s, including DeMille's monumental remake of *The Ten Commandments* (Paramount, 1956), but the parts were inconsequential. Sensing her talents could be better utilized elsewhere, she called it quits.

The final four decades of the glamorous Woodbury's life were spent with her beloved family and pursuing her myriad of interests. In 1963, she helped form the Valley Players Guild in Palm Springs. The group staged over 100 plays during a 20+ year period, and in the process became an important forum for developing up-and-coming young actors and showcasing veteran performers. Joan served as production manager, director, choreographer, writer, and, occasionally, as actor for the Guild. In the latter capacity she shined in several V.P.G. productions, notably the acclaimed *The Shanghai Gesture* and *I Remember Mama*. Joan found great personal satisfaction and joy guiding the group, a fulfillment she never knew as a film actress. In a 1979 interview with Jess Hoaglin, published in *The Hollywood Reporter*, she expressed her pride in what she had accomplished. "Our theater is doing very well, going into its 17th season. We will soon have our new theater in Palm Desert in a community center of shops, malls, etc. I am very proud to say that we will celebrate our 100th production in January, 1980 with *Plaza Suite*. I am a very proud Mama!"

On October 20, 1971, Joan married radio personality Charles Raymond Mitchell in Las Vegas. Mitchell shared her interest in the arts and local theater, and devoted his time to the Valley Players Guild. The couple loved to travel the world and spend time in Catalina Island. They moved to Desert Hot Springs in the late 1970s. During the mid-1980s illness forced the effervescent star to give up her job maintaining the Valley Players Guild. In November 1988 the Desert Theater League presented Joan with its first Lifetime Achievement Award for outstanding accomplishments. She was too ill to attend the presentation, but confided to friends she was "thrilled to bits," citing it as "the most gratifying phase of my life."

Joan Woodbury died at her home of respiratory failure on February, 22, 1989, age 73. She was survived by her husband Ray, three daughters, and four grandchildren. When announcing her death her friend, local *Desert Weekly* columnist Lloyd Chester, cited Joan's many accomplishments in and out of the entertainment world then added these appropriate sentiments: "She may have been 'The Queen of Bs' to thousands of film fans, but to us she was "'The Queen of Hearts.'"

BEHIND THE SCENES

THE CREATOR

J. DONALD WILSON (1904–1984)

To say Whistler's "father" J. Donald Wilson was a man of many talents would be a gross understatement. Writer, producer, director, actor, announcer, pioneer broadcasting executive, he literally made history in several entertainment categories on stage, screen, radio, and television. An intelligent, intellectually curious, unassuming man, the bespectacled Wilson always appeared as if he might be more at home in a classroom or a laboratory than on a soundstage or a movie set. But looks were deceiving. Behind the nerdish facade lay the inventive mind of a master entertainer, one who kept his trusty typewriter ablaze with an endless variety of quirky characters, elaborate criminal schemes, violent confrontations, and an occasional hatchet murder all in the name of entertaining his audience. Although his impact was substantive in multiple artistic realms, Wilson's greatest achievement was undoubtedly the Whistler, a mysterious otherworldly entity whose tales of terror combined the best elements of his work.

Born June 5, 1904, in Kansas City, Missouri, John Donald Wilson was an overachiever even as a youngster. At 10 he took up the clarinet, and was so good he became the youngest member of the legendary John Philip Sousa Marching Band. Entering radio in his teens, he became employed at The Blue Network, a subsidiary of NBC. During the late 1920s and throughout the 1930s he worked his way up in the ranks of the organization, functioning in a variety of capacities. During this time the ambitious, immensely creative young man moonlighted as an actor, radio scriptwriter, and announcer. Among his early acting credits were supporting roles on KECA's musical drama *King of Toy Mountain* (1933), KHJ's dramatic *Ben Franklin* (1934), and *Lux Radio Theater's* adaptation of "Mayerling" (1939). His early announcing credits included gigs on *The Adventures of Charlie Chan*.

The 1940s would be Wilson's most productive and successful decade during which he would achieve recognition in several creative spheres. In 1940, the Federal Communications Commission declared NBC a monopoly, formally splitting it into two networks, Blue and Red. A brief transitional period followed which ended in 1945 when the Blue Network officially became ABC (American Broadcasting Company). Legend has it Wilson was at least partially responsible for naming the ABC network which rewarded his natural ability and hard work with a position as executive vice president in charge of West Coast programming.

By the time he assumed his new executive job at ABC in the mid-1940s, the industrious Wilson had already chalked up several notable accomplishments during the decade. He'd performed all duties as a commander in the Naval Reserve, written scripts for several Navy documentaries and episodes of radio series, including *Suspense* (1943), served as a film narrator for a segment of Disney's delightful behind-the-scenes look at the animation process, *The Reluctant Dragon* (1941), and directed episodes of three radio programs, the adventure/drama *American Challenge* (Syndicated, 1940), the CBS comedy detective series *Miss Pinkerton* (1941), and *Treasury Star Parade* (Syndicated, 1942).

Wilson's master work, *The Whistler*, which debuted on CBS radio network May 16, 1942, and lasted for 13 years until 1955, appears to have been born during the latter 1930s or, at the latest, the summer of 1941. Records have yet to surface confirming the etiology of the Whistler character, the date of its genesis, and the specifics of its evolution into a radio series, but the striking similarities between Wilson's *Whistler* radio program and several literary, film, and radio projects which preceded it are not coincidental. Blending crime, psychological terror, and irony Wilson crafted a program designed to both terrify and intrigue.

Wilson wrote, produced, and directed *The Whistler* radio series for over a year. In the autumn of 1943, he turned the duties over to others and accepted Columbia's offer to serve as a consultant and furnish the story for an initial *Whistler* film. The feature, *The Whistler*, was released in March 1944 to popular applause and positive reviews. A few weeks later, on April 23, 1944, another of Wilson's creations, *The Adventures of Bill Lance*, debuted on the CBS network. A 30-minute radio crime drama featuring the daring exploits of a globe-trotting criminologist, Bill Lance, and his assistant, Ulysses Higgins, it was a minor hit lasting until September 1945. (It was revived by ABC in 1947–48.) In 1947 one of Wilson's works, a short story entitled *Destiny*, became the basis of Columbia's entertaining B crime movie *Key Witness*, a tale of assumed identities and murder starring John Beal.

During the latter 1940s, as ABC head of West Coast programming, Wilson attempted to duplicate the success of *The Whistler* with several other programs of both the adventure and suspense genres. None were as successful, but most were extremely entertaining. One of the best was *Dark Venture*, a Whistler-like anthology featuring stories of common folk who resort to criminality when faced with emotional upheaval and various challenges. The program, which explored the psychological aspects of criminal behavior, and frequently featured surprise "double twist" endings, lasted two years (1945–47).

In November 1948 Wilson's successful track record paid off in spades when ABC promoted him to the prestigious position of vice president in charge of national programming in New York. According to press releases, the move was made "to give New York more insight into Hollywood's program potential." It was a well-deserved honor, the culmination of years of hard work and loyalty. Unfortunately, it was short-lived. Less than one year later the company, in the midst of what it termed "streamlining operations," gave Wilson and one other executive their walking papers.

The disappointed former ABC executive moved back to the West Coast in 1950 where he immediately found work creating, producing, and directing radio and television for all the major networks. In 1950, he directed episodes of the NBC radio anthology *Presenting Charles Boyer*, and began producing and directing *The New Adventures of Nero Wolfe* (1950–51), the third radio incarnation of Rex Stout's orchid-growing crime solver, starring the inimitable Sydney Greenstreet.

In 1951 Wilson, the Renaissance man, became heavily involved in the production of television. Among his many early small screen credits were *Mark Saber* a.k.a. *The Mark Saber Mystery Theatre* (ABC, 1951–54), a 30-minute crime and mystery series chronicling the bravura efforts of a plainclothes New York police detective, Mark Saber (Tom Conway), and partner Sgt. Tim Maloney (James Burke) to solve complex crimes. A unique aspect of the program (which

Wilson concocted) involved the unusual devices (i.e. poison darts, radioactivity, and cyanide gas, etc.) used to commit the crimes. In a rare interview with *Los Angeles Times'* writer Walter Ames, Wilson discussed the series and the production of early TV. He said he utilized multiple radio techniques to cut costs and trim the length of his television programs. "Many hours can be saved during shootings if the director, finding his schedule running behind, can look at the script and make cuts right on the set without having to locate writers and producers."

On June 27, 1953, 49-year-old Wilson married film and radio actress/singer Christine McIntyre in Los Angeles. A talented opera-trained soprano, McIntyre had been a radio singer before breaking into the movies in 1937. In 1944, she signed a long-term contract with Columbia who put her to work in B westerns and two-reel comedies, most memorably as the beautiful blonde foil of the legendary Three Stooges. Miss McIntyre retired from films shortly after the couple's nuptials. Their long, happy union lasted over 30 years until Wilson's death. They had no children.

During the 1950s J. Donald adapted innumerable film and television properties for Don Sharp's Ambassador Productions. His last major credit came in 1959 when he produced *Shotgun Slade*, a syndicated half-hour TV series combining the detective and western genres. Several prominent critics found the program ingenious and stimulating, but it was not a success and disappeared nine months after its premiere.

Wilson retired from show business in the 1960s and went into the business world. He and Christine joined a group of real estate investors who purchased, renovated, managed, and sold apartment buildings in the Los Angeles area. For the remainder of his years the reserved, modest former radio executive and his gifted wife remained out of the spotlight. They moved several times, living in various apartment complexes which they developed. During his last years "J," as his wife called him, began experiencing heart-related problems which gradually worsened. On the morning of January 26, 1984, 79-year-old Wilson suffered a massive heart attack at the couple's residence in Van Nuys. He died in his wife's arms before paramedics arrived. Shortly before his death the well-respected organization Pacific Pioneer Broadcasters (of which he was a founding member) wanted to award him its ultimate prize, the Diamond Circle Award, for "important contributions to the industry." In typical low-key fashion, Wilson declined, saying he would be out of town on the date of the ceremony.

Wilson was survived by his widow, a nephew, and a niece. Grief stricken and traumatized, Christine's health deteriorated quickly. A few weeks after J's passing she was diagnosed with terminal cancer, and placed in a convalescent home. Christine McIntyre died less than six months after her beloved husband, on July 8, 1984, age 73. The couple was interred at Holy Cross Cemetery in Culver City, California.

THE DIRECTORS

WILLIAM CASTLE (1914–1977)

The Whistler
The Mark of the Whistler
Voice of the Whistler
Mysterious Intruder

When famed producer/director William Castle died in 1977, many newspaper obituaries dismissed his body of work, labeling him "master showman" and "shlockmeister." While it is true his films were not artistic masterpieces, and he *was* a marketing wizard, a self-described "PT Barnum," Castle was much more than a savvy salesman, and a purveyor of cheapies. In a 40+ year show-business career in which he wore a variety of hats, including editor, writer, actor, producer, director in theater, motion pictures, radio, and television, Castle exhibited a wide range of significant abilities that were supplemented by an uncommon respect and affection for his audience, and an earnest dedication to entertaining them. During his long tenure as a low-budget film director at Columbia Pictures at the outset of his career, he demonstrated great skill, manipulating every possible aspect of his cut-rate productions to set them apart from typical B product. In the latter 1950s he utilized his of wealth experience to make his own films; achieving fame and notoriety by producing and directing a collection of enormously successful horror shockers which he promoted with entertaining and inventive gimmicks.

Born William Schloss Jr., on April 24, 1914, in New York City, Castle grew up and was educated in the "Big Apple." A tall, awkward, withdrawn boy, he was not a good student and exhibited no particular talents. According to his autobiography, he was mercilessly teased about his name and lack of coordination; so much so his family sent him to camp hoping he might acquire poise and people handling skills. Young Bill hated the idea, but the experience worked out well. Although he couldn't play sports, his ability to contort his body (putting his legs around his neck) apparently won him respect, acceptance, and some much-needed confidence. His first experience

William Castle.

with the horror genre came at age eight when his father took him to see Wilton Luckaye's stage performance of *The Monster*. According to Castle, "I clutched my father's hand in abject terror, finally embarrassing the hell out of him by wetting myself."

As a child Bill suffered successive tragedies when his mother died of pneumonia in 1924 and his father succumbed to a heart attack one year later. Sent to live with his older sister and her husband, the youngster's grief and self-loathing manifested itself in bizarre behavior and several "death-defying stunts" like jumping into the Hudson River. At a low point in 1927, Bill got his first real taste of show business when he attended the Broadway production of *Dracula* starring Bela Lugosi. Young Schloss was so mesmerized he attended the show again and again, eventually working up the courage to head backstage to meet its star. Lugosi apparently liked the boy enough to allow him to view the production from backstage and to recommend him for a position as an assistant stage manager in the road company version two years later. The experience would have a profound effect. Bill had found his life's calling in the nick of time.

After the tour ended the newly named William Castle (Castle was the English equivalent of Shloss) managed to find work as an actor. Extremely ambitious and always willing to exaggerate or fabricate to achieve a goal, Castle claimed to be the nephew of Samuel Goldwyn to secure a role on Broadway in the revival of *An American Tragedy*. Later, he became the show's stage manager, and then played three other Broadway roles in the mid-1930s in *Ebb Tide, No Small Frontier,* and *Oliver Twist*. In between acting assignments, he worked in various menial jobs and did impressions of Hollywood stars in small nightclubs.

By 1937, the desire to become part of the motion picture industry became a driving force in Castle's life. After an unsuccessful attempt to find employment in Hollywood, he returned to New York, where a fortuitous encounter with Orson Welles in 1939 indirectly helped make Castle's moviemaking dream a reality. Having inherited $25,000 from his father's estate, the persuasive Bill convinced the actor/director to allow him to acquire the rights to his Stoney Creek Theater in Connecticut where Welles' Mercury Players tested plays before Broadway. Castle's initial production, *Not for Children* (which he also penned), caught the attention of Samuel Marks of Columbia Pictures. Apparently, Marks saw something special in the audacious young man, and convinced Harry Cohn to sign Castle to a "seven-way contract" at $50 a week.

The pact allowed the studio to assess Castle's abilities while giving him the chance to learn the movie business from several perspectives. After two years experience in a variety of capacities; as an actor: *He Stayed for Breakfast* (1940), *The Lady in Question* (1940); dialogue director: *Music in My Heart* (1940); scriptwriter: *North to the Klondike* (on loan to Universal, 1942); short subject director: *Mr. Smug* (1943), Columbia gave Castle the chance to direct his first feature-length picture, the *Boston Blackie* series entry *Chance of a Lifetime* (1943). Realizing it might be his first and only opportunity to prove himself, Castle gave it his all, but the script was deficient and the film unpopular. Castle expected Cohn to fire him after critics savaged it. Instead, King Harry rewarded him with another opportunity to direct a crime drama based on a popular radio series. Bill was thrilled and inspired by Eric Taylor's suspenseful screenplay for *The Whistler*, and determined to make it a success.

Innovative, imaginative, fast-paced, *The Whistler* (1944) was a hit with critics and the public. The surprisingly positive reception it received not only redeemed Castle with influential reviewers, but won him the respect of his boss who gave him more B directorial assignments. One of them was a loan to the King brothers at Monogram for an intriguing thriller which would turn out to be another of Castle's most fondly remembered Bs, *When Strangers Marry* a.k.a. *Betrayed* (1944), an early *noir* about a young waitress who marries a mysterious man who might be a killer. Both *The Whistler* and *When Strangers Marry* showcased Castle's flair for manipulating mood; creating and sustaining suspense through the innovative use of sets, lighting, unusual camera angles, and a plethora of contrivances, while eliciting strong performances from large casts.

The years 1943–48 would find Castle guiding a dozen entertaining Columbia Bs, mostly series' thrillers, including four *Crime Doctors*, three more *Whistlers*, and an entry in the *Rusty* series. In between Columbia assignments Castle directed an unsuccessful Broadway whodunit, *Meet a Body* (1944), worked as an associate producer and second-unit director on friend Orson Welles' classic *noir The Lady from Shanghai* (Columbia, 1947), and married Ellen Falk on March 21, 1948. By all accounts the marriage was a happy one, lasting until Castle's death. Bill and Ellen had two daughters, Georgianna in 1954, and Terry in 1958.

In 1949, William Goetz and Leo Spitz of Universal International Pictures acquired Castle's Columbia contract. At first the director was enthusiastic. He liked Goetz and the laidback atmosphere of the studio; and was certain the company intended to promote him to bigger budget features. His optimism was unfounded. During the director's two-year stint at UI (1949–51), he was assigned six more programmers all save one mediocre. The standout was *Johnny Stool Pigeon* (1949), a nifty *noir* with a good cast and an above-average script chronicling attempts to crack an international drug ring.

In 1953, Bill Castle returned to Columbia at the behest of Cohn and B impresario Sam Katzman, but his fortunes remained unimproved. In the next three years he directed a mind-numbing 18 low-to-mid-budget pictures handicapped by undernourished screenplays. Most were beautifully photographed Technicolor costume adventures like *Serpent of the Nile* (1953), *Charge of the Lancers* (1954), *Drums of Tahiti* (1954), or westerns such as *Fort Ti* (1953, filmed in 3-D), and *Masterson of Kansas* (1954). Castle's best film of his Columbia II period was the action-packed crime drama *The Houston Story* (1956), a minor gem about a morally challenged oil driller who gets mixed up with mobsters.

When his contract expired in 1956, Castle turned his attention to television. In 1956–58 he directed episodes of various TV series, including 10 well-received entries of *Men of Annapolis*, a collection of dramas depicting the adventures of American soldiers, sailors, and airmen during World War II. Bill enjoyed working in TV, but by the latter 1950s was anxious to return to filmmaking, and wanted to produce his own motion pictures. According to his autobiography, a visit to a movie theater one stormy night to see Clouzot's psychological classic *Diabolique* (1955) was the catalyst which initiated the second major phase of his career. After viewing the large throngs waiting in the rain to see the picture, and witnessing their reaction, Castle reportedly told his wife. "I want to scare the pants off America. When that audience gave that final collective scream, I knew that's where I wanted to take them—only I want louder screams, more horror, more excitement."

After months searching for the right story from which to produce his first motion picture, Castle settled on the horror novel *The Marble Forest*, the tale of a doctor's frantic search for his missing daughter believed to be buried alive. In order to purchase the film rights and have $90,000 to make the picture, he mortgaged his home and enlisted the aid of his friend, writer Robb White, who anted up part of the cash and wrote the adaptation. Filmed in nine days by a largely unknown cast, the minor chiller *Macabre* was released by Allied Artists. In the first of many gimmicks, Castle concocted to promote his movies, the producer/director insured each ticket buyer with a $1,000 life insurance policy from Lloyds of London in case they died of fright during the picture. Although the *New York Times* derided *Macabre* as "a somber tepid shocker," box-office receipts totaled $5 million.

The cigar-chomping Castle achieved his greatest fame during the period 1959–65 producing and directing eleven features, mostly thrillers. Many starred obscure film and television actors and were aimed at the teen and young adult audience. All were lifted by the experienced director who manipulated all aspects of his productions to create and maximize a mood of terror. There were no deep meanings in Castle's films. They were made to entertain not to inspire or educate. Although there were a few common themes, such as inheritances, old houses, locked rooms, handicapped adults, dark humor, there were no essential threads running between them except Castle's expertise, his brief appearances in them (a la Hitchcock), and of course his trademark gimmicks.

Bill followed *Macabre* with the extremely popular *House on Haunted Hill* (Allied Artists, 1959), featuring Vincent Price as a millionaire who volunteers to pay selected guests $10,000 to survive one night in a haunted house. Castle sold the tense, atmospheric thriller with a gimmick he called "Emergo": twelve-foot skeletons placed in boxes next to theater screens which emerged on wires to fly over moviegoers. Castle's penultimate film, *The Tingler* (Columbia, 1959), also starred Price. The story of a doctor who believes fear generates a living creature in the body deemed powerless when a person screams, it was a box-office sensation which literally electrified its audiences. Castle's gimmick, "Percepto," consisted of wires hooked up to certain rows of theater seats which gave filmgoers a small electrical

Poster for *House on Haunted Hill* (Allied Artists, 1959).

shock at opportune moments.

More hit horrors and inventive Castle gimmicks followed in quick succession. The "spirited" *13 Ghosts* (Columbia, 1960) featured "Illusion-O," 3-D type glasses; the creepy *Psycho*-esque *Homicidal* (Columbia, 1961), a "fright break"; and the gothic thriller *Mr. Sardonicus* (Columbia, 1961) a "Punishment poll." Critics scoffed at all Castle's pictures, but he would have the last laugh, one which extended all the way to the bank.

A desire to expand his repertoire inspired the 48-year-old director to hire television actor/comedian Tom Poston, some expert supporting casts, and talent writers to produce two largely comedic projects, *Zotz* (Columbia, 1962) and *The Old Dark House* (Columbia, 1963). Sandwiched in between the Poston comedies was the international intrigue adventure *13 Frightened Girls* (Columbia, 1963). All were unsuccessful.

In 1964, Castle returned to the horror genre. His vehicle was *Strait-Jacket* (Universal International), a frightening Robert Bloch-penned tale of a former ax murderess who, after years in a mental hospital, returns home to more bloodletting and mayhem. Castle had always dismissed the notion of hiring big name movie actors to appear in his productions, but after three successive failures decided his new project needed extra oomph. Trading gimmicks for star power, he inked a contract with veteran actress Joan Blondell to play the unfortunate heroine Lucy Harbin. When Blondell bowed out due to an "injury," Castle replaced her with the legendary Joan Crawford.

Despite initial demands, Castle found working with Crawford a pleasurable experience. The filming went so well Joan agreed to headline a tour of major cities to promote it. Critics were not impressed with the finished product, but the tour was well attended, and the film was a box-office hit, the last of Castle's directorial career. Unfortunately, his two star-studded follow-ups, *The Night Walker* (Universal International, 1964), with Barbara Stanwyck and Robert Taylor, and the frightening *I Saw What You Did* (Universal International, 1965), also starring Crawford, were box-office losers.

Convinced filmgoers were finally tiring of the horror genre, Castle made four more unproductive attempts to branch out into comedy and adventure films. He won surprisingly positive reviews for the suspenseful *Let's Kill Uncle* (1966), the ghostly comedy *The Spirit is Willing* (1967), the all-star gangster spoof *The Busy Body* (1967), and the sci-fi thriller *Project X* (1968), but the films were major flops which left the irrepressible director contemplating the end of his career. In his memoirs he recalled this difficult period. "My small empire was beginning to collapse and by 1967, I was ready to throw in the towel . . . Desperately I started to search for the miracle that would save my career. I had to find something, anything—or I'd be

Castle traded gimmicks for star power in *Strait-Jacket* (Columbia, 1964), starring Joan Crawford. Back left is Leif Erickson.

out of the business. Then from heaven, the miracle appeared. Or was it from hell?"

The miracle from hell was Ira Levin's horrific bestseller, *Rosemary's Baby*, about an unsuspecting young wife whose pregnancy becomes a cause for alarm when her husband becomes involved with witches. After reading the galley proofs from Random House, Castle immediately purchased the film rights, and approached Paramount Pictures. A deal was struck which gave him $250,000, 50% of the profits, and the opportunity to produce and direct with one caveat, he meet with Polish director Roman Polanski (*Repulsion, Knife in the Water*), whom both Paramount and novelist Levin preferred to helm the picture. Initially unimpressed with Polanski, Castle eventually handed the directorial duties over to the 35-year-old who also penned the screenplay.

Castle assembled a 24-carat cast headed by Mia Farrow to enact the intensely macabre story of *Rosemary's Baby* (1968). His patience and high regard for Polanski were sorely tested during the filming.

A stubborn perfectionist who possessed a specific vision of how he wanted the film made, Polanski had running battles with many involved parties; but the result was a masterful suspense film aided by a superb script, great performances, and attention to detail. Critics and audiences hailed the picture as one of the best horror films of all time. Produced for 2.3 million, box-office receipts totaled more than 30. After a lifetime of trying to make a great film, Bill Castle had at last produced a movie which was both a critical *and* a box-office smash.

Unfortunately, his triumph was short-lived. After being forced by illness to bow out as director of the Neil Simon-penned comedy *The Out of Towners*, Castle's career quickly declined. Some of his latter projects had merit, like the prison break drama *Riot* (1969) and the well-produced TV anthology series *Ghost Story* (1972–73), but none approached the quality of *Rosemary's Baby*.

An exuberant, good-humored man who loved his work, and never took himself too seriously, Castle pressed ahead. The last three years of his life (1974–77) would be among his most productive. In 1974 he produced, directed and acted in *Shanks*, an unusual tale of a deaf mute (mime Marcel Marceau) who brings dead people back to life to fight a malevolent motorcycle gang; then one year later, produced and appeared in the disaster film *Bug* (1975) about deadly cockroaches. When he wasn't busy behind the camera, hyperactive Castle was appearing in front of it: as a movie executive in the TV drama *The Sex Symbol* (1974), a film director in John Schlesinger's *Day of the Locust* (1975), and a producer in Hal Ashby's acclaimed satirical comedy *Shampoo* (1975). In 1976 Castle published his memoirs, aptly titled *Step Right Up, I'm Gonna Scare the Pants Off America*. In later years he found time to buy homes in the L.A. area, rehab them, and then sell them at a tidy profit.

Castle was developing another suspense thriller, *2,000 Lakeview Drive*, for MGM in December 1976, when he collapsed. Paramedics were called, but when they failed to revive him sufficiently, transported him to Culver City Hospital where he remained in intensive care for two days. After a short recuperation, he returned to work. He described the incident as "congestion," but it apparently was some form of heart attack. Six months later, on May 31, 1977, after dining at his Beverly Hills home, 63-year-old William Castle suffered a second attack and died a short time later at the U.C.L.A Medical Center. He was survived by his wife Ellen and two daughters. Memorial services were held in Los Angeles on June 3, and interment was in Forest Lawn Memorial Park in Glendale, California.

Although he never achieved the success and critical acceptance he hoped for, William Castle's talent and influence as a producer, director, and businessman are not to be scoffed at. While no one equates his legacy with masters like Hitch, Ford, Wyler, etc., he was more than just a purveyor of cheap schlock. His films, including many of his early Columbia Bs, are well-crafted and exceedingly entertaining. Because of his years of experience and knowledge of all aspects of the process, he was able to elevate them.

Castle's reputation, both inside and outside the film industry, has steadily increased over the decades since his death. In recent years many film enthusiasts from across the country have gathered to celebrate his legacy in film festivals, which include screenings and discussions. Such noted filmmakers as John Waters, Joe Dante, and Robert Zemeckis have also cited Castle as a major influence. Dante's *Matinee* (Universal, 1993), a delightful comedy/drama about a bigger-than-life, cigar-chewing B filmmaker, was a valentine to Castle, as were many of Waters' films like *Polyester* (New Line Cinema, 1982) promoted with the help of "Odorama."

In 1999 director Zemeckis, along with producer Joel Silver, formed Dark Castle Entertainment to make pictures which celebrate the spirit of William Castle. Their first production was a remake of *House on Haunted Hill* with Castle's daughter Terry as co-producer. In 2007 a documentary about the producer/director, *Spine Tingler! The William Castle Story*, helmed by Jeffrey Schwartz, was premiered at the American Film Institute Fest and won the Audience Award for Best Documentary. The self-described P.T. Barnum would no doubt be pleased he's still packing 'em in and putting on a good show!

William Clemens (1905–1980)

The Thirteenth Hour

In a favorable review of the mystery drama *Night of January 16* (Paramount, 1941) a prominent movie critic paid the film's director, B movie maven William Clemens, a rather offhanded compliment. At the end of his remarks the reviewer noted Clemens never made a really bad picture or a really good one. While the critique is basically factual, it is an inadequate assessment of a craftsman who helmed over 30 low-budget motion pictures in a decade-long career, including many well-made mystery and suspense movies which have stood the test of time. Clemens' finest films combine a fast pace with a mixture of suspense and comic elements.

Born William Barry Clemens, in Saginaw, Michigan, on September 10, 1905, the future director grew up in a rural community just outside Saginaw. After graduating from Saginaw High School in 1922, an interest in the art of filmmaking eventually landed the young man on the West Coast where he paid his professional dues by working for several years in various jobs for assorted movie studios. In 1931, Clemens achieved his first important break when RKO hired him as an editor for a group of low-budget westerns featuring Tom Keene.

His apparent talent soon attracted the brothers Warner who were making their own western series starring John Wayne. In 1932 Clemens signed with WB, where he would remain for almost a decade toiling in the company's low-budget unit headed by Bryan Foy, known to film buffs as "Keeper of the Bs." Editor Clemens prospered under Foy's leadership gaining marketable skills and valuable experience working on a wide variety of minor features which ran the gamut from westerns: *Ride Him Cowboy* (1932), *Man from Monterey* (1933); action adventures: *Devil Dogs of the Air* (1935); to dramas: *Oil for the Lamps of China* (1935), *I Found Stella Parish* (1935); comedies: *Kansas City Princess* (1934), *Page Miss Glory* (1935); and suspense thrillers: *Journal for a Crime* (1934), and *The Murder of Dr. Harrigan* (1936). As a Warners "cutter" Clemens had the opportunity to collaborate with some of the studio's most skillful directors, including Mervyn LeRoy, Lloyd Bacon, and William Keighley. In

Bonita Granville and Frankie Thomas in *Nancy Drew and the Hidden Staircase* (Warners, 1939).

1936, Foy rewarded Clemens' ability and hard work by promoting him to B movie director.

Clemens would helm 24 low-budget feature films for Warners in the next five years. Adept at handling actors and bringing a picture in on time and under budget, he surely earned his $300–$400 a week salary. Because he honed his cinematic skills in the cutting room, Clemens appeared to have a special knack for making a coherent film from an incoherent, undernourished script, and 60–70 minutes of footage.

Most his best WB films were crime dramas, mysteries, or comedies. Among them was a pair of suspenseful Perry Mason whodunits, *The Case of the Velvet Claw* (1936) and *The Case of the Stuttering Bishop* (1936), the melodramatic *Missing Witnesses* (1937), the insurance fraud meller *Accidents Will Happen* (1938), and two fluffy comedies, *The Footloose Heiress* (1937) and *She Couldn't Say No* (1940). Clemens' one notable drama at Warners was *Devil's Island* (1939). Similar to John Ford's *Prisoner of Shark Island* (Twentieth Century-Fox, 1936), it was a hard-hitting tale of a doctor (Boris Karloff) sentenced to life in a brutal penal colony for attending an escaped criminal. A well-made B feature with good performances, it earned critical applause and screenings at first-run houses.

Clemens most fondly remembered Warners' films were the quartet of Nancy Drew mysteries he made in 1938–39 (*Nancy Drew Detective, Nancy Drew—Reporter, Nancy Drew—Troubleshooter*, and *Nancy Drew and the Hidden Staircase*) starring spunky, charismatic Bonita Granville as the famed teen detective. Made on barebones budgets with thin, sketchy plots, Clemens somehow crafted four amiable, engaging, and thoroughly entertaining movies which remain highly watchable 70 years hence. His accomplishment was not inconsiderable. Capturing the ambience of 1930s small-town America, he cleverly blended mystery and comedy elements. Assisted by scenarist Kenneth Gamet, Clemens discarded the sophisticated Keene heroine and substituted a more juvenile Nancy, a typical teen who is intelligent and resourceful, but far from perfect. In its review of the last entry, *Nancy Drew and the Hidden Staircase, Variety* said it best: "Director William Clemens keeps the film moving at a speedy clip and gets in some nice comedy touches. He seems to have a special knack of making entertainment out of the weak Nancy Drew story material."

Lured by promises of a higher salary ($500 per week) and bigger budgets, the unassuming 5 ft. 10½ in. tall, brown-haired, 142-pound director moved to Paramount in 1941 where he made four low-to-medium budget motion pictures for producer Sol C. Siegel (1941–42). Three were standouts. Based on Ayn Rand's popular play, the mystery *Night of January 16* (1941) had a superb cast, a good script, and decent production values. Clemens utilized these assets to assemble a topnotch dualer which sustained suspense and audience interest while remaining true to the play. His direction was equally adept on *Night in New Orleans* (1942), an effective whodunit starring Preston Foster, and *Sweater Girl* (1942), a frothy campus musical comedy turned thriller about the baffling murders of a radio broadcaster and a well-known singer. In the latter, a remake of the 1935 Paramount mystery *College Scandal*, Clemens effectively mixed a mystery plot with liberal doses of comedy and two hit Frank Loesser songs.

Bill moved to RKO in 1943 at the behest of producer Maurice Geraghty. His assignments were to helm the 6th, 7th, and 8th entries of the studio's popular *Falcon* series, a group of murder mysteries built around an aristocratic sleuth portrayed by Tom Conway. Although the series was well-established, Clemens transitioned into the director's chair with ease, bringing his own unique flair and experience to bear. His entries, *The Falcon in Danger* (1943), *The Falcon and the Co-Eds* (1943), and *The Falcon Out West* (1944), are largely considered to be among the best of the entire group. Of the three, *The Falcon and the Co-Eds*, about the murders of a professor and dean at a quaint seaside girls' school, was particularly distinguished. Chockfull of red herrings, suspects, and thrilling twists and turns (including a suspenseful climax), it was a B movie lover's delight: a clever, compact, well-paced, 68-minute testament to Clemens skill.

Clemens followed the *Falcons* with another entertaining B detective yarn which would unfortunately be his last for his old employer, Warners. A snappy little number about the ax murders of a millionaire chemical manufacturer and his caretaker, *Crime By Night* (made in 1942, released in 1944) was distinguished by decent production values, an intriguing plot, and an exceptional cast lead by character actor Jerome Cowan as a ethically challenged detective and Jane Wyman as his jealous assistant/best girl. Clemens maintained interest throughout the 62-minute dualer by creating several effectively tense scenes interrupted by welcome comic relief supplied by delightful Wyman who cracks wise throughout. An example of Clemens' effective mixture of thrills and laughs can be found as Cowan and Wyman search the deceased's premises. In a particularly suspenseful moment Wyman cracks, "You and I are gonna stick so close together we could wear the same suspenders."

A combination of factors (discussed in Chapter 5) precipitated an upheaval within the movie industry during the late 1940s which ultimately led to the decline of the B movie, and the end of many notable film careers. Some low-budget directors managed to survive the revolution; some transitioned into the new, dynamic medium of television; and some simply retired and moved on. After making *Musical Shipmates* (1946), a 15-minute short featuring the United States Navy Orchestra, and the 7th Whistler, *The Thirteenth Hour* (Columbia, 1946), director Clemens opted to call it quits. His reasoning is unknown. After years of hard work, intense pressure, not to mention the disappointment of never being promoted to

A-level pictures, perhaps Clemens had simply had enough. What he did after his retirement from films at age 41 is also unclear. One source states he went into business for himself, but does not specify what type of business. Clemens died on April 29, 1980, in Los Angeles, California, age 74.

LEW LANDERS (1901–1962)

The Power of the Whistler

Amiable, dependable, hardworking B movie and television director Lew Landers would undoubtedly have smiled and nodded if he heard comedian Rodney Dangerfield's lamentations of "no respect." Despite one of the silver screen's most prolific careers and a reputation for being the "go-to guy" when movie studios needed product made quickly, efficiently and economically, Landers was never widely acknowledged for his talent and body of work by the motion picture industry or significant critics and historians. A retrospective analysis of his four-decade-long career (130+ films, 100+ series episodes) reveals this slight to be more than unfair. A master craftsman who understood the filmmaking process inside out, Landers' pictures were known for their quickened pace, well-staged action scenes, and on occasion for the innovative use of lighting and photography. If the majority were routine, forgettable it had more to do with the B movie structure under which Landers operated than any lack of ability and originality. Such B movie favorites as *The Raven, Pacific Liner, Return of the Vampire, The Power of the Whistler,* and *The Enchanted Forest* are but a few prime examples of Landers' under-appreciated skills.

Although he never achieved his goal of being a top-ranked director of grade-A films, Lew Landers accomplished a great deal in his relatively short 61-year lifespan. The journey began on the teaming streets of turn-of-the-century New York. Born Lewis Friedlander, on January 2, 1901, he was raised and educated in the Big Apple. Like most artistic souls he developed an interest in the performing arts while still very young. Initially aspiring to be an actor, he began performing at various school functions; and at age 11 secured employment with Universal Film Studios doing odd jobs. In 1913, the youngster was signed to a stock acting contract and made his film debut (billed as Lewis Friedlander) as Joe Binns, the farmer's son, in D.W. Griffith's dramatic *The Escape* (Reliance), then appeared in the two-reel comedy *Admission—Two Faces* (1914). Friedlander continued to work for Universal and act on stage at Temple and Catholic League productions after graduating from high school and enrolling in Columbia University in 1919. To makes ends meet, the industrious young man sold fire insurance.

Friedlander's dedication, work ethic, and potential apparently so impressed Universal Studio head Carl Laemmle he brought the young man to Hollywood in 1922, and gave him an opportunity to experience the filmmaking process from a number of perspectives. Between 1922–34 Louis slowly worked his way up the Universal ladder from production assistant, to assistant director, editor, scriptwriter, and second-unit director. In 1934, he began directing shorts and serials. His initial work, which included the 15-chapter western *Red Ryder* (1934) starring Buck Jones and the aerial adventure *Tailspin Tommy* (1936), showed promise.

Laemmle made Friedlander a feature film director in 1935. His first effort, *The Raven*, proved the wisdom of the promotion. The chilling story of a psychotic doctor/Poe enthusiast who seeks vengeance on the family of a woman who rejects his affections, it starred classic horror's two greatest stars, Bela Lugosi as the mad Doctor Vollin and Boris Karloff as his disfigured assistant Bateman. Aided by the talent and professionalism of his cast, technical team, and a noteworthy script, Landers built a compact, stylistic movie which manipulated mood and tone through the utilization of elaborate set pieces, unusual camera angles, shadows, light, and fog. There were several memorable moments in the 61-minute picture, but the standout was a powerful scene in which a horrified Bateman discovers Vollin has severely disfigured him following facial surgery. Enraged, he shoots his reflection in a room of full-length mirrors as Vollin laughs in sadistic pleasure. Made in three weeks for $135,000, Landers' debut film was an impressive achievement. Sadly, instead of rewarding the novice with bigger and better projects, Universal and future employers chose to exploit the young director's obvious ability to make a good film on a barebones budget by assigning him an endless series of low-budgeters, the lower the better.

During the filming of *The Raven* on March 31, 1935, 34-year-old Friedlander wed his long-time girlfriend, 29-year-old Carmen Bouche, in a civil ceremony in Los Angeles. The childless couple divorced in March 1945. In the early 1950s, Lew wed wife # 2, writer, former columnist Rosalind "Rolli" Roxi, who survived him. They had no children.

By the time he began directing motion pictures in mid-1930s Lew had developed his own technique, an efficient no-frills approach to making movies which would serve him well throughout his career in the Bs. Because he worked under strict time and budgetary limitations, he planned each day's shooting the night before and knew exactly how he would make things work. Although getting the job done on time was paramount, the affable Landers emphasized cordial, respectful working relationships with his cast and technical team. Typically 60–70 minutes in length, his pictures were characterized by a fast pace, use of stock footage, extent sets, and action sequences. Character development was often sacrificed in favor of action and movement.

Friedlander took a new name, Lew Landers, and left Universal in 1937. For the next few years he made the rounds of various studios, plying his multi-dimensional abilities. From 1937–39 he worked for RKO primarily on B action adventures and crime dramas. His collaborations with actors Chester Morris and Richard Dix, including *Flight from Glory* (1937), *Blind Alibi* (1938), *Twelve Crowded Hours* (1939), and *Sky Giant* (1938), are especially memorable.

Landers' best work of the RKO period, *Pacific Liner* (1939), also starred Morris as a ship's physician aboard a ocean liner which experiences a cholera outbreak confined to lowly crew members below decks. Boasting a credible script, topnotch performances, an elaborate ship set constructed by art directors Van Nest Polglase and Albert D'Agostino and realistic action sequences choreographed by Landers, it was a standout. Unlike most of Landers' films *Pacific Liner* contained a strong sociological component which the director exploited to the max. In the film's most memorable scene the bodies of dead crew members are burned in the furnace instead of receiving proper burial at sea to "protect" paying passengers from learning about the epidemic.

Landers demonstrated flair and talent in his first feature film, *The Raven* (Universal, 1935), starring horror masters Bela Lugosi and Boris Karloff.

Victor McLaglen and Wendy Barrie in *Pacific Liner* (RKO, 1939).

Landers made a dozen more B features for Universal and Republic during 1941–43. Most were routine "fillers" with robust action and sincere casts. Among them were such fan favorites as *Ski Patrol* (Universal–1940), an entertaining war drama about Russia's conflict with Finland prior to World War II, and *Back in the Saddle* (Republic, 1941), a rousing Gene Autry musical shoot-'em-up. Appearing in both was a talented former MGM contract player Edward Norris who began making B movies in the mid-1930s. In a series of interviews conducted by the author during the period 2000-2001, Norris recounted details of his long feature film career which included several low-budgeters directed by Lew Landers. "I really thought some of the B pictures we did were better than the As they had running with them because the Bs were never boring. They moved and the kids loved all the action. The B picture directors were mostly action directors . . . There were some really excellent ones like Phil Rosen, Oliver Drake, and Lew Landers. I admired their speed technique. They listened to the actors and respected them. They would take suggestions, anything to help a scene . . . I particularly admired Landers. He was a kind, respectful, and talented gentleman. He would always say, 'Do it the way you want to do it, and let's see.' If he liked it, he'd say, 'Do it just that way.' Landers was always interested in making the films as good as they could be, and the actors and technical people appreciated that. This was not true of many other B movie directors. I could name names if you like!"

In 1941 Columbia's head of production, Irving Briskin, hired the 39-year-old Lew as a contract director, thus beginning Landers' long, frequently stormy association with Harry Cohn who would employ him on and off for the next dozen years (1941–53). Although one could say it was a mutually beneficial relationship, clearly Columbia reaped the lion's share of the rewards. In most respects Landers was an ideal studio employee: compliant, amiable, competent, and incredibly hardworking. He thoroughly understood the filmmaking process, completed assignments with little complaint, and made a studio dollar stretch like few could. No wonder Columbia big whigs referred to him as "the go-to guy."

Lew made a mind-boggling 51 inexpensively produced, quickly manufactured features for the Cohn factory. There were notable exceptions, but the vast majority were entertaining and unremarkable.

John Litel, Ted Donaldson, and *Flame in My Dog Rusty* (Columbia, 1948).

Many of Landers' lesser efforts can be totally summed up by their colorfully descriptive titles, numbers like *Harvard, Here I Come* (1941), *I'm from Arkansas* (1944), *Revenue Agent* (1950), and *The Big Gusher* (1951).

A better opportunity occasionally presented itself, and the experienced Lew took full advantage. Such was the case of funny comedies like *The Stork Pays Off* (1941), *The Boogieman Will Get You* (1945); topical flag-wavers: *Stand By All Networks* (1942), *Submarine Raider* (1942), *Atlantic Convoy* (1942); adventures: *California Conquest* (1952); thrillers: *The Power of the Whistler* (1945), *Man in the Dark* (1953); and several stylish horror mysteries, *Murder in Times Square* (1943) and *Return of the Vampire* (1944).

Among the Columbia contract players Lew worked with at the time was young Ted Donaldson, a gifted child actor who'd made a name for himself on radio and on stage prior to striking cinematic gold in such time-honored movie classics as *Once Upon a Time* (Columbia, 1944) and *A Tree Grows in Brooklyn* (Twentieth Century-Fox, 1945). Signed by Cohn in 1943, the 10-year-old eventually became the star of a Columbia series of family-oriented adventure/dramas about a young boy and his beloved German shepherd, Rusty. Donaldson worked with Landers three times, *The Son of Rusty* (Columbia, 1947), *My Pal* (RKO, 1947), and *My Dog Rusty* (Columbia, 1948); and in 2009 recalled the director's congeniality and professionalism. "His reputation as a nice man was fully deserved. I would go further and say a kind man, though I don't remember any specific instances of his kindness. It was more the ease with which he worked and the respect he had for all his colleagues. He knew what he wanted, and was always clear in expression, though receptive to suggestions of an actor. I suspect like some others of his breed and generation, he was a better director than I knew, though obviously not one with the genius of Kazan or the highly gifted Alexander Hall whose subtlety, both with actors, camera setup, and movement reminded me of Wyler . . ."

Lew's legendary good nature would be sorely tested by Columbia on a regular basis. In 1944 he became so frustrated he left the studio in protest over its insistence he train other directors like Oscar "Budd" Boetticher, William Castle, and Henry Levin while shooting his own features in 10–12 days. He eventually returned to work at Columbia, but never forgot the humiliation. His last Columbia film was *Man in the Dark* (1953).

In the midst of the acrimony, the productive Landers continued making B feature films for other studios. Outside of Columbia his most interesting movies were made at poverty row's PRC. Highlights included the tense, intriguing melodrama *Shadow of Terror* (1945), the compelling underworld meller *Crime Inc.* (1945), and *The Enchanted Forest* (1945), a touchingly beautiful Technicolor drama of a lost child who learns about nature and the meaning of life when he is raised by an old hermit. The latter is particularly memorable for its affecting script based on a story by John Lebar, and well-mounted wild animal sequences staged by Landers.

Although his private life was low-key, devoid of scandal, Lew was the subject of several newspaper stories during the 1940s and 1950s having to do with his favorite hobby, making home movies. Aided by his trusty 8mm, Landers recorded details of making each of his films; things like outtakes, rehearsals, screen goofs, gags, game playing, and offstage giggles. Included were process shots of how particular films were constructed and behind-the-scenes footage of technicians working their magic.

Like most of his contemporaries Landers also worked in television. Although he preferred film and continued to make motion pictures, the veteran director told interviewers he found directing TV both challenging and fulfilling. His television credits included popular series of all genres. There were comedies: *Meet Corliss Archer* (1954), *Topper* (7 episodes, 1954); dramas: *Dr. Christian* (2 episodes, 1957), *Rescue 8* (1959); crime dramas: *Highway Patrol* (10 episodes, 1955–59); mysteries: *Mr. & Mrs. North* (7 episodes, 1952–54); adventures: *Terry and the Pirates* (9 episodes, 1953), *Casey Jones* (4 episodes, 1957–58), and many westerns: *The Adventures of Kit Carson* (9 episodes, 1951–53), *Tales of the Texas Rangers* (16 episodes, 1955–57), *Mackenzie's Raiders* (9 episodes, 1958–59), *Colt 45* (3 episodes, 1960), *Maverick* (2 episodes, 1959–60), and *Bat Masterson* (4 episodes, 1959–61), etc. Among the last projects of his long career were two episodes of the classic western *Sugarfoot* starring Will Hutchins. In a 2010 interview, Mr. Hutchins told the author he admired Landers despite being upbraided by him for being late on the set one day. "Lew Landers, a worthy subject, a quiet craftsman. Wish I'd told him how much I appreciated his work! Recently reviewed a nifty print of one of his *Sugarfoots*, "The Long Dry" with Robert Armstrong. I liked it! I remember I was tardy one day during the time we were shooting it. He yelled at me, 'Who do you think you are showing up so late!' 'Will Hutchins,' I replied lamely. Later, he invited me to visit him in Palm Springs."

Landers' post-Columbia film credits were undistinguished lowercase projects with substandard production values, and/or inept scripts. The most that can be said of features like *Captain John Smith and Pocahontas* (United Artists, 1953) and *Captain Kidd and the Slave Girl* (Allied Artists, 1954) is they moved and contained color photography. Lew's final film, *Terrified* (Crown International, 1963), released after his death, was perhaps the best of this lot. A masked maniac grade-Z cheapie, it had a genuinely creepy vibe, and contained surprisingly scary scenes.

Landers had just completed *Terrified* when he collapsed and died of a heart attack at his residence in Palm Springs, California, on December 16, 1962, at age 61. Funeral services were held at the Pierce Brothers in Beverly Hills followed by cremation. Landers

Lew Landers (left) poses with Lucille Ball and John Agar for a publicity shot on the set of *The Magic Carpet* **(Columbia, 1951).**

was survived by his wife, Rosalind, and two stepdaughters, Mrs. Bernadette Wolfe and Palm Springs columnist-radio commentator Gloria Greer.

Although he will forever be associated with low-budgeters, and be ridiculed by elitist writers and critics, the truth is B movie director extraordinaire Lew Landers was a very talented man who made a significant contribution to the film industry by the sheer magnitude of his work, by his tutelage of many important directors and actors, and for the knowledge, professionalism, and enthusiasm he brought to the art of making motion pictures. His beloved home movie hobby was perhaps the most concrete reflection of the joy and immense pride he took in his work. "Sometimes I just sit in my living room in the dark all alone and watch my home movies," he once told an interviewer. "I get more of a thrill out of looking at these pictures than out of anything else. My entire life's work comes before me on the screen."

D. ROSS LEDERMAN (1894–1972)

The Return of the Whistler

D. Ross Lederman was one of many journeyman directors working in 1930s and 1940s Hollywood who specialized in B genre films, primarily westerns and thrillers. Like the other *Whistler* directors profiled in this volume, he was a conscientious and efficient technician. His work is generally characterized by continuous movement, use of stock footage, familiar sets, and action sequences. Lederman's best films possess a certain stylistic energy derived from the skillful use of montage, well choreographed gun battles, fisticuffs, chase sequences, and other scenes of violence. Many believe Lederman's professional preoccupation with brutality, turbulence, and discord was a reflection of his personality. A confrontational individual (both on a personal and professional level), he often forged antagonistic, mutually contemptuous relationships with those around him; including many of the actors and creative personnel he worked with.

Born in Lancaster, Pennsylvania, on December 12, 1894, David Ross Lederman was the only child of Luke and Laura Ross Lederman. Young David's severe asthma necessitated the family's move to Venice, California, in 1904, where David's father found work as a department store manager. According to several sources, David's parents were distant and his childhood unhappy. Many believe his detachment from family significantly impacted his work and relationships.

By the time he entered high school David's health had improved. An athletic young man, he excelled in sports, especially baseball. He was also interested in the arts and motion pictures. In 1915, he combined his athletic and artistic interests by becoming an extra (doing stunts) in Mack Sennett's Keystone Kops series, then secured a position as assistant to the second assistant director on D.W. Griffith's *Intolerance* (1916). Throughout the next decade Lederman worked in various capacities as "field assistant," then assistant director, at Warner Brothers. Hardworking, disciplined, always eager to please, he delighted his frugal bosses by developing several time-saving, moneymaking measures, even writing a field manual for assistant directors, setting forth efficient, cost-effective methods of checking up on productions, and techniques for organizing shots and sequences.

During his first years at Warners Lederman learned the ropes from such distinguished pros as Lewis Milestone, Lloyd Bacon, and especially Roy Del Ruth.

Lederman's private life was considerably less organized. On September 22, 1920, he married Marcella Brush. Within a year she was filing for divorce alleging violence and cruelty. According to Wheeler Winston Dixon's 2006 *Film Criticism* article, "A Cinema of Violence: the Films of D. Ross Lederman," "The women in Lederman's world were to be dominated, exploited, or ignored . . ." The couple separated and reconciled six times. In April 1923, Marcella claimed her husband, "choked and struck her and professed a hearty aversion for her women friends." In 1924 she asserted more abuse, and said Lederman often refused to speak to her. He countered by denying the charges and claiming his wife's frequent litigations were keeping him poor. The couple finally divorced in 1925.

Amid the marital woes Lederman also made headlines when he was charged with assault by a man who claimed the director attacked him on the set of one of his films. The charges were later dismissed, but the incident fed a growing perception of Lederman as "difficult." In 1926 the misogynistic D. Ross married for a second time to former actress Frances Dee Warner (no relation to the Warner Brothers). They had one daughter, Joan D., born on August 8, 1927. Several sources assert Lederman's second marriage was no happier than the first. The couple divorced in 1944. Lederman never remarried, and remained estranged from his only child until shortly before his death.

In 1927 32-year-old D. Ross Lederman became a feature film director at Warner Brothers. His first effort, the rousing children's adventure *A Dog of the Regiment* (1927) starring Rin Tin Tin, was a success with the public and Jack Warner who admired the young director's ability to make an entertaining film on a miniscule budget. For his part Lederman was equally awed by his ruthless, manipulative boss whom he considered a role model. Lederman followed with several Rinty adventures including *The Million Dollar Collar* (1929) the famous canine's sound debut.

In 1931, Lederman was hired by poverty row's Mascot Pictures to helm the western serial *Phantom of the West* starring Tom Tyler. The success of the venture caught the eye of another movie tyrant,

Harry Cohn, who signed the up-and-comer to a contract. Lederman would work for Columbia and Warner Brothers off and on for the next 20 years. At Columbia he directed over 40 low-budget motion pictures. All emphasized action over characterization and plot. At the beginning of his Columbia tenure Lederman worked almost exclusively in westerns starring Tim McCoy and Buck Jones. Demonstrating an aptitude for choreographing gunfights, fistfights, and galloping chase scenes, his exciting 60 to 65-minute oaters were hits. Unfortunately, the director wasn't nearly as popular. During his early years at Columbia Lederman cemented a reputation for being an inflexible taskmaster renown for piecing together a movie on time and under budget at all costs. This netted him gold stars from Cohn but frequently earned him enmity from the actors and technicians he worked with. McCoy reportedly despised Lederman and attempted to defy him whenever possible. The legendary John Wayne (with whom the B movie director worked in his early Columbia days) put it this way, "You know, I loved that old son-of-a-bitch, but he [Lederman)] was the meanest man I ever knew."

Cohn gradually expanded Lederman's repertoire by assigning him crime dramas like *High Speed* (1932) starring Buck Jones, *State Trooper* (1933) with Regis Toomey, and two mysteries, *Girl in Danger* (1934) and *The Crime of Helen Stanley* (1934). The latter, which starred Ralph Bellamy as a determined detective on the trail of the killer, was typical of Lederman's work. Produced in eleven days for considerably less than $100,000, it was a compact, modestly entertaining dualer with a threadbare plot, lots of action, mundane dialogue, made with leftover sets, and stock footage (both film and music).

Throughout the remainder of the 1930s Lederman continued to dazzle Cohn with the quantity of his output. Crime thrillers became his specialty, but his best films of the 1930s (made for Columbia and on loan to Warner Brothers) included other genres. Among them were *Red Hot Tires* (Warner Brothers, 1935), an action-packed racing quickie with an exciting climactic car race, *Dinky* (Warner Brothers, 1935), a heartwarming drama of the devotion between a mother and son, and *Come Closer, Folks* (Columbia, 1936), a well-acted comedy about a shyster salesman's love for a prim department store manager. In between Columbia and WB jobs Lederman helmed *Tarzan's Revenge* (Twentieth Century-Fox, 1938), an atypically low-key jungle adventure starring Olympic champions Glenn Morris and Eleanor Holm.

Lederman returned to Warners for a three-year stint in 1941. There he would make several memorable B movies beginning with the amusing comic thriller *The Body Disappears* (1941), followed by a succession of violent wartime espionage thrillers, mysteries, and crime dramas which featured a lightning pace and montages compressing time and narrative. Highlights included the murder mystery *Shadows on the Stairs* (1941), the gangster melodrama *Bullet Scars* (1942), two intense war-related suspensers, *Busses Roar* (1942) and *Adventures in Iraq* (1943), and the breakneck-paced crime drama *The Racket Man* (Columbia, 1944).

The two best films of Lederman's Warners' years, and perhaps his career, were *Strange Alibi* (1941) and *The Gorilla Man* (1943). For anyone who questions his talent these rough-and-ready programmers are must-sees. The former, an amazingly downbeat, often vicious, tale of a righteous cop's (Arthur Kennedy) dedicated quest to expose police corruption and infiltrate the mob, boasts breathless pacing, relentless violence, skillful montages, several memorable sequences, and topnotch performances. The latter, a wartime espionage tale featuring John Loder as a wounded British Army captain who ends up in a hospital run by Nazi agents, was likewise violent and inventive with nonstop action and unusual camera angles. Both were expert, imaginative examples of B product at its best: art on the economy plan. It's hard to argue with writer Dixon, who hailed *Strange Alibi* as "a curiously compelling film that resonates in the memory long after the last violent scene has faded on the screen."

Unfortunately, not all of Lederman's work was as inspired. Sometimes his cost-effective speed technique worked to the detriment of a production; and his finished films seemed hurried or confusing. Such forgettable entries as *Passage to Hong Kong* (Warners, 1941), *Escape from Crime* (Warners, 1942), and *Find the Blackmailer* (Warners, 1943), and the vast majority of his late 1940s movies are prime examples. Unlike *Strange Alibi* these inexpensively-produced, 10-day "bottom fillers" looked as cheap as they were. In his illuminating volumes *The Detective in Hollywood* (1978) and *The Vanishing Legion* (1999), the normally positive author Jon Tuska professed little enthusiasm for Lederman's work. "Lederman was something of an oddity, his principal concerns throughout his career even throughout his many years at Columbia remained budget cutting for its own sake . . ."

Lederman's return to Columbia in the late 1940s coincided with the decline of the B movie. He seemed to know his days as a movie director were numbered; and whatever vitality he brought to the creative process of making movies dissipated. The results were multiple indifferent, laden, hurried-looking features, including several entries of well-loved Columbia series. Although some, like the *Boston Blackie* entry *The Phantom Thief* (1946), the murder mystery *Key Witness* (1947), and *The Return of the Whistler* (1948) contain excellent acting and one or two good scenes, they appeared to lack the vigor of Lederman's best endeavors. Tuska believes these films failed because their director "seemed to approach every assignment with no enthusiasm whatsoever . . ."

Mr. Lederman made one feature film in the 1950s, the cliché-ridden World War II drama *The Tanks Are Coming* (Warner Brothers, 1951), before turning his creative attentions to television. During an eight-year period (1952–60), he directed multiple episodes of several successful TV series. Among them were westerns: *The Range Rider* (6 episodes, 1952–53), *The Gene Autry Show* (11 episodes, 1951–54), *Annie Oakley* (6 episodes, 1956), *Shotgun Slade* (2 episodes, 1959–60); crime dramas: *State Trooper* (5 episodes, 1957), and *Border Patrol* (1959); and one memorable adventure: *Captain Midnight* (6 episodes, 1954–55).

When television work became less plentiful in the early 1960s, the veteran director retired. Since work had always been his refuge, its absence was costly. By the latter 1960s Lederman was experiencing multiple health problems. For a time he resided with his old friend and boss Bryan Foy before his ailments forced a move to the Motion Picture Country Home and Hospital in Woodland Hills, California, where he died on August 24, 1972, of kidney and heart ailments. Shortly before his death, he attempted a brief, rather unsatisfactory, reconciliation with daughter Joan who had become a noted interior designer. Joan told author Dixon she brought her 16-year-old son along to meet his grandfather, but Lederman never asked the boy about his life, only spoke of himself.

Although Lederman's film work was largely ignored in its day, his catalog of 80+ features is receiving new and welcome attention today. Opinions remain mixed regarding his legacy, however. In 2006, Dixon cited Lederman for his "audacious visual stylization and bizarre, often surrealistic compression of narrative and character." He believes Lederman's fast-paced, often-violent films were essentially the result of his troubled life, personal unhappiness, frustrations, and inner rage. Others view the controversial D. Ross in a decidedly less favorable way; as a competent, but uninspired studio employee who substituted a frenetic pace and violent action for creativity. There is truth in both assessments.

GEORGE SHERMAN (1908–1991)

The Secret of the Whistler

Diminutive producer/director George Sherman contributed an amazing body of work in a lifetime in the movie business. At one time or another, this dedicated, hardworking artisan held down every cinematic job imaginable from lowly messenger boy to producer. In the process he gained a unique and valuable understanding of the filmmaking process which would serve him well in a career which lasted four decades and included over 100 features. Sherman's finest films were renowned for their careful plot development and movement, well-choreographed action sequences, and later, for their lush on-location color photography. Unlike most B movie directors, Sherman eventually graduated to more upscale features.

Sherman's personal story resembles a Horatio Alger tale. Born George Sherman, on July 14, 1908, in New York City, his interest and ambition to become involved in motion pictures developed early. At age 13, he found work as a messenger boy for First National Attractions, a film exhibitors company. When the organization started producing motion pictures at the old Biograph Studios in the Bronx, George was hired as an office boy by studio manager Hugh McCollum who later became a noted short subjects producer.

When First National moved to Burbank, California, in 1927, Sherman's boss, Al Rockett, promised him a job if he would relocate. George worked his way out to the West Coast as a bell boy on the steamer, S.S. Magnolia; and, true to his word, Rockett hired him as an office assistant. Six months later director Frank Lloyd selected Sherman as his personal assistant, then second assistant director.

George moved to the Mack Sennett Studios in 1929 where he worked as an editor on two-reel comedies, then as assistant director to George Marshall. In 1935, he began freelancing as an assistant director working mainly at Republic and RKO in westerns and musicals. His first chance to direct came in 1937 when writer/director Ewing Scott was injured in an auto accident; and Sherman was asked to take over the reins of RKO's low-budget western comedy *Hollywood Cowboy* (1937). The film was a success, guaranteeing there would be many more such opportunities for the industrious 29-year-old.

In 1937, on the recommendation of director Joe Kane (with whom George worked on *Melody Trail* in 1935), Republic hired Sherman to take over directorial duties of the successful Three Mesquiteers western series so Kane could work with Republic's new cowboy star Roy Rogers. During his seven-year tenure at Republic (1937–44) George made over 50 low-budget features, mostly westerns, establishing a reputation as a consummate B movie professional, renown for, "making 'em fast but good." Under the most challenging circumstances (i.e. minuscule budgets, short shooting schedules, barebones scripts, etc.) he crafted respectable programmers which were entertaining and highly profitable. His formula westerns were engrossing, fast-paced, and frequently innovative, effectively balancing plot and action.

Sherman's Republic highlights included 22 Mesquiteer entries, five Gene Autry cowboy musicals, including two of his best, *Mexicali Rose* (1939) and *Colorado Sunset* (1939), and a succession of oaters starring Don "Red" Barry. A difficult and combative actor, Barry was detested by many Republic directors, but not the laidback George. In fact, he and Barry shared a warm rapport which lasted through 18 motion pictures. Perhaps the 5 ft. 1 in. Sherman, whom Gene Autry once described as "about the size of a popcorn kernel," could relate to the challenges of the feisty, defensive, yet talented 5 ft. 4 in. Barry.

From left to right: George Sherman, Willard Parker, and Evelyn Keyes on the set of *Renegades* (Columbia, 1946).

While working on Barry westerns George married nonprofessional Corrine Autra in 1942 and set up housekeeping in Newport Beach, 50 miles from Hollywood. The couple adopted two daughters, Judy and Luana in the mid-1940s, and had their own daughter Suzanne in 1947. After their divorce in the 1970s, Sherman married a second time, to actress/writer Cleo Ronson, and had another daughter. His second union would be a happy and productive one. Sherman and Ronson eventually formed their own production company and collaborated on television scripts.

In 1942, the up-and-coming director received a promotion of sorts when Republic plucked him from the old west and gave him the opportunity to direct and co-produce a group of mysteries and adventures they planned to make faster and cheaper than westerns. With major assists from talented writers like Curt Siodmak and Republic technicians, Sherman demonstrated a surprising flair for making compact, fast-paced B thrillers. Among the best of these quickies were *The London Blackout Murders* (1942), which featured John Abbott as a surgeon murdering supposed Nazi sympathizers during the London blitz, and *A Scream in the Dark* (1943), with Robert Lowery on the trail of a black widow suspected of killing several husbands.

Sherman's non-westerns were so well-received Republic studio chief Herbert Yates rewarded him with a raise, and one of the most difficult assignments of his career, to make a movie actress of Czech-born skating champion Vera Ralston. Sherman worked with Ralston on two low-to-medium-budget features: the horror film *The Lady and the Monster* (1944) and the espionage melodrama *Storm Over Lisbon* (1944). Both had redeeming qualities, but were hamstrung by Ralston's inexperience and thick accent.

Rumor had it Sherman exited Republic in 1944 because he didn't want to work with Ralston again. Whatever the reason, George signed with Columbia in 1945 and spent the period (1945–1948) cranking out low-to-medium-budget movies which ranged from crime thrillers: *The Crime Doctor's Courage* (1945) and *The Secret of the Whistler* (1946); musical comedies: *Talk About a Lady* (1946) and *The Gentleman Misbehaves* (1946); to Technicolor adventures and westerns: *The Bandit of Sherwood Forest* (1946) and *Renegades* (1946). The best of them was the old west melodrama *Relentless* (1948), about a cowboy (Robert Young) falsely accused of murder on a quest to locate the real perpetrator before being captured by a determined sheriff. Aided by a good script, beautiful color photography, and expert performances, Sherman created a rich, realistic movie effectively mixing plot and character development with a healthy dose of rousing action.

The excellent reviews he garnered for *Relentless* undoubtedly inspired Universal International's interest in Sherman. Signing a pact with the studio, he spent the next seven years at U.I. (1948–55)

A scene from Sherman's western *The Hard Man* (Columbia, 1957), starring, from left to right: Lorne Greene, Guy Madison, and Valerie French.

helming over 20 medium-budget motion pictures, mostly action-packed westerns and adventures. Many of his better U.I. oaters took a more modern view of the old west, especially in their depiction of American Indians as rational, often sympathetic, figures whose conflicts with white settlers were frequently the result of broken promises and violence perpetrated on them. Among the best examples were *Tomahawk* (1951), *Comanche Territory* (1950), and *Chief Crazy Horse* (1955). Other adventure highlights included the exciting Exodus tale *Sword in the Desert* (1949) and the fascinating Nazi interrogation melodrama *Target Unknown* (1951). In between adventure assignments Sherman again surprised Hollywood insiders by helming a trio of superior noir thrillers for U.I., including *Larceny* (1948), *The Raging Tide* (1951), and *The Sleeping City* (1950). The latter, a grim, disturbing melodrama chronicling crimes in a metropolitan hospital, and the cynical, hardnosed cops who investigate them, is largely considered one of Sherman's finest.

In 1955 Sherman began freelancing. His initial effort, the

big-budget post-Civil War drama *Count Three and Pray* (Columbia, 1955), proved overly ambitious, but many of his mid-1950s B+ features were entertaining and successful. Among them were the sizzling adventure/drama *The Treasure of Pancho Villa* (RKO, 1955, filmed in Mexico), the racially-charged western *Comanche* (United Artists, 1956, also filmed in Mexico), and *The Hard Man* (Columbia, 1957), a western character study involving a former Texas Ranger-turned-deputy sheriff who battles a cattle baron.

By 1960, Sherman was dividing his time between directing motion pictures and producing feature films and television. He worked for various studios during the 1960s and for his own production company, Shergari Corporation, formed in 1959. His solo directorial ventures included the well-received Audie Murphy western *Hell Bent for Leather* (Universal International, 1960), the Maurice Chevalier, Jayne Mansfield comedy *Panic Button* (1963, made in Italy), and the sentimental drama *Smoky* (Twentieth Century-Fox, 1966). Among his solo production credits were the John Wayne western *The Comancheros* (Fox, 1961) and the underwater fantasy comedy *Hello Down There* (Paramount, 1965). Sherman both produced and directed several westerns and adventures, such as *Ten Days to Tulara* (United Artists, 1958), filmed in Mexico, and *Son of Robin Hood* (1959), made in Great Britain.

Throughout the 1950s and 1960s George also worked as a director and producer on television. Among his many TV directorial credits were episodes of such acclaimed series as *Rawhide* (2 episodes, 1959), *The Naked City* (5 episodes, 1962–63), and *Route 66* (3 episodes, 1962–63). His TV production projects included 26 episodes each of two hit youth-oriented adventure series, *Daniel Boone* (directed 11 episodes, 1965–67) and *Gentle Ben* (directed one episode, 1967–68).

Suffering from heart problems and other ailments, Sherman scaled back his work schedule in the 1970s, concentrating his energies on his family, writing scripts with his wife Cleo, and making various television appearances discussing his career. He was basically retired in 1971 when old friend John Wayne lured him back to direct *Big Jake* (National General), a western set in 1910 Texas involving the kidnapping of a wealthy rancher's son (Wayne) by a bloodthirsty gunrunner (Richard Boone). Filmed in the wilds of Mexico, *Jake* proved an ordeal for the frail Sherman, but the tough, hardworking George persevered; and with the help of his pal Duke (who filled in for him on the days he was unable to shoot) he completed the picture.

Although some critics gave *Big Jake* a thumbs down for "a thin script," "gratuitous violence," and "lackadaisical direction," theirs was a minority opinion. Superbly directed, sumptuously photographed, enthusiastically enacted by a veteran cast, and brilliantly scored by Elmer Bernstein, *Big Jake* became the biggest hit of George Sherman's career, a fitting cap on a lifetime devoted to the art of making motion pictures. Afterward, the veteran producer/director worked on three television projects. In 1977, he directed episodes of two crime dramas, *Nashville 99* and *Sam*, and one year later produced the acclaimed biopic *Little Mo* about the life of tennis star Maureen Connolly.

Eighty-two-year-old George Sherman died on March 15, 1991, at the Cedars-Sinai Medical Center in Los Angeles of heart and kidney failure. Survivors included wife Cleo, four daughters, and eight grandchildren. There were no memorial services; and his body was cremated. While filming one of his latter movies an interviewer once asked Sherman why he continued to direct. His response was poignant and revealing. He said, "I make films for many reasons. One, it's the only thing I know. It's my occupation, my life, my career."

PRODUCER, WRITERS, CRAFTSMAN

MISCHA BAKALEINIKOFF (1890–1960)

MUSIC DIRECTOR: All eight *Whistler* films.
(His work on the first three was uncredited.)

One of Hollywood's most industrious, dependable, and unheralded talents was Russian-born conductor and composer Mischa Bakaleinikoff. Born on November 10, 1890, in Moscow, he was a music student at the conservatory when the Russian Revolution commenced. The turmoil eventually led Mischa and brother Constantin to flee their native land. They lived in Manchuria and Shanghai prior to emigrating to the U.S. in 1926. By 1931 both were in Hollywood where Mischa landed a job at Columbia Pictures and his brother at RKO.

Bakaleinikoff would be one of Harry Cohn's most productive and valued employees for the next 29 years. Beginning as a double bass violin player in the orchestra, he gradually worked his way up to composer, and then music director for Columbia's B unit. In the latter capacity he functioned as a supervisor, conducting music written by others for a particular film, assembling existing music from the Columbia library, or composing bits as "bridges" between library music. Among his best-known credits were entries in the *Whistler, Boston Blackie, Blondie,* and *Jungle Jim* series, and several notable B+ items, including *The Big Heat* (1953) and three memorable sci-fiers: *It Came from Beneath the Sea* (1955), *Earth vs. Flying Saucers* (1956), and *Twenty Million Miles to Earth* (1957). His music was noted for its unique heavy brass sound.

The industrious Mr. Bakaleinikoff had just completed work on the Three Stooges feature *Have Rocket Will Travel* (1959) when he died of complications of lung cancer in Los Angeles, on August 2, 1960, age 69. He was survived by his wife, Yvonne, two sons, Tony and William, and two daughters, Victoria and Annie. A string ensemble from Columbia played at his funeral service. Bakaleinikoff was buried at Forest Lawn Memorial Park in Glendale, California.

REGINALD "REG" BROWNE (1911–1981)

EDITOR: *The Mark of the Whistler.*
The Power of the Whistler.

California native Reginald Browne was a skilled film and television editor who worked in Bs for the greater part of three decades (mid-1940s–1970) for various studios, primarily Columbia and Eagle-Lion. His talent for assembling entertaining, coherent films on barebones budgets, often utilizing stock footage, was exemplary. In addition to the two *Whistler* entries, his significant credits were *Appointment in Berlin* (Columbia, 1943), *Cry of the Werewolf* (Columbia, 1944), *The Fighting Stallion* (Eagle-Lion, 1950), and *The Marshal's Daughter* (United Artists, 1953).

When the demand for his services in feature films waned in the latter 1950s, Browne turned his creative attentions to television. For a time, while serving as supervising editor for several TV projects, including westerns *Judge Roy Bean* (1956) and *26 Men* (1957–59), he tried his hand at directing and acting. By the 1960s he had returned to editing films exclusively. His latter credits were mostly low-budget westerns and sexploitation features like *Four Fast Guns* (Universal, 1960), *The Gay Deceivers* (Fanfare, 1969), and his last credit, *The Curious Female* (Fanfare, 1970). He died of a heart attack in Los Angeles at 69, on May 13, 1981. He was survived by a son Reg. Jr. and daughter, Linda Lee.

RUDOLPH FLOTHOW (1895–1971)

PRODUCER: All *Whistler* features
(except *The Power of the Whistler*).

Renowned for his efficient, no-frills approach to making motion pictures, German-born film and television producer Rudolph Flothow was involved in the making of over 300 feature films and in excess of 200 television projects during a 40+ year career which encompassed several filmmaking jobs.

Born and educated in Frankfurt, Flothow came to the U. S.

during the early teens. By 1915 he had entered the motion picture industry as an employee of Paramount Pictures in New York. During the latter teens and 1920s he worked for Fox and other studios, before landing a job as assistant production manager at M.H. Hoffman's Tiffany Stahl in 1929. It was at Tiffany, and later at Hoffman's Allied Pictures, that Flothow began perfecting his ability to produce entertaining, highly profitable programmers with exceedingly low-budgets. Hoffman promoted Flothow to production manager when Allied became Liberty Pictures in 1934. Flothow's Liberty credits included *School for Girls* (1934), *Sweepstake Annie* (1935), and the Ellery Queen whodunit *The Spanish Cape Mystery* (1935). When Liberty was folded into Republic Pictures in 1935, Flothow and Hoffman parted ways. One year later Flothow was hired by independent producer Larry Darmour, who specialized in low-budgeters and serials distributed by Columbia. Flothow became associate producer at Darmour Inc. in 1937.

When Larry Darmour died suddenly in 1942, Flothow became head of production at Darmour Inc. In that capacity he took over the reins of various projects, including Columbia's *Ellery Queens*, the *Crime Doctor*, and *Whistler* series. In 1943, Flothow became officially employed as a B producer at Columbia where he worked for the next eight years. In addition to the aforementioned, Flothow produced entries in the *Lone Wolf* and *Boston Blackie* series, and many other entertaining low-budget items like *Key Witness* (1947), *The Devil's Henchmen* (1949), *Prison Warden* (1949), *Al Jennings of Oklahoma* (1951), *Criminal Lawyer* (1951), and five cliffhanger serials, *The Phantom* (1943), *The Desert Hawk* (1944), *Black Arrow* (1944), *The Monster and the Ape* (1945), and, notably, *Batman* (1943).

After leaving Columbia in 1951 Flothow utilized his time-tested talents to produce projects for the small screen. During the mid- to latter 1950s he served as producer for 52 episodes of the African adventure series *Ramar of the Jungle* starring Jon Hall (1953–54), served as production manager on multiple episodes of *Fury* (1955–56) and *The Count of Monte Cristo* (1956), and produced *The New Adventures of Charlie Chan* (1957–58).

Beginning in 1953 Flothow re-cut episodes of *Ramar of the Jungle* to assemble three theatrical films released by Lippert, the most notable being *Phantom of the Jungle* (1955). Flothow's last major credit came in 1963 when he worked as production manager for his old friend, writer/director Sam Fuller, on the lurid melodrama *Shock Corridor* (Allied Artists, 1963). Flothow died on December 21, 1971, in Culver City, California, age 76. His son and namesake, Rudolph Flothow (1926–2007), was a noted educator.

RICHARD LANDAU (1914–1993)

STORY: *The Secret of the Whistler.*

Richard Landau was a prolific film and television writer. Among his notable motion picture credits were *Back to Bataan* (RKO, 1945), *Christmas Eve* (United Artistsm, 1947), *The Crooked Way* (United Artists, 1949), *Roadblock* (RKO, 1951), *Stolen Face* (Lippert, 1952), *The Quartermass Xperiment* (Hammer/United Artists, 1955), *Voodoo Island* (United Artists, 1957), *Pharaoh's Curse* (United Artists, 1957), and *Frankenstein 1970* (Allied Artists, 1958). Beginning in the early 1950s Landau also penned scripts for television, becoming one of the medium's most in-demand writers. His small screen credits included episodes of such noted series as *Wanted: Dead or Alive, Adventures in Paradise, Bonanza, Hawaiian Eye, Rawhide, The Green Hornet, Ben Casey, Ironside,* and *The Six Million Dollar Man.*

GEORGE MEEHAN (1891–1947)

CINEMATOGRAPHY: *The Mark of the Whistler.*
Voice of the Whistler.

Brooklyn-born cinematographer George Meehan entered the movie business during the teens as a mechanic and tester. In 1913, Henry Lehrman of Fox studios took an interest in Meehan and made him an assistant cameraman. By 1922, Meehan had graduated to full cameraman on various films, mostly second features and shorts. Although he made a handful of movies for RKO and Twentieth Century-Fox, Meehan worked almost exclusively for Harry Cohn at Columbia Pictures (1934–47). A mainstay of the studio's famed B unit, Meehan churned out scores of programmers of all genres productively and skillfully. Today, he is best known for photographing entries in the *Boston Blackie* and *Whistler* series, innumerable Tim McCoy, Charles Starrett, and Bill Elliott westerns, and multiple classic Three Stooges shorts. Meehan was still working for Cohn when he died of a heart attack on February 10, 1947 in Hollywood. He was survived by a wife and daughter.

L.W. O'CONNELL (1890–1985)

CINEMATOGRAPHY: *The Power of the Whistler.*

L.W. O'Connell was a prolific American cinematographer who lensed over 170 feature films and shorts in a career spanning over three decades. Born and educated in Chicago, Lewis William O'Connell entered films in the teens, first as a production assistant then assistant director. After demonstrating skill as a photographer in the Mary Pickford drama *Missing* (1918), King Vidor's western *The Sky Pilot* (1921), and the Colleen Moore comedy *Come On Over* (Goldwyn, 1922), O'Connell was much in demand.

By the late 1920s, often billed as William O'Connell or L. William O'Connell, he had established a reputation as a topnotch cinematographer, renown for his ability to interpret the spirit of the material and for his attention to detail. Among his diverse early credits were the Clara Kimball Young comedy/drama *Enter Madame* (Metro, 1922), the Victor McLaglen western *The Beloved Brute* (Vitagraph, 1924), and the melodramatic classic *The Bells* (Chadwick, 1926).

O'Connell worked for Fox during the latter 1920s through 1935. Although he contributed distinguished work on projects as varied as the Warner Baxter drama *Such Men Are Dangerous* (1930), the Shirley Temple musical drama *Baby Take a Bow* (1934), and the mystery *Charlie Chan in London* (1934), it was on loan to Howard Hughes for the 1932 gangster epic *Scarface, The Shame of a Nation* (United Artists) that O'Connell made his greatest impact. His stylish innovative photography on *Scarface* won him universal respect, and is considered the best work of his long career.

Between 1936 and 1940 O'Connell became employed by Warner Brothers' B unit, where he photographed programmers including installments of the *Nancy Drew* and *Penrod and Sam* series. In 1941, he joined the staff of Columbia. During a five-year tenure working for Harry Cohn he also lensed several memorable low-budgeters, including *Murder in Times Square* (1943), *Return of the Vampire* (1944), *Cry of the Werewolf* (1944), entries in the *Blondie*, *Lone Wolf*, and *Whistler* series, and several classic Three Stooges shorts. In 1946, O'Connell moved to Monogram, where he received recognition for his work on the violent crime thriller *Decoy* (1946). He retired from films in 1952. O'Connell died in Pinopolis, South Carolina, in February 1985, age 94.

HANS RADON (1891–1977)

ART DIRECTOR: *Mysterious Intruder.*
The Secret of the Whistler.
The Thirteenth Hour.

German-born art director Hans Radon entered films in 1936. By the mid-1940s he became employed by Columbia's B unit, working primarily on the studio's popular *Crime Doctor*, *Rusty*, and *Whistler* series. Radon's atmospheric sets for the three *Whistler* films constituted the highlight of his brief career in the movies which ended in 1947. After he quit making movies, Radon became a successful businessman. He died at age 85, on October 10, 1977, at Presbyterian Hospital in Los Angeles. Cause of death was listed as a gastrointestinal hemorrhage.

RAYMOND SCHROCK (1892–1950)

SCREENPLAY: *The Secret of the Whistler.*
The Thirteenth Hour.

Prolific scenarist, editor, playwright, Raymond Schrock contributed stories and/or screenplays for over 150 feature films. A native of

Goshen, Indiana, Schrock was educated at the University of Illinois. A college gridiron star, he played professional football for three years, was a coach at Winona College, and worked as an editor and reporter at a Chicago newspaper before landing an associate editor's job at *Photoplay* magazine. By 1910, Schrock had begun writing scenarios for various stage and motion picture stars. He officially entered films in 1915, adapting many of his previous works for the cinema. During the silent era Schrock worked for several companies in all genres. His notable efforts included multiple Hoot Gibson westerns; comedies: *Never Say Quit* (Fox, 1919) and *Burn 'Em Up Barnes* (Mastodon, 1921); and the horror classic *The Phantom of the Opera* (Universal, 1925), which he co-adapted from the Gaston Leroux novel. During the mid-1920s he became editor-in-chief at Universal.

Schrock wrote screenplays for MGM and Fox prior to signing with Warners in 1939. At WB he worked in Bryan Foy's B unit composing both stories and scripts. Later, he became employed at Columbia and minor studios writing for low-budgeters, mainly westerns and crime films. His memorable sound credits included entries in Warners' *Brass Bancroft*, Fox's *Charlie Chan*, Columbia's *Crime Doctor* and *Whistler* series, as well as several fondly remembered Bs: *Hell Below* (MGM, 1933), *Secret Service of the Air* (Warners, 1939), *Devil's Island* (Warners, 1940), *Wild Bill Hickok Rides* (Warners, 1942), Crime Inc. (PRC, 1945), *The Missing Corpse* (PRC, 1945), and *Blonde Ice* (Film Classics, 1948).

The prolific Mr. Schrock had just begun working in television when he died suddenly at his Hollywood home of a heart attack on December 12, 1950. He was 58 years old.

PHILIP TANNURA (1897–1973)

CINEMATOGRAPHER: *Mysterious Intruder.*
The Return of the Whistler.

Noted B movie cinematographer Philip Tannura lensed over 120 feature films and shorts, and many television episodes and specials during a six-decade long movie career which began in 1911 when he was hired as a child actor in several Edison shorts. He worked at Edison as a lab assistant and still man until 1917 when director Alan Crosland chose him to photograph the drama *The Apple Tree Girl*. He later became chief cameraman at Edison before volunteering for the Army Signal Corps. During World War I he served as a photographer in Siberia.

By the mid-1920s Tannura was back working as a cinematographer at Paramount's Astoria Studios. In 1926, he became employed by FBO, where he made a name for himself as a gifted artisan, adept at capturing the director's vision and the mood of the script. Because he worked almost exclusively in second features, Tannura developed the ability to ply his craft under a tight time and budgetary structure.

After a brief, unsuccessful try at directing (Pathé short comedies, 1929), Tannura returned to Paramount who sent him abroad in 1930. In England, he eventually worked at Gaumont, British Lion, etc., on several memorable minor films, including the backstage drama *Charing Cross Road* (British Lion, 1935) and multiple melodramas: *Moscow Nights* (London Films, 1935), *Love from a Stranger* (Trafalgar, 1937), and *Dinner at the Ritz* (New World, 1937).

When World War II commenced, Tannura returned to America where he toiled in Columbia's B unit, lensing many memorable programmers, both feature length and shorts, during a decade-long tenure (1941–51). Among them were several entries in the *Lone Wolf, Boston Blackie, Crime Doctor, Whistler, Blondie,* and *Rusty* series, and such diversities as *You'll Never Get Rich* (1941), *Sweetheart of the Fleet* (1942), *Reveille With Beverly* (1943), *City Without Men* (1943), *Out of the Depths* (1945), *Night Editor* (1946), and *Criminal Lawyer* (1951). Tannura also made a few notable movies for other studios during his Columbia years. Among them were the United Artists musical drama *Knickerbocker Holiday* (1944), PRC's superb B melodrama *Strange Illusion* (1945), Monogram's biopic *The Babe Ruth Story* (1948), and Film Classic's sci-fi meller *The Flying Saucer* (1950).

After his departure from Columbia, Tannura worked in television for 15 years, serving as director of photography for TV movies, specials, and for several popular television series, including *The George Burns and Gracie Allen Show* (1951–52), *The Bob Cummings*

Show (1955), *The Jack Benny Program* (1953–61), and *Family Affair* (1966). Philip Tannura died in Beverly Hills, California, on December 7, 1973, age 76.

ERIC TAYLOR (1897–1952)

SCREENPLAY: *The Whistler.*
SCREENPLAY & STORY: *Mysterious Intruder.*

Chicago-born scenarist and short story writer Eric Taylor penned stories and scripts for over 50 films in a 16-year movie career. Not much is known about his early life, but apparently he did not begin writing professionally until he was in his late twenties. In 1928, he penned the first of several stories for the noted pulp-fiction publication *Black Mask*; and became employed as a Hollywood screenwriter in 1936. After working briefly for Republic (1936–38), he freelanced for the remainder of his career. Although he produced scripts of all genres, his specialty was crime dramas, mysteries, and horrors. Producer Larry Darmour and his successor, Rudolph Flothow, whose independently-produced features were released through Columbia, procured Taylor's services on a regular basis. Known for his ability to write quickly and articulately, Taylor won kudos and respect for composing scripts and stories for various Columbia Bs produced at Darmour Inc., especially entries in the *Ellery Queen, Crime Doctor,* and *Whistler* series. Taylor also worked directly for Columbia and Universal. Taylor died suddenly of a heart attack on September 8, 1952, while on a vacation in San Francisco following the release of the spy melodrama *Big Jim McLain* (Warners, 1952) which he co-wrote. He was 55.

Taylor's other notable cinematic credits included stories and/or screenplays for *Navy Blues* (Republic, 1937), *Lady in the Morgue* (Republic, 1938), *Black Friday* (Universal, 1940), *The Ghost of Frankenstein* (Universal, 1942), *The Phantom of the Opera* (Universal, 1943), *Son of Dracula* (Universal, 1943), *Dick Tracy Meets Gruesome* (RKO, 1947), *North of the Great Divide* (Republic, 1950), and two TV series, *The Roy Rogers Show* (1952) and *Adventures of Kit Carson* (1951–52).

Aubrey Wisberg (1909–90)

Screenplay: *The Power of the Whistler.*

British-born writer and film producer Aubrey Wisberg grew up in Savannah, Georgia, where his parents moved after the family immigrated to the United States during the teens. Graduating from Columbia University in New York, Wisberg worked as a newspaper writer and radio dramatist in the U.S., Great Britain, and Australia, and as a diffusionist in Paris before moving to Hollywood in the early 1940s.

An ambitious, hard-working individual, Wisberg penned dozens of screenplays and stories, mostly in the war, adventure, and mystery genres during the 1940s and 1950s. At one time or another he worked for most of the major studios, but was primarily employed by Columbia, RKO, and Twentieth Century-Fox in their B units. Among his credits were war dramas: *Submarine Raider* (Columbia, 1942), *They Came to Blow Up America* (Twentieth Century-Fox, 1943), *Out of the Depths* (Columbia, 1945); adventures: *Lady in the Iron Mask* (Twentieth Century-Fox, 1952), *At Sword's Point* (RKO, 1952), *The Desert Hawk* (Universal, 1950); melodramas: *So Dark the Night* (Columbia, 1946); and entries in the *Lone Wolf, Boston Blackie, Crime Doctor, Whistler,* and *Falcon* series. The highlight of Wisberg's screenwriting career came in 1945 when he penned the story for the Jack Benny comedy *The Horn Blows at Midnight* (Warners).

During the 1950s Wisberg teamed up with scenarist Jack Pollexfen to form Mid-Century Productions to make feature films. The duo became renowned for producing low-budget sci-fi and adventure movies released through United Artists. Among them were *The Man from Planet X* (1951), *The Neanderthal Man* (1953), *Captain John Smith and Pocahontas* (1953), and *Return to Treasure Island* (1956). Mr. Wisberg's last professional job was producing the adventure *Hercules in New York* (RAF, 1970) starring young Arnold Swartzenegger. He died of cancer in New York City, on March 14, 1990, age 79. He was survived by his wife, Barbara. In addition to his screen credits, Wisberg was also the author of several war and adventure books, including *Patrol Boat 999, Savage Soldiers, This is the Life,* and *Bushman at Large.*

THE WHISTLER'S EXTENDED FAMILY

The following are vital statistics for various acting and technical contributors not previously profiled. The actors' birth and death dates are followed by the character they played. When an actor appeared in more than one Whistler film, his statistics are listed under the first.

THE WHISTLER (1944)

WRITING AND TECHNICAL:
JAMES S. BROWN (1892–1949) CINEMATOGRAPHER
SIDNEY CLIFFORD (1902–86) SET DECORATOR
WILBUR HATCH (1902–69) COMPOSER, CONDUCTOR
GEORGE VAN MARTER (1910–63) ART DIRECTOR

OTHER PLAYERS:
WILLIAM "BILLY" BENEDICT (1917–99) — DELIVERY BOY
CLANCY COOPER (1906–75) — BRIGGS
BYRON FOULGER (1899?–1970) — FLOPHOUSE CLERK
ROBERT E. HOMANS (1874–1947) — DOCK WATCHMAN
ROBERT EMMETT KEANE (1883–1981) — CHARLES MCNEAR
CY KENDALL (1898–1953) — GUS THE BARTENDER

THE MARK OF THE WHISTLER (1944)

WRITING AND TECHNICAL:
GEORGE BRICKER (1898–1955) – WRITER
JOHN DATU (1896–1985) – ART DIRECTOR
CORNELL WOOLRICH (1903–68) – WRITER

OTHER PLAYERS:
WILLIE BEST (1916–62) — MEN'S ROOM ATTENDANT
EDGAR DEARING (1893–1974) — BANK GUARD
HOWARD FREEMAN (1899–1967) — M.K. SIMMONS
ARTHUR SPACE (1908–83) — SELLARS

Minerva Urecal (1894?–1966)—Woman Sweeping the Stairs
Matt Willis (1913–89)—Perry Donnelly

THE POWER OF THE WHISTLER (1945)

Writing and Technical:
Leonard S. Picker (1910–61)—Producer

Other Players:
John Abbott (1905–96)—Kaspar Andropolous
Murray Alper (1904–84)—Joe Blainey
Nina Mae McKinney (1909–67)—Flotilda, the maid
Loren Tindall (1921–73)—Charlie Kent

VOICE OF THE WHISTLER (1945)

Writing and Technical:
Wilfred H. Pettit (1910–48) – Writer

Other Players:
Tom Kennedy (1885–1965) – Ferdinand
Gigi Perreau (1941–) – Bobbie

MYSTERIOUS INTRUDER (1946)

Other Players:
Harlan Briggs (1890–1952) – Brown
Paul Burns (1881–1967) – Edward Stillwell
Edith Evanson (1896–1980) – Mrs. Ward
Selmer Jackson (1888–1971) – Dr. Connell

THE SECRET OF THE WHISTLER (1946)

WRITING AND TECHNICAL:
ALLEN SIEGLER (1892–1960)—CINEMATOGRAPHER

OTHER PLAYERS:
CHARLES TROWBRIDGE (1882–1967)—DR. WINTHROP
RAY WALKER (1904–80)—JOE CONROY
BARBARA WOODELL (1910–97)—NURSE

THE THIRTEENTH HOUR (1947)

WRITING AND TECHNICAL:
VINCENT FARRAR (1905–50)—CINEMATOGRAPHER

OTHER PLAYERS:
ERNIE ADAMS (1885–1947)—MCCABE
CLIFF CLARK (1893–1953)—POLICE CAPTAIN LINFIELD
MARK DENNIS (1932–)—TOMMY BLAIR
ANTHONY WARDE (1908–75)—RADFORD

THE RETURN OF THE WHISTLER (1948)

WRITING AND TECHNICAL:
EDWARD BOCK (1901–75)—WRITER
GEORGE BROOKS (1903–57)—ART DIRECTOR
MAURICE TOMBRAGEL (1913–2000)—WRITER

OTHER PLAYERS:
ANN DORAN (1911?–2000)—SYBIL
WILTON GRAFF (1903–69)—DR. GRANTLAND
OLIN HOWLIN (1896–1959)—JEFF ANDERSON
ANN SHOEMAKER (1891–1978)—MRS. BARKLEY
EDDY WALLER (1889–1977)—SAM, THE GARDENER

BIBLIOGRAPHY

BOOKS

Balk, Alfred. *The Rise of Radio, from Marconi through the Golden Age.* McFarland & Company, 2006.

Bansak, Edmund, and Robert Wise. *Fearing the Dark: The Val Lewton Career.* McFarland & Company, 1995.

Castle, William. *Step Right Up! I'm Gonna Scare the Pants off America.* G.P. Putnam and Sons, 1976.

Cocchi, John. *Second Features.* Carol Publishing, 1991.

Dick, Bernard F. *The Merchant Prince of Poverty Row: Harry Cohn of Columbia Pictures.* University of Kentucky Press, 1993.

Dick, Bernard F. *Columbia Pictures, Portrait of a Studio.* University of Kentucky Press, 1992.

Dix, Robert. *Out of Hollywood: The Autobiography of Robert Dix.* Ernest Publishing, 2009.

Dunning, John. *On the Air, The Encyclopedia of Old Time Radio.* Oxford University Press, 1998.

Franklin, Joe. *Classics of the Silent Screen.* Citadel Press, 1959.

Grams, Martin Jr. *Radio Drama: A Comprehensive Chronicle of American Network Programs, 1932-62.* McFarland & Company, 2000.

Hagen, Ray and Laura Wagner. *Killer Tomatoes.* McFarland & Company, 2004.

Hamann, G.D. *Richard Dix in the 30's.* Filming Today Press, 2008.

Halliwell, Leslie. *Halliwell's Filmgoer's Companion – 12th Edition.* Harper Collins, 1995.

Hannsberry, Karen Burroughs. *Bad Boys, The Actors of Film Noir.* McFarland & Company, 2003.

Hannsberry, Karen Burroughs. *Femme Noir, Bad Girls of Film.* McFarland & Company, 1998.

Howard, Kathleen. *Confessions of an Opera Singer.* Alfred A. Knopf, 1918.

Jarvis, Mary J. *A Reader's Guide to the Supernatural Novel.* Gale Group, 1997.

Juran, Robert A. *Old Familiar Faces.* Movie Memories Publishing, 1995.

Katz, Ephraim. *The Film Encyclopedia*, 3rd Edition. Harper Collins, 1998.

Keaney, Michael F. *Film Noir Guide: 745 Films of the Classic Era 1940-1959.* McFarland & Company, 2003.

Lamparski, Richard. *Whatever became of . . .* Eleventh Series. Crown Publishers, 1989.

Langman, Larry. *A Guide to Silent Westerns.* Greenwood Publishers, 1992.

Larkin, Rochelle. *Hail, Columbia.* Arlington House, 1975.

Lasky, Betty. RKO, *The Biggest Little Major of Them All.* Roundtable Publishing, 1984.

Law, John W. *Scare Tactic, The Life and Films of William Castle.* Writers Club Press, 2000.

Levine, Caroline. *The Serious Pleasures of Suspense: Victorian Realism and Narrative Doubt.* University of Virginia Press, 2003.

Liebman, Roy. *The Wampus Baby Stars.* McFarland & Company, 2000.

Lowe, Denise. *An Encyclopedic Dictionary of Women in Early American Films 1895–1930.* Taylor & Francis Inc., 2004.

Lyons, Arthur. *Death on the Cheap, The Lost B Movies of Film Noir.* Da Capo Press, 2000.

McClelland, Doug. *The Golden Age of "B" Movies.* Charter House Publishers, 1978.

Miller, Don. *B Movies.* Ballantine Books, 1973.

Miller, Leo. *The Great Cowboy Stars of Movies & Television.* Arlington House, 1979.

Parish, James Robert. *Hollywood Character Actors.* Arlington House, 1978.

Pitts, Michael. *Famous Movie Detectives.* Scarecrow Press, 1979.

Pitts, Michael. *Famous Movie Detectives II.* Rowman & Littlefield, 1991.

Pitts, Michael. *Western Movies: A TV and Video Guide to 4,200 Genre Films.* McFarland & Company, 1986.

Quinlan, David. *The Illustrated Guide to Film Directors*. Barnes & Noble Books, 1983.

Quinlan, David. *The Film Lover's Companion*. Carol Publishing, 1997.

Quinlan, David. *Quinlan's Illustrated Directory of Film Character Actors*. B.T. Batsford Ltd., 1985.

Ragan, David. *Who's Who in Hollywood 1900–1976*. Arlington House, 1976.

Renzi, Thomas C. *Cornell Woolrich, From Pulp Fiction to Film Noir*. McFarland & Company, 2006.

Rothal, David. *The Singing Cowboys*. A.S. Barnes & Company, 1978.

Selby, Spencer. *Dark City, Film Noir*. McFarland & Company, 1984.

Shipman, David. *The Great Movie Stars, The Golden Years*. De Capo Press, 1979.

Siegel, Scott and Barbara Siegel. *The Encyclopedia of Hollywood*. Facts on File, 1990.

Silver, Alain, and Elizabeth Ward. *Film Noir: An Encyclopedia Reference to the American Style*. Overlook Press, 1998.

Slide, Anthony. *Silent Players, A Biographical and Autobiographical Study of 100 Silent Film Actors and Actresses*. University of Kentucky, 2002.

Terrace, Vincent. *The Complete Encyclopedia of Television Programs 1947–1976*. A.S. Barnes and Company, 1976.

Thomas, Bob. *King Cohn*. Barry & Rockcliff, 1967.

Tuska, Jon, *The Detective in Hollywood*. Doubleday, 1978.

Weaver, Tom. *It Came From Weaver Five*. McFarland & Company, 1996.

Weiss, Ken, and Ed Goodgold. *To Be Continued . . .* Crown Publishers, 1972.

Wilt, David. *Hardboiled in Hollywood, Five Black Mask Writers and the Movies*. Bowling Green University Press, 1991.

ARTICLES

Barber, Rowland. "The Lady in Red, the Designated Heavy, and the Texas Outlaws." *TV Guide*, November, 1973.

Bodeen, Dewitt. "Richard Dix." *Films in Review*, October, 1966.

Briggs, Colin. "Million Dollar Eyeful." *Classic Images*, No. 324. June, 2002.

Buchanan, Joan. "Whistler Producer DOESN'T Tell All." *Radio Life*, March 21, 1948.

Burke, Marcella. "Richard Dix—the Pioneer." *Screen Play*, 1931.

Cannon, Regina. "How Rich and Virginia Were Married." *Modern Screen*, October, 1934.

Davis, Charles E. "Regis Toomey: Death Takes Holiday as Career Flourishes." *Los Angeles Times*, October 13, 1963.

Digg, J. "Nina Foch on Columbia." *Los Angeles Times*, October 8, 2008.

Dixon, Wheeler Winston. "A cinema of violence: the films of D. Ross Lederman." *Film Criticism*, Spring, 2006.

Hannah, Sara. "Who Hides Behind 'The Whistler's' Mask?" *Radio Life*, February 8, 1952.

Hare, William. "Mike Mazurki, The Man of a Thousand Roles." *Hollywood Studio*, 1976.

Haven, Lee. "The Story of the Girl Who Married Richard Dix." *Photoplay*, May, 1932.

Herzog, Dorothy. "Columbus Dix." *Photoplay*, July, 1926.

Hill, Angela. "Give 'Em Hill, 97 Year Old Magician Has Many Tricks Up His Sleeve." *Oakland Tribune*, January 9, 2009.

Hoaglin, Jess L. "Where Are They Today—Joan Woodbury." *The Hollywood Reporter*, January 3, 1975.

Johnson, Erskine. "Dix Nixed Five Times, But Back." *Ironwood Daily Globe*, December 23, 1944.

Kelly, Bill. "Mike Mazurki, Hollywood's Favorite Tough Guy. *American Classic Screen*, 1982.

Kendall, Robert. "John Calvert's African Movie Venture: An Interview with 'The Falcon.'" *Classic Images*, July, 1998.

Kingsley, Grace. "Matinee Idol? You Bet He Is." *Los Angeles Times*, May 22, 1921.

Maltin, Leonard. "Conversations: Mary Brian, part 2." *Leonard Maltin's Movie Crazy*, Autumn, 2002.

Martin, Elliot. "I'm No Ladies' Man." *Photoplay*, June, 1930.

McPherson, Jim. "How Fond is My Memory." *Toronto Sun*, November 24, 1991.

McPherson, Jim. "The Lady With the Walk: Lenore Aubert." *Toronto Sun*, 1987.

McPherson, Jim. "A 'star' is Buried Here." *Toronto Sun*, November 28, 1993.

McPherson, Jim. "W.C. Fields' Funny Foil." *Toronto Sun*, December 13, 1987.

McClay, Howard. "Column." *Los Angeles Daily News*, August 14, 1952.

Meienberg, L. Paul. "Tala Birell: The Glamour of Intrigue." *Films of the Golden Age*, Fall, 1999.

Othman, Frederick. "Hollywood's Busiest Actor." *Hollywood Citizen News*, March, 1944.

Parsons, Louella. "For Jeff Donnell—Life is a 'Two-Ring' Circus." *Los Angeles Examiner*, August 14, 1955.

Phillips, Cheryl Kellogg. "The Untouchable." *Los Angeles Times West Magazine*, September 17, 2006.

Scott, John L. "Janis Carter Battles Back to Singing Role." *Los Angeles Times*, 1951.

Seymour, Blackie. "The Whistler." *Classic Images* No. 372, June, 2006.

Stumpf, Charles. "Claire Du Brey: 42 Years in Films." *Classic Images* No. 307, January, 2001.

Van Neste, Dan. "Chasing Rainbows in Dreamland: The Life and Career of Gloria Stuart." *Films of the Golden Age*, Spring, 2007.

Van Neste, Dan. "Ed Norris: Baby Face Gangster." *Films of the Golden Age*, Summer, 2001.

Van Neste, Dan. "Maverick in White Satin: Karen Morley." *Films of the Golden Age*, Spring, 2004.

Van Neste, Dan. "The Shrink Who Didn't Blink: The Story of Columbia's Crime Doctor Series." *Films of the Golden Age*, Fall, 2002.

Weaver, Tom. "In His Father's Footsteps: An Interview with Robert Dix." *Classic Images* No. 338, August, 2003.

Online Resources

Classic Images. http://classicimages.com

Glamour Girls of the Silver Screen. www.glamourgirlsofthesilverscreen.com

Golden Silents. www.goldensilents.com

Internet Broadway Database. www.ibdb.com

Internet Movie Database. www.imdb.com

Jerry Haendiges' Vintage Radio Logs. http://www.otrsite.com/radiolog/

Miller, Ron. "Two Classic Mystery Series." 2007. http://www.thecolumnists.com/miller/miller609.html

Old Time Radio Network. www.otr.net/

Radio Goldindex. radiogoldindex.com

Where Yesterdays Live. www.whereyesterdayslive.com

www.robertdix.com

www.tv.com

INDEX

Abbott, Bud – 196p
Abbott, John – 71-72, 79, 361, 376
Abbott and Costello Meet the Killer, Boris Karloff (1949) – 196
Absolute Quiet (1936) – 272
Accidents Will Happen (1938) – 341
Ace of Aces (1933) – 173
Ace the Wonder Dog – 176
Action in Arabia (1944) – 195
Adams, Ernie – 377
Adamson, Al – 304
Adam 12 (tv series) – 310
Addio Mimi (1947) – 212
Admiral Was a Lady, The (1950) – 288
Admission – Two Faces (1914) – 345
Adventures in Iraq (1943) – 356
Adventures in Paradise (tv series) – 368
Adventures of Bill Lance (radio) – 325
Adventures of Bullwhip Griffin, The (1967) – 296
Adventures of Champion (tv series) – 233
Adventures of Charlie Chan (radio) – 324
Adventures of Ellery Queen (tv series) – 144
Adventures of Huckleberry Finn, The (1981) (tv movie) – 297
Adventures of Kit Carson, The (tv series) – 351
Adventures of Martin Eden, The (1942) – 29
Adventures of Sherlock Holmes (book) – 11
Adventures of Superman (tv series) – 265, 283
Adventures of the Flying Cadets (1943) (serial) – 309
Adventures of the Texas Kid (1954) – 201
Agar, John – 208, 352p
Air Mail (1932) – 228
Air Force (1943) – 287
Aldrich, Robert – 310
Alfred Hitchcock Hour (tv series) – 146
Alfred Hitchcock Presents (tv series) – 114, 146, 316
Algiers (1938) – 320
Alias Boston Blackie (1942) – 32p
Alias Mr. Twilight (1946) – 189
Ali Baba and the Forty Thieves (1944) – 245
Ali Baba Goes to Town (1937) – 257
Alibi (1929) – 307
Al Jennings of Oklahoma (1951) – 367

Index

All About Eve (1950) – 299
Allen, Fred – 146
Allen, George W. – 35-37, 40
Allen, Rex – 235, 253
Allied Pictures – 367
All Men Are Enemies (1934) – 238
Alper, Murray – 71, 376
All's Fair in Love (1921) – 161
All the King's Men (1949) – 142
Alyn, Kirk – 28
Americana (play) – 256
American Broadcasting Company (ABC) – 325-326
American Challenge (radio) – 325
American Empire (1942) – 179
American Madness (1932) – 22
American Tragedy, An (play) – 331
Ames, Adrienne – 214
Ames, Walter – 327
Amis, Suzy – 231p
And Baby Makes Three (1949) – 211
Anderson, Maxwell – 268
Andy Griffith Show, The (1967) – 316
Angels With Dirty Faces (1938) – 17
Ankrum, Morris – 227
Annie Get Your Gun (1950) – 303
Annie Oakley (tv series) – 357
Anthony Adverse (1936) – 302, 319
Apache Chief (1949) – 235
Apple Tree Girl, The (1917) – 372
Appointment in Berlin (1943) – 366
Appointment With Murder (1948) – 246
Arabian Nights (1942) – 287
Are These Our Parents? (1944) – 245
Are You Afraid of the Dark? (tv series) – 146
Argosy (magazine) – 134
Arizona (1940) – 308

Arizona Bushwhackers (1968) – 292
Arizona Cowboy, The (1950) – 253
Arizona Terrors (1942) – 216
Arizonian, The (1935) – 173
Arlen, Richard – 144-145
Armstrong, Robert – 351
Arnello Affair, The (1947) – 322
Arnow, Max – 26, 258
Arsene Lupin (1932) – 222
Arthur, Jean – 25
Ashby, Hal – 338
As the Devil Commands (1932) – 257
Astor, Mary – 307
Asylum (1972) – 147
Atlantic Convoy (1942) – 349
At Sword's Point (1952) – 374
Aubert, Lenore – 131-132, 134, 137, 138p, 140p, 193-197, 193p, 196p
Autry, Gene – 28, 175, 233, 235, 281, 348, 359
Autumn Crocus (play) – 237
Avalanche (1946) – 298
Awful Truth, The (1937) – 22

Babe, Thomas – 283
Babe Ruth Story, The (1948) – 288, 372
Baby Take a Bow (1934) – 257, 369
Back in the Saddle (1941) – 348
Back to Bataan (1945) – 368
Bacon, Lloyd – 340, 354
Bad Boys, The Actors of Film Noir (book) – 7, 148
Bad Men of Tombstone (1949) – 281
Badlands of Dakota (1941) – 179-180
Bakaleinikoff, Mischa – 82, 93, 110, 121, 131, 365
Balcon, Michael – 175

Ball, Lucille – 176, 177p, 261, 352p
Ball of Fire (1941) – 277-278
Ballard, Lucien – 25
Bandit of Sherwood Forest, The (1946) – 361
Banker's Daughter, The (play) – 225
Banks, Joan – 39
Banks, Lionel – 25
Bannon, Jim – 121-122, 127, 232-234, 232p
Bansak, Edmund G. – 42, 46
Bardette, Trevor – 48-49, 53, 56, 58p, 131, 133, 135, 138p, 234-236, 235p
Bari, Lynn – 320
Barrie, Mona – 110, 116, 118p, 236-241, 237p
Barrie, Wendy – 347p
Barry, Don "Red" – 210, 215-216, 217p, 359
Barrymore, Ethel – 314
Barrymore, John – 222, 225, 242
Barrymore, Lionel – 222, 225
Bartholomew, Freddie – 229
Barton, Charles – 24
Bates, Jeanne – 25-26
Batman (serial) – 28, 367
Batman (tv series) – 297
Baxter, Warner – 25, 33p, 369
Beal, John – 326
Beau Geste (1939) – 302
Beery, Noah – 161
Beery, Wallace – 168, 222, 223p
Behind the Mask (1946) – 252
Behind the Rising Sun (1943) – 302-303
Bellamy, Ralph – 355
Belle of the Nineties (1934) – 294

Bells, The (1926) – 369
Bells of Capistrano (1942) – 265
Bells of St. Mary's, The (1945) – 316
Beloved Enemy (1936) – 224
Beloved Brute, The (1924) – 369
Ben Casey (tv series) – 368
Benaderet, Bea – 234
Benedict, William "Billy" – 48-49, 375
Bengal Tiger (1936) – 291
Benny, Jack – 146, 374
Bennett, Constance – 307
Berkeley, Busby – 228
Bernstein, Elmer – 364
Best, Willie – 60, 375
Best of the Badmen (1951) – 291
Best Years of Our Lives, The (1946) – 265
Betrayed (1944). (see *When Strangers Marry*)
Beverly Hillbillies, The (tv series) – 297
Big Boy (play) – 286
Big Carnival, The (1951) – 271
Bigelo Theatre (tv) – 278
Biggers, Earl Derr – 11-12, 166
Biggest Thief in Town, The (play) – 315
Big Gusher, The (1951) – 349
Big Heat, The (1953) – 365
Big Jake (1971) – 363-364
Big Jim McLain (1952) – 373
Big Street, The (1942) – 291
Birell, Tala – 71-72, 78, 241-243, 241p
Biscuit Eater, The (1940) – 288
Bitter Sweet (play) – 237, 312
Bitter Tea of General Yen, The (1933) – 22
Black Arrow (1948) – 316

Black Arrow (1944) (serial) – 367
Black Camel, The (book) – 11
Black Friday (1940) – 373
Black Fury (1935) – 224, 291
Black Hand (1950) – 303
Black Mask (magazine) – 11, 54, 64, 98, 102, 373
Black Room, The (1935) – 29
Black Sabbath (1963) – 146
Black Shield of Falmouth (1954) – 316
Blackmer, Sidney – 27p
Blake, Pamela – 93, 95, 97, 104, 197-202, 198p
Blind Alibi (1938) – 176, 346
Blind Justice (1986) (tv movie) – 283
Bloch, Robert – 336
Blonde from Brooklyn, The (1945) – 216
Blonde Ice (1948) – 207, 371
Blondell, Gloria – 39
Blondell, Joan – 207, 336
Blondie (film series) – 30, 142, 365, 370, 372
Blondie Goes to College (1942) – 30p
Blood Alley (1955) – 296
Blood and Sand (1941) – 302
Blood on the Sun (1945) – 316
Blore, Eric – 31p
Blossoms in the Dust (1941) – 265, 277
Blue Gardenia, The (1953) – 261
Bluebeard's Eighth Wife (1938) – 194
B Movies (book) – 23-24, 46
Bob Cummings Show, The (tv series) – 372
Bock, Edward – 121, 127, 131, 134, 136, 377
Bodeen, Dewitt – 161

Body Disappears, The (1941) – 204, 356
Boetticher, Oscar "Budd" – 350
Bombardier (1943) – 245, 291
Bonanza (tv series) – 283, 297, 304, 368
Boogieman Will Get You, The (1942) – 260, 350
Boone, Richard – 363
Border Rangers (1950) – 201
Born on the Fourth of July (1989) – 202
Born to be Bad (1950) – 278
Born to the Saddle (1953) – 224
Born Yesterday (1950) – 142
Boston Blackie (film series) – 30, 32, 142, 288, 332, 357, 365, 367, 369, 372, 374
Boston Blackie (tv series) – 201, 283
Boston Blackie Booked on Suspicion (1945) – 216
Boston Blackie's Chinese Venture (1949) – 322
Bow, Clara – 307
Brace Up (1918) – 264
Brandt, Joe – 20-21
Brass Bancroft (film series) – 371
Brenda Starr, Reporter (1945) (serial) – 321-322
Brent, George – 207
Bricker, George – 60, 63-65, 375
Bride of Frankenstein (1935) – 18
Bridge on the River Kwai, The (1957) – 142
Bridges, Lloyd – 25, 31p, 213
Briggs, Harlan – 93, 95, 99, 376
Bring On the Girls (1945) – 271
Briskin, Irving – 23-24, 26, 41, 348
Brissac, Virginia – 33p

Britton, Mozelle – 258
Bromley, Sheila – 145
Bronze Bell, The (1921) – 264
Brooke, Hillary – 145
Brooks, George – 131, 377
Brooks, Leslie – 5, 46, 110-114, 116, 117p, 118p, 119p, 202-208, 203p, 205p, 206p, 214
Brown, Clarence – 221
Brown, Gilmor – 227
Brown, Himan – 13
Brown, James S. – 48, 56, 375
Brown, Joe E. – 253, 307
Brown, Johnny Mack – 321
Brown, Tom – 144-145
Browne, Reginald "Reg" – 25, 60, 66, 71, 366
Browning, Tod – 18
Brownsville Herald (newspaper) – 51
Brother Orchid (1940) – 288
Brother Rat (play) – 280
Buccaneer, The (1958) – 296
Buckskin Frontier (1943) – 179
Bud Abbott and Lou Costello Meet Frankenstein (1948) – 194, 196, 196p
Bunco Squad (1950) – 273, 282
Bug (1975) – 338
Bulldog Courage (1935) – 319
"Bulldog Drummond" (fictional character) – 12
Bulldog Drummond (film series) – 29
Bullet Scars (1942) – 309, 356
Bullets or Ballots (1936) – 291
Bullfighters, The (1945) – 288
Burke, Billie – 264
Burke, James – 326
Burke's Law (tv series) – 310

Burn 'Em Up Barnes (1921) – 371
Burns, Paul – 93-94, 100, 104, 106p, 376
Busch, Mae – 191
Busses Roar (1942) – 356
Busy Body, The (1967) – 336
Butch Minds the Baby (1942) – 288
Butler, David – 157

Cabot, Bruce – 298p
Caged (1950) – 299
Cagney, James – 228, 266, 308
Caine Mutiny, The (1954) – 142
Caine, Sir Hall – 161
Caldwell, Dwight – 25, 90, 93, 110, 121, 131
California Conquest (1952) – 349
Call of the Canyon (1923) – 163
Call of the Wild, The (1935) – 319
Calvert, John – 46, 60, 62-64, 66, 69p, 70p, 243-248, 244p
Camden Courier Post (newspaper) – 253
Cameron, James – 227, 230
Cameron, Rod – 253
Canyon Passage (1946) – 252
Capra, Frank – 21-22, 292, 296
Captain Hates the Sea, The (1934) – 242
Captain John Smith and Pocahontas (1953) – 351, 374
Captain Kidd and the Slave Girl (1954) – 351
Captain Midnight (1942) (serial) – 28
Captain Midnight (tv series) – 357
Captain Scarface (1953) – 269
Cardwell, James – 82-83, 85, 87-89, 92p, 131-132, 134-135, 137, 138p, 248-253, 249p

Carey Treatment, The (1972) – 310
Carolina (1934) – 238
Carradine, John – 248
Carroll, Nancy – 165p
Carter, Janis – 46, 60-61, 63-64, 66, 68, 69p, 71-72, 74p, 75-76, 78, 80p, 81p, 208-214, 209p
Carter, Mrs. Leslie – 187
Case of the Curious Bride, The – 11
Case of the Stuttering Bishop, The (1936) – 341
Case of the Sulky Girl, The – 11
Case of the Velvet Claw, The (1936) – 341
Casey Jones (tv series) – 351
Cass Timberlane (1947) – 240
Castle, William – 5, 24, 41-42, 46-48, 50-57, 60, 63-66, 75, 77-78, 82, 85-89, 93, 96-100, 103-104, 115, 137, 246, 329-339, 330p, 350
Catman of Paris (1946) – 195
Cat's Paw, The (1934) – 257
Cavalcade of America (tv) – 261, 265, 310
C. B. C. Productions – 20
Centerfold Girls, The (1974) – 297
Center Stage (tv) – 213
Chadwick, Helene – 161
Champ, The (1931) – 168
Challenge to Be Free (1976) – 297
Chance of a Lifetime (1943) – 52, 332
Chandler, Chick – 145
Chandler, Jeff – 39
Chandler, Raymond – 11
Chaney, Lon Jr. – 144, 196, 304
Change of Heart (1937) – 229
Chapman, Edythe – 163

Chapman, Marguerite – 146
Charge of the Lancers (1954) – 333
Charge of the Light Brigade, The (1936) – 302
Charing Cross Road (1935) – 372
Charisse, Cyd – 317
"Charlie Chan" (fictional character) – 4, 11-12
Charlie Chan (film series) – 29, 142, 371
Charlie Chan at the Circus (1936) – 302
Charlie Chan at the Race Track (1936) – 257
Charlie Chan at Treasure Island (1939) – 235
Charlie Chan in Honolulu (1938) – 287
Charlie Chan in London (1934) – 238, 369
Charlie Chan on Broadway (1937) – 320
Charlie Chan's Murder Cruise (1940) – 265
Chase, Charlie – 29
Chasing Danger (1938) – 320
Cherokee Strip (1940) – 179
Chester, Lloyd – 323
Chevalier, Maurice – 363
Cheyenne (1947) – 291
Cheyenne (tv series) – 310
Cheyenne Autumn (1964) – 296
Chicago Teddy Bears, The (tv series) – 296
Chicago Tribune (newspaper) – 303
Chick Carter, Detective (1946) (serial) – 201
Chicken Every Sunday (play) – 315
Chief Crazy Horse (1955) – 362
Chinese Cat, The (1944) – 321

Christian, The (1923) – 125, 161
Christie, Agatha – 11, 192
Christmas Eve (1947) – 368
Cigarette Girl (1947) – 205
Cimarron (1931) – 2, 167-170, 169p, 176, 180
Cinderella Man, The (play) – 156
Cipher Bureau (1938) – 320
Cisco Kid, The (tv series) – 201
Citizen Kane (1941) – 86, 88
City Detective (tv series) – 253
City Without Men (1943) – 188, 205, 372
Clark, Cliff – 121, 377
Clarke, Everett – 39-40
Classic Images (magazine) – 245
Claxton, William F. – 144
Clemens, William – 46, 121, 124, 126-127, 340-344
Clifford, Sidney – 98, 60, 71, 90, 375
Climax (tv series) – 144, 269
Close Call for Boston Blackie (1946) – 216
Close Call For Ellery Queen, A (1942) – 27
Clyde, Andy – 29
Cocchi, John – 46, 75
Cohan, George M. – 166, 307
Cohn, Harry – 1-2, 18, 20-29, 41-43, 52, 100, 136, 141-142, 175, 181-182, 202, 204, 211-212, 246, 258-259, 331-333, 348-349, 355, 365, 368, 370
Cohn, Jack – 20-21, 141-142
Colbert, Claudette – 22p, 194
Colgate Theatre (tv) – 191
College Widow, The (play) – 155
Collins, May – 162

Collins, Wilkie – 11
Collyer, Bud – 213
Colorado Sunset (1939) – 359
Columbia Broadcasting System (C.B.S.) – 13, 34, 325
Columbia Pictures Corporation (studio) – 1-2, 4-6, 10, 12, 15, 17-19, 20-33, 41-43, 45-48, 52-53, 60, 63-64, 66, 71, 78, 82, 87, 90, 93, 97-99, 110, 122, 124-125, 131, 135-136, 141-142, 175, 181-182, 186, 189-191, 195, 202, 204-207, 209, 211-214, 216, 218, 224, 229, 233, 242, 246, 252, 258-261, 281, 298, 321, 325-327, 329, 331-332, 348-351, 355, 357, 361, 365-367, 369-374

    Budgets of – 21, 23-24
    B Unit – 4-5, 23-34
    Contract players – 25-26
    Early history – 20-23
    High budget pictures – 31-23
    In the 1950's – 142
    Personnel – 21-33
    Production costs – 21, 23-24
    Production details – 23-27
    Serials – 28
    Series films – 29-33
    Short subjects – 28-29
    Westerns – 28

Comanche Territory (1950) – 362
Comancheros, The (1961) – 363
Come Closer, Folks (1936) – 355
Come On Over (1922) – 369
Confessions of an Opera Singer (book) – 274

Confessions of Boston Blackie (1941) – 321
Conquerors, The (1932) – 170
Conreid, Hans – 39
Conte, Nicholas – 188
Convicts 4 (1962) – 283
Conway, Tom – 246, 326, 343
Cooper, Gary – 277, 302
Cooper, Clancy – 48, 375
Corby, Ellen – 145
Corn is Green, The (play) – 314
Corn is Green, The (1945) – 315
Cornell, Ann – 247-248
Cornell, Katherine – 214, 267
Cornered (1945) – 312
Corpse Came C.O.D., The (1947) – 207, 233
Corpse Vanishes, The (1945) – 268
Corvette K225 (1943) – 287
Costello, Dolores – 161
Costello, Don – 48-49, 54-55
Costello, Lou – 196p
Council Bluffs Nonpareil (newspaper) – 85
Count of Monte Cristo, The (tv series) – 367
Count Three and Pray (1955) – 363
Cover Girl (1944) – 207
Cowan, Jerome – 343
Coward, Noel – 210
Crabbe, Buster – 28, 201
Craig, James – 200
Crashing Hollywood (1937) – 287, 320
Crawford, Joan – 336, 337p
Crazy House (1943) – 288
Creeper, The (1948) – 287
Creepshow (1982) – 147

Creepshow 2 (1987) – 147
Crime By Night (1944) – 343
Crime Doctor (film series) – 30, 33, 41, 142, 240, 332, 367, 370-374
Crime Doctor's Courage, The (1945) – 361
Crime Doctor's Strangest Case, The (1943) – 33p, 291
Crime Inc. (1945) – 350, 371
Crime of Dr. Forbes, The (1936) – 229
Crime of Helen Stanley, The (1934) – 355
Criminal Lawyer (1951) – 296, 367, 372
Crisp, Donald – 315
Cronjager, Eddie – 162, 167
Crooked Way, The (1949) – 316, 368
Crook's Convention, The (play) – 301
Crosland, Alan – 372
Crusades, The (1935) – 302
Cry Danger (1951) – 309
Cry of the City (1948) – 278
Cry of the Werewolf (1944) – 291, 366, 369
Cuban Love Song, The (1931) – 222
Cukor, George – 22
Curious Female, The (1970) – 366
Currier, Mary – 110-111, 113, 115-116, 117p, 254-255, 254p
Curtis, Ken – 260
Curtis, Tony – 261
Curtiz, Michael – 17, 224
Cutter's Trail (1970) (tv movie) – 304
Cyclone Kid, The (1942) – 216
Cynthia (1947) – 278

Da (play) – 283
D'Agostino, Albert – 346

Dakota Incident (1956) – 309
Dana, Viola – 191
Dance Night (play) – 280
Dangerfield, Rodney – 344
Dangerous Business (1946) – 218
Dangerous Curves Ahead (1921) – 161
Dangers of the Canadian Mounted (1948) (serial) – 233
Daniel Boone (tv series) – 363
Daniels, Bebe – 162, 166
Dannay, Fredric – 11-12
Dante, Joe – 339
Dante's Inferno (1935) – 257
Dark City (1949) – 296
Dark Venture (1956) – 248
Dark Venture (radio) – 326
Dark Victory (1939) – 255
Darmour, Lawrence "Larry" – 4, 23, 42-43, 367, 373
Darnell, Linda – 188
Datu, John – 46, 60, 66, 71, 90, 375
Daughter of the Jungle (1949) – 252
Davis, Bette – 315
Davis, Jack – 110, 118p
Dawn on the Great Divide (1942) – 239
Day of Reckoning (1933) – 173
Day of the Locust (1975) – 338
Daybreak (1931) – 222
Dead of Night (1945) – 146
Dearing, Edgar – 60, 66, 131, 135, 375
Death on the Cheap (book) – 46, 147
Death Takes a Holiday (1934) – 276
Death Valley Days (tv series) – 310
December Bride (tv series) – 310
Decoy (1946) – 370
Deerslayer, The (1943) – 235

De Havilland, Olivia – 228
Del Ruth, Roy – 354
Demarest, William – 260
De Mille, Cecil B. – 157, 163, 271, 283, 296, 308, 321-322
Dennis, Mark – 121, 123, 127, 377
Denny Reginald – 33p
De Santis, Joseph – 188
Desert Bandit (1941) – 216
Desert Hawk, The (1950) – 374
Desert Hawk, The (1944) (serial) – 367
Deslys, Gaby – 300
Desperadoes, The (1943) – 28
Destination Big House (1950) – 265
Destination 60,000 (1957) – 261
De Sylva, Buddy – 210-211
Detective in Hollywood, The (book) – 46, 356
Devil Commands, The (1941) – 29
Devil Dogs of the Air (1935) – 340
Devil is Driving, The (1937) – 175
Devil on Wheels, The (1947) – 252
Devil Ship (1947) – 287
Devil's Cargo, The (1948) – 246
Devil's Henchmen, The (1949) – 295, 309, 367
Devil's Island (1939) – 341, 371
Devil's Mask, The (1946) – 189, 233
Devil's Playground, The (1937) – 175
Devil's Squadron (1936) – 29, 175
Diabolique (1955) – 333
Dick, Bernard – 28
Dickson, Gloria – 33p
Dick Tracy (1945) – 235, 295
Dick Tracy (1990) – 297
Dick Tracy Meets Gruesome (1947) – 373

Dick Tracy's Dilemma (1947) – 273
Dietrich, Marlene – 242
Dime Detective (magazine) – 11
Dinehart, Alan – 48, 57, 58p, 255-258, 256p
Dinehart, Alan Jr. – 258
Dinehart, Alan III – 258
Dinky (1935) – 355
Dinner at Eight (1933) – 222
Dinner at the Ritz (1937) – 372
Disney, Walt – 29, 325
Disney's Wonderful World (tv series) – 292
Dive Bomber (1941) – 309
Dix, Richard – 1-2, 4-5, 8, 25, 41-43, 45, 47, 48-53, 55-56, 58p, 59p, 60-61, 63-65, 68p, 69p, 70p, 71-72, 74p, 75-76, 78, 80p, 81p, 82-83, 85, 88-89, 91p, 93-94, 96-98, 100, 104, 106p, 107p, 108p, 109p, 110-114, 116, 117p, 118p, 119p, 121-122, 124-127, 135-137, 141, 150, 152, 153-185, 153p, 158p, 159p, 160p, 164p, 165p, 169p, 171p, 174p, 177p, 181p, 189, 289, 346

    Aiding careers of others – 161-162
    Children – 1-2, 172, 184-185
    Cimarron – 167-170
    Columbia period – 181-182
    Death – 184
    Early years – 155-157
    Goldwyn period – 157, 161-162
    Illnesses – 166, 180, 182-184
    Later years – 180-184
    Marriages – 171-172
    Paramount period – 162-166
    RKO period – 166-176
    Stage work – 155-157

Dix, Richard Jr. – 172, 183-184
Dix, Robert – 1-2, 156, 162, 166-167, 170, 172, 178-185
Dix, Sara Sue – 172, 183-184
Dix, Mrs. Virginia (Webster) – 172, 178, 183-184
Dixon, Wheeler Winston – 354, 356-358
Dmytryk, Edward – 24, 98, 295, 302
Dobov, Paul – 145
Dr. Broadway (1942) – 287, 321
Dr. Christian (tv series) – 269, 351
Dr. Christian Meets the Women (1940) – 215
Dr. Jekyll and Mr. Hyde (1931) – 168
Dr. Kildare (tv series) – 262, 316
Dr. Renault's Secret (1942) – 303
Dr. Socrates (1935) – 291
Dr. Terror's House of Horrors (1965) – 147
Dog of the Regiment, A (1927) – 354
Donaldson, Ted – 349-350, 349p
Donna Reed Show, The (tv series) – 316
Donnell, Jeff – 71-72, 74p, 78, 80p, 81p, 258-263, 259p
Donovan, King – 144
Donovan's Reef (1963) – 296
Don't Gamble With Strangers (1946) – 273
Doomsday Flight, The (1966) (tv movie) – 283
Doran, Ann – 131, 133, 138p, 145, 377

Doris Day Show, The (tv series) – 310
Double Face (1954) – 213
Double Indemnity (1944) – 271
Doucette, John – 145
Doughboys in Ireland (1943) – 216, 260
Doughgirls, The (play) – 312
Down to Earth (1947) – 218
Downs, Cathy – 145
Doyle, Arthur Conan – 11-12
Dracula (play) – 331
Dracula (1931) – 18
Dracula vs. Frankenstein (1971) – 304
Draegerman Courage (1937) – 291
Dragnet (radio series) – 252
Dragnet (tv series) – 265
Drake, Oliver – 348
Drake, Tom – 279
Dreifuss, Arthur – 24
Dressler, Marie – 264-265
Drifter, The (1917) – 264
Drums of Tahiti (1954) – 333
Duane, Michael – 45, 110, 112, 114, 116, 117p, 118p, 131-132, 134-135, 137, 138p, 139p, 140p, 141, 186-192, 186p, 190p
DuBarry Was a Lady (play) – 211
Du Brey, Claire – 110-111, 116, 118p, 263-266, 263p
Duck Soup (1933) – 229
Duff, Howard – 39, 145
Duncan, Pamela – 145
Dunne, Irene – 167, 169p, 184
Durbin, Deanna – 278
Dvorak, Ann – 222

Eagle-Lion – 207, 233, 366
Eagle Squadron (1942) – 315
Eagle's Brood, The (1935) – 319
Earth vs. Flying Saucers (1956) – 365
Easy Come, Easy Go (1928) – 165p
Easy Come Easy Go (1947) – 316
Ebb Tide (play) – 331
Edgley, Leslie – 121, 125, 127-128
Eggerth, Marta – 212
Eight Girls in a Boat (1934) – 199, 319
Eldredge, Florence – 173, 272
Elephant Stampede (1951) – 283
Elgin Hour, The (tv) – 213
"Ellery Queen" (fictional character) – 11-12
Ellery Queen (film series) – 30, 367, 373
Ellery Queen and the Murder Ring (1941) – 239
Ellington, Duke – 250
Elliott, Bill – 39, 369
Elliott, Cathy – 39
Elliott, Gordon "Wild Bill" – 201
Ellis, Edward – 176
Enchanted Forest, The (1945) – 344, 350
Engels, Wera – 174p
Enter Madame (1922) – 369
Erickson, Leif – 336p
Errand Boy, The (1961) – 310
Errol, Leon – 29, 199
Escape, The (1914) – 345
Escape By Night (play) – 280
Escape from Crime (1942) – 356
Escape from Terror (1955) – 218
Estabrook, Howard – 167-168
Evans, Maurice – 314
Evanson, Edith – 93, 376
Evil Town (1987) – 310
Exquisite Sinner (1926) – 264

Eyes of the Underworld (1943) – 179

Face Behind the Mask, The (1941) – 29
Falcon, The (film series) – 141, 246-247, 343, 374
Falcon and the Co-Eds, The (1943) – 343
Falcon in Danger (1943) – 343
Falcon in Mexico, The (1944) – 255
Falcon Out West, The (1944) – 343
Falcon Pictures – 246
Falschmunzer Am Werk (1951) – 197
Family Affair (tv series) – 373
Famous Movie Detectives (book) – 46
Fantasy Island (tv series) – 262, 310
Farmer's Daughter, The (1947) – 316
Farrar, Vincent – 121, 124, 127, 377
Farrell, Glenda – 257
Farrow, John – 199
Farrow, Mia – 337
Fata Morgana (play) – 221
Fathers and Sons (play) – 283
Faversham, William – 156
F.B.I., The (tv series) – 262
Fearing the Dark: The Val Lewton Career (book) – 42, 46
Feather Your Nest (tv) – 213
Federal Man (1950) – 201
Fellows, Edith – 262
Femme Noir (book) – 148
Ferber, Edna – 167
Field, Margaret – 145-146
Field, Virginia – 145
Fields, Stanley – 169p
Fields, W.C. – 274, 276-277
Fighting Coward, The (1935) – 319
Fighting Gringo, The (1917) – 264
Fighting Stallion, The (1950) – 366

Fighting Sullivans, The (1944) (see *Sullivans, The*)
Film Criticism (magazine) – 354
Film Daily (newspaper) – 50, 62, 85, 97, 124, 246
Film Encyclopedia (book) – 147
Films in Review (magazine) – 161
Films of the Golden Age (magazine) – 26
Find the Blackmailer (1943) – 356
Finger Points, The (1931) – 308
First is Last (play) – 157
First Love (1939) – 278
First Time, The (1952) – 240
Fitzgerald, Michael – 201
Five Little Peppers (film series) – 30
Five Little Peppers in Trouble, The (1940) – 255
Flame – 349p
Flame of the West (1945) – 321
Flash Gordon (tv) – 243
Fleming, Victor – 163
Flesh (1933) – 222, 223p
Flight Angels (1940) – 215
Flight from Glory (1937) – 346
Flint, Sam – 33p
Flothow, Rudolph – 41-43, 48, 60, 64, 82, 85, 93, 97, 103, 110, 112, 121, 124, 128, 131, 134, 136, 141, 366-368, 373
Flying Leathernecks (1951) – 212
Flying Saucer, The (1950) – 372
Foch, Nina – 25-27, 192
Folies Bergere (1935) – 319
Follow That Girl (1917) – 264
Footloose Heiress, The (1937) – 341
Forbidden Planet (1956) – 184
Force of Impulse (1961) – 304

Ford, Glenn – 240
Ford, John – 296, 312, 314, 341
Ford, Wallace – 145
Forest Rangers, The (1942) – 309
Forman, Bill – 39, 144
Forrest, Otto – 44, 48, 60, 71, 82, 93, 110, 121
Fort Ti (1953) – 333
Forty Guns (1957) – 185
Forty Naughty Girls (1937) – 320
Foster, Preston – 157, 179, 184, 342
Foulger, Byron – 48, 82, 87, 89, 110, 115-116, 145, 375
Four Fast Guns (1960) – 366
Four Star Playhouse (tv series) – 265, 292, 310, 316
Fox, William – 301
Foy, Bryan – 17, 340, 357, 371
Framed (1947) – 212
Francis, Kay – 236, 238
Frankenstein (1931) – 18
Frankenstein 1970 (1958) – 368
Franz, Arthur – 145-146
Freeman, Howard – 60, 65-66, 375
French, Valerie – 362p
French Key, The (1946) – 295
Freulich, Henry – 25
Friday the 13th (1980) – 78
Friedlander, Lewis (see Landers, Lew)
Friganza, Trixie – 286
From Here to Eternity (1953) – 142
Frome, Milton – 145
Front Page Detective (tv series) – 201
Frou Frou (play) – 300
Full Confession (1939) – 199
Fuller, Sam – 368
Fuller Brush Girl, The (1950) – 261

Fury (tv series) – 367

G' Men (1935) – 308
Gable, Clark – 22p, 183, 245, 274
Gabriel Over the White House (1933) – 222
Gallant Blade, The (1948) – 189
Gallaraga, Martin – 82, 91p
Gamet, Kenneth – 342
Gangs Inc. (1941) – 321
Gangster, The (1947) – 281
Garbo, Greta – 221, 225, 241-242
Gardner, Earle Stanley – 11
Garfield, John – 279, 281
Garnett, Tay – 297
Gasoline Alley (film series) – 30
Gates, Nancy – 143p, 145
Gauthier, Eva – 278
Gavin, John – 304
Gay Deceivers, The (1969) – 366
Gay Defender, The (1928) – 164
Gay Falcon, The (1941) – 312
Geisha Boy, The (1958) – 292
Gene Autry Show, The (tv series) – 357
General Died at Dawn, The (1936) – 271
General Electric Theatre (tv) – 316
General Hospital (tv serial) – 262
Gentle Ben (tv series) – 363
Gentleman Jim (1942) – 315
Gentleman Misbehaves, The (1946) – 361
George Burns and Grace Allen Show, The (tv series) – 372
George Gobel Show, The (tv series) – 261-262
George White's Scandals (play) – 286
Geraghty, Maurice – 342

INDEX

Gerard, Hal – 143p
Gerson, Betty Lou – 39
Get Smart (tv series) – 304
Gettman, Lorraine (see Brooks, Leslie)
Ghost of Frankenstein, The (1942) – 373
Ghost of Zorro (1949) (serial) – 201
Ghost Ship, The (1943) – 180-181, 181p
Ghost Story (tv series) – 338
Gibson, Hoot – 371
Gibson, Walter – 14, 36
Gidget Goes Hawaiian (1961) – 261
Gidget Goes to Rome (1963) – 262
Girl From the Rio, The (1939) – 224
Girl From Scotland Yard, The (1937) – 224
Girl From Wyoming, The (play) – 312
Girl in Danger (1934) – 355
Girl Trouble (1942) – 211
Girls About Town (1931) – 257
Girls of the Big House (1945) – 243
Glorious Fool, The (1922) – 161
Go Naked in the World (1961) – 283
Gobel, George – 261-262
Godsoel, Harold – 60, 66
Goetz, William – 333
Going My Way (1944) – 271
Gold Diggers of 1935 (1935) – 228
Gold Fever (1954) – 247
Golden Earrings (1947) – 195
Goldwyn, Samuel – 157, 194-195, 331
Goodman, Benny – 251
Goosebumps (tv series) – 146
Gordon, C. Henry – 176
Gordon, Gale – 39

Gordon, Michael – 24
Gorilla at Large (1954) – 283
Gorilla Man, The (1943) – 356
Gough, Lloyd – 224-225
Goulding, Edmund – 296
Gow, Gordon – 16-17
Graff, Wilton – 131, 377
Grant, Hank – 262
Granville, Bonita – 278, 341p, 342
Grapes of Wrath, The (1940) – 268
Great Gatsby, The (play) – 272
Great Guy (1937) – 273
Great Jasper, The (1933) – 173, 174p
Great Jessie James Raid, The (1953) – 233
Great Missouri Raid, The (1951) – 233
Great Moment, The (1944) – 271
Great Wallendas, The (1978) – 213
Greatest Show on Earth, The (1952) – 283
Green, Anna Katherine – 11
Green, Angela – 145
Green, Dorothy – 144-145
Green Acres (tv series) – 304, 310
Green Flame, The (1920) – 264
Green Hat, The (play) – 267-268
Green Hornet, The (tv series) – 368
Greene, Lorne – 362p
Greenstreet, Sydney – 326
Grey, Zane – 2, 163, 173
Griffith, D.W. – 345, 353
Guestward Ho! (tv series) – 304
Guilfoyle, Paul – 60-61, 63, 66, 68p, 266-269, 267p
Guinan, Texas – 286
Gun Fire (1950) – 201
Gung Ho! (1943) – 287, 303
Gunsmoke (tv series) – 260, 269, 283, 292

Guys and Dolls (play) – 297
Guys and Dolls (1955) – 309

Hale, Barbara – 262
Hale, Jonathan – 145
Hale, Monte – 201, 235, 252
Half Breed, The (1952) – 212
Hall, Alexander – 350
Hall, Jon – 367
Hall, Porter – 46, 60-61, 63, 66, 269-272, 270p
Hallmark Hall of Fame (tv) – 261
Hammerstein, Oscar II – 307
Hammett, Dashiell – 11
Hampden, Walter – 266
Hanged Man, The (1964) (tv movie) – 304
Hanley, Jimmy – 174p
Hannsberry, Karen Burroughs – 7, 147-152
Hard Man, The (1957) – 362p, 363
Hardboiled in Hollywood (book) – 102
Harding, Ann – 170
Hare, William – 294-295
Harper's Bazaar (magazine) – 274, 276
Harriet (play) – 315
Hart, Moss – 189
Harvard Here I Come (1941) – 349
Hast, Walter – 157
Hatch, Wilbur – 39, 43, 60, 71, 82, 93, 110, 121, 131, 375
Hatchet Man, The (1932) – 302, 305
Have Rocket Will Travel (1959) – 296, 365
Having Wonderful Crime (1945) – 195
Hawaiian Eye (tv series) – 368
Hawk, The (play) – 156
Hawks, Howard – 22

Hayes, Bernadine – 121, 123-124, 127, 128p, 272-274, 273p
Hayes, George "Gabby" – 177p
Hayworth, Rita – 25, 204, 207, 218
He Stayed for Breakfast (1940) – 332
He Walked By Night (1949) – 252
Heat's On, The (1943) – 257
Hell Bent for Leather (1960) – 363
Hello Down There (1965) – 363
Hercules in New York (1970) – 374
Hell's Highway (1932) – 171
Helton, Percy – 145
Henry, William – 201
Here Comes Mr. Jordan (1941) – 255
Here Comes the Navy (1934) – 228
Here Comes Trouble (1936) – 238
Here Comes Trouble (1948) – 322
Here I Am a Stranger (1939) – 176
Hermit's Cave (radio series) – 13
Hesse, Paul – 204
Hi Diddle Diddle (1943) – 312
High Sierra (1941) – 17, 291
High Speed (1932) – 355
Highway By Night (1942) – 291
Highway Patrol (tv series) – 269. 351
Highway 13 (1948) – 200
Hill, George Roy – 191
Hills of Home, The (1948) – 316
Hillyer, Lambert – 24
His Girl Friday (1940) – 22, 271, 308
His Greatest Gamble (1934) – 173
His Woman (1931) – 290
Hit Parade of 1937 (1937) – 277
Hit the Deck (play) – 307
Hit the Road (1941) – 291
Hitchcock, Alfred – 17, 77, 199, 334, 339
Hitchhiker, The (tv series) – 146

Index

Hoaglin, Jess – 323
Hobart, Rose – 33p
Hoedown (1950) – 261
Hoffman, M. H. – 367
Holiday (1938) – 22
Holliday, Judy – 142
Hollywood Cowboy (1937) – 359
Hollywood Reporter (magazine) – 63, 97, 112, 133, 246, 262, 323
Hollywood Studio (magazine) – 294
Holm, Eleanor – 356
Holt, Jack – 238
Homans, Robert E. – 48, 55, 375
Homicidal (1961) – 335
Honky Tonk (1941) – 245
Honor Bright (play) – 280
Hope, Bob – 195
Hopkins, Arthur – 156-157
Hopkins, Miriam – 144-145
Hopper, Hedda – 188, 245-246
Horn Blows at Midnight, The (1945) – 374
Hound of the Baskervilles – 11
House on Haunted Hill (1959) – 334, 335p
House on Haunted Hill (1999) – 339
House UnAmerican Activities Committee a.k.a H.U.A.C. – 224-225
House Without a Key – 11
Houston Story, The (1956) – 333
How Green Was My Valley (1941) – 312, 314-315
Howard, Cy – 304
Howard, John – 145, 210
Howard, Kathleen – 5, 46, 93, 95, 103-104, 274-279, 275p
Howard, Leslie – 267

How's Your Love Life (1970) – 208
Howlin, Olin – 131-132, 137, 377
Hughes, Howard – 212, 222, 369
Hughes, Mary Beth – 208
Hull, Josephine – 187
Human Jungle, The (1951) – 309
Human Side, The (1934) – 272
Hunted Men (1938) – 302
Hunter, Anne (see Vale, Nina)
Huston, John – 17, 291
Huston, Walter – 222
Hutchins, Will – 351
Hutton, Robert – 143p, 145

I Am a Fugitive from a Chain Gang (1932) – 171
I Can Get it for You Wholesale (1951) – 288
I Dream of Jeannie (tv series) – 292, 304
I Found Stella Parish (1935) – 340
I Just Kept Hoping (book) – 230
I Killed That Man (1941) – 321
I Love a Bandleader (1945) – 205
I Love a Mystery (film series) – 30, 189, 233, 240
I Love a Mystery (radio series) – 13
I Love a Mystery (1945) – 233
I Love Trouble (1948) – 211, 218
I Love You (play) – 157, 166
I Married an Angel (play) – 210
I Married an Angel (1942) – 211
I Met Him in Paris (1937) – 239
I Remember Mama (play) – 322
I Saw What You Did (1965) – 336
I Wanted Wings (1941) – 287
I Wonder Who's Kissing Her Now (1947) – 195

I'll Sell My Life (1941) – 321
I'm From Arkansas (1944) – 349
I'm From the City (1938) – 268, 287
Icebound (1924) – 163
Idiot's Delight (1939) – 274
Illegal Traffic (1938) – 302
In a Lonely Place (1950) – 261
In Old Cheyenne (1941) – 321
In the Glitter Palace (1977) (tv movie) – 230
Independent, The – 75
Independent Film Journal, The (magazine) – 97
Inner Sanctum Mysteries (radio series) – 13, 36, 75
Inspiration (1931) – 221
Intolerance (1916) – 353
Intruder in the Dust (1949) – 271
Invisible Man, The (1932) – 18, 228, 231p
Ireland, John – 145
Irene (play) – 286
Ironside (tv series) – 368
Irwin Allen's Adventures of a Queen (1975) (tv movie) – 230
Is Everybody Happy? (1943) – 188
Island in the Sky (1938) – 199
Island of Lost Men (1939) – 302
It Ain't Hay (1943) – 288
It Came from Beneath the Sea (1955) – 365
It Came From Weaver Five (book) – 53
It Happened in Hollywood (1937) – 175
It Happened One Night (1934) – 22p
It's About Time (tv series) – 296
It's a Gift (1934) – 277
It's a Living (tv series) – 310
It's a Mad, Mad, Mad, Mad World (1963) – 296
It's Great to Be Young (1946) – 205

Jack Benny Program, The (tv series) – 373
Jack Slade (1953) – 233
Jackie Robinson Story, The (1950) – 288
Jackson, Selmer – 93, 376
Jane Eyre (1935) – 265
Janis, Elsie – 300
Jason, Will – 144
Jealousy (1945) – 224
Jergens, Adele – 25-26, 190p
Jesse James (1939) – 265
Jimmy the Gent (1934) – 257
Joan of Arc (1948) – 255
John Calvert – Magic and Adventures Around the World (book) – 248
Johnny Guitar (1954) – 235
Johnny O'Clock (1947) – 233, 281-282
Johnny Stool Pigeon (1949) – 333
Johnson, Erskine – 300
Johnstone, Bill – 14, 39
Jolly Roger, The (play) – 266
Jolson, Al – 286
Jolson Sings Again (1949) – 299
Jones, Buck – 28, 239, 355
Jordan, Dorothy – 171
Josette (1938) – 242
Journal For a Crime (1934) – 340
Joy, Leatrice – 161
Joy Ride (1958) – 309
Juarez (1939) – 265
Judge Roy Bean (tv series) – 366

Julius Caesar (1953) – 268
Jungle Jim (film series) – 30, 365
Jungle Queen (1945) (serial) – 243
Just Off Broadway (1942) – 211

Kane, Joe – 359
Kansan, The (1943) – 179
Kansas City Bomber (1976) – 288
Kansas City Princess (1934) – 340
Kansas Cyclones (1941) – 216
Kansas Raiders (1950) – 282
Karloff, Boris – 13, 341, 345, 347p
Karns, Roscoe – 298p
Katz, Ephraim – 147
Katzman, Sam – 23, 316, 333
Kazan, Elia – 350
Keane, Robert Emmett – 48, 131, 135, 375
Keaney, Michael – 147
Kearns, Joseph – 39
Keaton, Buster – 29
Keene, Tom – 340
Keeper of the Bees (1947) – 189
Keighley, William – 340
Kellogg, John – 121, 123-124, 127, 128p, 151, 279-284, 280p
Kelly, Paul – 145
Kendall, Cy – 48, 71, 79, 375
Kendall, Robert – 245-246
Kennedy, Arthur – 356
Kennedy, Tom – 82, 89, 376
Kentucky (1938) – 224
Key Largo (tv) – 304
Key Witness (1947) – 357, 367
Keyes, Evelyn – 25, 360p
Kick In (1931) – 307
Kid Comes Back, The (1938) – 291
Kid Millions (1934) – 229

Kiepura, Jan – 212
King, Dennis – 307
King Cohn (book) – 21
King of Alcatraz (1938) – 302
King of Burlesque (1935) – 238
King of the Zombies (1941) – 321
Kingsley, Grace – 156
Kirkwood, Joe Jr. – 218
Kiss Before the Mirror, A (1933) – 228
Kiss Me Deadly (1955) – 102
Kiss Tomorrow Goodbye (1950) – 291
Kitty Foyle (1940) – 255
Kline, Benjamin – 25
Knickerbocker Holiday (1944) – 372
Knife for the Ladies, A (1974) – 284
Knock On Any Door (1949) – 298
Knowles, Patric – 144-145
Kojak (tv series) – 225, 283
Kolchak: The Night Stalker (tv series) – 262
Kraft Television Theatre (tv series) – 191, 292
Kramer, Stanley – 296
Kruger, Otto – 135, 141
Kung Fu (tv series) – 225

La Cava, Gregory – 162-163, 178, 184
Ladd, Alan – 200
Ladies Love Danger (1935) – 238
Ladies of Leisure (1930) – 22
Lady and the Monster, The (1944) – 361
Lady For a Day (1933) – 22
Lady from Shanghai, The (1947) – 332
Lady in Question, The (1940) – 332
Lady in the Iron Mask (1952) – 374
Lady in the Morgue (1938) – 373

Laemmle, Carl – 18, 345
Lahr, Bert – 211
Lake, Arthur – 30p
Lamour, Dorothy – 195
Land of Plenty (2004) – 230
Landau, Richard H. – 110, 115, 368
Landers, Lew – 5, 24, 46, 71, 75, 77-78, 176, 344-352, 352p
Lane, Allan "Rocky" – 235
Lane, Charles – 93, 95, 104
Lane, Richard – 5, 32p, 131-132, 134, 137, 139p, 284-289, 285p
Lang, Fritz – 291
Larceny (1948) – 362
La Rocque, Rod – 163
Lasky, Jessie – 156-157
Last Parade, The (1931) – 22
Last Sunset, The (1961) – 310
Last Train to Madrid (1937) – 224
Late George Apley, The (1947) – 278
Laura (1944) – 278
Law, John Phillip – 265
Lawful Larceny (play) – 256
Lawless Empire (1945) – 246
Lawman (tv series) – 269
Lawyer Man (1932) – 257
Leavenworth Case, The – 11
LeBar, John – 350
LeBaron, William – 157, 166-168, 184
Lederer, Francis – 319
Lederman, David Ross – 24, 131, 134, 136-137, 353-358
Lee, Manfred – 11
Lemmon, Jack – 142
Leonard Maltin's Movie and Video Guide – 46
Leroux, Gaston – 371

LeRoy, Mervyn – 17, 319, 340
Lesser, Sol – 260
Let Us Be Gay (play) – 237
Let's Fall in Love (1933) – 242
Let's Kill Uncle (1966) – 336
Levin, Henry – 350
Levin, Ira – 337
Lewis, Jerry – 292
Lewis, Ted – 188
Lewton, Val – 42
Liberty Pictures (studio) – 367
Life of the Party, The (1937) – 287
Life with Luigi (radio series) – 303-304
Lifeline (play) – 315
Light in the Sky, The (play) – 242
Lights of New York (1928) – 17
Lights Out (radio series) – 13
Lights Out (tv series) – 144
Lil' Abner (play) – 297
Lion's Den (1936) – 319
Litel, John – 349p
Little Brother, The (play) – 157
Little Caesar (1931) – 17
Little Man What Now? (1935) – 228
Little Mo (1978) (tv movie) – 364
Little Nelly Kelly (play) – 307
Little Shepherd of Kingdom Come (1961) – 185
Littlest Rebel, The (1935) – 224
Lives of a Bengal Lancer, The (1935) – 302
Living Ghost, The (1942) – 321
Living on Love (1937) – 320
Llewellyn, Richard – 314
Lloyd, Frank – 161, 264
Loder, John – 356
Loesser, Frank – 309, 342

Index

Loftus, Cecilia – 187
Logan, Jacqueline – 162
London Blackout Murders, The (1942) – 361
Lone Ranger, The (tv series) – 283
Lone Star (1952) – 235
Lone Wolf (film series) – 29-30, 31p, 142, 240, 243, 367, 370, 372, 374
Lone Wolf (tv series) – 144
Loretta Young Show, The (tv series) – 316
Los Angeles Times (newspaper) – 26, 156, 184, 212, 284, 327
Lost Horizon (1937) – 23
Lost Squadron, The (1932) – 171, 171p
Louisiana Hayride (1944) – 288
Love Doctor, The (1929) – 166
Love From a Stranger (1937) – 372
Love, Honor and Behave (1938) – 239
Love, Honor and Oh Baby! (1940) – 240
Love Letter, The (1999) – 230
Love On the Run (1936) – 239
Lovejoy, Frank – 39
Lovin the Ladies (1930) – 166
Lowe, Edmund – 222
Lowery, Robert – 28, 201, 361
Lubitsch, Ernst – 194
Luce, Claire Booth – 312
Luckaye, Wilton – 330
Lugosi, Bela – 188, 330, 345, 347p
Lux Radio Theatre (radio) – 324
Lyons, Arthur – 46, 134, 147

Macabre (1958) – 334
Macao (1952) – 235
MacDonald, Kenneth – 71, 73, 187
Mackenna's Gold (1969) – 235
Mackenzie's Raiders (tv series) – 351
MacLane, Barton – 46, 93, 95, 96-97, 104, 107p, 144, 150, 289-292, 290p
MacLean, Douglas – 157
Macpherson, Jeanie – 157
Mad Bull (1976) (tv movie) – 297
Mad Martindales, The (1942) – 278
Madison, Guy – 362p
Magers, Boyd – 201
Magic Carpet, The (1951) – 352p
Magic of Lassie, The (1978) – 297
Maher, Wally – 39
Mahoney, Jock – 28, 261
Maisie Gets Her Man (1942) – 200
Majestic Pictures (studio) – 42
Malone, Joel – 40, 144
Maltese Falcon, The (1941) – 17, 291
Maltin, Leonard – 24, 46, 51, 86, 113
Man from Headquarters (1942) – 321
Man from Monterey (1933) – 340
Man From Planet X, The (1951) – 374
Man From U.N.C.L.E., The (tv series) – 304
Man in the Dark (1953) – 349-350
Man of Conquest (1939) – 176-179, 177p
Man of Iron (1935) – 291
Man On the Flying Trapeze (1935) – 277
Man They Could Not Hang, The (1939) – 29
Man Who Came to Dinner, The (play) – 194
Man Who Came to Dinner, The (1942) – 204

Man's Favorite Sport (1964) – 310
Manhattan (1924) – 163
Mankiewicz, Joseph L. – 309
Mannix (tv series) – 316
Mansfield, Jayne – 363
Mara, Adele – 32p
Marble Forest, The (book) – 334
Marceau, Marcel – 338
March, Fredric – 168
Marcus Welby M.D. (tv series) – 262
Marine Raiders (1944) – 291
Marines Fly High, The (1940) – 176
Mark Saber Mystery Theatre, The (radio) – 326
Mark of the Whistler, The (1944) – 41, 60-70, 68p, 69p, 70p, 149, 154, 181, 208, 211, 243, 246, 266, 268-269, 271, 329, 366, 368, 375-376
Marks, Samuel – 331
Marks, Sherman – 40
Marshall, George – 359
Marshal's Daughter, The (1953) – 366
Mascot Films (studio) – 308, 354
Mass Appeal (1984) – 230
Masterson of Kansas (1954) – 333
Matt Helm (tv series) – 262
Matinee (1993) – 339
Maverick (tv series) – 316, 351
Maxwell, Elsa – 245
Mayer, Louis B. – 221, 223
Maynard, Ken – 28
Mazurki, Mike – 93-94, 96-97, 103-104, 150, 292-297, 293p
McCambridge, Mercedes – 39
McClay, Howard – 308
McClure, Gladys – 214
McCoy, Tim – 28, 319, 355, 369
McCrea, Joel – 171p

McDonald, Frank – 144
McDowell, Roddy – 315
McGraw, Charles – 145-146
McIntire, John – 39
McIntyre, Christine – 327-328
McKenna, Kenneth – 187
McKinney, Duane (see Duane, Michael)
McKinney, Nicholas – 191-192
McKinney, Nina Mae – 71, 79, 376
McLaglen, Victor – 229, 301, 347p, 369
McPherson, Jim – 197, 278, 317
McTaggart, Bud – 199
Medal for Benny, A (1945) – 303
Meehan, George – 25, 46, 60, 66, 82, 87, 90, 368-369
Meet a Body (play) – 332
Meet Corliss Archer (tv series) – 351
Meet John Doe (1941) – 308
Melody Trail (1935) – 359
Memphis is Gone (play) – 283
Men Against the Sky (1940) – 176
Men and Women (1925) – 163
Men of Annapolis (tv) – 333
Menken, Helen – 188
Merchant Prince of Poverty Row, The (book) – 28
Merlene of the Movies (1981) (tv movie) – 230
Merman, Ethel – 211
Merrick, Lynn – 46, 82-83, 85, 89, 91p, 214-219, 215p, 217p
Merrick, Marilyn (see Merrick, Lynn)
Merry-Go-Round (play) – 256
Merry Wives of Reno (1934) – 255
Metro Goldwyn Mayer (MGM) (studio) – 2, 4, 15, 173, 195, 200, 204, 220-223

Mexicali Rose (1939) – 359
Mickey Rooney Show, The (tv series) – 310
Midsummer Night's Dream, A (play) – 228
Milestone, Lewis – 281, 354
Miller, Ann – 317
Miller, Arthur – 304
Miller, Don – 23-24, 46, 51, 63, 75, 97
Miller, Gilbert – 315
Miller, Marvin – 39
Million Dollar Collar, The (1929) – 354
Million Dollar Hotel, The (2000) – 230
Millionaires in Prison (1940) – 268
Miracle at Morgan's Creek, The (1944) – 271
Miracle on 34th Street (1947) – 271
Mirage, The (play) – 256
Miss Grant Takes Richmond (1949) – 211
Miss Mink of 1949 (1949) – 268
Miss Nobody (1926) – 264
Miss Pinkerton (radio) – 325
Miss Polly (1941) – 277
Missing (1918) – 369
Missing Corpse, The (1945) – 371
Missing Juror, The (1944) – 233
Missing Witnesses (1937) – 341
Mission Impossible (tv series) – 316
Mitchum, Robert – 52
Mohawk (1956) – 316
Mohr, Gerald – 39
Monkey Business (1931) – 229
Monogram (studio) – 199, 252, 261, 308, 321, 332, 370

Monster, The (play) – 330
Monster and the Ape, The (1945) (serial) – 367
Monster Maker, The (1944) – 243
Montgomery, Robert – 221
Moon Over Las Vegas (1944) – 257
Moonstone, The – 11
Moore, Clayton – 28, 201
Moore, Colleen – 369
Moore, Dennis – 201
Moorehead, Agnes – 14
Morley, Karen – 5, 46, 121-122, 124-127, 129p, 219-225, 220p, 223p
Morosco, Oliver – 156-157
Morris, Chester – 25, 32p, 176, 307, 346
Morris, Glenn – 356
Moscow Nights (1935) – 372
Motion Picture Guide (book) – 51, 98, 134
Motion Picture Herald (magazine) – 75, 112, 124
Movita – 199
Mowery, Helen – 8, 93-94, 96-97, 104, 106p, 107p, 298-299, 298p
Mr. & Mrs. North (tv series) – 351
Mr. and Mrs. Smith (1940) – 199
Mr. Deeds Goes to Town (1936) – 22
Mr. Doodle Kicks Off (1938) – 287
"Mr. Magoo" (cartoon series) – 29
Mr. Moto (film series) – 29
Mr. Peebles and Mr. Hooker (play) – 315
Mr. Sardonicus (1961) – 335
Mr. Smith Goes to Washington (1939) – 22, 271
Mr. Smug (1943) (short film) – 332

Mr. Winkle Goes to War (1944) – 287
Mrs. Miniver (1942) – 315
Mrs. Parkington (1944) – 243
Mummy's Ghost, The (1944) – 291
Muni, Paul – 222
Munsters, The (tv series) – 289, 297
Murder Among Friends (1941) – 239
Murder By the Clock (1931) – 308
Murder He Says (1945) – 271
Murder in Times Square (1943) – 349, 370
Murder My Sweet (1945) – 98, 150, 295
Murder of Dr. Harrigan, The (1936) – 340
Murder of Roger Ackroyd, The – 11
Murder She Wrote (tv series) – 230
Murders in the Rue Morgue – 11
Murphy, Audie – 282, 363
Music in My Heart (1940) – 332
Musical Shipmates (1946) (short film) – 343
My Dear Children (play) – 242
My Dog Rusty (1948) – 349p, 350
My Favorite Year (1982) – 230
My Man Godfrey (1957) – 261
My Mother the Spy (tv movie) – 230
My Pal (1947) – 350
My Sister Eileen (1942) – 260
Mysterious Affairs at Styles – 11
Mysterious Intruder (1946) – 93-108, 106p, 107p, 108p, 115, 150, 154, 182, 197, 201, 274, 278, 289, 291-292, 298, 305, 311-312, 329, 370-371, 373, 376
Mysterious Mr. M, The (1946) (serial) – 201
Mysterious Traveler (radio series) – 146

Mystery of the White Room (1939) – 320
Mystery Woman (1935) – 238

Nabonga (1944) – 291
Nagana (1933) – 242
Nagel, Conrad – 218
Naish, J. Carrol – 5, 45, 48-51, 53, 55-57, 58p, 59p, 116, 299-305, 300p
Naked City, The (tv series) – 363
Nancy Drew (film series) – 342, 370
Nancy Drew, Detective (1938) – 342
Nancy Drew and the Hidden Staircase (1939) – 341p, 342
Nancy Drew, Reporter (1939) – 342
Nancy Drew, Trouble Shooter (1939) – 342
National Broadcasting Company (NBC) – 191, 213, 261, 292, 324-325
Navy Blues (1937) – 373
Navy Blues (1941) – 204, 287
Nashville 99 (tv) – 364
Neanderthal Man, The (1953) – 374
"Nero Wolfe" (film series) – 29
Never Give a Sucker an Even Break (1941) – 239
Never Say Quit (1919) – 371
Never the Twain Shall Meet (1931) – 222
New Adventures of Charlie Chan, The (tv series) – 304, 367
New Adventures of Nero Wolfe, The (radio) – 326
New York Confidential (1955) – 296
New York Herald Tribune (newspaper) – 63

New York Times (newspaper) – 334
New York World Telegram (newspaper) – 50
Night and the City (1950) – 296
Night Editor (1946) – 76, 211, 260, 372
Night Gallery (1969) – 147
Night Gallery (tv series) – 146
Night in New Orleans (1942) – 342
Night Must Fall (play) – 187
Night of January 16 (1941) – 340, 342
Night Slaves (1970) (tv movie) – 283
Night Spot (1938) – 320
Night to Remember (1942) – 260
Night Walker, The (1964) – 336
Night's Lodging, A (play) – 157
Nightmare (1956) – 316
Nightmare Alley (1947) – 296
Nine Girls (1944) – 206, 216-217, 260
No Man of Her Own (1950) – 299
No Marriage Ties (1933) – 173
No Place For a Lady (1943) – 99
No Small Frontier (play) – 331
Nobody's Children (1940) – 255
Nolan, Jeanette – 39
Nolan, Lloyd – 302
Norris, Edward – 25-27, 27p, 348
North of the Great Divide (1937) – 274
North of the Great Divide (1950) – 373
North Star, The (1943) – 268, 315
North to the Klondike (1942) – 332
Not For Children (play) – 331
Not Guilty (1921) – 157
Nothing But the Truth (1929) – 165

Novarro, Ramon – 161
Now Voyager (1942) – 265

O'Brien, George – 161
O'Connell, L.W – 5, 46, 71, 75, 77, 369-370
O'Conner, Donald – 179
Of Mice and Men (play) – 297
Oil For the Lamps of China (1935) – 340
Old Dark House, The (1932) – 228
Old Dark House, The (1963) – 336
Old Maid's Baby, The (1919) – 264
Oliver, Edna May – 161, 167, 171, 173
Oliver Twist (play) – 331
Omaha Trail, The (1942) – 200
Once Upon a Time (1944) – 349
One and Only, The (1978) – 288
One Dangerous Night (1943) – 243
One in a Million (1936) – 199
One Mysterious Night (1944) – 211
One Night in the Tropics (1940) – 278
One Night of Love (1934) – 238
One of Many (1917) – 157
One Step Beyond (tv series) – 283
O'Neil, Nance – 167
Only Angels Have Wings (1939) – 22
Only Yesterday (1934) – 228
Order Please (play) – 242
Orient Express (tv) – 243
Orphans (1987) – 284
O'Sullivan, Maureen – 143p, 144-145
Other Men's Women (1931) – 307
Our Daily Bread (1934) – 223
Our Man Flint (1966) – 317
Out of Hollywood (book) – 172, 185
Out of the Blue (1947) – 287

Out of the Depths (1945) – 233, 372, 374
Out of Towners, The (1970) – 310, 338
Outcasts of Poker Flat (1937) – 287
Outer Limits, The (tv series) – 146
Outlaws, The (tv series) – 292
Overland to Deadwood (1942) – 205
Overman, Lynne – 302

Pacific Liner (1939) – 344, 346, 347p
Padden, Sara – 131, 134, 138p
Page Miss Glory (1935) – 340
Panama Hattie (play) – 211
Panama Lady (1939) – 273
Panic Button (1963) – 363
Pantomime Quiz (tv series) – 200
Paramount Pictures (studio) – 2, 15, 125, 161-166, 179, 195, 200, 224, 227, 250, 289, 302, 307, 337, 342, 367, 372
Parker, Willard – 360p
Parks, Larry – 25
Parole Inc. (1948) – 252
Parsons, Lindsey – 144
Parsons, Luella – 245
Partridge Family, The (tv series) – 262
Passage to Hong Kong (1941) – 356
Passport Husband (1938) – 320
Passport to Destiny (1944) – 195
Passport to Suez (1943) – 31p
Patsy, The (play) – 256
Patterns (tv) – 191
Paxton, Bill – 231p
Pearce, Adele (see Blake, Pamela)
Peggy (1916) – 264
Penalty, The (1941) – 287
Penner, Joe – 287

Penrod and Sam (movie series) – 370
Perreau, Gigi – 82, 89, 376
"Perry Mason" (fictional character) – 11
Perry Mason (film series) – 29
Perry Mason (tv series) – 262, 292, 297, 299, 310
Personality Kid (1946) – 189
Persons in Hiding (1939) – 302
Petticoat Junction (tv series) – 310
Pettit, Wilfrid H. – 82, 87-88, 376
Petty Girl, The (1950) – 278
Peyton Place (tv series) – 283
Phantom, The (1943) (serial) – 367
Phantom Killer (1942) – 321
Phantom of Crestwood (1932) – 222
Phantom of the Jungle (1955) – 368
Phantom of the Opera, The (1925) – 371
Phantom of the Opera, The (1943) – 373
Phantom of the West (1931) (serial) – 354
Phantom Thief, The (1946) – 357
Pharaoh's Curse (1957) – 368
Philadelphia Story, The (play) – 312
Philo Vance (film series) – 29
Photoplay (magazine) – 276, 371
Pichel, Irving – 221
Picker, Leonard S. – 71, 376
Pickford, Mary – 369
Pitts, Michael – 51
Plainsman, The (1936) – 271
Pleasure of Honesty, The (play) – 301
Plunder of the Sun (1953) – 240
Plymouth Adventure (1952) – 316
Pocketful of Miracles (1961) – 292, 296

Polanski, Roman – 337-338
Polglase, Van Nest – 346
Police Woman (tv series) – 225
Pollexfen, Jack – 374
Polyester (1982) – 339
Poor Little Rich Girl (1936) – 229
Pop Always Pays (1940) – 199
Port of New York (1949) – 281
Portrait of Jennie (1949) – 86
Post, Guy Bates – 187
Poston, Tom – 336
Poverty of Riches, The (1921) – 161
Powell, Dick – 150, 228, 281
Power of the Whistler, The (1945) – 46, 71-81, 74p, 80p, 81p, 149, 154, 182, 208, 241, 258, 260, 344, 349, 366, 369, 374, 376
Prairie, The (1947) – 195
Present Arms (play) – 286
Presenting Charles Boyer (radio) – 326
Price, Vincent – 334
Pride and Prejudice (1940) – 225
Priestley, Robert – 104
Prince and the Pauper, The (1937) – 291
Prince of Thieves (1948) – 189, 190p
Princess Comes Across, The (1936) – 271
Prison Farm (1938) – 271
Prison Nurse (1937) – 274
Prison Warden (1949) – 367
Prisoner of Shark Island (1936) – 229
Prisoner of the Pines (1917) – 264
Private Lives (play) – 237
Private Secretary (tv series) – 265
Producers Releasing Corp. (PRC) (studio) – 308, 321, 350
Professional Soldier (1936) – 229

Project X (1968) – 336
Public Defender, The (1931) – 170
Public Enemy, The (1931) – 17

Quarterback, The (1926) – 163, 289
Quartermass Xperiment (1955) – 368
Queen of the Mob (1940) – 302
Quicksand (1950) – 288
Quicksands (1923) – 164
Quiet Please (radio series) – 146

Rack, The (1956) – 235
Racket Man, The (1944) – 356
Radar, Allan – 86-87
Radio Life (magazine) – 37
Radio World (magazine) – 36
Radon, Hans – 25, 46, 93, 100, 104, 116, 121, 370
Raft, George – 222
Raging Tide, The (1951) – 362
Ragtime Cowboy Joe (1941) – 215
Raiders of Ghost City (1944) (serial) – 309
Rains, Claude – 231p
Raintree County (1957) – 317
Ralston, Vera – 361
Ramar of the Jungle (tv series) – 367
Rand, Ayn – 342
Random Harvest (1942) – 315
Range Rider, The (tv series) – 201, 357
Rauscher, William V. – 248
Raven, The (1935) – 344-346, 347p
Rawhide (tv series) – 310, 363, 368
Ray, Aldo – 261
Ray, Nicholas – 212, 261
Razor's Edge, The (1946) – 255
Readick, Frank – 14

Reagan, Ronald – 311
Reagan, Nancy – 311
Rebecca of Sunnybrook Farm (1937) – 229
Reckless Age (1944) – 278
Red Hot Tires (1935) – 355
Red Ryder (1934) (serial) – 345
Redhead from Manhattan (1943) – 188
Redskin (1928) – 125, 164
Reid, Wallace – 161
Reinhardt, Max – 214, 228, 242
Reis, Irving – 291
Relentless (1948) – 291, 361
Reluctant Dragon, The (1941) – 325
Remember Pearl Harbor (1942) – 315
Rendevous (play) – 290
Renegades (1946) – 360p, 361
Rennie, James – 272
Reno (1939) – 176
Republic Pictures (studio) 28, 176-178, 215-216, 252, 261, 348, 359, 361, 373
Rescue, The (1917) – 264
Rescue 8 (tv series) – 351
Return of the Durango Kid, The (1945) – 246
Return of the Vampire (1944) – 188, 344, 349, 370
Return of the Whistler, The (1948) – 131-140, 138p, 139p, 140p, 141, 152, 186, 189-190, 193, 196, 234, 248, 284, 353, 357, 371, 377
Return to Treasure Island (1954) – 272, 374
Reveille With Beverly (1943) – 29, 372
Revenue Agent (1950) – 349
Reynolds, Burt – 317

Rich People (1929) – 307
Richard Diamond, Private Detective (tv series) – 265, 310
Richmond, Kane – 28
Ride Him Cowboy (1932) – 340
Rifleman, The (tv series) – 316
Rin Tin Tin – 354
Rio Rita (1929) – 166
Riot (1969) – 338
Riskin, Robert – 21
Ritter, Tex – 199, 320
Ritz Brothers – 229
RKO (studio) – 15, 168, 170-171, 173, 175-176, 180, 195, 199-200, 209, 211, 215, 267-268, 286-287, 320, 340, 342, 346, 374
Roadblock (1951) – 368
Roaming Lady (1936) – 268
Roar of the Dragon (1932) – 170
Roaring Twenties, The (1939) – 17
Roberts, Dorothy – 39, 43, 48, 144
Robin Hood of El Dorado (1936) – 302
Robin Hood of Texas (1947) – 281
Robinson, Edward G. – 305
Rodeo (1952) – 233
Rogers, Ginger – 302
Rogers, Roy – 235, 359
Rogue's Tavern (1936) – 319
Roman Hat Mystery, The – 11
Roman Scandals (1934) – 228
Ronson, Cleo – 359, 363-364
Rooney, Mickey – 288
Rorke, Hayden – 146
Rose Marie (play) – 307
Rosemary's Baby (1968) – 337-338
Rosen, Phil – 348
Roundup, The (1941) – 179

Route 66 (tv series) – 363
Roy Rogers Show, The (tv series) – 373
Ruben, J. Walter – 162, 166, 173
Ruggles, Wesley – 167
Run For Cover (1955) – 235
Russell, Rosalind – 211
Rusty (film series) – 240, 332, 349-350, 370, 372
Rutherford, Ann – 24-25, 175
Ryan, Irene – 145

Sabotage Squad (1940) – 26, 27p
Sahara (1943) – 303
Saint, The (film series) – 268
Saint in Palm Springs, The (1941) – 268
Saint Takes Over, The (1940) – 268
Saint Saens, Camille – 14
San Antone Ambush (1949) – 252
San Quentin (1937) – 291
Sanders, George – 246, 268
Sanders, Hugh – 145-146
Santa Fe (1951) – 211
Saratoga Trunk (1945) – 195
Scandal Sheet (1938) – 271
Scandal Sheet (1940) – 26
Scarface, The Shame of a Nation (1932) – 222, 225, 369
Schlesinger, John – 338
Schlitz Playhouse of Stars (tv) – 269, 299
School For Girls (1934) – 367
Schrock, Raymond – 5, 24, 110, 112-113, 115, 121, 127, 370-371
Schwartz, Jeffrey – 339
Science Fiction Theatre (tv) – 269, 299
Scott, Ewing – 359
Scott, Randolph – 178, 211

Scott, Vernon – 297
Scream in the Dark, A (1943) – 361
Screaming Eagles (1956) – 185
Sea Hawk, The (1924) – 264
Sea Hound, The (1947) (serial) – 201
Sea Hunt (tv series) – 269, 299
Sea of Grass (1947) – 235
Seagull, The (play) – 227
Search For Danger (1949) – 246-247
Second Features (book) – 46
Second Fiddle (1939) – 257
Secret of the Blue Room (1933) – 228
Secret of the Whistler, The (1946) – 109p, 110-119, 117p, 118p, 119p, 127, 151, 154, 182, 186, 189, 202, 205, 236, 254-255, 264-265, 358, 361, 368, 370, 377
Secret Service (1931) – 170
Secret Service Investigator (1948) – 235, 281
Secret Service of the Air (1939) – 371
Secrets of a Secretary (1931) – 270
Selznick, David O. – 170, 222
Sennett, Mack – 353
Separate Rooms (play) – 257
Sergeant and the Spy, The (1954) – 213
Serpent of the Nile (1953) – 333
Seven Days Ashore (1944) – 257
Seven Keys to Baldpate (1930) – 166
Seven Miles from Alcatraz (1942) – 243
Seven Women (1966) – 296
Seventh Cross, The (1944) – 268
77 Sunset Strip (tv series) – 292
Sex Symbol, The (1974) – 338
Shadow (fictional character) – 13-15, 36, 44

Shadow, The (radio series) – 13-15, 36, 44
Shadow of a Doubt (1935) – 308
Shadow of Fu Manchu (radio series) – 13
Shadow of Terror (1945) – 350
Shadowed (1946) – 189
Shadows in the Night (1944) – 27
Shadows on the Stairs (1941) – 356
Shady Lady (1945) – 278
Shaggy D.A., The (1976) – 288
Shampoo (1975) – 338
Shanghai Cobra, The (1945) – 252
Shanghai Gesture, The (1941) – 295
Shanghai Gesture, The (play) – 301-322
Shanks (1974) – 338
She Couldn't Say No (1940) – 341
Shearer, Norma – 161
Sheekman, Arthur – 229
"Sherlock Holmes" (fictional character) – 11-12
Sherman, George – 5, 24, 46, 110, 112, 115, 216, 358-364, 360p
She's Dangerous (1937) – 242
Shirley, Anne – 199
Shock Corridor (1963) – 368
Shoemaker, Ann – 131-132, 134, 137, 138p, 377
Shooting Straight (1930) – 166
Shopworn (1932) – 307
Shot in the Dark, A (1941) – 309
Shotgun Slade (tv series) – 327, 357
Siegel, Sol – 176, 342
Siegler, Allen – 110, 116, 377
Sierra Passage (1951) – 233
Silence, The (1975) (tv movie) – 283
Silver, Joel – 339

Silver Chalice, The (1954) – 247
Silver River (1948) – 291
Simmons, Jean – 309
Sin Flood, The (1921) – 161
Sinatra, Frank – 13
Singleton, Penny – 30p
Siodmak, Curt – 175, 361
Six Million Dollar Man, The (tv series) – 368
Skelton, Red – 200
Ski Patrol (1940) – 348
Skirts Ahoy (1952) – 261
Skullduggery (1970) – 317
Sky Giant (1938) – 176, 346
Sky Liner (1949) – 200
Sky Pilot, The (1921) – 369
Sleeping City, The (1950) – 362
Slightly Honorable (1940) – 257
Slightly Married (play) – 240
Smoky (1966) – 363
So Dark the Night (1946) – 374
So This is Love (1953) – 261
Sombrero Kid, The (1942) – 216
Some Like It Hot (1959) – 296
Something to Sing About (1937) – 239
Son of Dracula (1943) – 373
Son of Robin Hood (1959) – 363
Son of Rusty, The (1947) – 350
Son That Rose in the West, The (book) – 234
Song of Bernadette, The (1943) – 243
Song of Love (1947) – 243
Song of Songs (play) – 156
Song of the Gringo (1936) – 320
Song to Remember, A (1945) – 195
Sons of God's Country (1948) – 200
Sons of Katie Elder, The (1965) – 317
Sorority House (1939) – 199

INDEX

Sothern, Ann – 200
Sothern, E. H. – 155
Souls For Sale (1923) – 161
Space, Arthur – 60, 93, 95, 110, 118p, 375
Space Patrol (tv series) – 269
Spacek, Sissy – 284
Spade Cooley Show, The (tv) – 288
Spanish Cape Mystery, The (1935) – 367
Spanish Main, The (1945) – 291
Special Investigator (1936) – 173
Spellbound (1945) – 308
Spine Tingler! The William Castle Story (2007) – 339
Spirit is Willing, The (1967) – 336
Sporting Goods (1928) – 163
Stage Door (1937) – 199
Stagecoach Express (1942) – 216
Stand By All Networks (1942) – 349
Stanwyck, Barbara – 277-278, 307, 336
Starrett, Charles – 28, 233, 235, 298, 369
Stars on Parade (1944) – 216
State Trooper (tv series) – 357
State Trooper (1933) – 355
Steinbeck, John – 297
Steiner, Max – 167
St. Elsewhere (tv series) – 283
Step Right Up . . . (book) – 52, 338
Stevens, Craig – 144-145
Stingaree (1934) – 173
Stokey, Michael Jr. – 200, 202
Stokey, Mike – 200
Stolen Face (1952) – 368
Stone, George E. – 32p
Stork Pays Off, The (1941) – 349

Storm Over Lisbon (1944) – 240, 361
Storm Over the Andes (1935) – 238
Stout, Rex – 29, 326
Stowe, Harriet Beecher – 315
Straight-Jacket (1964) – 336, 337p
Stranded (1935) – 291
Strange, Glenn – 196
Strange Alibi (1941) – 356
Strange Case of Dr. Rx, The (1942) – 239
Strange Fascination (1952) – 240
Strange Frequency (tv series) – 146
Strange Illusion (1945) – 309, 372
Strange Love of Martha Ivers, The (1946) – 281
Stranger, The (1924) – 163
Strauss, Robert – 145
Street of Women (1932) – 257
Stuart, Gloria – 5, 46, 48-49, 51, 53, 55, 58p, 226-231, 226p, 231p
Studio One (tv) – 316
Study in Scarlet, A (1933) – 257
Stump the Stars (tv) – 200
Sturges, Preston – 271
Submarine Raider (1942) – 349, 374
Such Men Are Dangerous (1930) – 369
Sued For Libel (1939) – 287
Sugarfoot (tv series) – 269, 351
Sullavan, Margaret – 228
Sullivans, The (1944) – 249, 251
Sullivan's Travels (1941) – 271
Sunny (1941) – 287
Sunset Serenade (1942) – 321
Superman (1948) (serial) – 28
Suspense (radio series) – 146
Suspense (tv series) – 144, 197, 213
Suspense in the Cinema (book) – 16, 47

Swanton, Harold – 40, 144
Swartzenegger, Arnold – 374
Sweater Girl (1942) – 342
Sweepstake Annie (1935) – 367
Sweet and Low Down (1944) – 251
Sweet Rosie O'Grady (1943) – 257
Sweet Smell of Success (1957) – 261
Sweetheart of the Campus (1941) – 277
Sweetheart of the Fleet (1942) – 29, 321, 372
Swing Out With the Blues (1944) – 216
Sword in the Desert (1949) – 362
Swordsman, The (1948) – 189

Tailspin Tommy (1936) (serial) – 345
Talbot, Lyle – 201, 257
Tales From the Crypt (tv series) – 146
Tales From the Crypt (1972) – 147
Tales From the Dark Side (tv series) – 146
Tales from the Dark Side, the Movie (1990) – 147
Tales of Terror (1962) – 146
Tales of the Texas Rangers (tv series) – 351
Tales That Witness Madness (1973) – 147
Talk About a Lady (1946) – 361
Tamiroff, Akim – 302
Tanks Are Coming, The (1951) – 357
Tannura, Philip – 5, 25, 46, 93, 97, 100, 104, 131, 371-373
Tap Roots (1948) – 298
Target Unknown (1951) – 362
Tarzan (film series) – 29
Tarzan and the Amazons (1945) 291

Tarzan and the Huntress (1947) – 291
Tarzan's Revenge (1938) – 356
Taylor, Eric – 5, 12, 24, 41, 48, 51, 53-56, 93, 97-100, 102-103, 332, 373
Taylor, Estelle – 167
Taylor, Robert – 336
Temple, Shirley – 229
Ten Cents a Dance (1945) – 246
Ten Commandments, The (1923) – 163
Ten Commandments, The (1956) – 322
Ten Days to Tulara (1958) – 363
Ten Little Indians (tv) – 192
Tennessee Johnson (1942) – 109
Tenth Avenue Angel (1948) – 316
Terhune, Max – 177p
Terrified (1963) – 351
Terry and the Pirates (tv series) – 351
Tess of Storm Country (1961) – 269
That Midnight Kiss (1948) – 303
That's My Story (1937) – 273
Them! (1954) – 253
There Goes My Girl (1937) – 287, 320
There's Always a Woman (1938) – 29
They Came to Blow Up America (1943) – 374
They Died With Their Boots On (1940) – 308
They Fought in the Creature Features (book) – 26
They Got Me Covered (1943) – 195
They Never Come Back (1932) – 308
They Won't Forget (1937) – 234
Thief of Damascus (1952) – 261
Thin Man (film series) – 4, 29
Thin Man (radio series) – 12

Thin Man, The (1934) – 270
Thin Red Line, The (1998) – 202
13 Frightened Girls (1963) – 336
13 Ghosts (1960) – 335
Thirteenth Hour, The (1947) – 54, 120-130, 120p, 129p, 130p, 136, 141, 151, 154, 182, 219, 232, 272, 279, 281, 305, 309, 340, 343, 370, 377
This Gun For Hire (1942) – 200
This is My Affair (1937) – 257
Thomas, Bob – 21
Thomas, Frankie – 341p
Thompson, Marshall – 145-146
Three Hours to Kill (1936) – 229
3 is a Family (1944) – 260
Three Mesquiteers (film series) – 359
Three Musketeers, The (1939) – 229
Three Sons (1939) – 199
Three Stooges (shorts) – 28, 327, 365, 369-370
Thriller (tv series) – 146
Thrilling Detective (magazine) – 11
Thunder in the Night (1935) – 224
Thundering Herd, The (1933) – 290
Tiffany/Stahl (studio) – 367
Tight Shoes (1941) – 287
'Til We Meet Again (1940) – 215, 308
Tillie and Gus (1933) – 290
Time Out For Murder (1938) – 229
Time to Kill (1942) – 287
Tindall, Loren – 71-72, 78, 80p, 376
Tingler, The (1959) – 334-335
Titanic (tv) – 191
Titanic (1997) – 226, 230, 231p
To Have and to Hold (1922) – 264
To the Last Man (1923) – 163
To the Shores of Tripoli (1942) – 287

Today I Hang (1942) – 239
Tokyo Joe (1949) – 252
Tomahawk (1951) – 362
Tombragel, Maurice – 131, 134, 136, 377
Tombstone, The Town Too Tough to Die (1942) – 179
Tomorrow is Another Day (1951) – 283
Tonight and Every Night (1945) – 204
Too Many Girls (1940) – 199
Toomey, Regis – 93-94, 96, 102, 108p, 121-122, 150-151, 305-311, 306p, 355
Top Man (1943) – 179
Topper (tv series) – 351
Tora! Tora! Tora! (1970) – 262
Torch Song (1953) – 268
Torchy Blane (film series) – 291
Toronto Sun (newspaper) – 278
Torture Garden (1967) – 147
Tourneur, Maurice – 161
Tover, Leo – 173
Tracy, Sterling – 40
Tragedy At Midnight, A (1942) – 239
Trail of Laredo (1948) – 233
Trail of the Vigilantes (1940) – 271
Transatlantic Tunnel (1935) – 173-175, 174p
Trapped By Boston Blackie (1948) – 26
Travis, Richard – 201
Treasure of Pancho Villa, The (1955) – 363
Treasure of the Sierra Madre (1948) – 292
Tree Grows in Brooklyn, A (1945) – 349
Trial of Mary Dugan, The (play) – 290

Trilogy of Terror (1975) (tv movie) – 147
Tropic Thunder (2008) – 202
Trouble at Midnight (1938) – 274
Trowbridge, Charles – 110, 377
Tucker, Sophie – 250
Tunnel, The (1935) (see Transatlantic Tunnel)
Tuska, Jon – 46, 63, 97, 113, 356-357
Tuttle, Frank – 162, 200
Tuttle, Lurene – 39
Twelfth Night (play) – 227
Twelve Crowded Hours (1938) – 176, 177p, 346
Twelve O'Clock High (1949) – 281
Twentieth Century (1934) – 22
Twentieth Century Fox (studio) – 2, 4, 15, 189, 211, 224, 229, 236-239, 251, 257, 301, 314, 374
24 Hours (1931) – 308
Twenty Million Miles to Earth (1957) – 365
26 Men (tv series) – 366
Twice Told Tales (1963) – 146
Twilight Zone, The (tv series) – 146
Twilight Zone, the Movie (1983) – 147
Twinkle Twinkle (play) – 307
Two Gun Sheriff (1941) – 215
Two Latins from Manhattan (1941) – 321
Two O'Clock Courage (1945) – 287
Two Senoritas from Chicago (1943) – 205
Tyrant of the Sea (1950) – 316

Uncanny, The (1977) – 147
Uncle Vanya (play) – 283
Unconquered (1947) – 265
Undercover Doctor (1939) – 302
Underground Agent (1942) – 205
Union Pacific (1939) – 308
United Artists (studio) – 15, 374
Universal International (studio) – 333, 361-362
Universal (studio) – 2, 15, 17-18, 20, 28, 179, 196, 215, 227-229, 242, 281, 345-346, 348, 371
Unknown, The (1946) – 224
Unknown Guest, The (1943) – 200
Untouchables, The (tv series) – 283, 304
Unwritten Code, The (1944) – 255
Upper World (1934) – 302
Urecal, Minerva – 60, 66, 82, 89, 376
Utah Trail, The (1938) – 199

Vague, Vera – 28
Vale, Nina – 8, 93, 95-97, 101, 104, 107p, 311-312, 311p
Valley of Decision, The (1945) – 255
Vance, Louis Joseph – 29
Vanderbilt Revue, The (play) – 286
Vanishing American, The (1925) – 125, 163-164, 164p
Vanishing Legion, The (book) – 356
Van Marter, George, – 375
Van Zandt, Philip – 145
Variety (magazine) – 50, 75, 85, 96, 113, 134, 216, 238, 320
Velez, Lupe – 188
Very Honorable Guy, A (1934) – 257
Vice Squad (1953) – 271
Vickers, Martha – 145
Vidor, Charles – 207, 223-224
Vidor, King – 223, 369

View from the Bridge, A (play) – 304
Vincent, Russ – 208
Violets Are Blue (1986) – 284
Virginia (play) – 240
Virginian, The (tv series) – 283
Voice of the Whistler (1945) – 82-92, 91p, 92p, 149-150, 154, 182, 214, 216, 248, 252, 312, 316, 329, 368, 376
Von Sternberg, Josef – 264, 294-295
Voodoo Island (1957) – 368
Vorkapich, Slavko – 170
Voyage to the Bottom of the Sea (1961) – 310
Vye, Mervyn – 145

Waco (1952) – 201
Wagon Train (tv series) – 297, 304, 316
Walk in the Sun, A (1946) – 251, 281
Walk Into My Parlor (play) – 188
Walker, Ray – 110, 112, 116, 118p, 377
Walker, Walter – 174p
Wallace, Richard – 212
Waller, Eddy – 131, 133, 137, 139p, 377
Walsh, Raoul – 17, 291
Waltons, The (tv series) – 230
Wanger, Walter – 320
Wanted: Dead or Alive (tv series) – 304, 368
War Arrow (1953) – 233
Warde, Anthony – 121, 377
Warming Up (1928) – 162-163
Warner Brothers Pictures (studio) – 2, 5, 15, 17-18, 204, 215, 290-291, 309, 340-343, 353-356, 370-371

Warner, Jack – 354
Washington Masquerade (1932) – 222
Waters, John – 339
Wayne, John – 175, 178, 199, 212, 317, 340, 355, 363-364
Weaver, Tom – 26, 53
Wednesday's Child (1934) – 223
Welles, Orson – 13-14, 86, 331-332
Wellman, William – 17, 170, 173, 296
Wenders, Wim – 230
Werker, Alfred – 252
West, Mae – 294
West, Roland – 307
West of the Pecos (1934) – 173
Western Union (1941) – 291
Whale, James – 18, 228
What Price Glory? (1926) – 301
Wheel of Life, The (1929) – 165
When Strangers Marry (1944) – 52, 87, 332
"Whistler" (fictional character) – 4, 7, 11, 13-15, 18, 35-39, 86, 325
Whistler (film series) – 1-2, 5-7. 10-19, 30, 35, 41-47, 141-143, 147-148, 181-182, 189, 191, 240, 281, 325, 332, 365, 367, 369-374

    Ending of the series – 141-142
    Legacy – 7, 144-147
    Noir elements – 5, 44, 147-152
    Origins – 10-19
    Overview – 41-47
    Production details – 41-43

Whistler, The (radio series) – 1, 6-7, 11-15, 34-40, 57, 128, 135, 144, 325-326

Whistler, The (tv series) – 7, 144-146, 292
Whistler, The (1944) – 41, 47p, 48-59, 58p, 59p, 148-149, 154, 181, 226, 229, 234, 255, 299, 317, 321, 329, 332, 373, 375
White Heat (1949) – 266
White, Jules – 28
White, Robb – 334
Who Is Hope Schuyler? (1942) – 211
Who Killed Aunt Maggie? (1940) – 239
Why Girls Leave Home (1945) – 268
Wife of Monte Cristo, The (1946) – 195
Wilcoxon, Henry – 320-322
Wild Bill Hickok Rides (1942) – 371
Wildcat Bus (1940) – 268
Wildcats (1986) – 230
Wilder, Billy – 296
William, Warren – 31p
Williams, Bill – 278
Williams, Emlyn – 314-315
Williams, Grant – 208
Williams, Rhys – 82-83, 85, 89, 91p, 312-317, 313p
Willis, Matt – 60, 62-63, 69p, 70p, 376
Wilson, J. Donald – 6, 10, 12-13, 18, 35, 40-41, 48, 54, 60, 71, 93, 110, 121, 131, 144, 324-328
Wilson, Lois – 162-163, 166-167
Wilt, David – 102-103
Windsor, Marie – 145, 262
Winged Victory (play) – 189
Winninger, Charles – 145
Winterset (1936) – 267-268
Wisberg, Aubrey – 24, 71, 79, 374

Wise, Robert – 42, 86
Withers, Isabel – 93, 131, 135
Withers, Jane – 278
Woman in White, The – 11
Woman of Distinction, A (1950) – 211
Woman on Pier 13, The (1949) – 211
Womanhandled (1926) – 162-163
Women, The (play) – 312
Women in the Night (1948) – 243
Wood, Douglas – 82, 87
Woodbury, Joan – 48-49, 55, 317-323, 318p
Woodell, Barbara – 110, 144, 377
Woods, Donald – 39, 86
Woolrich, Cornell – 11, 60, 63-65, 131, 134-136, 141, 375
World Changes, The (1933) – 257
Wyler, William – 350
Wyman, Jane – 309, 343
Wynters, Charlotte – 292
Wyoming Outlaw (1939) – 199

Yank in Libya, A (1942) – 321
Yankee Doodle Dandy (1942) – 204
Yankee Fakir (1947) – 322
Yates, Herbert – 361
Yellow Dust (1936) – 173
Yellow Men and Gold (1922) – 161
You Can't Buy Luck (1937) – 287
You Can't Take It With You (play) – 187
You Were Never Lovelier (1942) – 204
You'll Never Get Rich (1941) – 372
Young, Clara Kimball – 369
Young, Robert – 361
Young Donovan's Kid (1931) – 170
Young People (1940) – 277
You're In the Army Now (1941) – 204, 309

You're Telling Me (1934) – 277
Youth on Parade (1942) – 216
Youth on Trial (1945) – 246, 255

Zane Grey Theater (tv) – 310

Zanesville Sunday Times (newspaper) – 63
Zanuck, Darryl – 211
Zemeckis, Robert – 339
Zotz (1962) – 336

www.ingramcontent.com/pod-product-compliance
Lightning Source LLC
Chambersburg PA
CBHW050831230426
43667CB00012B/1956